Pro SharePoint 2010 Solution Development

Combining .NET, SharePoint, and Office 2010

Ed Hild and Chad Wach

Apress®

Pro SharePoint 2010 Solution Development: Combining .NET, SharePoint, and Office 2010

ISBN-13 (pbk): 978-1-4302-2781-6

ISBN-13 (electronic): 978-1-4302-2782-3

Printed and bound in the United States of America 9 8 7 6 5 4 3 2 1

Trademarked names may appear in this book. Rather than use a trademark symbol with every occurrence of a trademarked name, we use the names only in an editorial fashion and to the benefit of the trademark owner, with no intention of infringement of the trademark.

Distributed to the book trade worldwide by Springer-Verlag New York, Inc., 233 Spring Street, 6th Floor, New York, NY 10013. Phone 1-800-SPRINGER, fax 201-348-4505, e-mail orders-ny@springer-sbm.com, or visit www.springeronline.com.

For information on translations, please e-mail rights@apress.com, or visit www.apress.com.

Apress and friends of ED books may be purchased in bulk for academic, corporate, or promotional use. eBook versions and licenses are also available for most titles. For more information, reference our Special Bulk Sales–eBook Licensing web page at www.apress.com/info/bulksales.

The information in this book is distributed on an "as is" basis, without warranty. Although every precaution has been taken in the preparation of this work, neither the author(s) nor Apress shall have any liability to any person or entity with respect to any loss or damage caused or alleged to be caused directly or indirectly by the information contained in this work.

The source code for this book is available to readers at www.apress.com.

I'd like to thank my family for cheering me on while I took on the challenge of writing this book. I'd like to thank my son for giving me an excuse to play laser tag and other fun activities. I'd like to thank my baby daughter for always saying "bye-bye" when I leave and enthusiastically saying "Daddo!" when I return. I'd like to thank my wife for being my best friend and for not always frowning when I spent too much time working on the book. –Ed Hild

To Sharon and Maddie, I am inspired by both of you every single day. –Chad Wach

Contents at a Glance

Contents

About the Authors

■**Ed Hild** is a Technology Architect at the Microsoft Technology Center in Reston, VA, specializing in Portal and Collaboration solutions. At the MTC, he meets daily with both commercial- and public-sector customers to discuss business requirements and map them to the Microsoft platform. He helps customers understand product features, best practices, and necessary customizations for them to realize SharePoint's full potential. Ed has previously presented at Microsoft Dev Days, Tech Ed, and Microsoft SharePoint Conference events as well as many local area user groups. He published an advanced SharePoint developer book through Apress titled *Pro SharePoint Solution Development* and was included in the MSPress *Microsoft Office SharePoint Server 2007 Best Practices* book. Ed's previous experiences include a high school teacher, government contractor, Microsoft Certified Trainer, and lead developer at a Microsoft partner.

■**Chad Wach** is a Solutions Architect on the Microsoft Federal Civilian Team focused on helping Microsoft's Federal customers and partners understand and take full advantage of the Microsoft platform. He holds a B.S. in Computer Science and an M.S. in Software Engineering; this with his more than 15 years of working with the Microsoft platform enables him to provide insight and direction in how to use SharePoint and Office as a foundation for building line of business applications in the Enterprise.

About the Technical Reviewer

■**Alex Starykh** is a Technology Architect at Microsoft. His specialties include technology and applications related to collaboration, integration, and business intelligence. Alex works with many commercial and public sector customers, helping them to envision and design solutions. Prior to joining Microsoft, he spent many years consulting with a variety of vertical industries. Alex has also taught numerous IT classes to help customers realize the full value of the technologies they used. He is a frequent presenter at many industry conferences and local user groups.

Introduction

When we first proposed this book, we set a goal of writing a different kind of SharePoint book. We did not want a reference that repeated the software development kit, nor did we want a how-to book that explained how to configure the out-of-the-box functionality. Instead, we envisioned a book that helped developers apply the Microsoft Office platform to customer problems. Since Chad and I work at the Microsoft Technology Center in Virginia, we have a unique opportunity to work with a wide variety of customers, in both the commercial and public sectors, who are trying to realize a benefit from incorporating Office technologies into their enterprises. Many of these customers are not just seeking installation or configuration advice. Instead, the focus is on how the Microsoft Office platform will make their workers more efficient, their processes more repeatable, and their businesses more profitable. For these customers, the technology must be applied to their specific challenges.

With the release of Office 2010, Microsoft gives the developer a complete platform (both client and server) for generating documents, automating processes, enhancing collaboration, and integrating line-of-business data. This platform includes not only the latest releases of SharePoint products and technologies, but also a new set of desktop applications. More importantly, these applications are extendable by .NET developers. This book walks through solutions to common customer challenges and utilizes both the client and server technologies of the Office 2010 platform, including Microsoft Office 2010, Microsoft SharePoint Server 2010, and Visual Studio 2010.

Since we, too, are developers, we recognize that often you buy a book just for that one code sample or chapter you need to complete a project. Unfortunately, many books don't support that approach and have a single huge example that builds throughout the book. As much as possible, we have designed our solutions to be self-contained within their own chapters. We anticipate that you will see something you can immediately relate to or that has a high priority for you. Go ahead and skip to that chapter and read that solution. Make sure you come back, though; the other chapters are just as interesting!

After the first few chapters, which introduce the technologies and outline the book, the remaining chapters each present a real-world customer problem and its solution. In every chapter we will introduce the problem, give you examples of customers who typically have this problem, provide you with an overview of the solution, and a complete walk-through. Accompanying this text is a download of completed solutions on the Apress web site (in the Source Code/Download section of http://apress.com). In each chapter we also highlight some of the key concepts you will likely use again, and list extension points for enhancing the solution. Finally, each chapter contains a set of links for further reading on the topics included in the solution.

So what are we going to build? The solutions combine the familiar interface of the desktop applications with the server capabilities of SharePoint. The solutions include items such as custom web parts, Office add-ins, SharePoint features, InfoPath forms, workflow, Business Connectivity Services, Outlook form regions, Excel Services, Silverlight, Bing Maps Mashups, and the Open XML file format. But this isn't a complete list. In most cases, a solution is not just any one of these items, but a combination that meets the customer's needs.

Who This Book Is For

This book is for developers looking to apply the Microsoft Office platform (both client and server) to their own solutions. We didn't set out to write a reference book; instead we focused on how the features and services of Office and SharePoint can be leveraged. Therefore, we assume the reader is already familiar with .NET code. Ideally the reader has also been exposed to some sort of development with Microsoft Office and at least used a SharePoint team site. We do provide a few background chapters for developers new to these areas or unfamiliar with the enhancements of the latest releases. If you are a developer who has always wanted to build solutions that dynamically build Office documents, automate processes, enhance collaboration, and integrate line-of-business data, then this book is for you. If you want to learn how to construct solutions that combine items like custom web parts, Office add-ins, SharePoint features, InfoPath forms, workflow, Business Connectivity Services, Outlook form regions, Excel Services, Silverlight, Bing Maps, and the Open XML file format, then this book is for you. If you ever wanted a book that focused on solutions and treated Microsoft Office 2010, Microsoft SharePoint Server 2010, and Visual Studio 2010 equally, then this book is for you.

Downloading the Code

The source code for this book is available to readers at `www.apress.com` in the Source Code/Download section of this book's home page. Please feel free to download all the code there. You can also check for errata and find related titles from Apress.

Contacting the Authors

You can contact the authors by e-mail. Ed Hild's e-mail address is `edhild@microsoft.com` and Chad Wach's e-mail address is `chad.wach@microsoft.com`. Additionally, Ed maintains a blog (`http://blogs.msdn.com/edhild`) that has more SharePoint code examples, best practices, and general collaboration information. You can also find Chad's blog at `http://chad.wach.us/blog`.

CHAPTER 1

■■■

Office Business Applications

It is sometimes difficult to remember the corporate office of the recent past. Think back about 10 or maybe 15 years. For many of us, that isn't so long ago. However, from a technology perspective, it's an era as distant as the dark ages. Sure, personal computing was taking off and the Internet was in its infancy, but most companies did not yet have a web site, and the average business user had little exposure to the technologies that seem commonplace today. Remember when only the technically proficient used spreadsheets? When e-mail was a productivity tool and didn't require labor-intensive filing and sorting? The point of this trip down memory lane is to lend some perspective as to how far workers have come in embracing the technology solutions IT offers. The fact is, the amount of information workers have to interact with increases regularly, as does the proliferation of often-siloed software systems built to cope with that information. Today, many organizations find themselves in a state where information and labor are duplicated. Often, workers take more time finding and constructing information than analyzing it and making decisions. This is where technology now has an opportunity—the opportunity to provide smarter tools that focus on the work corporate business users actually need to accomplish. It is with this in mind that this book will explore common challenges and scenarios and their solutions.

Companies often believe the average business user isn't going to find new technologies or solutions easy enough to use. Though there is some truth in that, history has shown that the information worker will adapt if the solution delivers a true value. What is more interesting is the behavior of the next generation of workers. After Hurricane Katrina, we had the opportunity to perform some community service in the New Orleans area. Some of our team helped restore houses, others helped local services restore computer networks, and we got to visit area schools to provide something similar to a career day for the students. Before we walked into the classrooms, the principals told us that most of the families who had the means left the area and didn't come back and that we should not have high expectations about how much technology the students had been exposed to. Of course, we didn't listen and asked the same questions we always ask students:

1. How many of you have cell phones?

   Almost every student had one. And most were comfortable discussing the phone as a multipurpose device. I quickly learned to turn off my Internet browser access when the students were playing with my phone. Most of the students had sent text messages and used their phones for music.

2. How many of you can type faster than you can write?

   Again, almost every hand in the room was raised.

3. How many of you use a computer daily?

> The hands remained raised. During our time there, many students asked us questions about their home networks. Even with middle-school kids, they were the ones setting up the networks for their families.

This past year, I picked up my son at the bus stop after the first day of third grade. Most of the older kids walked off the bus with cell phones in hand, responding to text messages. And this was an elementary school bus! Our school experience is evidence that not only will the average corporate business user pick up a new technology if we can provide a solution that delivers value, but that our workforce will more and more include users who have been exposed to a fair amount of technology outside of the office. Still, we do have to be aware that many workers don't want to learn something completely new. Because of this, this book will focus on solutions that customize tools that have been a staple on the corporate desktop. The solutions in this book will extend the most familiar Microsoft Office tools: Word, Excel, Outlook, PowerPoint, Access, and Visio.

Why focus on Microsoft Office? For the information worker, Microsoft Office has a proven value that few other technologies can compare with. Word, Excel, Outlook, and PowerPoint have been on the corporate desktop for more than a decade and users are comfortable working with them. Microsoft itself is using this strength to address the needs of enterprises, relating to how they create, organize, and search information. At the heart of these enterprise application servers are Microsoft SharePoint products and technologies.

Specifically, the name SharePoint is attached to two server-side applications: SharePoint Foundation is a Windows Server component that provides collaboration features designed to deliver Web-based sites for teams and groups of users. These sites provide a focal point for activities, such as planning a meeting, reviewing a document, or completing a business process. Microsoft SharePoint Server extends this foundation to provide enterprise-level features such as search, records management, content management, personalization, application integration, social networking, data visualization, and so on. There is a reason that SharePoint is a part of the Microsoft Office platform—these products extend the Microsoft Office desktop applications to provide services that an organization needs beyond document creation. The server applications integrate seamlessly into the Microsoft Office desktop applications. As a result, organizations can connect information workers, service their collaboration needs, and help them locate information—all from within the same document, spreadsheet, presentation, or e-mail they are working on.

The latest versions of the Microsoft Office desktop tools and application servers provide an incredible range of features and functionality out of the box, and they integrate more completely than any previous release. However, as organizations apply these technologies to their business processes or to solve specific problems, there may still be some gaps because of the nuances inherent in the way a company wants to use them. This is where the application developer enters center stage. The mistake often made here is that the application developer builds a solution completely removed from the user's familiar environment. To be successful, a solution needs to be highly integrated with the Office desktop tools, and to leverage SharePoint's services as well. There is no reason, for example, to build a custom database application that stores documents and their metadata, and provides versioning capabilities. Such features are available with any SharePoint document library. And as for the interface, why ask a user to close the document he is working on to go to some other thick Windows client or custom web page?

Historically, developers have avoided customizing the Office tools for several reasons. The first is that such solutions are notoriously difficult to construct. This is in large part due to the lack of a sophisticated development environment. Developers focused on C++, Visual Basic, or C# are typically not exposed to VBA, the development model within Office, and therefore lack the comfort level needed to build effective solutions. Microsoft Visual Studio Tools for Office (VSTO) bridges this chasm. VSTO is a runtime library that provides a layer of abstraction between the .NET developer and the Microsoft Office primary interop assemblies. This layer helps hide some of the COM particulars from .NET developers and enables them to build .NET solutions for Office using Visual Studio, focusing on their solutions, not on interop plumbing. In addition to making the code simpler, VSTO provides a designer experience. For example, when building an Excel-based solution, Excel is loaded into Visual Studio and the spreadsheet becomes the design surface. This means a developer can drag and drop her familiar Windows forms controls right onto the spreadsheet, set their properties, and add a code-behind. This is the expected experience for the Windows or Web developer. Many of the examples in this book will utilize Visual Studio Tools for Office.

Another milestone that promotes new development opportunities is the switch from Office documents that rely on proprietary binary file formats to those using formats that are open and built on XML. This change first arrived with Microsoft Office 2007, whose files rely on an Open XML format. Very often, developers find themselves in a situation where a solution requires the generation of a document, spreadsheet, or presentation based on data in a SQL database, web service, or other external application. Previously, most solutions relied on automating Office, which required the application to be installed on the server. Not only were these solutions extremely difficult to scale, but in most circumstances they were not recommended by Microsoft. With the Open XML file format, developers can build server-side document-generation solutions that don't require having the Office application on the server.

So this book is about building solutions on top of the Microsoft Office platform, meaning that the solutions will incorporate SharePoint, Office, and VSTO. This is a book for the developer community. We assume an average level of experience building .NET applications and some familiarity with Office and SharePoint.

The three chapters following this one (Chapters 2, 3, and 4) provide an overview of SharePoint, the new SharePoint 2010 development tools, and Office development topics. Almost all of our chapters have a "Further Reading" section at the end in case you want more information on the topics covered there.

This book is not meant to be a reference manual that teaches you every feature of these technologies; instead it shows you common solution patterns through scenarios that could apply to any organization. If you are an expert in these technologies, feel free to skim the overview chapters or even skip them and jump straight to the scenario/solution ones (Chapter 5 and onward). We tried to make each of our solution chapters capable of standing on its own, so you can read them in any order, focusing on the scenarios that most interest you.

You might think that, with all of this technology, we will be building solutions never dreamed of before. However, that really isn't the case. The solutions we will construct are ones that developers have been struggling to deliver for some time. What has changed over time are the tools available for constructing these solutions. With the 2010 releases, you will see how much easier it is to build the solutions and how much less code it takes.

The solutions we will construct have their humble beginnings in custom VBA applications. Many VBA solutions are brought into businesses by a technology-savvy business user who loves to record macros and see the code they emit. Such users are able to put together a document or spreadsheet that turns into a mission-critical application. Unfortunately for the organization, such applications become difficult to manage and deploy. They typically haven't been designed with performance and security in mind, and debugging has been largely a process of trial and error. Even though these VBA applications are rather primitive, they tend to be a huge success. The reason is that they are designed to make the information worker's job easier and they can be deployed rather quickly. They are integrated into the Office applications and were built by someone intimately involved with the challenges faced in the workplace.

A level above VBA applications are solutions developed using the COM interfaces exposed by Office. These tend to be application add-ins that run within an Office tool or an application that automates Office. An add-in is essentially a custom library that Office loads as the application launches. The add-in can then extend the Office tool to provide additional functionality. An example could be an Excel add-in that puts a button on the toolbar that, when pressed, loads data from an external source into the spreadsheet. The add-in model is a powerful one that continues into the managed code solutions created by VSTO. The biggest differences between COM and VSTO add-ins are the improvements in the development experience and the benefits of .NET code bases over COM.

Developers have also built solutions that rely on automating an Office tool. An example of this would be custom code that loads the Word application (`Word.Application`) and automatically begins to construct a document based on a data source. Such applications tend to be deployed on servers where this work can be done on behalf of the user. The main problem with these solutions is that they will not scale, because automating Word in this manner is equivalent to each user logging on to the server and opening the application directly. Moreover, this kind of server-based automation of Office is something Microsoft has always advised against.

Microsoft Office 2003 presented an application type called smart documents, which were supposed to solve the information integration and duplication challenge. Smart documents took advantage of the task pane and Office 2003's support for XML. An example of such an application would be a Word document that, through a custom task pane, allows a user to select data from another application. That data is then placed appropriately into the document based on the document's XML schema. Smart documents were first presented as COM applications in which the task pane was HTML with an XML file detailing the controls that were to be loaded. Later, the first version of VSTO for Visual Studio 2003 provided a .NET programming option, but only for Word, Excel, Outlook, and InfoPath. These types of applications got "smart" in their name because of their similarity to smart clients. In smart client applications, a thick client relies on external resources such as web services. This model has many appealing advantages, including deployment scenarios and support for disconnected clients. Visual Studio 2010 and .NET continue to evolve solutions of this type, and expose this development model to many more Office applications.

Solutions developed on the Microsoft Office platform are termed Office Business Applications, or OBA. The OBA team at Microsoft has documented common patterns that solutions incorporate to deliver integration, a rich experience, and data reduction for the information worker. These patterns can be grouped into the categories displayed in Table 1-1. As we introduce you to the scenarios in the book, we will describe which of these patterns the solutions implement. (Often there is not a single pattern used, but rather a combination.) For more information on these patterns and OBA, visit the OBA developer portal at `http://msdn2.microsoft.com/en-us/office/aa905528.aspx,` and read an article in *MSDN Magazine* on the solution patterns at `http://msdn.microsoft.com/en-us/magazine/cc337889.aspx`.

Table 1-1. Categories of Office Business Application Patterns

Pattern Category	Description
Office Applications as a Reach Channel	Using Office to present data from other systems in an effort to simplify access or reduce duplication of effort
Document Integration	Automating the generation of documents with data from another system or processing the documents to extract data
Composite User Interface	Bringing together data from disparate resources into a single tool for the end user
Complementary Document Workflow	Providing the ability to incorporate ad-hoc workflow into other line-of-business processes

Pattern Category	Description
Discovery Navigation	Providing the ability to search and navigate through data of other systems
Collaborative Site	Using a SharePoint site to represent an instance of a structured process
Application-Generated Tasks and Notifications	Consolidating task requests from systems into Microsoft Outlook

You've just read about the need for these solutions, the technologies we have access to, and how we may have built them in the past. Now let's focus on the information-worker problems we will solve in this book. We've designed each solution not to rely on code presented in another chapter. Therefore, you will be able to read these chapters in any order depending on how appealing you find the problems.

Overview of the Solutions Chapters

Chapter 5: Beyond the Spreadsheet—Organizations often have large sets of spreadsheets. Some of these spreadsheets get dedicated teams to update them and distribute them on a regular basis. Other spreadsheets just get lost on file shares. In this chapter, we show you how to breathe new life into to Excel spreadsheets making them more interactive with automatically up to date data. This will include automatically generating new spreadsheets with data, providing an effective way to navigate a large number of data visualizations, and new methods of collaborating on portions of the spreadsheet.

Related OBA patterns: Document Integration, Composite User Interface, Discovery Navigation

Chapter 6: Merging SharePoint List Data into Word Documents— Organizations often have sets of document templates that are used throughout their enterprise. It is not unusual for several of these templates to share common data elements. At the same time, the list structures in SharePoint sites are increasingly being used to store records of data that might have previously been in local spreadsheets or Access databases. In this chapter we show you how to leverage the Open XML file format to insert a list item into a Word document so that its fields are displayed in designated locations.

Related OBA pattern: Document Integration

Chapter 7: Automating Document Assembly—By storing a document in a SharePoint library, users are able to collaborate and benefit from features such as versioning, metadata, and security. What if an organization has a document consisting of several fragments that need to be completed by different users concurrently and go through different approval processes or processing? In this chapter we will build a proposal tool that enables a user to search the SharePoint profile data to insert requests for résumés When the proposal is saved, each résumé request becomes an assigned task for the corresponding employee. When each one completes the task and attaches his résumé, it is merged back into the larger proposal document. We will also show how you can then take the final proposal and automatically convert it to a PDF on the server.

Related OBA patterns: Document Integration, Discovery Navigation, Office Application as a Reach Channel, Application Generated Tasks and Notifications

Chapter 8: Extending PowerPoint to Build a Presentation Based on Site Content—SharePoint Foundation supports collaboration for a particular team of users or a business process by providing team sites. Often, the users involved with such processes have to present their progress to the organization or to upper management. In this chapter, we will extend Microsoft PowerPoint with a wizard that allows the user to have presentation slides containing site content inserted into their presentation automatically.

Related OBA patterns: Office Applications as a Reach Channel, Document Integration, Composite User Interface

Chapter 9: Building a Presentation Server-Side within a Web Part—When an organization uses a team site to represent an instance of a business process, it often has to report the status of that process in the form of a presentation. That presentation usually includes content from the lists within the site. For types of presentations that happen frequently, the organization has likely adopted a template that is always used and orders the slides and information in a specific manner. In this chapter, we will build a web part that takes a PowerPoint template and populates the slides with content from a SharePoint site. This all happens on the server with a simple click of a button.

Related OBA pattern: Document Integration

Chapter 10: Surfacing Line-of-Business Data in Outlook—Information workers are often put into an environment where they need several tools that contain silos of duplicate data. They often have to jump in and out of these tools, copying and pasting data from one screen to the next. In this chapter we will show you how to leverage the Business Connectivity Services (BCS) functionality of Microsoft SharePoint Server to seamlessly integrate a line-of-business system with SharePoint. This will allow the data to be used in web parts and columns of lists, and will support search indexing. We will also show you how to extend this integration into Microsoft Outlook, providing the end-user with the external data in a familiar tool. We will then extend Outlook's functionality so that it provides single place for decision-making and acting on the data. This customization will include an Excel chart in the Outlook form for visualizing the data that will be generated by leveraging SharePoint's Excel Services functionality. The customization will also enable the user to create follow-up tasks from the Outlook form.

Related OBA patterns: Office Applications as a Reach Channel, Discovery Navigation, Composite User Interface, Application-Generated Tasks and Notifications

Chapter 11: Site Provisioning Workflows—The ability for a user to self-provision a site or site collection is one of the more powerful enabling features of SharePoint. It is also one of the most frequent features that organizations try to insert governance policies. In this chapter, we show you how an organization can utilize workflows to add controls to the site creation process. We will start with envisioning a process as a flow diagram in Visio and then import it into SharePoint Designer where the workflow will be constructed. We will also show you how you can build new custom workflow actions for SharePoint Designer in Visual Studio. Once the workflow is complete, we will take the solution full-circle and use a Visio diagram to visualize the status of the workflow.

Related OBA patterns: Office Applications as a Reach Channel, Complementary Document Workflow, Application-Generated Tasks and Notifications

Chapter 12: Rapid SharePoint Application Development with Access—Microsoft Access has always been an excellent Rapid Application Development (RAD) tool for building desktop data-centric applications, but it has been challenged when the need arises to move the application to the Web or to support a shared multi-user environment. With the release of Office 2010, the combination of SharePoint, Access, and Access Services now provides the ability to publish an Access database application to the Web. In this chapter, we show how, with Access, you can quickly create a SharePoint site for tracking assets.

Related OBA pattern: Collaborative Site

Chapter 13: Using Visio Services to Visualize Data—Visio has long been used by information workers as a canvas to create drawings that represent a wide range of ideas and systems. However, after implementation, the Visio drawing usually gets discarded. In this chapter, we show you how to breathe more life and achieve even greater value from Visio drawings by using them for data visualization. We will show you how to connect Visio drawings to information stored across disparate repositories, how to conditionally format a drawing based on values found there, and how to share the result with a wide audience through SharePoint's Visio Services feature.

Related OBA patterns: Composite User Interface, Discovery Navigation

Chapter 14: Building Mashups—Mashups are a Web 2.0 technique of taking data from multiple sources a combining them into a single presentation. The result provides greater insight than viewing each of the data sources individually. In this chapter, we use Bing Maps as the surface for the mashup. We then bring together data from a SharePoint list, a KML file, and a geocoded RSS feed all onto the surface of the map. This solution also includes an extension of SharePoint's out-of-the-box contact list so that when new items are added, their address is automatically geocoded.

Related OBA patterns: Discovery Navigation, Composite User Interface

Finally, Chapter 15 entitled **Realizing the Vision** will sum things up revisiting the importance of the solutions.

Development Environment Requirements

There are many options for a development environment and through the course of writing this book we used almost all of them at one point in time. When we first started, we relied on a virtualized environment. This gives the developer a sandbox to implement the solutions presented in the book. Because Microsoft SharePoint Server 2010 is a 64-bit application, we chose to host this virtual environment on a Windows Server 2008 machine with its Hyper-V virtualization features. We allocated 5GB of RAM to the machine and used an external E-SATA drive to host the virtual disk independent of the host machine. This does create quite the hardware requirement. As the Office 2010 and SharePoint 2010 bits neared release, we simplified our environment by installing SharePoint 2010 directly onto a 64-bit workstation using Windows 7 (could also use Windows Vista). This technique is discussed in Chapter 3. This is also why you see several different styles of Urls in the code references.

The reason we used a variety of approaches is that we began writing this book well before the final release of Office and SharePoint 2010, which meant we were constantly loading new versions and juggling multiple images. Hyper-V in Windows Server 2008 simplified the management of all of this. If you are going to match the Hyper-V configuration, you should have a recent machine that supports virtualization with about 8GB of RAM, and an external drive for the virtual machines is recommended. The virtual machine was our domain controller and included Microsoft SQL Server 2008. The virtual machine ran Microsoft SharePoint Server 2010 with its enterprise features enabled. This was also our development environment, and Microsoft Office Enterprise 2010, Microsoft SharePoint Designer 2010, and Microsoft Visual Studio 2010 Ultimate were also installed. The Windows 7 environment was similar in that it contained Office, SharePoint, Visual Studio, and SQL Server, but we used the domain our laptop was already joined to. In SharePoint, we used a single web application to host the intranet and enabled all of the shared service applications. In addition to these core products, we installed several SDKs, toolkits, and the like, including:

- SharePoint Server 2010 SDK

- The .NET Framework (versions 2.0, 3.5 SP1, and 4.0)

- All SharePoint 2010 prerequisites (installed as part of the SharePoint installation process)

- Word Content Control Toolkit from Codeplex - `http://www.codeplex.com/dbe`

- Open XML SDK 2.0 March 2010 - `http://msdn.microsoft.com/en-us/library/bb448854(office.14).aspx`

CHAPTER 2

■ ■ ■

SharePoint 2010: Overview and New Features

SharePoint is the name Microsoft has given to its collaboration platform. The name actually refers to a number of applications, though today most people use it to refer to the two prominent server applications: SharePoint Foundation 2010 and SharePoint Server 2010. But you'll also find it used for desktop applications such as SharePoint Designer and SharePoint Workspace (formerly Groove).

It is SharePoint Foundation that serves as the base for the platform, and it is actually a component of the Windows Server operating system. SharePoint Foundation provides core functionality, such as the ability to quickly provision collaboration sites, and a sophisticated document repository featuring collaboration necessities such as versioning, checkin/checkout, and a metadata system.

Whereas SharePoint Foundation provides collaborative sites to facilitate teams of users, SharePoint Server supplies more features to the enterprise. With SharePoint Server, the focus is on distributing information, social networking, application integration, search, business intelligence, and managing an enterprise's content. Enterprises get a platform designed for their intranet, extranet, and Internet environments.

In this chapter, we take a moment to reflect on SharePoint's history and then give you an overview of the new features. The idea is to get you up to speed on the new areas and terminology, not to replace the thorough introduction you can get from other resources. We'll focus on the big changes in the products' functionality and refer you to solutions later in the book that leverage them, along with lots of links for you to do more reading on your own. We'll exclude the Visual Studio 2010 Tools for SharePoint from this chapter as they are so pivotal in many of the solutions in this book that we gave them their own chapter (Chapter 3).

History of SharePoint Technologies

To understand the products as they exist today, it is important to review their history. Each product has a different heritage and only recently have the products been so seamlessly aligned and integrated. Before the term portal grew in popularity, developers sought to use Microsoft Outlook as a foundation to provide access to different systems and data, and most of the attention was focused on creating views that aggregated information from different applications into a single display. These views were made up of page components, and were organized much like the Outlook Today view. Microsoft provided SDK material and soon developers were building components to be loaded into the Outlook interface—a technique known as building digital dashboards. This allowed developers to build reusable components that could be arranged on the dashboard to provide a view of data across the enterprise. These components were the beginning of the web parts we know today. Developers used them to query databases and to display charts, data, and other key information.

Early in the Web era, Microsoft released a FrontPage server application that ran on top of Internet Information Services (IIS) and relied on the FrontPage HTML-design tool for administration and customization. One of the compelling features of FrontPage server was that it shipped with web site templates. Thus an organization could quickly create new sites that automatically had some application functionality, such as calendaring and task lists. These web sites would be ready for use after simply running a wizard. This eliminated the labor-intensive processes of web designers and application developers, dramatically decreasing the time it took to deploy a web site. The result was especially powerful for a straightforward web site that was going to be used by a small number of users for a short period of time.

For many organizations, such a site is not worth the effort and cost of a full-blown web-development endeavor. These FrontPage sites eventually evolved into a product named SharePoint Team Services, or STS, which was still based on Active Server Page (ASP) technology. With the .NET evolution, Windows SharePoint Services (WSS) arrived, and the version 2 features were released as a component of the server operating system. This led to a proliferation of organizations using this application's ability to create collaboration sites based on templates for teams of users. Windows SharePoint Services (version 3) was released as part of the 2007 wave of Office products and was built on top of ASP.NET 2.0. Though it still provided the foundation layer for the SharePoint stack, this release gave developers increased capabilities for customizing the solution so it could match a particular customer business process. Developers gained access to master pages, web parts, authentication providers, list and library event handlers, custom workflows using Windows Workflow Foundation, and much more.

Microsoft SharePoint Portal Server (SPS) 2001 was the first release of enterprise collaboration services that were to complement the agile team sites. This portal product was also based on ASP technology and focused on creating workspaces. With a workspace, the product provided a document repository as well as a web site where an organization could set up a site structure or taxonomy for organizing its information. The focus here was that documents should be categorized and that users would browse the category terms to locate their documents of interest. This category-based interface was a popular one for Web-based search engines at the time, such as Yahoo!. Included in this release was a search service as well as a Web-based component platform supporting web parts. A major difference between this version and the ones that would follow is that SharePoint 2001 did not rely on SQL Server for storage. Instead the repository was more like Exchange 2000 and was called the Web Storage System.

Like Windows SharePoint Services, SharePoint Portal Server received a major facelift with the move to the .NET platform. Microsoft SharePoint Portal Server 2003 gave organizations the ability to create enterprise portals. These portal sites relied on the WSS foundation for their document-repository needs and added new features for the enterprise, including a search that could index not only content stored within its repositories but also other content stores, such as file shares, web sites, and Microsoft Exchange public folders. SharePoint 2003 folded the workers of the system into the content mix as well. The services of My Sites and user profiles allowed the system to capture information about an organization's users and provided an application that let users view each other's profiles from within the system, access documents they shared, and locate users by attributes such as proficiency in a particular language. In fact, a user could be returned as a search result item along with documents and sites. SharePoint Portal Server 2003 also extended the web-part interface provided by WSS by incorporating a personalization service that allowed for a page to hide or show specific web parts to specific audiences of users. SharePoint's single-sign-on service provided an application-development framework for translating security contexts between the logged-in user and that user's credentials to an external application whose data was used by a web part. Ultimately, SharePoint Portal Server 2003 completed the touch points a user would have with his organization's information. Whereas WSS answered the needs for teams of users, SPS provided the services to meet the needs of the overall organization, divisions, and even the individual.

Microsoft Office SharePoint Server 2007 (MOSS) extended the capabilities of SPS 2003 by adding enterprise features to the platform. Built on the success of the 2003 release, this product expanded into new areas. The definition of content management was expanded to include web content and records management. In fact, the addition of web content management meant that MOSS swallowed whole the product capability of Microsoft Content Management Server. This was a benefit to customers in that there was no longer a need to support two separate products and platforms for content management. It also eliminated the need to glue the two products together for a complete offering. Moreover, MOSS 2007 integrated electronic forms into its definition of content, solving a key problem for InfoPath in the process. InfoPath, introduced in Office 2003, was a great product for quickly building forms without code but was limited in that the user filling out the form also had to have the InfoPath client application. MOSS solved this problem by automatically generating a web-based equivalent of the form using its InfoPath Forms Services feature.

MOSS 2007 also expanded to play a pivotal role in business intelligence by allowing users to visualize their data in dashboards. A major part of this functionality was Excel Services which, much like Forms Services, allowed users to publish their spreadsheets to the server. Once the spreadsheets were published, the rich charting and visualization capability of Excel could be utilized through web-based web parts that could still maintain their connection to data sources. Furthermore, MOSS 2007 became an integration platform with the inclusion of the Business Data Catalog (BDC). This feature enabled the surfacing of line-of-business data from external systems, such as Oracle databases, SAP, or other applications, into a SharePoint environment with the developer only having to describe the external system through XML. The surfaced data could find its way into dashboards via web parts, search, and even metadata columns—all without the developer having to write a line of code. For more information on SharePoint's history, read the reflections of Microsoft Corporate Vice President for SharePoint Server, Jeff Teper's blog post: `http://blogs.msdn.com/sharepoint/archive/2009/10/05/sharepoint-history.aspx`.

SharePoint 2010 Overview

Microsoft's tag line for the SharePoint 2010 release is "The Business Collaboration Platform for the Enterprise and the Web." The key word for us is *Platform*. Think of all of the other words that could have been chosen: application, product, server, suite, and so forth. However, none of these other terms adequately describes what enterprises are doing with the software or Microsoft's vision regarding the direction of the product. The software has evolved beyond a set of out-of-the-box capabilities to a set of application-level services that enterprises and their developers mold into business solutions. SharePoint is no longer about just setting up an intranet and publishing documents. The 2010 release of these technologies is about providing a rich set of capabilities that can be combined and extended to make a business more effective. Figure 2-1 is Microsoft's depiction of the SharePoint 2010 feature areas. We will spend some time in each, providing an overview and discussing some of the extension points for developers.

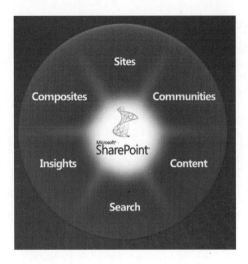

Figure 2-1. SharePoint 2010 feature areas

Sites

In SharePoint, the "site" provides a context for the users interacting with the information within it. This context could be a particular team, department, event, or an instance of a business process. The site provides a wrapper that relates all of the content (lists, document libraries, and web parts) to a specific purpose. The ability to provision these sites quickly has always been one of the strengths of the platform. These sites can be self-provisioned with no need for developers to hold many months of requirements-gathering sessions before building a custom solution. In fact, this is the focus of Chapter 11, which not only looks at site templating but also examines how to inject workflow into the site provisioning process so you can have self-service along with process and auditing.

In the 2010 release, SharePoint sites provide the user with an enhanced web experience. The most obvious improvement is the ribbon interface, which first made its appearance in the Office client applications in Office 2007. The ribbon makes the organization of commands uniform between the web and desktop interfaces, a great help to users. Of course, as developers, you've been able to extend the ribbon in the desktop applications (described in more detail in Chapter 4), and that extension point will continue in with the SharePoint web experience. Figure 2-2 shows the SharePoint ribbon extension you will build in Chapter 3. The same technique will also be used in the solution you'll build in Chapter 6.

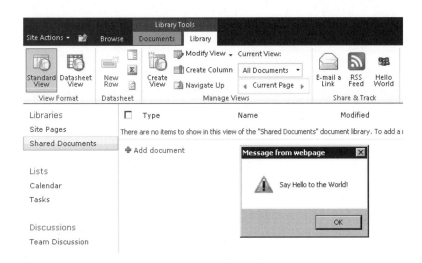

Figure 2-2. *Customizing SharePoint's ribbon*

Another significant improvement in the 2010 release is the AJAX behavior of the pages. AJAX stands for asynchronous JavaScript and XML. For end users, this means the web interface behaves more like a traditional Windows Forms application that updates only appropriate controls. Not only is the out-of-the-box experience enhanced, your customizations can leverage it as well. Chapter 9 shows you how to build an AJAX-style web part, and Chapter 13 layers data over a web-based Visio document using the new JavaScript-based SharePoint API. There are also new dialog and notification techniques that reduce page refreshes. These are used in Chapter 5.

With each release of SharePoint, the Office client applications become more integrated into the sites its files participate in. The new backstage interface that appears when users click the File menu eases adoption by removing some of the mystery of how to get a document into SharePoint. As shown in Figure 2-3, from this interface a user can easily perform actions such as saving the file to a SharePoint site, setting metadata, starting a workflow, and more. We will even extend this interface in Chapter 7.

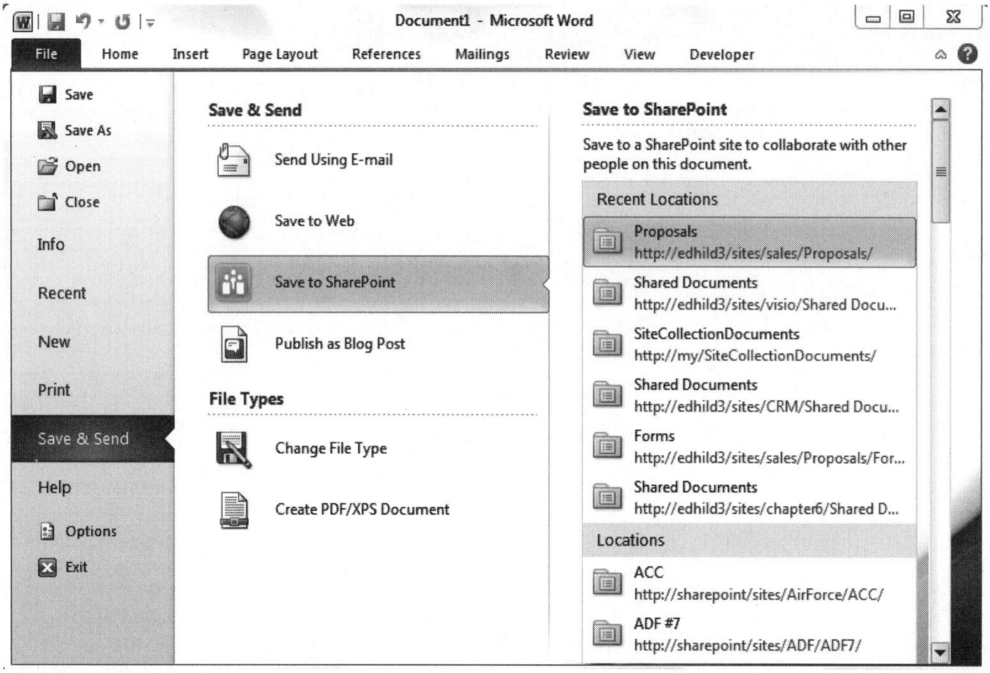

Figure 2-3. *The Office backstage interface*

In addition to streamlining the interaction between the server and desktop applications, SharePoint 2010 also enables scenarios that were problematic in the past. Users with low-bandwidth connections often found it difficult to interact with their SharePoint sites. Now in the 2010 release, these sites can make it to the desktop much more efficiently than before. For example, the user can start with the web-based versions of Word, Excel, PowerPoint, or OneNote installed in the SharePoint environment to preview a file before deciding to download it. As the remote user browses the SharePoint sites, a combination of Windows 7 and Windows Server 2008 R2 together provide a branch cache solution that accelerates the experience. The acceleration is due to the remote user's ability to potentially retrieve the HTML, JavaScript, images, and other files from a peer instead of across the wide area network. If the user changes a downloaded file and saves it back to the server, the save is actually asynchronous to a local cache where a delta is created and sent to the server. The Office clients are even more capable of taking content offline. Microsoft Outlook and SharePoint Workspace (formerly Microsoft Groove) play a large part in offline scenarios. In Chapter 10 you will see how SharePoint 2010 enables a user to take line-of-business data offline. Use the following links for more details on these improvements:

- Introduction to the Office 2010 Backstage View for Developers

  `http://msdn.microsoft.com/en-us/library/ee691833(office.14).aspx`

- SharePoint 2010 Sites (Video on New Features)

  `http://sharepoint2010.microsoft.com/product/capabilities/sites/pages/`
  `top-features.aspx`

- Windows Server 2008 R2 and BranchCache

  `http://www.microsoft.com/windowsserver2008/en/us/branch-cache.aspx`

- See What's New in Microsoft SharePoint Workspace 2010

  `http://www.microsoft.com/video/en/us/details/755f7866-f95c-4d8a-a904-d80154413444`

Communities

Ever since SharePoint Portal Server 2003 included the "my site" functionality, the SharePoint platform has been more than just a web-based file share. The product focuses on engaging people, and this continues with My Sites, which are still a feature of SharePoint Server 2010. The user profile store still exists, and surfaces itself as a sort of electronic business card, and there is still a personal dashboard where users can organize web parts for quick access to information they check regularly. The main difference in the 2010 release is how My Site becomes the center hub for a user to get updates on activities and events within their enterprise, along with the increased number of ways users can participate socially. There are now many different ways users can contribute, participate, and share beyond the documents themselves. For example, users can tag any piece of content, whether list item, document, or even the web page. These tags become social since a user is able to see what colleagues are tagging as a roll-up on their My Site. Users can also rate content and share bookmarks. My Sites now even have a note board, which Facebook users will relate to writing on someone's wall. Of course, there are also enhanced blogs and wikis. In fact, every page in a SharePoint 2010 site has a wiki-like editing experience. And the new team blog enables multiple people to publish blog posts. The bottom line is that social networking tools have definitely become popular in the public domain, and SharePoint 2010 brings these features to the enterprise. They are all ways to get your users involved, integrated, and participating in the environment. User tags, ratings, and profile data also becomes a wealth of information you can leverage in your own solutions. In Chapter 13, we integrate user profile data into a Visio diagram. And in Chapter 7, we integrate a people search into a task pane of Microsoft Word. Use the following link for a video on SharePoint 2010 Communities features `http://sharepoint2010.microsoft.com/product/capabilities/communities/pages/top-features.aspx`.

Content

In SharePoint 2010, the content repository gets too many enhancements to list. Nevertheless, we will touch on some of the really big items you will surely want to be aware of when reading through the solutions in this book. The most important improvement is one you might rarely actually see—scale. SharePoint 2010's content repositories have been tested well beyond the limits that were practical in the previous release. Almost everyone working with SharePoint 2007 was aware of the recommended threshold of 2,000 items in a list or folder of a document library. This was not a hard ceiling, but if a solution pushed much past this limit, the user experience would begin to degrade. It seems difficult to imagine returning more than 2,000 items in a single view of a page, but we have seen lots of customers try. Such an operation can be a problem for a farm because it can be very taxing on the SQL Server and SharePoint web front end to generate this view of data for just one user. So taxing, in fact, that other users of the environment may suffer long page loads or dropped requests even with trivial actions. In SharePoint 2010, it is possible to have lists where the number of items is measured in millions. This scale is achieved by first realizing that users won't browse through millions of items like they browse a file system. Retrieving items from a large list will be done by specifying filters against metadata properties (another improvement described a bit later). Of course, it's still possible for a user to specify a filter that returns more items than you want to allocate resources for, but in SharePoint 2010, there is a farm configuration setting where you can specify the desired threshold limit. This will vary in different environments based on the hardware and server configuration, but it gives the administrators confidence that SharePoint will defend itself from queries that could drag down performance. If a query exceeds the threshold, the user will be informed and asked to indicate additional filters to the query to bring it under the limit.

Another major change in the 2010 release is that metadata is everywhere—and we're not talking about just simple columns of data on a file. In SharePoint 2010, you can create hierarchical enterprise metadata term stores for use in your enterprise. In addition to this top-down approach, SharePoint also provides a bottom-up solution where users can submit their own terms through tagging, creating a folksonomy of metadata. This metadata can also be used for navigation instead of the typical folder navigation approach. Figure 2-4 shows the administrative interface for the term store management tool.

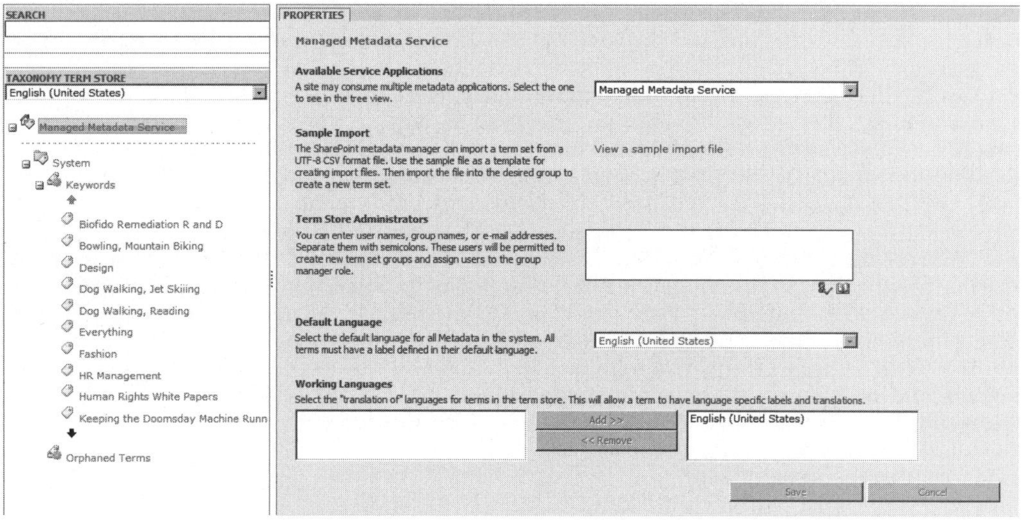

Figure 2-4. SharePoint 2010 Term Store Management Tool

In previous versions of SharePoint, metadata and other many other features were focused on a particular item. You could set metadata for an item, send an item through a workflow, version an item, and so on. But customers often asked how to operate on a set of items as a single unit. SharePoint 2010 answers this question with the new feature called document sets. A document set can be treated as a single item, with its contained files taking on some of the behavior of the set. You can cascade metadata across the items in a set, have the set go through a workflow, or version the entire set. Of course, not every item in the set has to be the same type. Figure 2-5 shows you the welcome page of a document set which contains several different types of files.

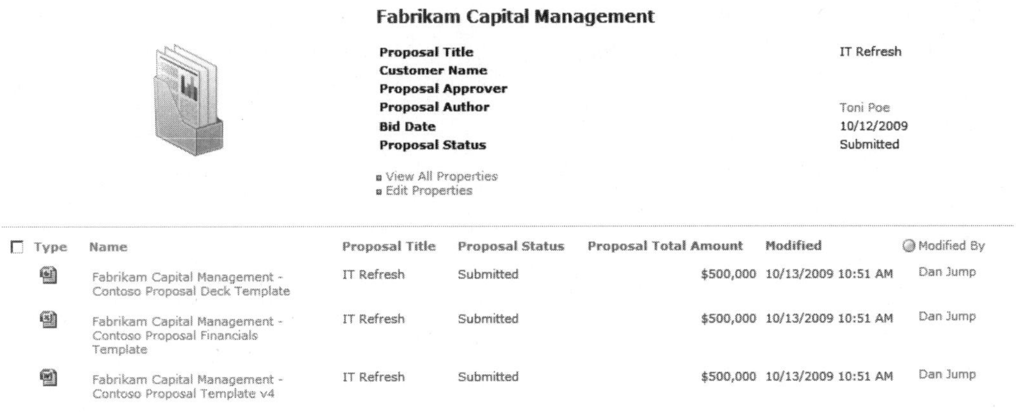

Fabrikam Capital Management

Proposal Title	IT Refresh
Customer Name	
Proposal Approver	
Proposal Author	Toni Poe
Bid Date	10/12/2009
Proposal Status	Submitted

■ View All Properties
■ Edit Properties

☐ Type	Name	Proposal Title	Proposal Status	Proposal Total Amount	Modified	◎ Modified By
📄	Fabrikam Capital Management - Contoso Proposal Deck Template	IT Refresh	Submitted	$500,000	10/13/2009 10:51 AM	Dan Jump
📄	Fabrikam Capital Management - Contoso Proposal Financials Template	IT Refresh	Submitted	$500,000	10/13/2009 10:51 AM	Dan Jump
📄	Fabrikam Capital Management - Contoso Proposal Template v4	IT Refresh	Submitted	$500,000	10/13/2009 10:51 AM	Dan Jump

Figure 2-5. Document sets

Other improvements in the content repository include additional support for digital asset management and enhanced records management. For records management, the enhancements give you additional routing capability. You can also choose to manage the records separately or manage retention in-place where the content was created. Also, there is a new server-side Word Automation Service that allows you to do conversions of Microsoft Word documents in ways similar to the options in Word's save-as dialog. This enables you to automate, say, converting files to PDF, XPS, or older versions of Microsoft Word. We will kick off this service from code as part of the solution in Chapter 7.

The workflow story with SharePoint 2010 is also more complete. In previous versions, there was a distinction between enterprise class workflows and ad-hoc, one-off solutions. Enterprise workflows that were going to be used in different lists, sites, or site collections had to be created using Visual Studio. However, a savvy end user could use SharePoint Designer to create a workflow for a specific list. What was missing, and what SharePoint 2010 provides, is the ability to promote the end-user workflow to an enterprise one. In fact, you can start with a Visio diagram, prototype the solution using SharePoint Designer, and then import that into Visual Studio for final development. Figure 2-6 shows a workflow at the beginning of this process in Visio. These techniques are used in the solution in Chapter 11.

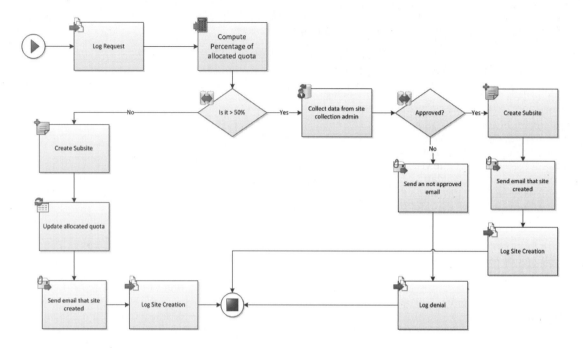

Figure 2-6. Building a SharePoint workflow in Visio

Use the following link for a video about SharePoint 2010 Content features `http://sharepoint2010.microsoft.com/product/capabilities/content/pages/top-features.aspx`.

Search

Ever since the SPS 2001 release, SharePoint has included Microsoft's enterprise search solution, which is not concerned only about searching content within SharePoint's databases, but also provides a single interface to search across an enterprise's content repositories. This means that file shares, web sites, and even data that is normally locked into line-of-business applications are all capable of being indexed and surfaced through a SharePoint interface. With the 2010 release, SharePoint's search interface becomes much more interactive. Users can narrow a search result through refiners, see related queries, and perform more advanced searches including by using wildcard support. Users can also subscribe to a search result as an RSS feed, ask to be alerted through e-mail or text message if new items for the search are found, or bookmark it to rerun the search later. The SharePoint search engine is also more broadly accessible in that searches can be performed from the browser, smartphone device, or from a desktop running Windows 7. One of our favorite new search features is in people search where you can phonetically spell a user's name. No more hunting through the Global Address Book looking for the right spelling of Shawn. We will leverage the search functionality in Chapter 7. Use the following link for a video about the SharePoint 2010 Search features: `http://sharepoint2010.microsoft.com/product/capabilities/search/pages/top-features.aspx`.

Insights

The Insights portion of the wheel in Figure 2-1 refers to the functionality in SharePoint 2010 that helps users make decisions based on data visualizations. This includes features like Excel Services, Performance Point Services, Visio Services, and PowerPivot. Excel Services was introduced in MOSS 2007 and its focus was to enable users who leverage Excel to build visualizations of their data to share through a SharePoint page. In this scenario, a spreadsheet is connected to a data source and the user builds the visualization and then publishes it to the SharePoint server. Once it's on the server, SharePoint enables users to view and interact with elements of the spreadsheet without ever downloading the file in Excel. The interface is a thin client that uses DHTML, JavaScript, and images. There are lots of potential advantages to sharing the visualization in this manner. First, the server can continue to connect to the original data source, updating the visualization so the user sees the most recent result. If the spreadsheet were just e-mailed around, this would not be possible unless all users had access and connectivity to the data source. By publishing to the SharePoint server, you can also hide elements of the spreadsheet that you don't want to share, such as sheets of background data, and you can prevent access to formulas. Chapter 5 focuses on spreadsheets and Excel Services. All of the Excel Services functions continue in SharePoint 2010 and, in addition, you can access the spreadsheet in Excel Services through a REST API. REST stands for Representational State Transfer and means that Excel Services can render elements of the spreadsheet simply with a URL request. So, for example, the following URL would retrieve a chart from an Excel Services spreadsheet named `CRMSales.xlsx` `http://intranet/sites/crm/_vti_bin/ ExcelRest.aspx/Shared%20Documents/CRMSales.xlsx/model/charts('Chart%203')`. The result is a PNG image that can be used in other applications. This technique is shown in Figure 2-7 and is used in Chapter 10 to pull in a visualization of orders information into Outlook.

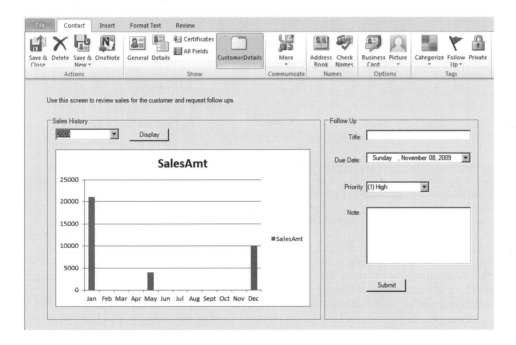

Figure 2-7. Embedding an Excel Services' visualization in another application

In addition to Excel Services, SharePoint 2010 includes Performance Point Services and support for SQL Server PowerPivot for SharePoint. Performance Point Services is a significantly enhanced version of the dashboarding capability that in the 2007 wave was offered as a separate product—Microsoft Performance Point. Performance Point Services includes a dashboard designer that allows you to build SharePoint pages containing many data visualizations with actions specifying what should change as the user interacts with the page. For example, using the dashboard designer, you could have a page with a scorecard that, when the user clicks a particular key performance indicator, causes other report web parts to load on the page that would display details specific to that metric. Figure 2-8 shows an example Performance Point Services dashboard.

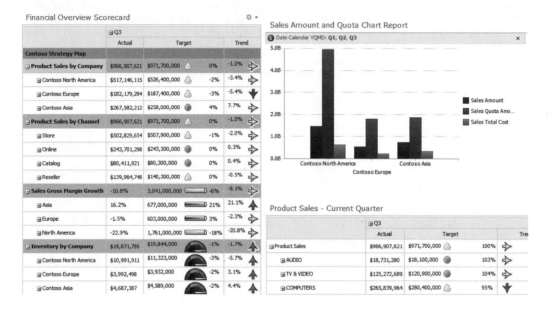

Figure 2-8. *A Performance Point Services dashboard*

SQL Server PowerPivot for Excel and SharePoint is actually a new solution for enabling users to analyze large datasets without having to build an OLAP cube. This offering brings an in-memory analysis engine that can be used by the Excel client or a SharePoint 2010 server should the spreadsheet be published there.

Another new data visualization technology in SharePoint 2010 is Visio Services. Much like Excel Services, this new feature enables you to connect a data source to a Visio document and then publish it to the server. Data sources could include SQL Server, Excel spreadsheets, and even SharePoint lists. Once on the server, the diagram is available through the browser, and you can add conditions to alter the appearance of the diagram based on the data. Figure 2-9 shows a floor-plan visualization you will build in Chapter 13. Notice how the conference room C-101 is available and that the printers are showing icons and overlays from other data sources.

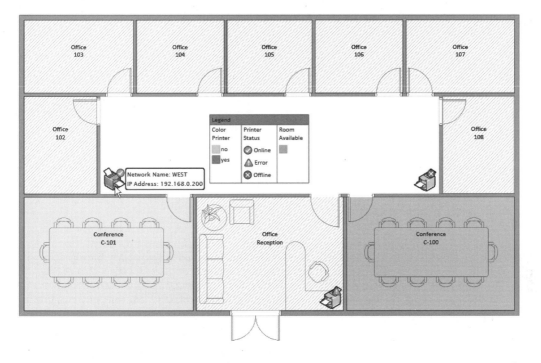

Figure 2-9. Visualizing data with Visio Services

Use the following link for a video on more about the SharePoint 2010 Insights features:
`http://sharepoint2010.microsoft.com/product/capabilities/insights/pages/top-features.aspx`.

Composites

The Composites portion of the wheel refers to the functionality in SharePoint 2010 that helps organizations bring together traditionally siloed applications into a seamless experience. This includes features like Business Connectivity Services, InfoPath Form Services, Access Services, and SharePoint Designer. Business Connectivity Services (BCS) in SharePoint 2010 represents the evolution of the Business Data Catalog (BDC) functionality that first appeared in MOSS 2007. The original BDC became the developers' best friend as it removed the need to reinvent the wheel over and over again to do the common tasks of integrating external data into the SharePoint environment. Instead of writing code, a developer could describe these external applications (whether database or web-services-based) with an XML file, including methods for how to retrieve the item, how to search for an item, and details on the makeup or attributes of the item. With the description, the BDC could make this data available to MOSS 2007 search, automatically provide web parts to view the external data on SharePoint pages, and use the data as metadata properties on SharePoint items. In SharePoint 2010, the BDC becomes the BCS and increases the scope of the application integration. While the BDC brought the data into SharePoint as read-only, BCS supports writing changes back to the original application. In fact, the Office 2010 desktop applications also play a part in BCS functionality. For example, the external content can be taken offline in Outlook or SharePoint Workspaces. We use this technique as part of the solution in Chapter 10. Microsoft Word can also use BCS data inline in documents. This technique is described in the solution in

Chapter 6. Figure 2-10 shows a Customers table from a SQL Server surfaced in SharePoint as an external list using the Business Connectivity Services functionality.

	CustomerID	FirstName	LastName	CompanyName	Address	City	State	Zip	Phone	WebPage
	1	Bob	Smith	Acme Inc	1 Acme Way	Baltimore	MD	21227	4102223333	http://www.acmeinc.com
	2	Jane	Doe	Test Corp	1 Test Rd	Seattle	WA	89203	4254445555	http://testcorp.com
	3	Kevin	Lost	Jump High Stores	2 Main St	Dallas	TX	57483	7103334444	http://www.jumphighstores.com

Figure 2-10. An external list in SharePoint

In addition to the enhanced functionality of BCS to bring in external data, the tooling also improves. In the previous versions, developers would either create the application definition XML file either manually or with a non-integrated tool. Now in the 2010 toolset, registering applications into BCS is integrated into SharePoint Designer and Visual Studio 2010. The experience in SharePoint Designer is easy and wizard-driven, but is limited to connecting to applications via SQL Server, web services, or a specific .NET class. As long as you stay within those boundaries, you can get your external application into SharePoint 2010 without writing a line of code, as you'll see in Chapter 10. If you need to connect to other types of applications, Visual Studio allows you to write some code for the integration and then still leverage the BCS infrastructure. In the 2010 release, SharePoint Designer takes on a larger role and often serves as a no-code method to rapidly bring applications together in your SharePoint environment.

Another composites feature is the improved InfoPath Forms Services. This feature also debuted in MOSS 2007. InfoPath had existed in Office 2003 only as a desktop application and was the centerpiece in Microsoft's electronic forms strategy. The appeal of InfoPath was that it could be used by non-developers and developers alike. A business savvy user could open up InfoPath, use its designer to lay out the form, and distribute the form to users who would use InfoPath to complete it. Developers could use the tool to connect to the web services of their applications. Once InfoPath inspected the description of the web service, it could automatically create a form. In either case, when users completed forms, InfoPath generated XML files containing their data that could easily be posted to other data sources or applications. The major problem, however, was that the InfoPath client was required both to design the form and to fill it out. This limited the tool to being used only within enterprises since you couldn't count on an external user having InfoPath. MOSS 2007's Form Services solved the problem by automatically creating a web-based equivalent of the form, including persisting any code a developer may have written. In SharePoint 2010, InfoPath Forms Services expands beyond traditional electronic forms. You can now use this service and InfoPath to design alternative forms for list items (view, edit, new). So instead of having to write custom web parts in Visual Studio in front of list items, developers can control the layout of the form, add advanced validation, incorporate other external data all through by using InfoPath to design the list item's form user interface. By the way, this form also goes with the list into SharePoint Workspace so the same user interface appears in the offline tool as the web interface. There is also an InfoPath form web part that is useful for composite applications. InfoPath Form Services is used as part of the solution in Chapters 5 and 11.

SharePoint 2010 also includes a feature called Access Services. Microsoft Access has long been a development tool with a lower bar of entry than Visual Studio or SQL Server. We can't tell you how often we've seen customers whose department-level Access database grew into a mission-critical application. Access is often used when a business user has a compelling need and requires a solution faster than an enterprise's developers can deliver. These types of applications often make a business more agile. The problem is that IT shops often clamp down on such activity because of how many times they have had to support these applications as they grow beyond the original intent. In SharePoint 2010, Access Services is the answer that promotes an Access application into a web-based, SharePoint-based solution. Not only do the tables and data find their way into SharePoint lists, but even the Access forms get converted into SharePoint pages. This can increase the reach of the solution and provide IT with a path to reduce governance risks. Access Services is the focus of Chapter 12. Figure 2-11 shows the creation of a web-based database in Access that could be published to SharePoint.

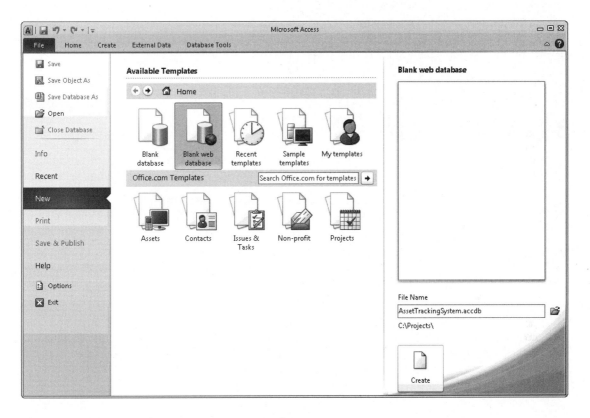

Figure 2-11. Creating a Web Database in Microsoft Access 2010

SharePoint 2010's out-of-the-box support for Silverlight makes it easier for developers to build interactive experiences that bring together data from multiple sources. In Chapter 5, we will use Silverlight to provide an interactive, graphical experience for the user to navigate the charts contained in Excel spreadsheets of a document library. As shown in Figure 2-12, the solution in Chapter 14 brings together several data feeds into a single mashup on top of Bing Maps.

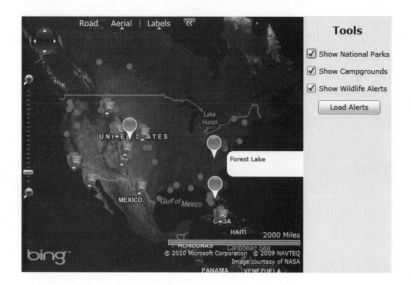

Figure 2-12. *Creating a Mashup with Silverlight and Bing Maps*

Use the following link for a video about the SharePoint 2010 Composites features
`http://sharepoint2010.microsoft.com/product/capabilities/composites/pages/top-features.aspx.`

Leveraging the Platform

This by no means is a complete guide to SharePoint 2010. If you are new to the SharePoint world, we highly recommend spending some time with some overview books or the materials on `http://sharepoint.microsoft.com`. When we introduced this chapter, we called out the importance of SharePoint 2010 as a platform, and the solutions presented in this book take this to heart. We don't simply stick to out-of-the-box functionality, but show how the features of SharePoint and Office along with the .NET framework enable developers to build effective solutions for information workers. In the next chapter, we dive deeper and take a closer look at the SharePoint development support in Visual Studio 2010.

CHAPTER 3

▪▪▪

SharePoint Development with Visual Studio 2010

With the release of SharePoint 2007, the product matured from a set of out-of-the-box features to a platform enterprises could build on and adapt to meet their exact needs. Successful platforms deliver value to an organization through a rich set of capabilities that can be extended and customized to align with key business processes and objectives. The quality of tooling to support development against the platform is a critical ingredient of this success as well. Development targeting SharePoint 2007 can be challenging at times, due largely to the lack of integrated and familiar tool support. SharePoint 2007 developers were required to hand-code large XML files, master multiple tools, and have deep understanding of the intricacies of the platform to perform even the simplest of tasks. Fortunately, SharePoint 2010 and Visual Studio 2010 together ease development significantly with features such as enhanced APIs, integrated tooling, and expanded deployment options that allow developers to focus more on the solution and less on the plumbing. In fact, there are so many new features, an entire book could easily (and likely will) be written on this topic alone.

SharePoint for the Professional Developer

For the professional developer, writing code is a critical aspect of the daily routine, and for many, it can even be a form of art and personal expression. Moreover, most developers hate to write the same code twice; we continually look for ways to be more productive and to accelerate development to bring our solution to market more quickly. As discussed in Chapter 2, SharePoint delivers a rich set of capabilities across six key workloads: Sites, Communities, Content, Search, Insights and Composites. SharePoint also provides a common foundation in support of these workloads to answer common crosscutting concerns, such as authentication and authorization, storage, scale, provisioning of services, and governance controls. SharePoint 2010 and the associated tools promote the increased productivity and accelerated development developers are looking for.

Some aspect of these six workloads will surface in most applications being developed today. For example, an approval process could be managed in SharePoint before orders are routed through an ERP system. The value in building such applications in whole or in part as SharePoint solutions is that you don't have to continually reinvent the wheel. By taking advantage of SharePoint as an application platform, you can focus your attention on the differentiating and business-value aspects of your solutions.

A Brief History of SharePoint Development

Windows SharePoint Services (WSS) 3.0 and SharePoint 2007 were released in late November of 2006, and while they offered developers an extremely rich platform on which to build some very compelling solutions, there was a gap—the toolset developers have come to expect and depend on when building .NET applications was limited and disjointed for projects targeting SharePoint. The initial development experience included manually editing XML files and running command-line tools and scripts for packaging and deployment. What the professional developer wanted and needed was the richness that Visual Studio provides, including IntelliSense and the familiar build, deploy, and debug process often referred to as the F5 experience.

In March of 2007, Microsoft released Visual Studio Extensions for WSS (VSeWSS) version 1.0 for Visual Studio 2005. The extensions provided SharePoint-specific project and item templates within Visual Studio as well as the familiar F5 behavior, but the experience was clunky compared with developing a typical ASP.NET application; still required lots of manual editing of XML files; and hid too much from the developer to the extent that some configuration files could not be accessed without breaking the project. And while the install package included a standalone application called the SharePoint Solution Generator that enabled developers to point to an existing site to generate a VSeWSS project based on the source site, many items, such as workflows, were not covered by the tool's examination of site elements.

In February of 2008, VSeWSS 1.1 was made available for download. The new version introduced several key enhancements based on community feedback, including a new Web Solution Package (WSP) view that provided access to files previously hidden from developers; the ability to create empty features; support for Visual Basic; additional item templates; and general bug fixes. Around this same time, many developers were transitioning to Visual Studio 2008, which was not supported by the 1.1 release though Visual Studio 2008 did introduce two workflow templates targeted for SharePoint as part of the standard install. A few months later, in June of 2008, the release of VSeWSS 1.2 provided version 1.1 capabilities for the Visual Studio 2008 developer.

The current and final build of VSeWSS is version 1.3. Version 1.3 was released as a community technology preview in March of 2009 with an update expected soon, this version is for Visual Studio 2008 only and includes several key enhancements such as 64-bit support; more granular control over the build process; command-line build commands that could be included in an automated software development lifecycle (SDLC) process; conflict resolution; and support for external assemblies. Going forward, VSeWSS 1.3 and Visual Studio 2008 are Microsoft's recommended solution for developers continuing to work with WSS 3.0 and SharePoint 2007.

So far, we have focused on the tools and guidance provided by Microsoft, but the solutions developed by the community in support of the SharePoint developer are definitely worth noting. A quick search for SharePoint on `http://www.CodePlex.com,` Microsoft's open source project hosting website, returns hundreds of results, many of which are both standalone solutions and extensions tied into the Visual Studio environment, all designed to make developers more productive. The importance of contributions from the community will continue even with the updated tooling provided in SharePoint and Visual Studio 2010.

What's New in SharePoint for Developers

Tooling aside for a moment, SharePoint 2010 delivers a number of enhancements further solidifying its place as a robust application platform.

For one, the options for architecting and building custom solutions targeting SharePoint have been greatly expanded. In addition to the server-side APIs available in SharePoint 2007, SharePoint 2010 introduces the concept of a Client Object Model (Client OM). The Client OM takes many of the same capabilities offered by the server-side APIs and exposes them outside the boundaries of the server, packaged as libraries for .NET, Silverlight, and JavaScript. SharePoint is then exposed to the client-side APIs via web services, Windows Communication Foundation (WCF) services, and REST-based interfaces. Moreover, until now, when it came to retrieving data from SharePoint, complex Collaborative Application Markup Language (CAML) queries were the only choice. Now LINQ support has been added, allowing developers to work with a much more familiar query language.

From a UI perspective, the most noticeable change is the Ribbon interface, which is now consistent across all the Office 2010 servers and clients. The Ribbon includes support for features such as contextual tabs and, of course, is extensible, allowing you to customize buttons and behaviors. In addition, enhancements around master pages, CSS processing, and a new theming engine enable you to more easily create a rich and intuitive user experience; a new AJAX-style page overlay dialog substantially reduces the need for full page roundtrips; and Silverlight is supported out of the box with the Silverlight Web Part.

On the deployment side, SharePoint 2010 continues to use WSPs as the packaging and deployment mechanism, but extends this model to answer a resounding need for isolation. Isolation is critical for multi-tenancy scenarios or even for cases where discrete development teams within the same organization are targeting a shared instance of SharePoint. This isolation is supported through sandboxed solutions that provide governance controls and the ability to deploy a WSP to a specific site collection, ensuring that code is unable to reach beyond the scope of the site collection. In addition, once our solutions are deployed, we need to ensure they are meeting performance expectations. For this, SharePoint 2010 introduces the Developer Dashboard (Figure 3-1) to provide insight into the processing and performance metrics for each page request. Developers have the option of enabling verbose tracing for step –by-step execution details.

These are just a few of the highlights. For a more detailed look at what is new for developers, you can browse to `http://msdn.microsoft.com/en-us/sharepoint/ee514561.aspx`.

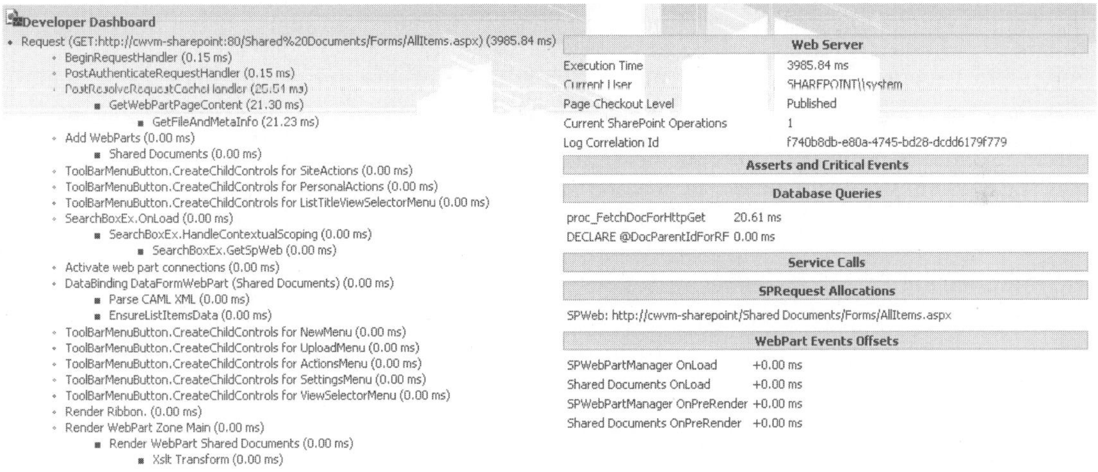

Figure 3-1. *The Developer Dashboard*

What's New in Visual Studio for SharePoint

While the platform enhancements are exciting and will greatly enhance productivity and flexibility when building solutions targeting SharePoint, the real news for the professional developer is the integration of the SharePoint tools into Visual Studio. When it comes to building tools for the professional developer, Microsoft's goal is to provide a productive environment by delivering a powerful and intuitive toolbox full of features like IntelliSense, visual designers, build and debugging support, rich project and item templates and wizards—in fact, all the tools we have come to expect and depend when we create a new Visual Studio project, regardless of the deployment target. This goal was a driving force behind the SharePoint tools for Visual Studio 2010; the key difference now is that the SharePoint tools are part of the Visual Studio release rather than a separate set of downloadable extensions. Just as was the case with VSeWSS, the SharePoint tools aim to abstract some of the complex implementation details from the developer, such as disregarding the structure of the 14 hive at design time and focusing more on logical groupings of related artifacts. Of course, developers always have direct access to the raw files when necessary.

Within Visual Studio 2008, developers were able to create SharePoint-specific sequential and state machine workflows, but this was the extent of the out-of-the-box template support. To those workflow templates, Visual Studio 2010 adds project template support for site definitions, list definitions, event receivers, content types, modules, visual Web Parts, Business Connectivity Services (BCS) models, and for creating a project by importing from an existing WSP or workflow. This last item is one of the most interesting—while the VSeWSS Solution Generator provided some ability to import from existing sources, the list of items available for import was limited. Selecting one of the new import project templates launches a wizard that lets a developer choose the site elements included in a WSP (which could be exported from an existing site) to be used to generate the initial project files. This could include conversion of declarative workflows, making a tool like SharePoint Designer a much more interesting option for prototyping before bringing a project into Visual Studio.

The most noticeable change is the support for visual design tools, providing a better experience around development and configuration of a SharePoint solution. By creating a visual Web Part, you no longer need to perform tasks such as adding controls in code. Package and feature configuration is now accomplished using the properties window and related designer, though the developer still has direct control over the generated XML. Package Explorer provides quick access to the structure of the WSP as it will be constructed by the packaging engine. Finally, Server Explorer (Figure 3-2) now natively supports SharePoint so browsing through and interacting with your local instance can be accomplished right inside Visual Studio.

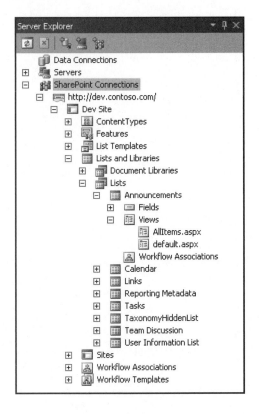

Figure 3-2. Browsing a SharePoint site using Server Explorer within Visual Studio

We are limited only by our imagination. With the SharePoint 2007 release, the community built and shared some very compelling tools to support the SharePoint developer, and the expectation is the community will continue to do so to fill the void where gaps exist. To support this scenario, Visual Studio exposes an extensibility framework for the SharePoint tools, providing a mechanism for the community to continue to enrich the toolset while taking advantage of functionality provided out-of-the-box.

Developers will also be happy to hear that the ability to install and run all requirements for SharePoint 2010 development on a client OS is now supported, thus removing the need to develop in a virtual environment or install a server OS on your development machine. Support is provided for 64-bit versions of Vista SP1 (or greater) and Windows 7.

For additional information on the SharePoint tools delivered as part of Visual Studio 2010, see `http://msdn.microsoft.com/en-us/library/ee330921(v=VS.100).aspx`.

Building Your First Project

OK, enough talk about all the great new tooling. Let's build and deploy a custom feature using the new SharePoint tools in Visual Studio. For this example we will create a new SharePoint feature that, when activated, will change the associated site title to Hello World, as well as create a new button on the Library tab of the Ribbon within the context of document libraries. This will not be a complex coding exercise, but should give you enough hands-on experience with the toolset for you to feel comfortable with the exercises in the remaining chapters, as well as serve as a starting point for projects you create on your own. Use the following steps to create your Visual Studio 2010 SharePoint tools project:

Creating the HelloWorld Project

1. Launch Visual Studio 2010 and create a new project based on the SharePoint 2010 Empty Project template, which you can find by browsing the Installed Templates tree using the path Visual C# ➤ SharePoint ➤ 2010. While you are there, browse through the other project templates for SharePoint 2010; you can click on each one for a description that will display to the right of the project template list.

■ **Tip** You may need to open Visual Studio with elevated privileges in order for Visual Studio to properly attach to the SharePoint worker process when debugging. To do this, right click on the Visual Studio icon in the start menu and select Run as administrator.

---

2. Using the drop-down above the project types, ensure you are targeting the .NET Framework 3.5.

3. Name your project HelloWorld and leave the default choice of creating a new solution with the same name. Your completed New Project dialog should look similar to Figure 3-3. Click OK to continue.

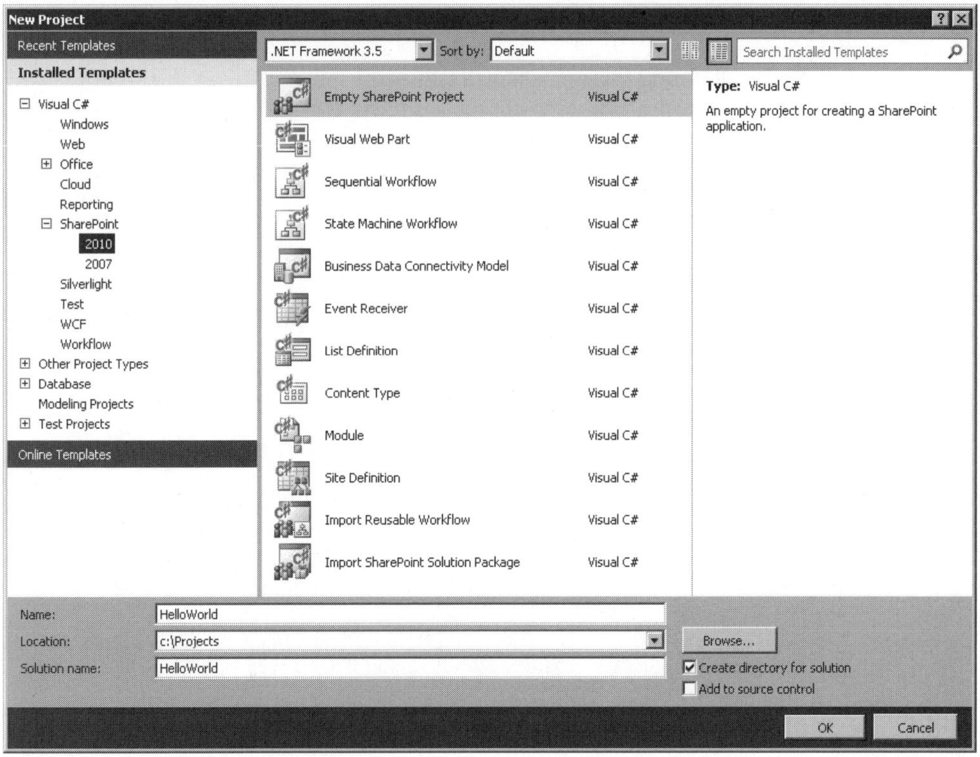

Figure 3-3. The New Project dialog for your HelloWorld project

4. Next the SharePoint Customization Wizard will prompt you for some additional information related to debugging and deployment. Enter the complete URL for the local site you will be using to debug this project and select the Deploy as a full-trust solution option as shown in Figure 3-4. Click Finish.

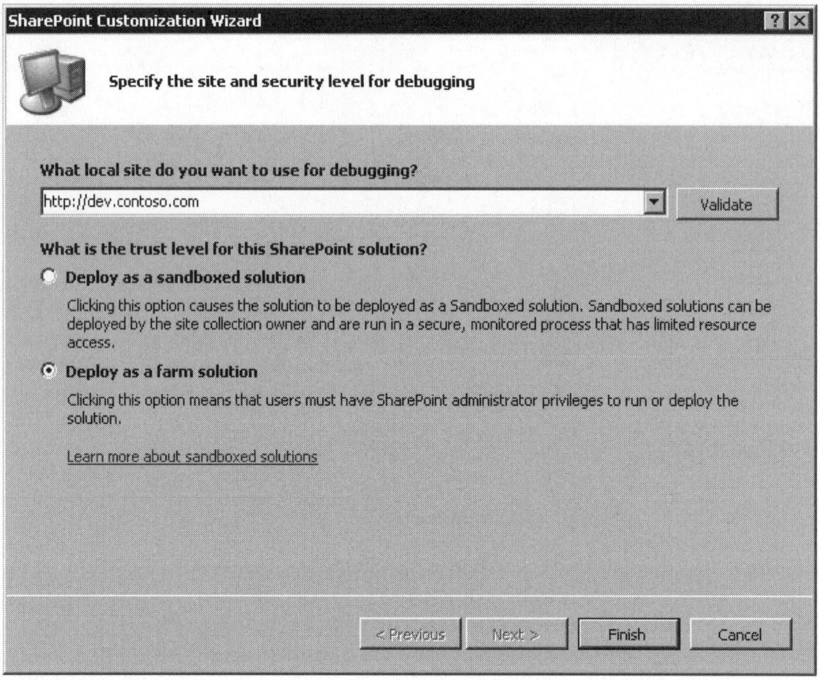

Figure 3-4. The SharePoint Customization Wizard

Exploring the HelloWorld Project

Your new project will be created with the appropriate references set, as well as the default files and folders as defined by the project template. By expanding the folders visible within the Solution Explorer, you should see a view similar to Figure 3-5. The Properties and References folders are common to all Visual Studio projects, whereas the Features and Package folders are specific to SharePoint projects. The SharePoint tools in Visual Studio provide an excellent mechanism for organizing SharePoint artifacts in a very logical way; we will add a few additional SharePoint-specific folders shortly.

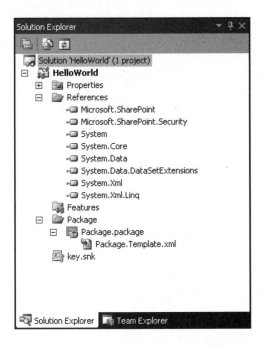

Figure 3-5. Your project view in the Solution Explorer

To explore a bit further, right-click on the HelloWorld project node, and notice a few additional menu options specific to SharePoint projects. The Deploy, Package, and Retract options give you more granular control over what actions of the build process you want to perform, and in fact the deploy option can be fully customized by modifying configuration settings in the properties window for the project. Open the project properties window and click on the SharePoint tab to view and customize the deployment steps. If you look at the Add menu item for the project, you'll see options to create some of the additional SharePoint-specific folders, such as Images and Layouts. By selecting the SharePoint Mapped Folder… option, you can create and manage any of the folders in the SharePoint install directory (often referred to as the 14 hive) as part of the project using a simple and intuitive dialog to make your selection.

Creating the HelloWorldFeature Feature

As previously mentioned, we want our feature to do two things when activated: change the title of the site and add a button to the Ribbon. The first task can be accomplished using an event receiver; the second requires a custom element. We will also want to reset all of our changes to their original state if the feature is deactivated. Let's begin by configuring a few properties of the Feature itself, then we will add an event receiver class and a custom elements file.

■ **Note** A Feature in SharePoint is simply a logical container used to package related code, resources, and configuration files. SharePoint then provides a framework for deploying and managing each feature within the environment. You can find additional information about SharePoint Features at `http://msdn.microsoft.com/en-us/library/ee537350(v=office.14).aspx`.

---

1. In Solution Explorer, right-click the Features node and select Add Feature. This will create a new feature named Feature1 and open the Feature Designer window.

2. Right-click on Feature1, select Rename, and change the name to HelloWorldFeature. This will rename all associated files as well.

3. In the Feature Designer window modify the Title, Description and Scope using the following values:

   Title: Hello World Feature

   Description: My first feature using the new SharePoint tools in Visual Studio.

   Scope: Web

   When you're done, you should see a view similar to Figure 3-6.

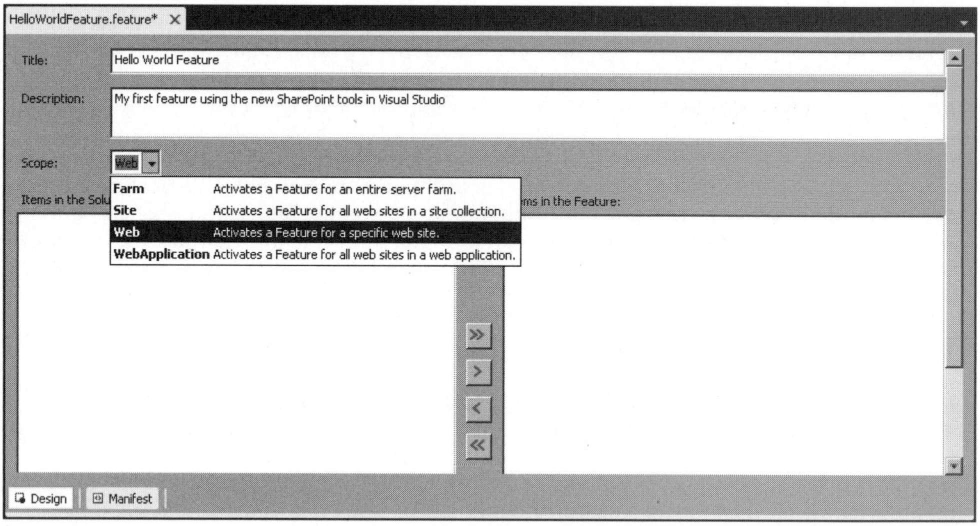

Figure 3-6. The HelloWorldFeature Feature Designer window after making updates

■ **Note** The Feature Designer window is one of the many visual designers provided as part of the SharePoint tools in Visual Studio. The visual designers allow you to update many of the settings without having to delve into the raw XML. Of course, you still have easy access to the XML by clicking on the *Manifest* tab in the lower left corner of the designer window for those cases when you require direct control over the XML.

4. Right-click HelloWorldFeature and select Add Event Receiver. A new class of type `SPFeatureReceiver` will be generated and opened in the code window. Make sure you don't change the `Guid` attribute value on the class as this is used during the packaging process to ensure this class is correctly associated with the Feature.

5. The Event Receiver lets you execute code at any of four key points in the lifespan of a feature—when the feature is activated, deactivating, installed, or uninstalling. We are interested in executing code when the HelloWorldFeature is activated or deactivating, so uncomment the `FeatureActivated` and `FeatureDeactivating` methods and feel free to remove the remaining commented lines in the class file.

6. Update the `FeatureActivated` method to read and store the existing site title and then to change the site title to Hello World using the code in Listing 3-1. This code will execute anytime the Feature is activated.

Listing 3-1. The updated FeatureActivated method

```
public override void FeatureActivated(SPFeatureReceiverProperties properties)
{
    SPWeb site = (SPWeb)properties.Feature.Parent; // current site
    site.Properties["SiteTitle"] = site.Title; // store the current title
    site.Properties.Update(); // save the updated property
    site.Title = "Hello World"; // set a new title
    site.Update(); // apply changes
}
```

7. Update the `FeatureDeactivating` method to restore the original site title value using the code in Listing 3-2. This code will execute anytime the Feature is deactivating.

Listing 3-2. The updated FeatureDeactivating method

```
public override void FeatureDeactivating(SPFeatureReceiverProperties properties)
{
    SPWeb site = (SPWeb)properties.Feature.Parent; // current site
    site.Title = site.Properties["SiteTitle"]; // restore origional title
    site.Update(); // apply changes
}
```

8. Right click on the HelloWorld project and select Add ➤ New Item, then add an
    Empty Element named `RibbonElement`. The Empty Project template can be
    found by browsing the Installed Templates tree using the path Visual C# ➤
    SharePoint ➤ 2010. Take the time to scroll through the other item templates
    for SharePoint 2010; you can click on each item template for a description that
    will display to the right of the item template list. Figure 3-7 shows the
    completed Add New Item dialog with a look at the some of the available item
    templates.

Figure 3-7. The Add New Item dialog

9. The Empty Element template will create a new node RibbonElement in the
    HelloWorld project that contains a single XML file named Elements.xml. The
    `Elements.xml` file should be open in the code window; if not, double-click the
    newly created `Elements.xml` file to view its contents. We will define a custom
    action within the element to create a new button on the Share & Track tab of
    the Ribbon. Update the `Elements.xml` file to match the XML in Listing 3-3.

Listing 3-3. CustomAction XML for creating a new Ribbon button.

```xml
<?xml version="1.0" encoding="utf-8"?>
<Elements xmlns="http://schemas.microsoft.com/sharepoint/">
  <CustomAction
    Id="Ribbon.Library.Actions.AddAButton"
    Location="CommandUI.Ribbon"
    RegistrationType="List"
    RegistrationId="101">
    <CommandUIExtension>
      <CommandUIDefinitions>
        <CommandUIDefinition
          Location="Ribbon.Library.Share.Controls._children">
          <Button Id="Ribbon.Library.Share.HelloWorldButton"
            Command="HelloWorldButtonCommand"
            Image32by32="/_layouts/images/ppeople.gif"
            LabelText="Hello World"
            TemplateAlias="o2" />
        </CommandUIDefinition>
      </CommandUIDefinitions>
      <CommandUIHandlers>
        <CommandUIHandler
          Command="HelloWorldButtonCommand"
          CommandAction="javascript:alert('Say Hello to the World!');" />
      </CommandUIHandlers>
    </CommandUIExtension>
  </CustomAction>
</Elements>
```

For a detailed discussion of the XML elements and attributes related to developing Features, see the
section titled Feature Schemas in the SharePoint SDK at `http://msdn.microsoft.com/en-us/library/`
`ms414322(v=office.14).aspx`. The `RibbonElement` needs to be associated with a feature in order to be
activated. Since we only have one feature in our project, this association should have been done
automatically. To confirm, double-click the HelloWorldFeature to open the Feature Designer window
and ensure the `RibbonElement` is included in the Items in the Feature pane on the right. As you can
imagine, the Feature Designer window makes it much easier to manage complex projects containing
multiple features and feature items since you can now manage these relationships without having to
manually edit raw XML. We will look at a similar designer to manage the package shortly. Your
HelloWorldFeature feature should look similar to Figure 3-8.

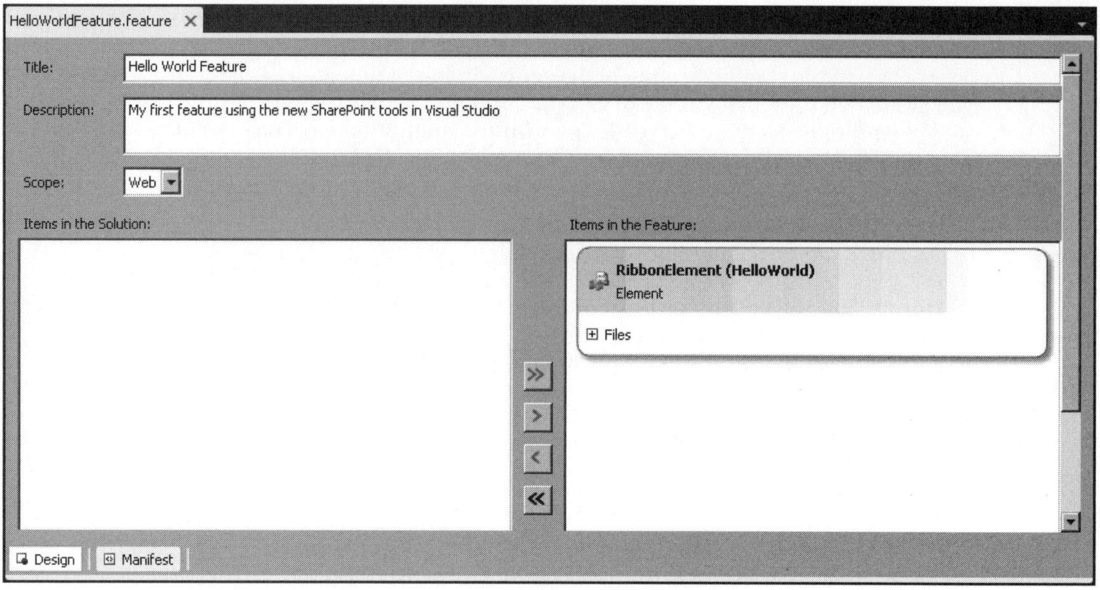

Figure 3-8. The HelloWorldFeature feature designer including the RibbonElement

Deploying the HelloWorld Project

We are now ready to build, deploy, and debug our project. During this process, Visual Studio— along with the SharePoint tools— will perform a standard build to generate assemblies, package necessary project items into the WSP, recycle the appropriate IIS app pool, retract any prior deployments of the project, install the new WSP, activate any features contained in the WSP, attach the debugger to the process, and open a browser window directed to the site selected for debugging. Of course, you have full control over this process and can customize by changing the order of steps, adding or removing steps, or specifying pre/post deployment commands to execute.

1. Double click the Package folder in the Solution Explorer to open the Package Designer window and ensure the correct project items have been specified to be included in the WSP. You should see your HelloWorldFeature in the Items in the Package pane on the right. Your HelloWorld package should look similar to Figure 3-9. Notice you are able to add the RibbonElement by itself or, as in this case, as a component of the Feature.

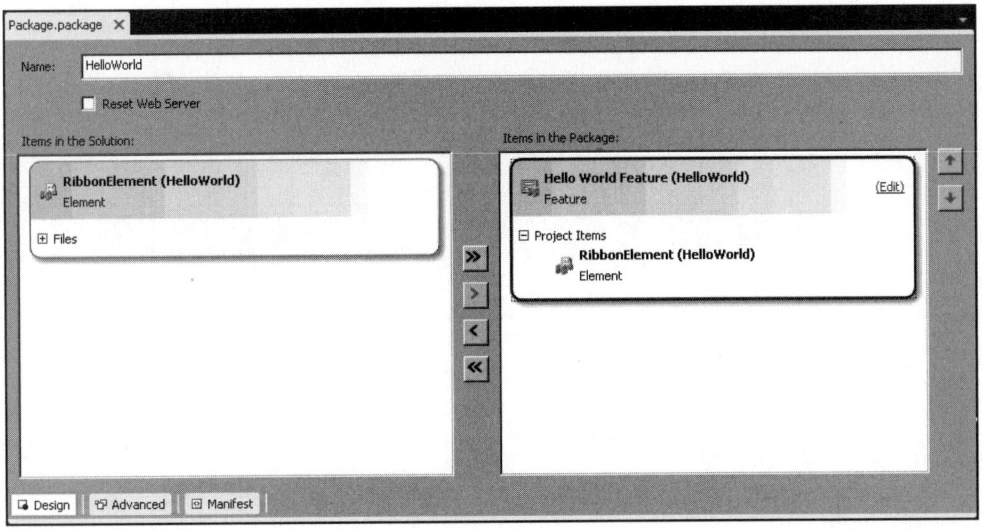

Figure 3-9. The HelloWorld package

2. Press F5 or select Start Debugging on the Debug menu to begin the build process. Use the Visual Studio output window to view feedback as each step of the build and deployment process is executed. If you aren't getting the feedback, make sure Build is selected in the Show output from dropdown in the output window. If this is the first time you have attempted to debug a project on the selected site, you will be prompted to enable debugging in the Web.config file.

■ **Note** By default, the deploy process will activate any features contained in your WSP. However, the activation occurs prior to attaching the debugger to the SharePoint process so breakpoints in a FeatureActivated method will not be hit. You can change this behavior by modifying the deployment configuration. To do so, right-click on your project and select Properties. In the project properties window, select the Deploy tab and change the Active Deployment Configuration to No Activation. This removes the activate step so you will need to manually activate your feature once the debugger is attached.

---

3. Once the debugger has been attached to the process, a new browser window will open to the site. If you elected only to deploy and not debug the solution, open a browser window and browse to the site you specified at project creation. The site title for your site should now be *Hello World*.

4. To view the newly added Hello World button, browse to any document library in the site and select the Library tab of the Ribbon. Your Hello World button should be visible next to the RSS Feed button in the Share & Track group. Click the Hello World button to execute the JavaScript code and display the alert box. Figure 3-10 shows a view of the site after performing this action.

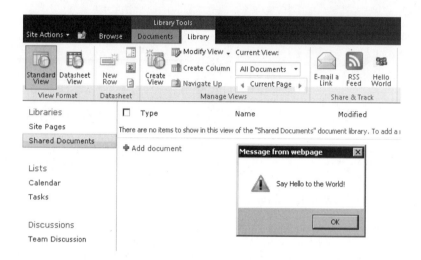

Figure 3-10. The new HelloWorld button and the alert box

Further Reading

- Visual Studio 2008 extensions for Windows SharePoint Services 3.0, v1.3 `http://www.microsoft.com/downloads/details.aspx?displaylang=en&FamilyID=fb9d4b85-da2a-432e-91fb-d505199c49f6`

- Debugging SharePoint Solutions `http://msdn.microsoft.com/en-us/library/ee231550(v=VS.100).aspx`

- SharePoint Foundation building blocks `http://msdn.microsoft.com/en-us/library/ee534971(v=office.14).aspx`

- Using the SharePoint client APIs `http://msdn.microsoft.com/en-us/library/ee537564(v=office.14).aspx`

CHAPTER 4

■ ■ ■

Microsoft Office Overview for Developers

Microsoft Office 2010 is the latest edition in a long line of productivity applications that have become commonplace on the desktops of information workers. Through the years, the Office brand has extended to new applications like InfoPath, Communicator, and OneNote, and it has also gained enterprise servers in SharePoint. Yet the core of Office continues to be Word, Excel, PowerPoint, and Outlook. Information workers use these four applications to generate a multitude of files that hold organizational information. With each new edition of this software suite, Microsoft focuses on the spreadsheets, documents, presentations, and e-mail, always enhancing the ways these items can participate in the enterprise, including collaboration, enterprise search, and interaction with business data and line-of-business systems. The 2010 release steps up the support for extension by developers. In this chapter, we will provide some insight into development opportunities with Office 2010 and point out which solutions in the book incorporate them.

History of Microsoft Office Development

When people are asked to describe developing with Microsoft Office, their first response generally involves Microsoft Visual Basic for Applications (VBA). This scripting language is the development environment for Office macros. Anyone who has tried to automate an Office application is familiar with the technique of starting a macro recording, performing the action they wish to automate, and then looking at the resulting script code. It is important to understand that VBA code is tightly integrated with the application it operates against. In fact, the code itself is persisted with the document.

Office developers are also familiar with COM add-ins. These are programs written in a language capable of producing COM objects, like Visual Basic, and are loaded by the Office application; they extend the application to include new functionality or specialized features. A COM add-in runs within the application and is capable of interacting with the Office application's object model.

Another technique Office developers use is *automation*. This is when the developer creates an external application that instantiates the Office application. The external application then uses the application's object model to have it perform certain actions. In some cases, the Office application is never shown to the user, even though it loads fully. Some developers use automation for server-based applications. Since the Office application must load in an automation scenario and Office applications are designed to support very limited concurrency, this solution does not scale and is not recommended by Microsoft.

With Microsoft Office 2003, the Office development environment was extended to managed code and the .NET languages. This meant that the Office applications could now interact with Web services. Plus, Word and Excel gained XML support with their ability to be attached to custom schemas and to save XML data. With this convergence, Office applications acquired behaviors normally associated with smart-client solutions. These behaviors extended Word and Excel, allowing users to interact with back-end data and systems while still in the context of their document or spreadsheet.

Shortly after Office 2003 debuted, Microsoft released an enhancement to Visual Studio called Visual Studio Tools for Office (VSTO), which allowed Office developers to use the powerful Visual Studio development environment. This reduced the complexity of developing with Office and provided a rapid application-development experience. Developers could drag familiar Windows controls onto the surface of Excel spreadsheets or Word documents and design user controls that could be loaded as document actions panes. This aligned the experience of Office development with the Web and Windows development experiences, and it meant that the community of .NET developers could, with little ramp-up time, tackle Office development. Just as web pages or forms have a code-behind file, documents and spreadsheets became the user interface with a .NET class file acting behind the scenes. The VSTO team also tried to satisfy developers' desire to automate the Office applications on the server by providing a ServerDocument object that allowed the insertion of a data island into documents. This did help, but was limiting in that developers could not manipulate the entire document's content. We will cover VSTO in a bit more detail later in this chapter.

Why Developers Should Care About Office

Developers should care about Microsoft Office because it has a proven value few other technologies can compare with. Word, Excel, Outlook, and PowerPoint have been on the corporate desktop for more than a decade and users are comfortable with them. This means that when you are presented with a challenge involving a document, spreadsheet, presentation, or e-mail, you should avoid the temptation to create a completely custom solution. Instead, you should look to develop a solution that integrates seamlessly with the environment the user is familiar with. Presenting this solution as an enhancement to Office aids user adoption and likely reduces the amount of code since you can take advantage of the Office application's functionality.

Development Opportunities with Office

Microsoft Office 2007 provided even more options for solution development and these options carry forward into Office 2010, so we will take some time to review them. The Office Open XML file format (described in the following section) opens up new possibilities for document generation on the server. Using this file format, developers are able to create or modify documents on the server without having to load the Office application. In fact, the Office applications don't even need to be installed on the server. This allows document-generation solutions to be server-based and scale to meet the needs of an enterprise.

Managed code solutions are also enhanced with Visual Studio Tools for Office. Now developers can create managed code add-ins and application task panes. They can extend Office's user interface—the *Ribbon*. Outlook forms also entered the managed code world, as they can be customized and extended with .NET code. This section is by no means a complete reference to Office development, so we will include links to external content you can read to learn more about specific topics that interest you. We'll also call out certain features that we'll incorporate into the solutions in the remainder of the book.

The Open XML File Format

Microsoft Office 2007 significantly changed the way developers look at Office files. In previous versions, Office files were stored in a proprietary binary format that captured serializations of in-memory data structures. The advantages of this technique were that it conserved space within the file and increased the speed at which the Office application could parse its contents. With Office 2007, Microsoft switched the default file format to an open, XML-based standard. This standard (called Office Open XML or just Open XML) was an output of Ecma International's Technical Committee 45; it was approved by the Ecma General Assembly on December 7, 2006 and became an ISO standard in April 2008. Since then, many companies have announced support for the Open XML format, including Novell's OpenOffice and Corel's WordPerfect Office X3 suite.

■ **Note** Ecma International was founded in 1961 as an industry association dedicated to the development of standards and technical reports that apply to information and communication technology as well as consumer electronics. Its members include many familiar companies such as Adobe, Microsoft, Intel, Sony, Yahoo!, IBM, Fujifilm, and Pioneer. This association has produced over 370 standards and 90 technical reports, of which more than two-thirds have gone on to become international standards or technical reports. Ecma is a major participant in "fast-tracking" standards through the process of other global standards bodies, such as ISO. To read more about Ecma, visit its web site: `http://www.ecma-international.org`.

Within Ecma, Technical Committee 45 took on the responsibility to standardize Office Open XML so that it can be used by other productivity applications and platforms. This committee is responsible for the standard, its documentation, and the comprehensive set of schemas. The committee includes representatives from Apple, Barclays Capital, BP, The British Library, Essilor, Intel, Microsoft, NextPage, Novell, Statoil, Toshiba, and the United States Library of Congress. To read more about this committee, including updates on their activities, visit its web site: `http://www.ecma-international.org/memento/TC45.htm`.

So why the change? One of the most interesting trends over the past few decades is the pace at which we are generating electronic information. This trend becomes disturbing when you realize that with a binary file format, the information is strongly tied to the specific versions of applications that generated them. With the long document retention policies many companies have, it becomes more difficult to maintain these documents reliably. Imagine if a document as important as the Declaration of Independence were written using Microsoft Word 95. For this reason, organizations and governments have been requesting that the technology industry reduce the dependencies of files on specific versions of specific applications by switching to an open format.

Of course, the new file format had to do more than fix such dependencies moving forward; it also had to address the billions of documents that already exist. This was an important goal of the Open XML initiative. The schemas for the format were designed to reflect existing documents. Microsoft has several efforts that will help in terms of adoption and backward compatibility. The Office Migration Planning Manager (OMPM) contains a set of tools to help organizations scan their documents and identify migration issues. One of the important tools in this set is the Office File Converter, which enables you to convert large quantities of files that use the binary format to the XML one. You can find more information about OMPM at `http://technet.microsoft.com/en-us/library/cc179179.aspx`.

Microsoft also provides an extension to older versions of Office that enables people to work with Open XML–formatted files. This extension is called the Microsoft Office Compatibility Pack, and it lets users open, edit, and save files in the Open XML format using Microsoft Office 2000, Office XP, or Office 2003. This is important because organizations often take more time to update their standardized desktops than to deploy new application servers. It means that developers will be able to use the new format on the server and in custom development projects even if the end user does not have Office 2007 or 2010. This add-on can be obtained at `http://www.microsoft.com/downloads/details.aspx?FamilyId=941B3470-3AE9-4AEE-8F43-C6BB74CD1466&displaylang=en`.

What does the Office Open XML file format mean to developers? It opens the possibility of generating or modifying an Office file from code without having to automate the Office application. Previously, developers would have to code against the Office application's API. When this was then run on a server, it was equivalent to a user launching the application and performing the necessary steps. These solutions did not scale well and Microsoft backed off of supporting them. However, with the Open XML format, Office files can be manipulated by modifying their XML structures. The Office application does not even have to be installed on the server. Even in Ecma's Open XML white paper (referenced in the "Further Reading" section of this chapter), the committee anticipated what developers would do with the format. Some of the new applications called out in the document were

- The ability for applications to generate documents automatically

- The extraction of data from documents to be consumed by line-of-business applications

- Enhancing accessibility options for users with special needs, such as the blind

- Using the documents on a variety of hardware, such as mobile devices

The best way to understand the Open XML file format is to make a copy of an existing file and explore how it is put together. Whether the file is a spreadsheet, a presentation, or a document, it is really a package of parts and items. Parts are pieces of content for the file, whereas items are metadata describing how the parts should be assembled and rendered. Most of these components are XML, making it possible for them to be manipulated through code. You can gain insight into the structure of an Open XML–based file by replacing its file extension with **.zip** since the file is really an ordinary Zip archive. We will use a PowerPoint presentation as an example to illustrate the structure of an Open XML file. Follow along by creating your own presentation with a few slides of content. Figure 4-1 shows the root of the archive for a PowerPoint presentation.

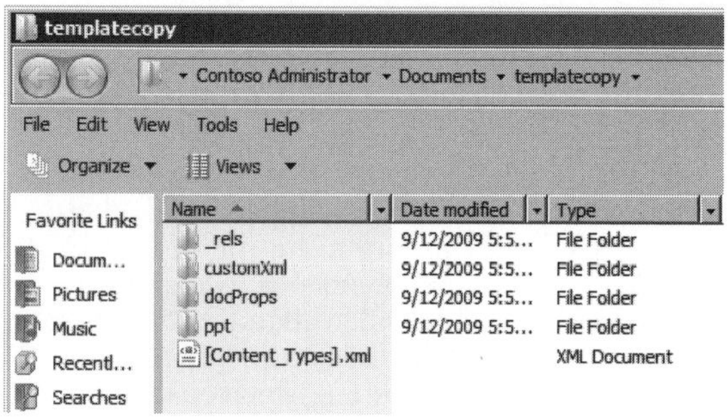

Figure 4-1. Examining the archive of a PowerPoint presentation

The XML file in the root is named `[Content_Types].xml` and it stores content-type directives for all the parts that appear in the archive. A content type contains metadata about a particular part or groups of parts and, more importantly, contains a directive as to how the application should render that part. For example, Listing 4-1 shows just a few lines from the file, but it clearly delineates how this file tells the rendering application which parts are slides, images, note pages, etc.

Listing 4-1. A Presentation's Content Types

```
<Override PartName="/ppt/slides/slide1.xml"
  ContentType="application/vnd.openxmlformats-
  officedocument.presentationml.slide+xml" />
<Default Extension="jpeg"
  ContentType="image/jpeg" />
<Override PartName="/ppt/notesSlides/notesSlide1.xml"
  ContentType="application/vnd.openxmlformats-
  officedocument.presentationml.notesSlide+xml" />
```

Of the parts in Listing 4-1, the slide parts are the most interesting to us. They store the presentation's content described using a markup language specific to presentations. This language is named PresentationML. It is XML-based and one of the easier Open XML file formats to understand because presentations have an obvious composition. A presentation is made up of the following:

- Masters for slides, notes, and handouts

- Slide layouts

- Slides and note pages

Open the `presentation.xml` file that is located in the ppt folder of the archive. Viewing this file in Internet Explorer displays XML similar to what's shown in Figure 4-2.

```
<?xml version="1.0" encoding="UTF-8" standalone="yes" ?>
- <p:presentation xmlns:a="http://schemas.openxmlformats.org/drawingml/2006/main"
    xmlns:r="http://schemas.openxmlformats.org/officeDocument/2006/relationships"
    xmlns:p="http://schemas.openxmlformats.org/presentationml/2006/main"
    saveSubsetFonts="1">
  - <p:sldMasterIdLst>
      <p:sldMasterId id="2147483660" r:id="rId2" />
    </p:sldMasterIdLst>
  - <p:sldIdLst>
      <p:sldId id="256" r:id="rId3" />
      <p:sldId id="257" r:id="rId4" />
      <p:sldId id="258" r:id="rId5" />
      <p:sldId id="259" r:id="rId6" />
    </p:sldIdLst>
    <p:sldSz cx="9144000" cy="6858000" type="screen4x3" />
    <p:notesSz cx="6858000" cy="9144000" />
  + <p:defaultTextStyle>
  </p:presentation>
```

Figure 4-2. The presentation.xml file

The `presentation.xml` file contains the list of slides (<p:sldLst>), references to the slide and notes masters, and the sizes of the slides (<p:sldSz>) and notes pages (<p:notesSz>). The sequence of the slide nodes is important; the rendering application will display them in the order they are listed here. Notice that each slide node, as well as the master nodes, has an r:id attribute. This identifier is a key to a specific relationship that will tell the rendering application where the part for this item is located. The relationship information for this presentation is stored in the `presentation.xml.rels` file located in the ppt_rels folder of the archive. Listing 4-2 is the XML node in this file that tells the application that the first slide's content is stored in `slide1.xml`.

Listing 4-2. Example of a Presentation Relationship

```
<Relationship
Id="rId3" Type="http://schemas.openxmlformats.org/officeDocument/↵
    2006/relationships/slide" Target="slides/slide1.xml"
/>
```

Following the relationship links, you can see that the contents of the slides are stored in the ppt\slides folder of the archive. When building solutions that work with the Open XML file formats, it is often useful to explore the archive to examine its contents before trying to manipulate it through code. In fact, you could extract these contents to a folder, modify them, and repackage them to a new Zip archive. Renaming this archive with a .pptx extension creates a new presentation, allowing you to see the changes in PowerPoint.

Within a slide, there are shapes marked up as <p:sp> in the XML. A shape could be the slide's title, a bulleted list of text, or even a table. Shapes are grouped into trees that you'll see as <p:spTree> elements in the XML. Figure 4-3 shows a sample slide that has a shape containing a bulleted list of three items.

```
- <p:sp>
  - <p:nvSpPr>
      <p:cNvPr id="3" name="Content Placeholder 2" />
    + <p:cNvSpPr>
    + <p:nvPr>
    </p:nvSpPr>
    <p:spPr />
  - <p:txBody>
      <a:bodyPr />
      <a:lstStyle />
    - <a:p>
      - <a:r>
          <a:rPr lang="en-US" dirty="0" smtClean="0" />
          <a:t>Item 1</a:t>
        </a:r>
      </a:p>
    - <a:p>
      - <a:r>
          <a:rPr lang="en-US" dirty="0" smtClean="0" />
          <a:t>Item 2</a:t>
        </a:r>
      </a:p>
    - <a:p>
      - <a:r>
          <a:rPr lang="en-US" dirty="0" smtClean="0" />
          <a:t>Item 3</a:t>
        </a:r>
      </a:p>
    </p:txBody>
  </p:sp>
```

Figure 4-3. A sample slide's XML

WordprocessingML is the Open XML markup language for documents. It defines a document as a collection of stories. Stories within a document can refer to the main document contents, its glossary, a header, or its footer. By examining the main document, `document.xml`, you'll find a body that contains paragraphs, each of which contains a collection of runs. A *run* is a continuous section of text that has the same properties. The text itself is stored within a text range, which is restricted to containing text only and can't have additional formatting, line breaks, tables, or graphics. The text range gets its formatting from the run or paragraph it is contained in. Figure 4-4 shows a portion of a WordprocessingML file. Notice the paragraph delimiters, the runs, and the text ranges.

```
- <w:p w14:paraId="2A327EFF" w14:textId="374B415D" w:rsidR="008405E1" w:rsidRDefault="008405E1">
    <w:bookmarkStart w:id="0" w:name="_GoBack" />
    <w:bookmarkEnd w:id="0" />
  - <w:r>
      <w:t>This trend becomes disturbing when you realize that a binary file format, the information is strongly tied to the specific versions of applications
         that generated them. With long retention policies, it becomes more difficult to reliably maintain these documents. For this reason, organizations and
         governments have been demanding the technology industry to reduce these risks by switching to an open format.</w:t>
    </w:r>
  </w:p>
```

Figure 4-4. Sample WordprocessingML

SpreadsheetML files are defined by a workbook part. Like a PowerPoint file whose presentation is made up of slides, workbooks are made up of worksheets. The workbook part includes information such as the file version and its collection of worksheets. Within a worksheet part, you'll find the sheet's data, containing rows of cells that have values. Figure 4-5 shows a simple spreadsheet we created to explore its Open XML structure.

	A	B	C
1	Sample	10	
2	Acme	20	
3	Generic	30	
4			

Figure 4-5. A simple Excel spreadsheet

Figure 4-6 shows a portion of the markup. Notice how the sheetData element contains row elements. Within each row element, there are cells (<c>) that have values (<v>). The reason you don't see the company names is that they are stored separately in a `sharedStrings.xml` part. This separation enables reuse since the file needs to store a string value only once, regardless of the number of cells that contain it.

```xml
<?xml version="1.0" encoding="UTF-8" standalone="yes" ?>
<worksheet xmlns="http://schemas.openxmlformats.org/spreadsheetml/2006/main"
  xmlns:r="http://schemas.openxmlformats.org/officeDocument/2006/relationships"
  xmlns:mc="http://schemas.openxmlformats.org/markup-compatibility/2006"
  mc:Ignorable="x14ac"
  xmlns:x14ac="http://schemas.microsoft.com/office/spreadsheetml/2009/9/ac">
  <dimension ref="A1:B3" />
+ <sheetViews>
  <sheetFormatPr defaultRowHeight="15" x14ac:dyDescent="0.25" />
- <sheetData>
  - <row r="1" spans="1:2" x14ac:dyDescent="0.25">
    - <c r="A1" t="s">
        <v>0</v>
      </c>
    - <c r="B1">
        <v>10</v>
      </c>
    </row>
  - <row r="2" spans="1:2" x14ac:dyDescent="0.25">
    - <c r="A2" t="s">
        <v>1</v>
      </c>
    - <c r="B2">
        <v>20</v>
      </c>
    </row>
  - <row r="3" spans="1:2" x14ac:dyDescent="0.25">
    - <c r="A3" t="s">
        <v>2</v>
      </c>
    - <c r="B3">
        <v>30</v>
      </c>
    </row>
```

Figure 4-6. Sample SpreadsheetML

Working with these large XML files can be a burden. To make it easier, download the schemas for the Open XML file formats so that Visual Studio's IntelliSense can help you create valid structures as you're modifying the files. The schemas are available for download at `http://www.microsoft.com/downloads/details.aspx?familyid=15805380-F2C0-4B80-9AD1-2CB0C300AEF9&displaylang=en`.

To let you build .NET applications that operate on Open XML files, Microsoft added a namespace to the .NET 3.0 Framework. The namespace is System.IO.Packaging and its classes are contained in the WindowsBase.dll assembly. You may have this assembly in your references dialog box in Visual Studio; if not, you can browse to it at `C:\Program Files\Reference Assemblies\Microsoft\Framework\v3.0\WindowsBase.dll`. Code that acts on Open XML files works much as you would if you were editing the file by hand. First the package must be opened and the file's main part located. In PowerPoint, the main part is the `presentation.xml` file. For spreadsheets, the main part is `workbook.xml` and for documents, it is `document.xml`. Once the main part is found, the relationship information helps the code locate the XML part with the content it wants to operate on. When this part is located, the XML part is loaded into an XML document, where it can then be read, manipulated, and saved back.

Fortunately, you won't have to do a lot of coding against the raw XML, an approach that was rather tedious and prone to error. To find areas of the files, you had to rely on XPath queries; and when you did make a change, there was no validation of your modified XML. To avoid these difficulties, we will leverage the Open XML Format SDK 2.0, which provides an object model that more closely represents the familiar objects of Office files. We will cover this SDK in the next section.

In addition to allowing you to modify or generate documents using the different markup languages, the Open XML standard supports having a custom XML folder that is capable of storing information. Within this folder, you or your applications can store your own XML data islands. Though all of the Office 2007 and 2010 files can store custom XML, Microsoft Word 2007 and 2010 have the added benefit of having a set of controls that can bind to the custom XML parts, displaying the data inline with the document. These controls are called *content controls* and they can be used to display data in the custom XML part, as well as serve as an input device for modifying the values there.

Several solutions in this book leverage the benefits of the Open XML file format. Chapter 6 works with Open XML Word documents and shows how to add content controls to the document to allow users to interact with its contents. The solution in Chapter 7 facilitates a document assembly scenario which also uses content controls that are placed in the document by a custom task pane. Chapter 9 leverages PresentationML to dynamically build a PowerPoint presentation by merging SharePoint list content with a presentation template.

The Open XML Format SDK

As you can see, working with the XML of Office files could involve a lot of XML manipulation. Once exposed to the format, developers usually raise several questions. How can I be sure my injected XML is valid? What about variations of the file format, since it continued to evolve after being released with Office 2007? Is there any better way of finding my way around than XPath queries? Isn't Microsoft going to make this any easier?

The answers to all of these questions are enhancements provided by the Open XML Format SDK 2.0 (which is used heavily in the solutions in Chapters 6, 7, and 9). You can download and install the SDK from http://msdn.microsoft.com/en-us/library/bb448854(office.14).aspx. The SDK includes an assembly, DocumentFormat.OpenXML, which provides an object model of strongly typed classes that are an abstraction from the actual XML markup, making your code easier to read and write. Listing 4-3, for example, takes just a few lines of code to create a new Microsoft Word document with a paragraph of text.

Listing 4-3. Creating a Word Document with the Open XML SDK

```
using (WordprocessingDocument doc = WordprocessingDocument.Create↵
        ("test.docx", WordprocessingDocumentType.Document))
{
  // Add main document part.
  doc.AddMainDocumentPart();

  // Create the Document DOM.
  doc.MainDocumentPart.Document =
      new Document(
        new Body(
          new Paragraph(
            new Run(
              new Text("Hello World!")))));

  // Save changes
  doc.MainDocumentPart.Document.Save();
}
```

It is important to realize that you still need to understand what the Open XML file format is all about in order to use the SDK. The classes it provides make it easier to write the code, but the underlying relationships of the package, its parts, and the content remain. This is why we took the time in the previous section to give you an overview. The SDK does reduce a lot of complexity, and as long as you refrain from writing code that modifies the XML directly, your changes will still be valid Open XML files. The classes provided by the SDK also support LINQ, so searching through parts to find specific elements is also easier than writing XPath queries. Your code will be more in the style of LINQ to XML. For example, the code in Listing 4-4 shows you how to query to find all tables within a slide of a PowerPoint presentation.

Listing 4-4. A LINQ-style Query for Finding Tables in a PowerPoint Slide

```
var tables = from table in slidePart.Slide.Descendants<Drawing.Table>()
             select table;
```

In addition to the object model, the Open XML Format SDK provides a tool to assist developers working with the Open XML file format. The Open XML SDK 2.0 Productivity Tool for Microsoft Office is installed by default at `C:\Program Files (x86)\Open XML Format SDK\V2.0\tool`. This tool can perform several functions. We will focus here on its ability to generate code. When you open an Open XML-based file, you can browse the structure of the file. Selecting a specific item shows you the XML for that portion of the file, as well as a generated function for creating that part of the file. We will use this repeatedly in the chapters where we manipulate Open XML files. Figure 4-7 shows this tool being used to create a function that creates a paragraph node for a bulleted list.

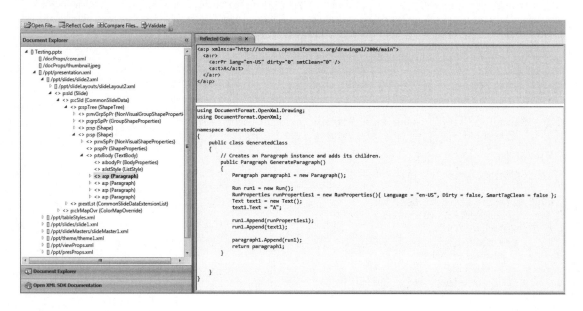

Figure 4-7. Using the Document Reflector tool

Moving Toward Managed Code

Microsoft Office is one of the world's most-used information-worker applications. That level of exposure and recognition has made these tools an enticing area for customization as developers like to extend a tool that users are already comfortable with. Developing with Microsoft Office has traditionally meant developing in a COM-based world. This began to change with Office 2003 when Microsoft shipped primary interop assemblies (PIAs) as part of the advanced installation. These PIAs opened Office to the .NET developer community and their managed code projects. A primary interop assembly enabled a Visual Studio developer to write code against the Office applications by adding a reference in the project. The assembly took on the responsibility of translating between the COM and managed code environments. Even with the PIAs, such development was not for the faint of heart. .NET developers often struggled—their code had to deal with the way Office maintained object lifetimes and they had to contend with lots of COM plumbing. Moreover, the managed code solution was limited to running outside the process of the Office application. What was missing was a layer between the PIAs and the developer's custom application. Microsoft Visual Studio Tools for Office (VSTO) fills that void. VSTO extends the Visual Studio environment to support the development of managed code solutions for Microsoft Office. With VSTO, the developer can create solutions that leverage Microsoft Office applications, including the construction of add-ins, custom task panes, action panes, ribbon customizations, and smart documents.

Visual Studio Tools for Office

The first version of VSTO was called Visual Studio Tools for Office 2003. This version was an add-on to Visual Studio .NET 2003 and it gave developers project types that let their code run in process with Word 2003 and Excel 2003. These project types let developers create applications by building on top of documents. You could select your project type as an Excel workbook, Word document, or Word template. By writing their customizations in the managed-code world, developers could leverage the power of the .NET languages C# and VB.NET. These languages were more appealing than VBA and provided powerful access to manipulate XML and connect to data stores through ADO.NET, plus support for web services. By running within Office, the resulting assembly could interact with application- and document-level events, command bars, and the document itself. An important limitation of these solutions was that they were not compatible with Office Standard Edition 2003 because some of the necessary elements, such as XML and smart documents, were not supported.

Over time, new versions of the Office, the .NET Framework, Visual Studio, and the VSTO runtime appeared and each improved the developer experience, bringing it closer to the experiences of developers using Visual Studio for web and Windows development. First appearing in Visual Studio 2005, VSTO literally brought Microsoft Word and Excel into Visual Studio and presented them as a designer surface (known as a document-level project or smart document). This continues today. As Figure 4-8 shows, when a developer is working on a workbook solution, Excel appears just as a form surface would to a Windows developer.

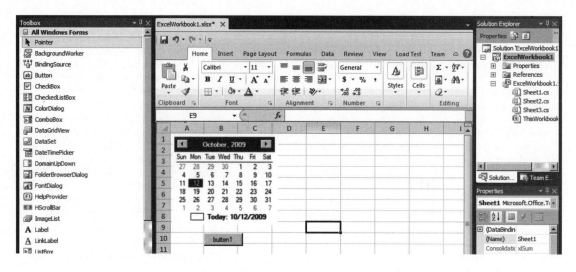

Figure 4-8. Microsoft Excel as a visual design surface

With the application as a design surface, the developer could drag Windows forms controls from the Visual Studio toolbox directly onto the spreadsheet or document. Double-clicking a button control took the developer to an event handler in a code-behind file. This made the Office development experience similar to that of Windows forms or ASP.NET, and gave Office developers a rapid application-development environment. In addition to the design surface, developers also gained access to application-level add-ins, task panes, smart tags, and the Ribbon interface, as well as expansion into other Office applications such as Visio and Outlook. However, with each release, a tighter relationship developed between Visual Studio, the .NET framework, Office, and the VSTO runtime. This means that as a developer, you need to be aware of dependencies on the applications you are writing.

- **VSTO 2003**: This version was released as an add-on for Visual Studio 2003, targeting development of Office 2003 solutions. It allowed you to build document-level projects for Excel and Word.

- **VSTO 2005**: This version was released with Visual Studio 2005, targeting development of Office 2003 solutions. It allowed you to build document-level projects for Excel and Word, as well as Outlook add-ins.

- **VSTO 2005 SE**: This version was an update for Visual Studio 2005, targeting development of Office 2003 and Office 2007 solutions. It allowed you to build add-ins for the 2003 version of Excel, Outlook, PowerPoint, Project, Visio, and Word, as well as the 2007 versions of Excel, InfoPath, Outlook, PowerPoint, Project, Visio, and Word. However, there was no support for document-level projects.

- **VSTO 2008**: This version was released with Visual Studio 2008, targeting development of Office 2003 and Office 2007 solutions. It allowed you to build the add-ins supported by VSTO 2005 SE along with document-level projects for the 2003 or 2007 versions of Excel and Word.

- **VSTO 2010**: This version was released with Visual Studio 2010, targeting development of Office 2007 and Office 2010 solutions. It allows you to build the previously mentioned add-ins and document-level projects for either Office 2007 or 2010. All of the code examples in this book use this version with Office 2010 as the target.

Developing with VSTO

This section describes the main types of development you can accomplish with Visual Studio Tools for Office. None of the descriptions here is of a complete project. Instead, this section establishes a baseline for the project types, a basic vocabulary, and some of the key code fragments you will find throughout our solutions in the remainder of the book. These examples are not specific to Visual Studio 2010, we will wait until the next section to discuss some of the specific enhancements VSTO 2010 and Office 2010 bring. With each development effort, we tell you which chapters contain solutions that incorporate that technique.

Add-Ins

Add-ins are defined by Microsoft Office Help as "supplemental programs that you can install to extend the capabilities of Microsoft Office by adding custom commands and specialized features." These programs run at the application level and are not tied to a specific document, spreadsheet, or presentation. In fact, the program can be loaded when the Office application starts, before any of these files are opened. Figure 4-9 shows the New Project dialog in Visual Studio 2010.

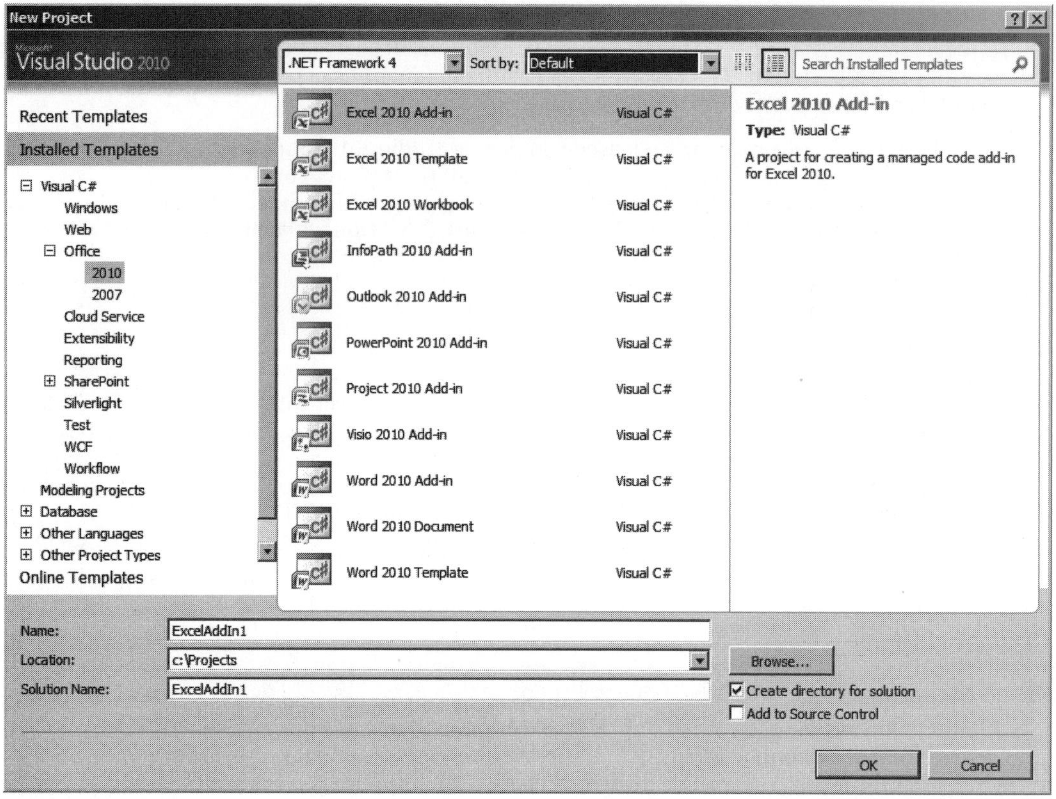

Figure 4-9. Creating an Office add-in project

Every add-in project includes a `ThisAddin` (`.cs` or `.vb`, depending on the language) file. This file includes the ThisAddin class, which is the root of your application. Within this class you can respond to events such as startup and shutdown, where you can include initialization and clean-up commands. Listing 4-5 shows some sample code from a ThisAddin class that sets up a task pane. This task pane is a user control that loads within the Office application, allowing a developer to display a custom user interface.

Listing 4-5. The ThisAddin Class

```
public partial class ThisAddIn
{
  public CustomTaskPane ctp;
  private void ThisAddIn_Startup(object sender, System.EventArgs e)
  {
    ctp = Globals.ThisAddIn.CustomTaskPanes.Add(new ucTaskPane(), "Custom Briefing");
```

```
    ctp.DockPosition = Office.MsoCTPDockPosition.msoCTPDockPositionRight;
    ctp.Width = 250;
  }
 private void ThisAddIn_Shutdown(object sender, System.EventArgs e)
 {
 }
```

With just a quick search on the Web, you can find a wide variety of Office add-ins for removing duplicate contacts in Outlook, creating surveys, redacting text in Word documents, and more. In this book, the solution in Chapter 9 creates a PowerPoint 2010 add-in to build presentation slides from the content in a SharePoint site. In Chapter 10, Outlook 2010 is extended, enabling customer data to be maintained as Outlook contacts, along with data visualizations of order trends.

Ribbon Customization

Before Office 2007, developers spent most of their efforts writing code utilizing the CommandBars object to create new buttons, extend menus, hide existing options, and make other user interface customizations. Microsoft Office 2007 introduced a new user interface for organizing these commands, called the R*ibbon*. The Ribbon occupies the top portion of most Office applications and provides a different experience from the layered menus and toolbars of previous Office releases. Figure 4-10 shows Microsoft Word 2010's Ribbon.

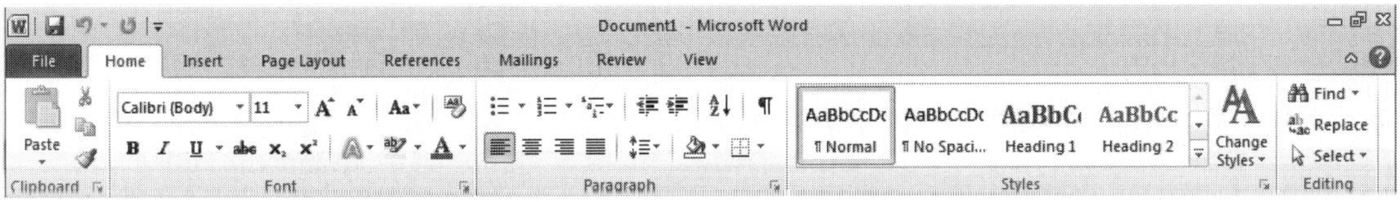

Figure 4-10. The Ribbon in Microsoft Word 2010

This interface provides a simpler experience for the user by improving the organization of commands and displaying a more graphical representation of options. One of the primary goals of the Ribbon interface is to surface functionality that users wanted but didn't know was there because of how buried or obscure that menu item was. The Ribbon also provides context sensitivity. That is, it will highlight certain tabs depending on the object you're focused on. For instance, the table tools are brought to your attention when you are in a table in a Word document. The controls on the Ribbon are broken up into tabs (Home, Insert, Page Layout, and so forth) and groups (Clipboard, Font, Paragraph, etc.).

VSTO opens the Ribbon interface to customization by the developer. In a project, you can select a custom ribbon from the Add New Item dialog of Visual Studio, as shown in Figure 4-11. There are two possible choices for building ribbon customizations: using a designer and working with the ribbon XML markup. The designer is adequate for most common scenarios and is used in Chapter 8. The XML markup option is useful when you need access to functionality that is not supported by the designer, which includes several 2010-specific features that we'll describe later. This approach is used in Chapter 7.

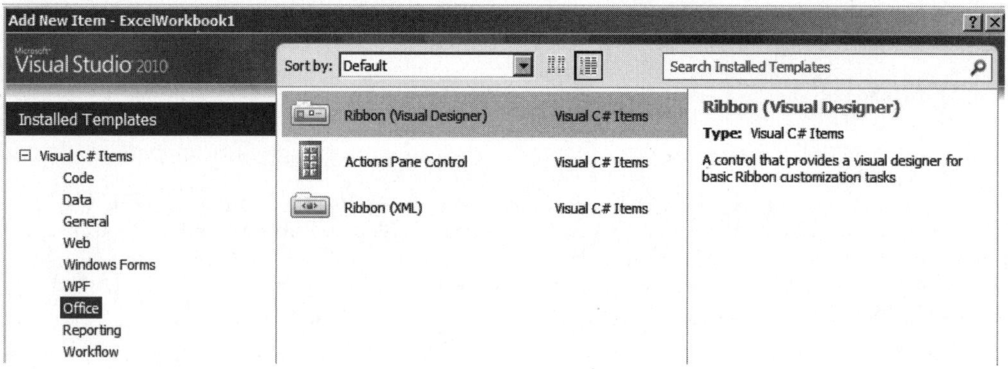

Figure 4-11. Adding a custom ribbon

Custom Panes

The concept of adding panes inside Office applications was introduced in Office 2003. The panes display in the same window as the application, usually off to the right-hand side of the document, e-mail, spreadsheet, or presentation. These panes can be scoped to the current open file or at the application level. When the pane is scoped to a file, we refer to it as an *actions pane*. When it is scoped to the application, we refer to it as a *task pane*. Actions panes are supported as part of the document-level projects. Task panes are associated with add-in projects. Panes provide an interface for the user to interact with, where the result usually has some impact on the user's current document. Office uses the pane interface for many tasks, such as browsing for clip art, searching through the Research pane, or displaying SharePoint site data. For developers, panes can be a method of extending the Office application with your own interface and process.

Office document-level projects can include custom actions panes. Fortunately, VSTO does most of the heavy lifting and provides you with an actions pane item template that can be added to your project. Figure 4-12 shows a sample actions pane control; the code necessary to load it is shown in Listing 4-6.

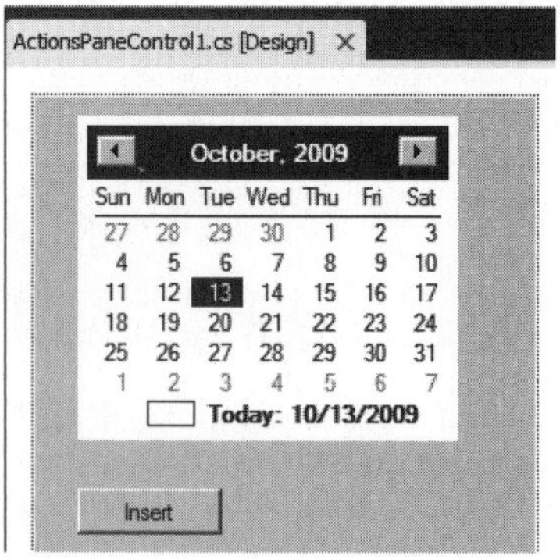

Figure 4-12. Constructing an actions pane control

Listing 4-6. Attaching the Actions Pane Control

```
public partial class ThisWorkbook
{
    ActionsPaneControl1 paneCtl1 = new ActionsPaneControl1();
    private void ThisWorkbook_Startup(object sender, System.EventArgs e)
    {
        this.ActionsPane.Controls.Add(paneCtl1);
        this.ActionsPane.Show();
    }
}
```

Once the control is loaded as an actions pane, it can interact with the host application (Excel) through Globals.ThisWorkbook. By placing code behind the control, you can manipulate the application or its document. For example, the code in Listing 4-7 responds by placing the selected date in the A1 cell of the current worksheet when the user clicks the Insert button.

Listing 4-7. Manipulating a Spreadsheet from an Actions Pane

```
private void btnInsert_Click(object sender, EventArgs e)
{
    if (Globals.ThisWorkbook.ActiveSheet != null)
    {
        Microsoft.Office.Interop.Excel.Worksheet current = null;
        string val = monthCalendar1.SelectionRange.Start.ToShortDateString();
        current = (Microsoft.Office.Interop.Excel.Worksheet) ↵
                  Globals.ThisWorkbook.ActiveSheet;
        current.Range["A1"].Value2 = val;
    }
}
```

Figure 4-13 shows the actions pane loaded to the right of the spreadsheet and the selected date inserted into cell A1.

Figure 4-13. The completed actions pane

Actions and task panes allow developers to inject their own interface and code into Office applications. The pane becomes like its own helper application to complete the document. PowerPoint 2010 is extended with a task pane in Chapter 8 so that slides can be built from SharePoint site content. The solution presented in Chapter 4 extends Microsoft Word 2010 so that a SharePoint people search can be performed to insert résumé requests into the document.

Outlook Form Regions

In addition to add-ins, ribbons, and task panes, Outlook 2007 introduced extensions through a new user interface element called *form regions*. Before Outlook 2007, developers who wanted to customize an Outlook form usually found themselves redesigning the entire form, even when all they wanted to do was add a few fields. In older versions of Outlook, these custom forms were deployed centrally on the Exchange server and often took too long to open. Developers also had a difficult time injecting their own code or script into the form. Enter Outlook form regions, which enable you to insert your own custom user interface into Outlook's inspectors. Do not confuse this approach with sending InfoPath forms through e-mail. Form regions are used to extend the user interface of Outlook.

In Visual Studio 2010, an Outlook form region is an item hosted by an Outlook add-in. Once you have an Outlook add-in project, you can create the form region in two different ways. As the dialog shows in Figure 4-14, when you add an Outlook form region item to the project, you can choose to design a new form in Visual Studio or import a form region that was designed in Outlook and exported as a Outlook Form Storage (OFS) file. Choosing a new form region lets you specify whether your region should appear separately from the original form or merge with it, what type of Outlook items should be matched with your form, and whether it should show up in read or compose scenarios.

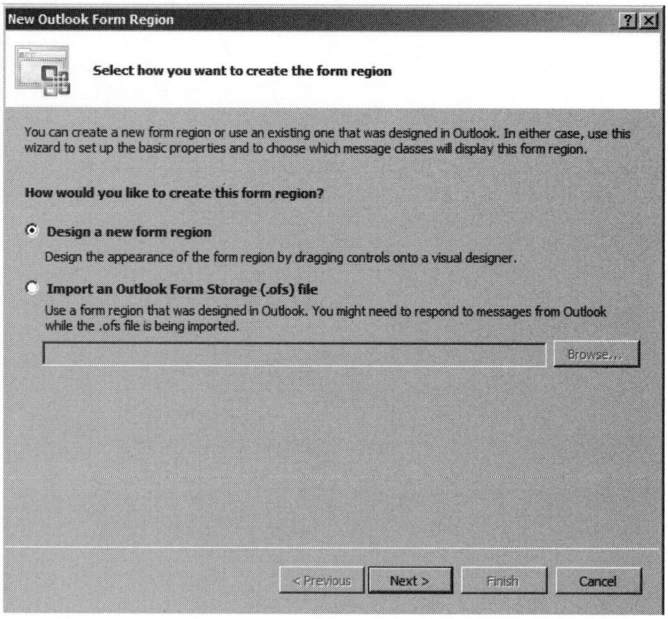

Figure 4-14. Adding a new region in Visual Studio

Once the form region is created, you can write code in it much as you would for any user control. Figure 4-15 shows a the custom form region you will create in Chapter 10, which is configured to display a chart of sales data for customers and allows the user to submit follow-up tasks, all from an Outlook contact form. This form region is accessed using the Show group in the ribbon.

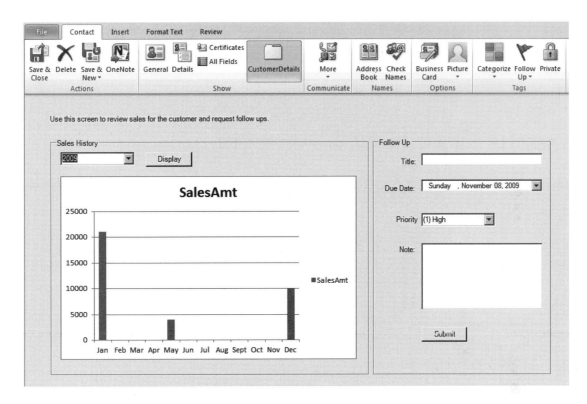

Figure 4-15. A custom form region displayed for customer contacts

Document-Level Projects

Document-level projects are solutions in which the application is a Word document or Excel spreadsheet and the technique used is often referred to as a *code-behind* document or a *smart document*. The difference between this type of solution and an add-in is that you are not just extending an Office application, but rather you're creating a tool from a specific file. The document or spreadsheet starts out with all of the traditional Office functionality and the developer can then drag new controls onto its surface, add custom code, add user-interface elements to an actions pane, and even cache data for offline access. Usually this type of solution is implemented to build a tool that helps an information worker create a complex document. Sales proposals and contracts whose contents likely come from many corporate resources are typical candidates for smart documents.

As shown earlier in Figure 4-8, Visual Studio Tools for Office provides a unique development environment for building document-level projects. When you start such a project, you have the option of creating a new file or importing an existing Word document or Excel spreadsheet. This is a useful feature for organizations that already have such assets and are looking to enhance them. Once in the designer, Windows form controls can be dragged onto the document's surface, and event-handler code can be placed in the code-behind. These projects also support data-binding the controls and caching of datasets for offline access. The result is an Office document with a code-behind assembly. Do keep in mind that the assembly is not contained within the document even if it is one based on the Open XML file format. Instead, the document includes a manifest that contains a pointer to where the code-behind assembly can be retrieved. This assembly location must be trusted by the code access security policies of the client. We will see this technique in action in Chapter 7 where we build a proposal tool out of a Microsoft Word 2010 document.

The 2010 Enhancements

In the earlier sections of this chapter, our examples could have been built with either Office 2007 or Office 2010. There are, however, benefits to targeting the newer platform. We will highlight a few of them in this section. To take advantage of these benefits, you must be targeting Office 2010 and using Visual Studio 2010.

Office 2010 includes a number of new user interface extensibility options, most designed to expand and enhance the ribbon programming model. A subtle improvement in the 2010 release is that developers can now make their custom ribbon tabs have the same context-sensitive behavior as the default tabs. Remember the earlier example of the table tools coming into focus when the user clicked on a table in Word? Now you can use code like the following to activate your own tab: `IRibbonUI.ActivateTab(string TabID)`. You need only specify the identifier of your custom tab to get the ribbon interface to bring it to the forefront.

Another user interface improvement is that your custom ribbon groups can now support the same scaling behavior of the out-of-the-box ones. Group scaling is the behavior that reacts when the Word Application window is either made larger or smaller. As the window decreases in size, commands change from using large icons to smaller ones or even rollup to a single command. This feature is increasingly important as computers continue to evolve into ever-smaller devices with much smaller screens. With the previous development tools, you customizations always stayed the same size. Now when you declare a custom ribbon group, you can simply set the autoScale property to true like this: `<group id="CustomGroup" autoScale="true">`. Figure 4-16 shows different renditions of the out-of-the-box Illustrations group, depending on the size of Word's window.

Figure 4-16. Group scaling functionality

Context menus and the new backstage user interface elements are also available to developers. With the 2010 toolset, the context menu (displayed when the user right-clicks) can also be extended using ribbon XML markup. In 2007, you still had to use command bars, which meant you had to mix approaches depending on where the user interface customization was to appear. The backstage user interface is the replacement for the pearl button that appeared in Office 2007 to provide functionality normally associated with the File menu. In Office 2007, the ribbon interface contained the actions the user would take within the document as they were authoring it. The File menu still showed up as a fly-out with menu options for saving, printing, setting permissions, and so on. The realization with the 2010 release is that users are spending increasing amounts of time working on their documents and the File menu just didn't provide enough real estate to make those functions easy to use. So now, clicking this button takes the user to an expanded interface where the actions take up most of the application space and a thumbnail of the file is displayed in the right hand corner. The backstage is basically the ribbon on its side where the tabs are now down the left-side of the screen. Just as with the rest of the ribbon interface, you can extend the existing tabs as well as create new ones. Figure 4-17 shows sort of a Hello World example of a backstage customization. The MyDocInfo button is the added functionality.

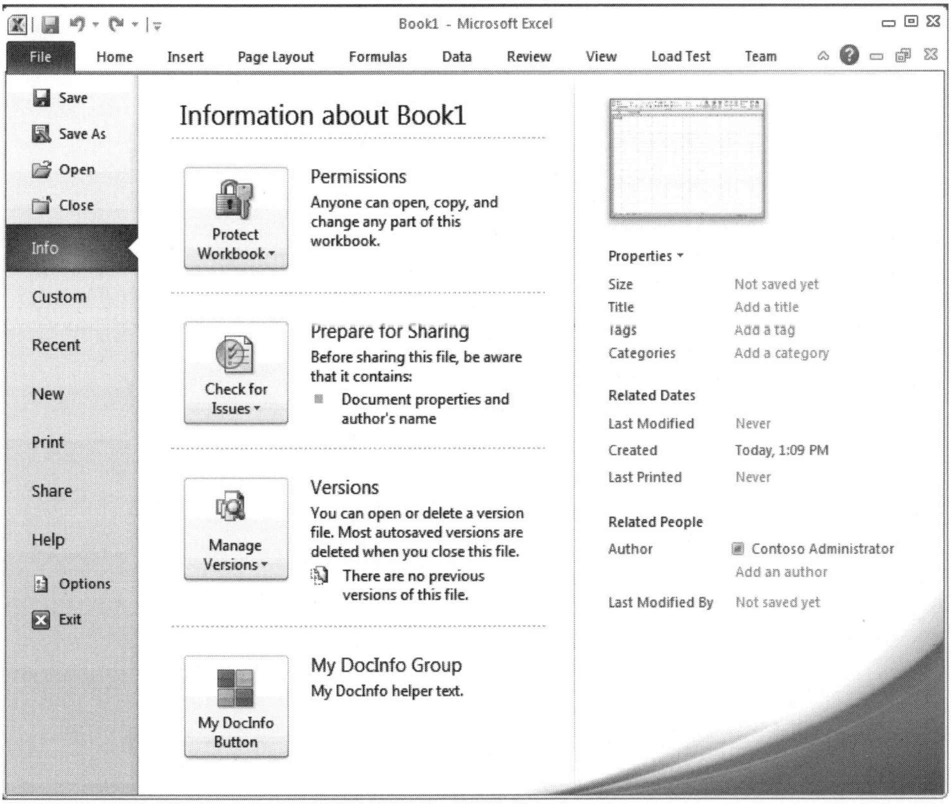

Figure 4-17. A backstage customization

Backstage customizations are defined using ribbon XML markup as well. Listing 4-8 shows the markup for the customization in Figure 4-17, which defines a new group **MyDocInfoGroup** on the Info tab. Chapter 7 includes a backstage customization.

Listing 4-8. Ribbon XML for Sample Backstage Customization

```
<customUI xmlns="http://schemas.microsoft.com/office/2009/07/customui">
<backstage>
  <tab idMso="TabInfo">
    <firstColumn>
      <group id="MyDocInfoGroup"
             label="My DocInfo Group"
             helperText="My DocInfo helper text.">
        <primaryItem>
          <button id="MyDocInfoButton"
                  label="My DocInfo Button"
                  imageMso="AppointmentColorDialog"
                  onAction="OnMyDocInfoButton"/>
        </primaryItem>
      </group>
    </firstColumn>
  </tab>
</backstage>
</customUI>
```

There are other reasons beyond user interface enhancements for using Office 2010 with Visual Studio 2010. In particular, using these tools gives you access to version 4 of the .NET Framework. In this release, there are several C# language enhancements that make developing Office solutions easier. The most impactful is that C# gains support for optional and named parameters. This feature is normally associated with Visual Basic and, in fact, it was the primary reason we chose to write the previous version of this book in VB.NET. In Office development, optional parameters show up all the time because COM supports them. Consider the code in Listing 4-9, which is what used to be necessary to have Word save a file.

Listing 4-9. C# Code to Save a Word File Before .NET Framework 4.0

```
object filename = "Test.docx";
object missing = "System.Reflection.Missing.Value;
doc.SaveAs(ref filename,
    ref missing, ref missing, ref missing,
    ref missing, ref missing, ref missing,
    ref missing, ref missing, ref missing,
    ref missing, ref missing, ref missing,
    ref missing, ref missing, ref missing);
```

With the .NET Framework 4.0, this code becomes far simpler. In fact, it could be just one line: `doc.SaveAs("Test.docx");`. Other language enhancements include named arguments, which are useful when you want to specify only a certain optional parameter or need to specify the parameters in a specific order. Named arguments are specified by preceding the passed value with the name of the parameter. Listing 4-10 is an example where we turn on case-sensitivity to a find operation of an Excel named range.

Listing 4-10. Named Arguments in C#

```
namedRange.Find("test", xlByRows, MatchCase: True);
```

Deployment also gets easier with the 2010 toolset. Two major improvements include multi-project deployment and fewer prerequisites. With multi-project deployment, you can now package up multiple Office customizations into a single ClickOnce deployment package. This means that if you have a solution that involves an Excel workbook, an Outlook add-in, and a Word add-in, they can be presented to the user as a single installation. Even after install, the combined projects will support update and uninstall operations as one application.

With Office 2010 solutions, you also have fewer prerequisites to worry about as you deploy your solutions to clients. There is no need to include setup or bootstraps for the VSTO runtime or primary interop assemblies. This is because the Office 2010 install takes care of getting the runtime on the user's machine, and the .NET 4.0 Framework supports embedding the interop types. Notice how the reference in Figure 4-18 shows that the interop types will be embedded (the default setting). For more on the deployment enhancements, watch Saurabh Bhatia's video from the PDC: `http://channel9.msdn.com/pdc2008/TL01/`.

Figure 4-18. Embedded interop types

Deployment Guidelines

In this book, all of our solutions are built with Visual Studio 2010 and Office 2010. However, with all the options of Visual Studio 2008 or 2010, Office 2007 or 2010, and the many versions of the .NET Framework, you may be wondering what to do to give you solution the widest client support. Here are a few guidelines on deployment, assuming you want your solution to run in both Office 2007 and Office 2010. For even more detail see `http://msdn.microsoft.com/library/ee712596(VS.100).aspx`.

- **Using Visual Studio 2008**: Choose an Office 2007 template when starting your project. Target the .NET Framework 3.5 SP1. Be careful about using P/Invoke statements as they could be different between the 32-bit and 64-bit versions of the applications. Bootstrap the Office 2007 PIA redistributable and the VSTO runtime 3.0 or higher (note the Office 2010 clients won't need them).

- **Using Visual Studio 2010**: Choose an Office 2007 template when starting your project. Target the .NET Framework 3.5 or 4. Be careful about using P/Invoke statements as they could be different between the 32-bit and 64-bit versions of the applications. Bootstrap the Visual Studio 2010 Tools for Office Runtime redistributable. If you target the .NET framework 3.5, then also bootstrap the Office 2007 PIA redistributable.

Further Reading

- Office Open XML Overview `http://www.ecma-international.org/news/TC45_current_work/OpenXML%20White%20Paper.pdf`

- Novell adds Microsoft's Open XML to OpenOffice `http://www.linux-watch.com/news/NS5248375481.html`

- OpenXMLDeveloper.org `http://openxmldeveloper.org/`

- VBA and Managed Code Extensions Compared `http://msdn.microsoft.com/en-us/library/ss11825b(VS.80).aspx`

- Office Development with Visual Studio `http://msdn.microsoft.com/en-us/vsto/default.aspx`

- Microsoft Visual Studio Tools for the Office System Power Tools `http://www.microsoft.com/downloads/details.aspx?FamilyId=46B6BF86-E35D-4870-B214-4D7B72B02BF9&displaylang=en`

- Microsoft Office 2010 Overview `www.microsoft.com/presspass/presskits/2010office/docs/OfficeOverviewFS.doc`

- See What's New in Microsoft Office 2010 `http://www.microsoft.com/showcase/en/us/details/6fc5abb1-d943-44ec-9b53-934e9b1cca0e`

- Common Tasks in Office Programming `http://msdn.microsoft.com/en-us/library/htx7t4k0(VS.100).aspx`

- Office Development in Visual Studio 2010 `http://msdn.microsoft.com/en-us/library/d2tx7z6d(VS.100).aspx`

- Brian Jones: Open XML `http://blogs.msdn.com/brian_jones/`

■ ■ ■

CHAPTER 5

Beyond the Spreadsheet

Just about everyone we speak with uses Microsoft Excel in one fashion or another. Information workers have become accustomed to modeling business calculations, analyzing information, or tracking data with spreadsheets and, typically, these spreadsheets are shared and distributed throughout the organization using e-mail, file shares, or, ideally, using SharePoint and Excel Services. SharePoint 2007 introduced Excel Services to overcome many of the challenges organizations face when building critical business processes around a spreadsheet, such as supplying a single source of the truth; saving bandwidth and processing resources by keeping much of the work on the server; and overcoming security issues by hiding formulas and publishing only what needs to be shared. SharePoint 2010 expands the scope of Excel Services, making it much easier to treat a spreadsheet as simply another data source for applications. With Excel Services, we have new ways to query data within a spreadsheet using REST, to interact with a spreadsheet hosted in a browser, and to easily integrate spreadsheets into a business process using web services.

For this chapter, we will detail how, as a developer, you can leverage Excel Services and find new ways to interact with and use spreadsheets that may otherwise sit forgotten in a file share.

Real-World Examples

We have encountered many customers whose users maintain and distribute large numbers of spreadsheets as part of the daily business process. Teams that coordinate floors of a hospital maintain spreadsheets of resources allocated to rooms. Housing companies maintain goals for production schedules. We have even worked with organizations that use Excel to manage all of their financials. One challenge is typical across all these cases—how to unlock the knowledge and information stored in the spreadsheets for sharing and collaboration with a broader audience, either internally or with external partners, without exposing information that should not be shared.

Solution Overview

For this solution, we will work with a spreadsheet used to manage the budget of an event, such as a conference or convention. The process begins when a user fills out a form to create a new event, which then generates a new spreadsheet to be used to keep track of income and expenses for the event.

Once we have a spreadsheet to manage the budget, we want to provide users a way to easily work with multiple spreadsheets. For this we will create an application that allows users to quickly browse all the charts currently stored within the budget spreadsheet. This provides a very visual way to see what is happening across several different spreadsheets at once, without having to spend a lot of time reviewing each spreadsheet individually. Users are bound to find areas they need to question when browsing the charts, so the application will also let them drill into the spreadsheet for further analysis and, at the same time, capture, store, and comment on a specific range of information within the spreadsheet.

Solution Walkthrough

This section details the major elements of the solution and the decisions we made as we were developing it. The walkthrough introduces you to the event budget spreadsheet that is the basis for our example. We will define seven named items in the spreadsheet, three ranges and four charts, which we will interact with using various methods exposed by Excel Services. Next, we'll create a document library in SharePoint to store the solution artifacts we'll be creating; here we'll save our spreadsheet to be used as a template, along with a second spreadsheet containing two ranges to be used as lookup values. We will use a form created in InfoPath to capture information and drive the creation of new event budget spreadsheets based on the REST and Web Service interfaces of Excel Services. Using SharePoint as a host, we will develop a dashboard using a Silverlight gadget to browse a list of spreadsheets and display available charts based on the user's selection. Finally, we will use a combination of the EWC JavaScript Object Model (JSOM) and the SharePoint client library to capture a range selection and write back a snapshot along with any user comments to a custom SharePoint list.

Introducing the Spreadsheet

For our example, we will work with an instance of the Event Budget spreadsheet template. This spreadsheet, shown in Figure 5-1, provides the ability to track various estimated and actual values for income and expenses associated with running an event such as a conference, and it includes several charts that provide visualizations into critical budget aspects, such as cost breakdown. The spreadsheet has one tab each for tracking Expenses and Income, and a summary tab with calculated values determined by the values entered on the other two tabs.

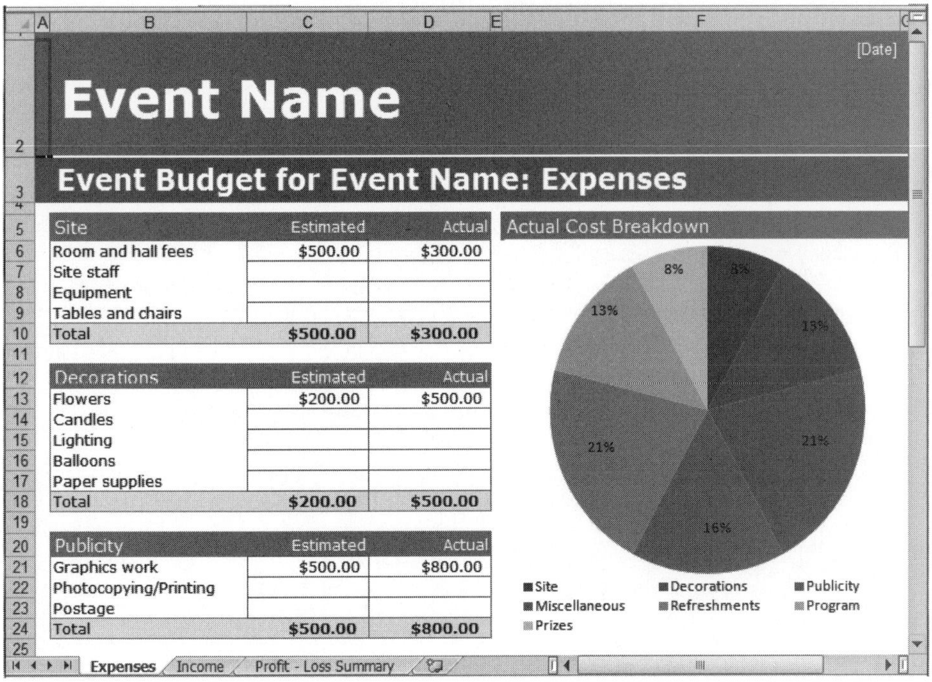

Figure 5-1. The Event Budget spreadsheet

You can obtain this template from the template download section of the Microsoft Office Online site at `http://office.microsoft.com/en-us/templates/TC103362741033.aspx`. If you have trouble downloading the template or you want to skip the chart and range modifications noted below you can use the copy, complete with updates, we have included in the Source Code/Download section of the Apress web site (`http://apress.com`). The file is named `Template.xlsx`. If you are using the version downloaded from Microsoft Office Online, you'll need to create three named ranges and modify the default chart names to match the remainder of the walkthrough. By explicitly defining ranges and naming these elements, we can access these components individually. The changes are outlined below:

1. With the Expenses tab selected, highlight all of the expense tables together, from the Site expenses section down to the Totals section, being sure to include all three columns (description, estimated, and actual).

2. Enter **ExpenseWorksheet** in the Name box, as shown in Figure 5-2, and press Enter. This will create a named range we can access directly.

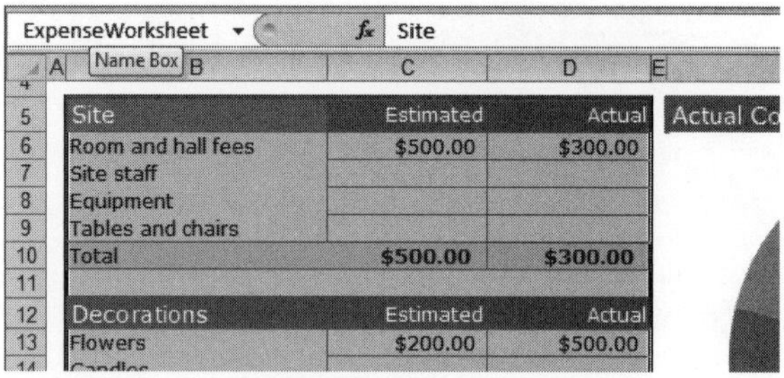

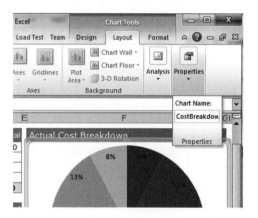

Figure 5-2. Creating a named range for the expense worksheet

3.   Select the Actual Cost Breakdown chart to bring up the Chart Tools tab set on the ribbon. Select the Layout tab and click the Properties drop-down to rename the chart **CostBreakdown**, as shown in Figure 5-3. Repeat this step to name the Estimated vs. Actual chart **EstimatedVsActual**.

Figure 5-3. Modifying the name of the Actual Cost Breakdown chart

Use steps 1 through 3 above to name the remaining elements as outlined in Table 5-1.

Table 5-1. Named Elements in the Event Budget Spreadsheet Broken Down by Worksheet

Worksheet	Range Name	Chart Name(s)
Expenses	ExpenseWorksheet	CostBreakdown EstimatedVsActual
Income	IncomeWorksheet	IncomeComparison
Profit-Loss Summary	ProfitLossSummary	ProfitVsLoss

We now have seven named elements in our spreadsheet that we can access quickly and directly using REST, Web Parts, or JSOM. Save your updated spreadsheet as `Template.xlsx`. You may also want to change the charts from 3D to 2D. Excel Services will not render the charts in 3D, and while a comparable 2D representation will be made, if you start with a 2D version you'll know up front exactly what you will be getting when viewed online. The template in the download directory has already been modified to use only 2D charts.

We need to create one additional spreadsheet that we'll use to supply lookup values during the Event Budget creation process. Create a new Blank Workbook in Excel and use the values in Table 5-2 to create two named ranges; save the spreadsheet as **Lookups.xlsx**.

Table 5-2. Named emelements in the Lookups spreadsheet

Range Name	Values
Regions	Midwest Northeast South West
EventTypes	Internal Partner Public

Storage for Our Solution Files

We have a number of options for how we deploy our solution, but because we're using several capabilities and services exposed by SharePoint, it makes the most sense to use SharePoint to host our solution. Even with this decision, there are multiple ways to get our solution into SharePoint, such as a custom feature deployed as a SharePoint Solution Package (WSP). Because we won't be deploying any binaries for this solution, we have chosen to simply store the artifacts we are creating in a standard SharePoint document library; this takes some of the complexity out of deployment and makes it very straightforward to link our artifacts to other elements, such as web parts. Chapters 3 and 14 go into more detail on other deployment options, such as using sandboxed solutions. Use the following steps to create the document library.

1. Open a browser and navigate to the SharePoint site you'll be using to host this solution.

2. From the Site Actions menu select New Document Library, which will bring up the Create dialog window shown in Figure 5-4. Type **EventBudgets** for the Name value and accept the default values for the remaining fields. Click Create.

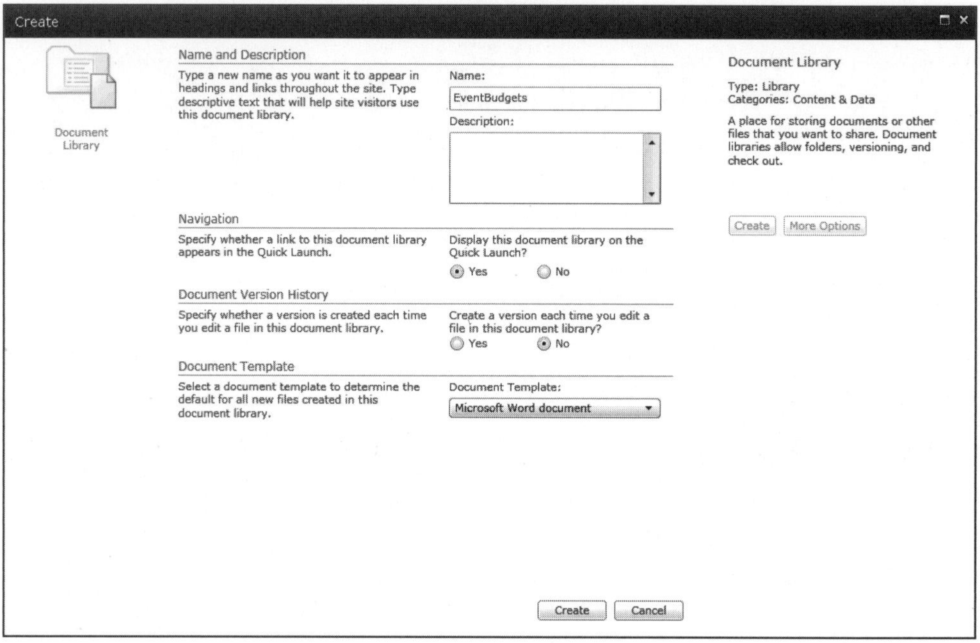

Figure 5-4. Creating the EventBudgets document library

■ **Note** We assume you are using the standard Team Site template for the SharePoint site where you are hosting your solution. Other templates may have slight variations in menu options and features enabled by default.

Supporting Business Process

So far we have developed a standard template and created a common storage location for Event Budget spreadsheets but we haven't done much to support the ability to create and manage the Event Budget process. Now for many organizations a standard template and a central storage location is a big step forward, but we want to do a bit more to automate some of the steps related to the creation of a new Event Budget, as well as provide some tools to give more insight into current state across all of the budgets being worked on. Let's start with the first half, adding some automation to the creation of the budget spreadsheet.

Create the Form

InfoPath is an awesome tool that provides a rapid development environment for building rich business forms. It uses XML for data storage and schema definition, provides a drag-and-drop designer, allows for no-code complex rules and actions, and supports data integration using standards such as REST, web services, and SQL out of the box. InfoPath is a logical choice for creating the first step in a business process—the initial data-capture step used to drive the remaining steps in the process. This is exactly where we will use InfoPath in our solution. We will develop a form to capture data related to a new Event, and once the form is submitted, we will create a new spreadsheet based on our template for managing the budget for the event. This will be a very loose process, just a step or two beyond a template alone. It will focus solely on managing the budget for the event, but this could easily be expanded to include steps such as approval, integration with an ERP system, or creation of a SharePoint site to manage all aspects of the event.

1. Open InfoPath Designer, select the Blank form template and click Design Form (Figure 5-5). Make sure you open InfoPath Designer and not InfoPath Filler. Filler is the new streamlined tool for 2010, for filling out existing forms only.

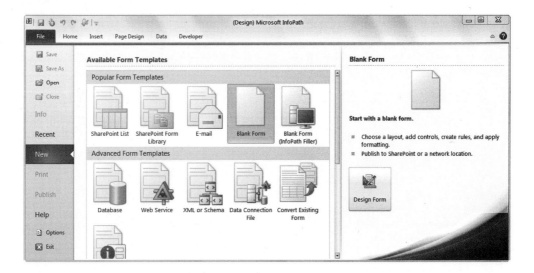

Figure 5-5. The Blank InfoPath form template

2. Add a title to your form by clicking the Click to add title text and typing **New Event Setup**.

3. Click the Add tables text to select the region where we want to add our form controls. Click the Insert tab of the ribbon and select one of the two column table templates; we used the Two-Column with Emphasis 4 template.

4. Regardless of the template you selected, you should have a table with three rows ready for labels and controls. Add labels and controls using Table 5-3. You'll find the available controls in the Controls section on the Home tab of the Ribbon. Once you add a control to the form, you can change the name using the properties screen; just right-click the control and select [control type] properties or click the Properties tab of the ribbon.

Table 5-3. Form Controls

Label	Control Type	Control Name
Event Type	Drop-Down List Box	eventType
Event Location	Drop-Down List Box	eventLocation
Event Name	Text Box	eventName

Your completed form should look similar to Figure 5-6. If you are new to InfoPath, feel free to take some time to look around. There are several more controls available beyond the drop-down list and text box, and you can quickly change the look of your form using the Themes available on the Page Design tab of the ribbon. Also, notice the Fields pane (click the Show Fields button on the Data tab if the pane is not visible). As you add and rename controls, new fields are created and updated; you are in essence building the XML schema the form will use to store its data. You can also import an existing schema and simply drag the fields from the Fields pane to create form elements as well. For a more in-depth look at InfoPath, check out the MSDN InfoPath Developer Center located at `http://msdn.microsoft.com/infopath`.

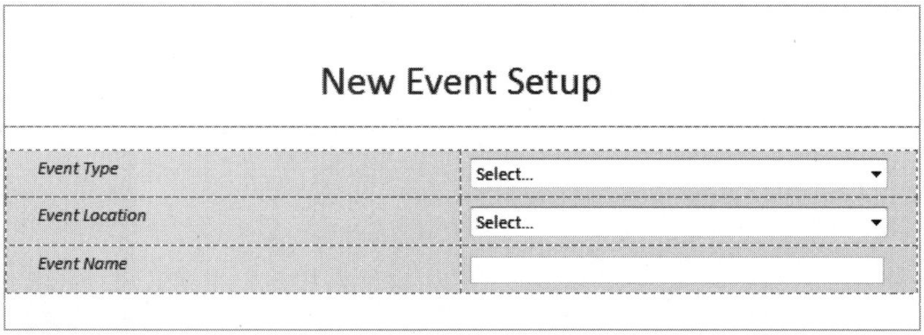

Figure 5-6. The form used for initial data capture related to new events

Add Lookups

In just a few steps we have created a decent-looking form, but it isn't very dynamic yet. Let's configure the drop-down lists to load their values from the Lookups.xlsx spreadsheet we created earlier. Thanks to the Excel Services REST interface and InfoPath's awareness of REST (both new features in SharePoint and InfoPath 2010), this will be amazingly easy. Use the following steps to create two data connections and bind them to the appropriate drop-down lists.

1. Right-click the eventType drop-down list and select Drop-Down List Box Properties… to bring up the properties window.

2. In the List box choices section, select the Get choices from an external data source option and click the Add… button to bring up the Data Connection Wizard.

3. The Create a new connection to: and Receive data radio buttons should be selected by default. Click Next to continue.

4. Select the REST Web service option as the data source and click Next.

5. Next we need to set the REST Web service URL. Enter a URL in the form `http://[siteroot]/_vti_bin/ExcelRest.aspx/EventBudgets/Lookups.xlsx/Model/Ranges('EventTypes')?$format=atom` where [siteroot] is the path to the top-level site where you are hosting your solution. This will return the Type range within the lookups.xlsx file we created earlier, formatted as an ATOM 1.0 feed. Click Next.

■ **Note** The Excel Services REST APIs provide direct access to named items (ranges, charts, tables, and pivot tables) of a spreadsheet via a URL. The return value is HTML, an ATOM feed, or a PNG image, depending on the parameters passed in the request. To browse a spreadsheet using the REST APIs, use the URL `http://[siteroot]/_vti_bin/ExcelRest.aspx/[Doc Lib]/[Spreadsheet]/Model`. For a detailed look at what you can do with Excel Services and REST, visit `http://msdn.microsoft.com/en-us/library/ee556413(v=office.14).aspx`.

6. Enter **Event Types** as the name for the data connection and Click Finish.

7. Finally, we need to select the location of the field in the return ATOM feed we'll use to populate the drop-down list. Click the button to the right of the Entries text box and select the **fv** node found at the path **entry/content/ns2:range/row/c/fv,** as shown in Figure 5-7, and click OK. Click OK one more time to close the properties window and complete the binding process.

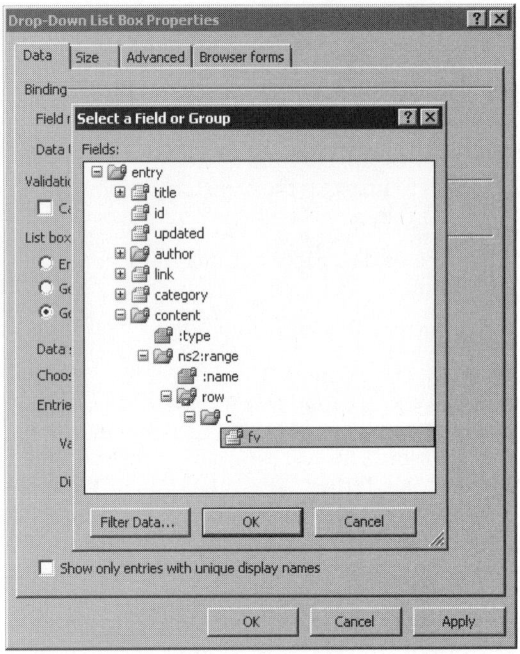

Figure 5-7. Selecting the field to bind the eventType drop-down list to

Repeat steps 1-7 above to bind the eventLocation drop-down to the Regions range in the lookups.xlsx spreadsheet substituting `http://[siteroot]/_vti_bin/ExcelRest.aspx/EventBudgets/Lookups.xlsx/Model/Ranges('Regions')?$format=atom` for the URL in step 5 and `Locations` for the connection name in step 6.

Click the Preview button on the Home tab to test your form; at this point, the drop-downs should include event type and location values from the lookups spreadsheet. This approach, storing our lookup data in an Excel spreadsheet, provides an easy way for users to manage lookup data using a well understood tool, and allows us to easily access this data using standards-based interfaces. It also demonstrates the power of both Excel Services and InfoPath—we did all this with no code. But this is only one option. InfoPath could easily be calling a web service or accessing a database to get this information, or we could use a mixture of all of these approaches within the same form.

Submitting the New Event

The final piece we'll add to our form is a submit behavior. For our solution, when a user submits the form, we want to create a new budget spreadsheet based on our Template.xlsx spreadsheet. This could, of course, include several additional steps—such as approvals—but we'll just open the template, write the event name entered in the form, and save a copy to the EventBudgets document library. And just as we did with the lookups, we will be able to take advantage of APIs provided by Excel Services, specifically the web services, to accomplish this without writing any code. To set this up, we'll first add a button to our form and enable the submit behavior for the button. Then we'll create a new rule associated with our submit button.

1. Click somewhere in the lower section of your form to set your cursor position, select the Home tab of the ribbon, and add a Button from the Controls section to the form.

2. Right-click on your new button and select Button Properties… to bring up the button properties window.

3. Change the action to Submit and click the Submit Actions button to bring up the Submit Options window.

4. Check the Allow users to submit this form option and select the Perform custom action using Rules option. Your Submit Options window should match Figure 5-8. Click OK.

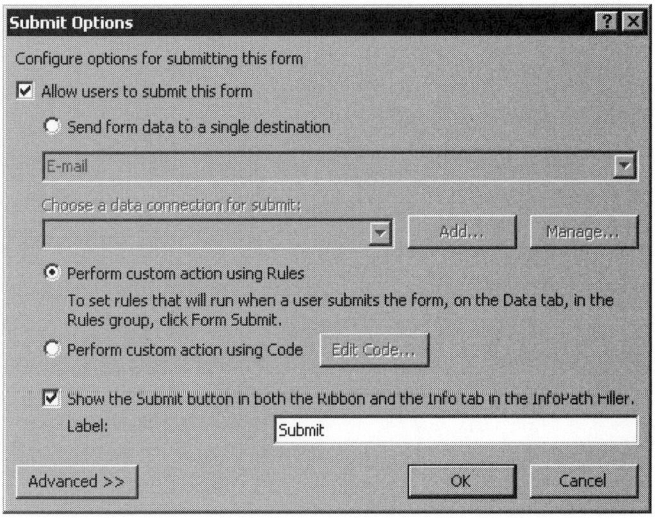

Figure 5-8. The Submit Options dialog

5. Click OK to close the Button Properties window. You should now see the Rules pane on the right side of your workspace set to manage the Form Submit rule; if the Rules pane is not visible, click the Form Submit button in the Rules section of the Data tab of the ribbon.

With the Submit button active and configured to run a set of rules and/or actions, we now need to specify exactly what actions should be run when the form is submitted. Here we will setup a series of calls to the Excel Services Web Service in order to create a new instance of the Event Budget spreadsheet.

1. Within the Rules pane select New ➤ Action and name the rule **Submit**.

2. In the Run these actions section, select Add ➤ Query for data (Figure 5-9) to bring up the Rule Details window. Click Add… to start the Data Connection Wizard.

Figure 5-9. Setting up the submit actions

3. Accept the default values and click Next. Click Next again on the following screen to select SOAP Web service as the source of the data.

4. Enter `http://[siteroot]/_vti_bin/ExcelService.asmx` for the location of the service where [siteroot] is the path to the site where you are hosting your solution. Click Next. InfoPath will query the service endpoint to retrieve a list of the available operations.

■ **Note** For more information on using the Excel Web Services in your custom applications, look at `http://msdn.microsoft.com/en-us/library/ms572330(v=office.14).aspx`.

---

5. In the list of available operations, select OpenWorkbook and click Next.

6. The next screen lets us set the values for the parameters being passed to the OpenWorkbook operation. Of the three parameters listed, we only need to provide a value for the workbookPath. Highlight the `tns:workbookPath` parameter and click Set Value… to bring up the Parameter Details dialog.

7. Here we want to set the Sample value field to be the path to the Event Budget template spreadsheet we stored in the EventBudgets document library. Enter the complete path to the template as shown in Figure 5-10 and click OK. InfoPath will use the sample value to query the endpoint and correctly build the schema for the data source.

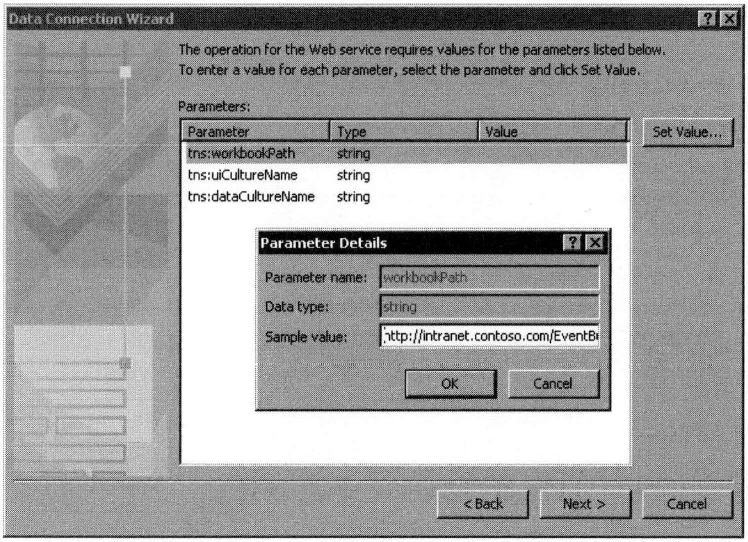

Figure 5-10. Setting parameters for the `OpenWorkbook` *operation*

8. Make sure the check box to store a copy of the data in the form template is not selected and click Next.

9. Accept the default value OpenWorkbook for the name of your new data connection and uncheck the box to automatically retrieve data when form is opened (we only want to make a call to the service on submit). Click Finish to create the new data connection and, finally, click OK to associate it with your action.

Every data connection created in InfoPath that returns data has an associated XML schema you can browse. Take a look at the Fields pane again and select OpenWorkbook (Secondary) from the Fields drop-down. Under the `myFields` root node you should see two additional nodes, `queryFields` and `dataFields`. The `queryFields` node contains the parameters that will be passed to the `OpenWorkbook` operation; we set a default value for the `workbookPath` value but you can also set any of these values at runtime using data from the form. The `dataFields` node contains any return values; we will need the session ID value stored in the `dataFields/tns:OpenWorkbookResponse/OpenWorkbookResult` field of the schema to correlate the remaining service calls. Let's complete the form submission process by adding actions to write the event name to our Event Budget spreadsheet and then to save the template as a new instance in our EventBudgets document library. First, however, we need to add four fields to our form data to be used as parameters for the calls, to write back the event name to the spreadsheet, and to save the spreadsheet.

1. In the Fields pane select Main from the Fields dropdown.

2. Right click the myFields node and select Add… to open the Add Field or Group dialog.

3. Enter **eventNameSheet** for the Name and **Expenses** for the Default value. Accept the defaults for the remaining options and click OK to add the new field.

Repeat steps 1-3 above to create fields named **eventNameCell** with a default value of `B2`, **workbookPath** without a default value, and **workbookType** with a default value of **FullWorkbook**. With our parameter values stored within our form data, we can now complete the submission process by adding the remaining actions. First we will add an action to update the value of the workbookPath field we just created.

1. Open the Form Submit rule again by clicking the Form Submit button in the Rules section of the Data tab of the ribbon

2. Within the Rules pane for the Form Submit rule, in the Run these actions section, select Add ➤ Set a field's value to bring up the Rule Details window.

3. Click the button to the right of the Field text box to open the field browser dialog and select the `workbookPath` field from the Main field set.

4. Click the button to the right of the Value text box to open the Insert Formula dialog. Enter the formula `concat("http://[siteroot]/EventBudgets/", my:eventName, " ", my:eventLocation, " Budget.xslx")` where [siteroot] is the path to the site where you are hosting your solution.

5. Click OK to save the formula and OK again to save the action.

■ **Note** The `workbookPath` field will be used as the file name for the new event budget spreadsheet we will be creating. However, we are not taking any extra steps to check for disallowed characters or doing anything to guarantee uniqueness beyond event name and location. Based on the settings we've used, if you attempt to save over an existing spreadsheet, submission will fail.

Finally we need to add the remaining Excel Services web service calls to complete the submit behavior for our form.

1. Within the Rules pane for the Form Submit rule, in the Run these actions section, select Add ➤ Submit Data to bring up the Rule Details window. Click Add… to start the Data Connection Wizard.

2. Accept the default values and click Next. Click Next again on the next screen to select To a Web service as the destination of your data.

3. Enter `http://[siteroot]/_vti_bin/ExcelService.asmx` for the location of the service where [siteroot] is the path to the site where you are hosting your solution. Click Next. InfoPath will query the service endpoint to retrieve a list of the available operations.

4. In the list of available operations select Set CellA1 and click Next.

For this operation we need to specify four parameters. The first parameter, `sessionId`, was returned by the `OpenWorkbook` operation and is used to correlate context across calls. We will associate the `sheetName` and `rangeName` parameters to the `evenNameSheet` and `eventNameCell` fields we just created. Finally we will pass the value event name entered by the user for the `cellValue` parameter.

1. For each parameter, highlight the parameter and double-click to open the field browser dialog. Use the values shown in Table 5-4 to set the parameter values to the correct fields. Figure 5-11 shows setting the sessionId parameter.

Table 5-4. Parameters for the `OpenWorkbook` *Operation*

Parameter	Field Set	Field Path
sessionId	openWorkbook	dataFields/tns:OpenWorkbookResponse/OpenWorkbookResult
sheetName	Main	eventNameSheet
rangeName	Main	eventNameCell
cellValue	Main	eventName

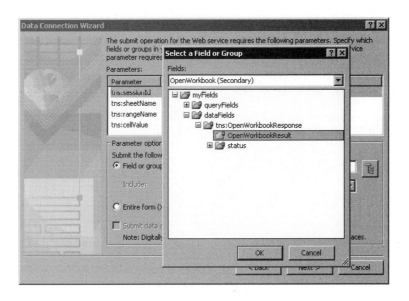

Figure 5-11. Setting the `sessionId` *parameter*

2. Once you have specified the element for each of the parameters, click Next.

3. Name your new data connection **WriteEventName,** then click Finish and OK to create the new data connection and associate it with your action.

Repeat steps 1-7 above to create two additional actions, one for the `SaveWorkbookCopy` operation and one for the `CloseWorkbook` operation; use the values in Table 5-5 for `SaveWorkbookCopy` and the values in Table 5-6 for `CloseWorkbook`. If for any operation a parameter is not called out in the table leave the element value empty.

Table 5-5. Parameters for the `SaveWorkbookCopy` operation

Parameter	Field Set	Field Path
sessionId	openWorkbook	dataFields/tns:OpenWorkbookResponse/OpenWorkbookResult
workbookPath	Main	workbookPath
workbookType	Main	workbookType

Table 5-6. Parameters for the `CloseWorkbook`

Parameter	Field Set	Field Path
sessionId	openWorkbook	dataFields/tns:OpenWorkbookResponse/OpenWorkbookResult

Our form is now complete. Your Rules pane should look similar to Figure 5-12, showing the set of actions we just finished creating for the Form Submit process. If you want to test your form to confirm everything is working as expected, select the Home tab of the ribbon and click the Preview button. After submission, you should find a new spreadsheet in the EventBudgets library.

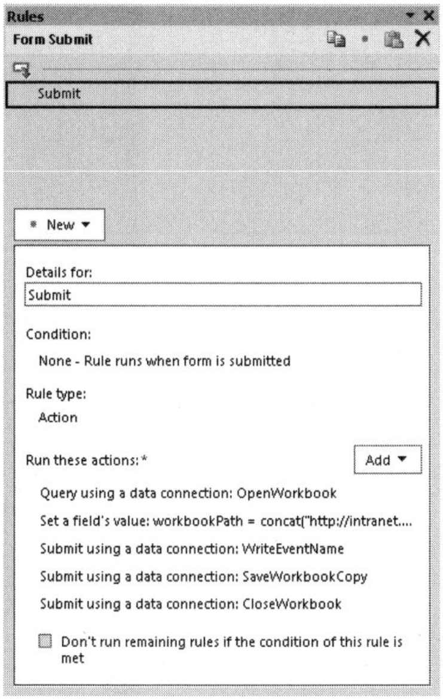

Figure 5-12. The rules pane showing the configuration for Form Submit

Deploying Our Form

The final step we need to take care of is publishing our form so others can use it. InfoPath provides several options for sharing forms, including e-mail, SharePoint, or a network location. To better support users in filling out forms, InfoPath 2010 now includes a standalone form-filler application that strips out the design tools. For our solution, we'll publish to the SharePoint site we are using to host our solution.

1. If you have not done so already, save your form.

2. Select the File tab of the ribbon to open Backstage, then select Publish from the options on the left.

3. Click the SharePoint Server button to start the Publishing Wizard, enter `http://[siteroot]/` (where [siteroot] is the path to the site where you are hosting your solution) and click Next.

4. Leave the default options to enable browser based forms and to publish to a form library and click Next.

5. Accept the default to create a new form library and click Next.

6. Type **NewEventForms** for the name and click Next.

7. The next screen lets you add columns and web part parameters based on values contained in the form. This is not something we need for our solution, but it is an option you should review further if you plan to do additional development with InfoPath and SharePoint. Click Next to continue.

8. Click Publish to complete the Wizard. Once your new form library has been created and the form published, you will have the option to open the form from the library. Check the box to open the form and click Close.

With the form open in the browser, you should see a view similar to Figure 5-13. Fill out the form and submit it to ensure all is working as expected. With our form completed and published and the ability for users to initiate the new event process, we now want to turn to managing the event budget spreadsheets we are creating.

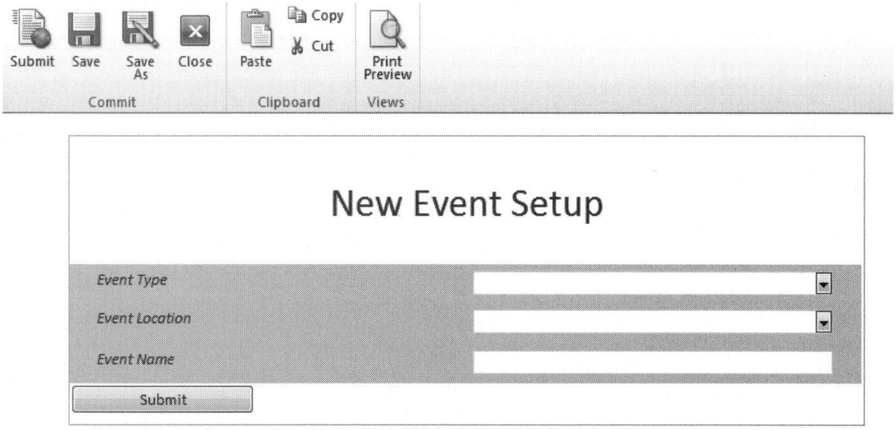

Figure 5-13. The New Event Setup form in the browser

Providing Insight

Data is only as valuable as the insights we are able draw from it, so the more easily accessible our data is and the more options we provide to work with it, the more valuable it becomes. We have provided a standard way to capture some initial information and have constructed a process to create a spreadsheet for capturing budget information based on a standard template. Now let's provide some tools to explore and work with the data.

Viewing the Spreadsheet

The first thing we need to do is create a simple web part page to view an instance of the event budget spreadsheet in the browser. We will construct the page such that the actual spreadsheet to be displayed will be determined by a query string parameter that will be important in a later step.

1. Open a browser and load the root site you are using to host your solution.

2. Open the Site Actions menu and select More Options… to open the Create dialog.

3. Find and select the Web Part Page item and click Create. If you are having trouble sorting through all of the available items, you can use the search box in the upper right of the dialog or select the Page link on the left side to filter the list of available items.

4. Enter **EventBudgetComment** for the name, select Header, Right Column, Body for the layout template, and select the Site Pages document library as the save location. Click Create.

The page template we selected has three web part zones, Header, Body, and Right Column. We will add the Excel Web Access (EWA) and Query String (URL) Filter web parts to the body zone and a Content Editor web part to the right column zone (we'll leave the header zone alone). We'll use the Excel web part to display our spreadsheet. We'll use the query string filter to pass a URL query string parameter containing the path to the spreadsheet we want to view to the Excel web part to set which spreadsheet to show.

1. Click the Add a Web Part text in the Body web part zone to bring up the web part selector at the top of the page.

2. Select Business Data as the category and Excel Web Access for the web part (Figure 5-14). Click Add to create an instance of the web part on our page.

Figure 5-14. Adding an Excel Web Access web part

3. Click the Add a Web Part text in the Body web part zone a second time to again bring up the web part selector at the top of the page.

4. Select Filters as the category and Query String (URL) Filter for the web part. Click Add to create an instance of the web part on our page.

5. Click the Open the tool pane link in the Query String (URL) Filter web part to configure the query string parameter we'll be using.

6. Enter **workbook** as the Query String Parameter Name. Click OK at the bottom of the tool pane.

7. You should now see some text stating the filter is not connected. Click the down arrow in the upper right of the filter web part to bring up the web part menu and select Connections ➤ Send Filter Values to ➤ Excel Web Access, as shown in Figure 5-15.

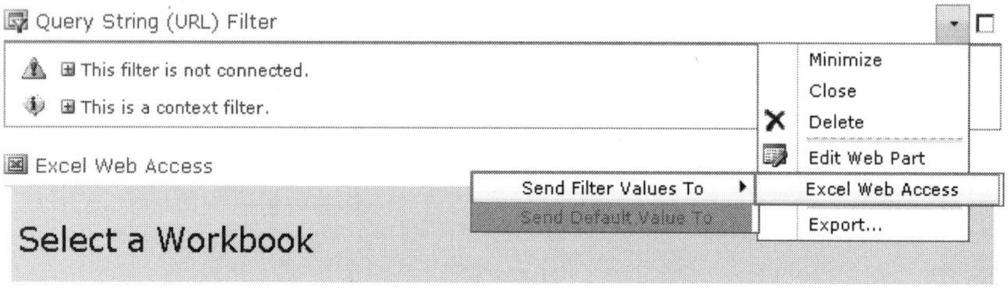

Figure 5-15. *Connecting the query string filter to the Excel web part*

8. In the Choose Connection dialog, accept the default connection type Get Workbook Url From and click Finish.

9. Click the Add a Web Part text in the Right Column web part zone to bring up the web part selector at the top of the page.

10. Select Media and Content as the category and Content Editor for the web part. Click Add to create an instance of the web part on our page.

11. Click the down arrow in the upper right of the Content Editor web part to bring up the web part menu and select Edit Web Part.

12. Enter `[siteroot]/EventBudgets/Comment.htm` for the content link; this file doesn't exist yet but we will be creating it shortly and adding it to the EventBudgets document library. Click Apply and then OK at the bottom of the tool pane.

13. Click the Stop Editing button on the Page tab of the ribbon to save the page.

To verify the filter is doing what it is supposed to do, set the location of your browser to `http://[siteroot]/SitePages/EventBudgetComment.aspx?workbook=/[subsite]/EventBudgets/Template.xlsx`, which should load the event budget template spreadsheet into the Excel web part. Feel free to modify the look of the page by updating the web part titles and adjusting the chrome.

Adding Comments

The page we just created is nice but doesn't do much yet, so let's add a bit more interactivity. Here we want to let users select a range within the spreadsheet and comment on what they are looking at, perhaps to ask a question about certain values or to request an update of specific items. We'll use a custom SharePoint list to save the comments to, along with a snapshot of the HTML representing the range and a link to the live data, by using the Excel Services REST APIs (for the snapshot and link) and the SharePoint JavaScript APIs. Let's begin with the custom list we will be using to store the comments.

1. Open the Site Actions menu and select More Options… to open the Create dialog.

2. Find and select the Custom List item, enter **EventBudgetComments** as the name and click Create.

3. Using Table 5-7, create three new columns to store comment information. You can add new columns by clicking the Create Column button found in the Manage Views section of the List tab on the ribbon.

Table 5-7. New columns for comments list

Column Name	Data Type
Comments	Multiple lines of text
CommentView	Multiple lines of text
CurrentView	Hyperlink or Picture

Next let's create the HTML file containing markup for a simple UI, as well as the JavaScript necessary to make all the magic happen. Create a new HTML file named **Comment.htm** in your favorite HTML editing tool, and add the HTML in Listing 5-1 to create a simple UI for our comment form. The class attributes refer to CSS styles included in the code download.

Listing 5-1. HTML to Specify the Comment UI

```
<script language="javascript" type="text/javascript">
</script>
<div class="commentWrapper">
    <div class="title">Range Comments</div>
    <div>Select a range, add your comments and click 'Save Comment'.</div>
    <div><span class="label">Current Range:</span> <span id="range"></span></div>
    <div class="label">Comments:</div>
    <div><textarea id="comments"></textarea></div>
    <div><input id="submitComment" type="button" value="Save Comment"
        onclick="SaveComment();" /></div>
</div>
```

Next, add the code in Listing 5-2 within the script block to declare the necessary variables.

Listing 5-2. Declaration of the Shared JavaScript Variables

```
var curRange; // currently selected range
var ewa; // reference to the Excel Web Access control (EWA)
var workbook; // path to the currently loaded workbook
var siteUrl = "http://[siteroot]/"; // complete site url
var siteRelativeUrl = "/" // subsite portion of the url will be '/' for root sites
var nid; // stores id of notifications being displayed
```

The first action we need to take is to get a reference to the EWA control on the page using the code in Listing 5-3. Here we are attaching to the **onload** event and then, once the page has been loaded, we are attaching to the application-ready event of the EWA control which will fire once the control and its content has finished loading.

Listing 5-3. The PageLoad Event Handler

```
window.attachEvent("onload", PageLoad);
function PageLoad() {
    // attach event to fire once EWA is loaded
    Ewa.EwaControl.add_applicationReady(GetEwa);
}
```

Once the control has been loaded, we need to save a reference to it using the **ewa** variable, then attach an event handler to the **activeSelectionChanged** event. This event will fire anytime a user selects a new range in the currently loaded spreadsheet. Add the code in Listing 5-4.

Listing 5-4. Getting a Reference to the EWA Control

```
function GetEwa() {
    // get a reference to the EWA, assume only one on page so using index 0
    ewa = Ewa.EwaControl.getInstances().getItem(0);
    // store the current workbook path without the site url
    workbook = ewa.getActiveWorkbook().getWorkbookPath().replace(siteUrl, "");
    // set initial range
    UpdateRange(ewa.getActiveWorkbook().getActiveSelection());
    // add event handler for selection change
    ewa.add_activeSelectionChanged(ActiveSelectionChanged);
}
```

When a user makes a range selection (or on initial load), we want to capture the current range value in A1 notation (**sheet!cellstart:cellend**). We will store this in the **curRange** variable for later user and write the value to the UI. Use the code in Listing 5-5 to implement this behavior; **ActiveSelectionChanged** is called when the event fires, and **UpdateRange** is where we do the work. Notice we are replacing the ':' character used in standard A1 notation with the '|' character; this is because a colon is invalid in a URL so the Excel team decided to replace it with the pipe for REST calls.

Listing 5-5. Capturing the Current Range Selection

```
function ActiveSelectionChanged(args) {
    // update current range based on selection
    UpdateRange(args.getRange());
}
function UpdateRange(range) {
    // store current range and update UI
    curRange = (range.getAddressA1().replace(":", "|"));
    document.getElementById("range").innerHTML = curRange;
}
```

Next use the code in Listing 5-6 to wire up the **onClick** event of the button. There is a lot going on here, but the code comments should help to explain each call. In a nutshell, the steps taken are to disable the submit button to prevent duplicate saves, notify the user of the action being taken, get the HTML representation of the range using the REST APIs, and, finally, save the comment and range information as a new entry in our EventBudgetComments list. Because all of the SharePoint client-side calls must happen asynchronously, we need to provide callback functions, one for success and one for failure, so we can take appropriate action once the call returns; the last line of code sets up the callbacks. For the notification, we are taking advantage of the new status and notification area in SharePoint. The Save completed successfully message in Figure 5-16 is an example of what a notification message looks like.

*Listing 5-6. Wiring up the Button's **onClick** Event*

```
function SaveComment() {
    // disable button
    document.getElementById("submitComment").disabled = true;

    // add sticky notification and store ref in nid var
    nid = SP.UI.Notify.addNotification("Saving Comment...", true);

    // get HTML for the range using Excel REST
    var rangeLink = siteUrl + "_vti_bin/ExcelRest.aspx/"
        + workbook + "/model/Ranges('" + curRange + "')";
    var request = new XMLHttpRequest();
    request.open("GET", rangeLink, false);
    request.send();
    var rangeHTML = request.responseText;

    // save new list item using SharePoint Client OM
    var context = new SP.ClientContext(siteRelativeUrl);
    var list = context.get_web().get_lists().getByTitle("EventBudgetComments");
    // create object to hold properties of the new list item
    var createInfo = new SP.ListItemCreationInformation();
    var listItem = list.addItem(createInfo);
    listItem.set_item("Title", "Range Comment");
    listItem.set_item("Comments", document.getElementById("comments").value);
    listItem.set_item("CommentView", rangeHTML);
```

```
        listItem.set_item("CurrentView", rangeLink);
        listItem.update();

        // make asynchronous call to perform save passing callback functions
        context.executeQueryAsync(
            Function.createDelegate(this, this.SaveCommentSucceeded),
            Function.createDelegate(this, this.SaveCommentFailed));
    }
```

■ **Note** Listing 5-6 includes several calls related to getting context and writing back a list item to SharePoint using the client OM. However, these calls are actually queued up and are not executed until the `executeQueryAsync` call, at which time the calls are bundled up and sent back to the server as a batch. This is an important distinction between programming against the SharePoint OM server-side vs. client-side, and one that is critically important to understand. Take a look at `http://blogs.msdn.com/ericwhite/archive/2009/11/20/using-the-sharepoint-2010-managed-client-object-model.aspx` for a detailed discussion of this topic.

Listing 5-7 shows the code we want to run once the call to `executeQueryAsync` completes successfully. Here we re-enable the button, remove the first notification (for the action being taken), and create a new notification alerting the user we were successful. Notice in the first call we made to `SP.UI.Notify.addNotification` we included two parameters, the message and a Boolean to specify stickiness. If the stickiness argument is true, it is our responsibility to remove the notification with a call to `SP.UI.Notify.removeNotification.` On the other hand, if it is false (which is the default value), SharePoint will remove the notification for us after approximately three seconds.

Listing 5-7. The Callback for Successful Execution of the `executeQueryAsync` *Call*

```
function SaveCommentSucceeded() {
    // enable button
    document.getElementById("submitComment").disabled = false;
    // clear save notification
    SP.UI.Notify.removeNotification(nid);
    // add success notification
    SP.UI.Notify.addNotification("Save completed successfullly");
}
```

The final bit of JavaScript, Listing 5-8, will execute if the call to `executeQueryAsync` is unsuccessful. Again we re-enable the button, remove the first notification, and then add a notification alerting the user to the failed save attempt.

Listing 5-8. The Callback for Unsuccessful Execution of the `executeQueryAsync` *Call*

```
function SaveCommentFailed() {
    // enable button
    document.getElementById("submitComment").disabled = false;
```

```
    // clear save notification
    SP.UI.Notify.removeNotification(nid);
    // add failure notification
    SP.UI.Notify.addNotification("Your save request failed!");
}
```

Save your Comment.htm file to the EventBudget document library. This is the file we configured as the source for the content editor on the EventBudgetComment page. With the file saved you can browse back over to the web part page we created earlier at `http://[siteroot]/SitePages/EventBudgetComment.aspx?workbook=/[subsite]/EventBudgets/Template.xlsx.` You should see the interface we just created displayed in the location where you added the content editor web part. The final page, including a spreadsheet and the comment form, is shown in Figure 5-16. Notice the notification in the upper right of the image. Highlight some cells within the spreadsheet, the range should be displayed just above the comment box. Click the Save Comment button and confirm a new list item is added to the EventBudgetComments list. You may notice the comment form has been stylized a bit; the `Comment.htm` file in the Source Code/Download section of the Apress web site (`http://apress.com`) also includes CSS style definitions which aren't included in the walkthrough but feel free to copy them from the download or create your own.

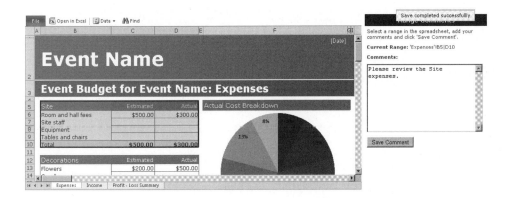

Figure 5-16. The EventBudgetComment page with the template spreadsheet loaded

Creating the Chart Browser

The next area we will focus on is a Silverlight application for browsing the charts associated with a specific spreadsheet. Silverlight is a great choice for building rich Internet applications, especially those that deal with media such as images and video. For this exercise we'll use the SharePoint client-side objects for Silverlight to retrieve a list of spreadsheets from a document library, and the Excel Services REST APIs to list and view the available chart images. We'll use SharePoint as the host so we can more easily integrate with the EventBudgetComment page we created in the previous section, but this could be easily refactored to run outside of SharePoint or to support browsing a set of spreadsheets from any document library. If you decide to take this route, you'll need to configure a cross-domain policy file on the server. See `http://msdn.microsoft.com/en-us/library/cc189008(VS.95).aspx` for more information.

1. Open Visual Studio and create a new Silverlight Application project named **ChartBrowser**, as shown in Figure 5-17.

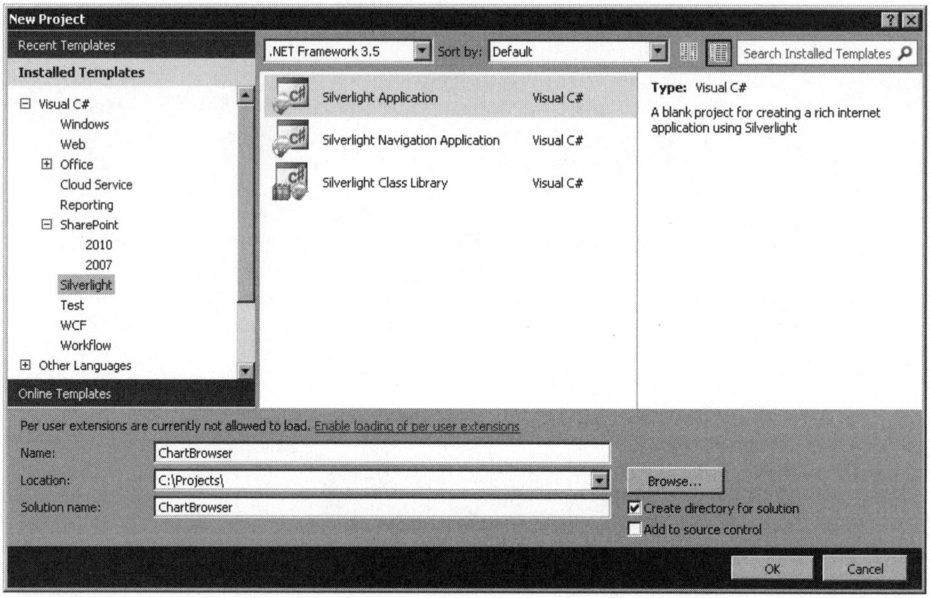

Figure 5-17. The New Project dialog

2. On the New Silverlight Application dialog, uncheck the box to host the Silverlight application in a new web site and click OK.

3. Right-click the References folder in the Solution Explorer window (select Solution Explorer from the View menu if it is not currently visible) and add references to the assembly `System.ServiceModel.Syndication` found on the .NET tab of the Add Reference dialog and click OK.

4. Right-click the References folder one more time and use the Browse tab to open the folder `[14hive]\Templates\Layouts\ClientBin` and locate the assemblies `Microsoft.SharePoint.Client.Silverlight` and `Microsoft.SharePoint.Client.Silverlight.Runtime`. Click OK.

With the project configured and references added, let's write some code. Let's first focus on the UI. We will add a list box to display a list of workbooks, a scroll viewer to display a list of chart thumbnail images, an image control to show the currently selected chart, and a button to allow users to view the currently selected spreadsheet (using the EventBudgetComment page). Open the `MainPage.xaml` file, which will be used to host our controls; this should open a designer window as well as a XAML editor. By default, you should have a Grid control surrounded by a UserControl. We will be adding markup within the Grid control tags. First, add height and width attributes to the Grid, **600** and **800** respectively, then add a ListBox control using the code in Listing 5-9. For the list box, we are specifying an event handler, `WorkbookSelected`, which will be called any time a user selects a different item in the list. We are also setting up the template for each item loaded in the list; in this case, it's a simple `TextBlock` control bound the `Name` property of the object we will be associating to the list a bit later.

Listing 5-9. Setting up the List Box

```
<ListBox HorizontalAlignment="Left" Name="workbookList" Width="250" Height="430"
        VerticalAlignment="Top" Margin="5" SelectionChanged="WorkbookSelected">
    <ListBox.ItemTemplate>
        <DataTemplate>
            <TextBlock Text="{Binding Name}" FontFamily="Verdana" FontSize="12" />
        </DataTemplate>
    </ListBox.ItemTemplate>
</ListBox>
```

■ **Note** For more information about using XAML in Silverlight, take a look at `http://www.silverlight.net/getstarted/` To find out more about data binding see `http://msdn.microsoft.com/en-us/library/cc189036(VS.95).aspx`.

Next, add a button using the code in Listing 5-10. The button, when clicked, will bring up a dialog window in SharePoint that displays the comment page we created earlier, loaded with the currently selected spreadsheet.

Listing 5-10. Adding a Button

```
<Button Content="View Workbook" Height="30" HorizontalAlignment="Left"
        Margin="140,440,0,0" Name="viewWorkbook"
        VerticalAlignment="Top" Width="115" Click="ViewWorkbook"/>
```

Just below the button we'll add a `ScrollViewer` (Listing 5-11) that allows users to scroll through thumbnails of all the chart images in the currently selected spreadsheet.

Listing 5-11. The Chart Image Scroller

```
<ScrollViewer Name="chartScroller" HorizontalAlignment="left" VerticalAlignment="bottom"
            Width="250" Height="120" Margin="5" VerticalScrollBarVisibility="Hidden"
            HorizontalScrollBarVisibility="Visible">
    <ItemsControl Name="chartList">
        <ItemsControl.ItemTemplate>
            <DataTemplate>
                <Border BorderBrush="Black" BorderThickness="1" CornerRadius="2"
                        Margin="2" Padding="2">
                    <StackPanel>
```

```
                    <Image Source="{Binding Id}" Width="80" Height="80"
                            MouseLeftButtonDown="ChartSelected"
                            HorizontalAlignment="Center" VerticalAlignment="Center"  />
                </StackPanel>
            </Border>
        </DataTemplate>
    </ItemsControl.ItemTemplate>
    <ItemsControl.ItemsPanel>
        <ItemsPanelTemplate>
            <StackPanel Orientation="Horizontal" HorizontalAlignment="left"
                        VerticalAlignment="Center" />
        </ItemsPanelTemplate>
    </ItemsControl.ItemsPanel>
    </ItemsControl>
</ScrollViewer>
```

The final UI element is a large image area. We want to provide a full-size view of a chart image when the user clicks on a thumbnail in the scroll viewer. Add the code in Listing 5-12 to support this.

Listing 5-12. *Enabling a Full-Size Chart Image*

```
<StackPanel HorizontalAlignment="Right" VerticalAlignment="Top" Width="535" Margin="5">
    <Image HorizontalAlignment="Center" VerticalAlignment="Center"
            Name="chart" Height="590" />
</StackPanel>
```

With our XAML written for the UI, we now turn our attention to the necessary code to load the data and handle the events. Open the `MainPage.xaml.cs` file and add the necessary `using` statements in Listing 5-13.

Listing 5-13. *Necessary Using Statements*

```
using Microsoft.SharePoint.Client;
using System.ServiceModel.Syndication;
using System.IO;
using System.Windows.Browser;
using System.Xml;
```

Next we need to add some class variables to set defaults and keep track of state across method calls, and define the `Workbook` type to store workbook information. We also need to define a delegate, named `UpdateUI` in this case. All network calls in Silverlight are required to be asynchronous and executed on a background thread. This means we need to define a delegate to be dispatched to once the background operation has completed and it is time to switch back to the UI thread. Finally, add a call to the `LoadSpreadsheets` method in the `MainPage` constructor; we will be creating this method next. Listing 5-14 details the code.

Listing 5-14. Defining a Workbook Type and a Delegate

```
ListItemCollection docs;
ClientContext context;
List list;
Workbook workbook;
string siteRoot = "http://[siteroot]/";

public struct Workbook
{
    public string Name { get; set; }
    public string FileName { get; set; }
}

private delegate void UpdateUI(bool success);

public MainPage()
{
    InitializeComponent();
    LoadSpreadsheets();
}
```

We'll be working with a few data elements in our form, the first of which is a list of spreadsheets (Listing 5-15). We need to query the EventBudgets document library to get a listing of all the budget spreadsheets currently in the library; to do this, we will use the SharePoint client object model to send a CAML query requesting all spreadsheets in the EventBudgets library where the built-in SharePoint field FileLeafRef contains the text Budget.

Listing 5-15. Getting the List of Spreadsheets

```
private void LoadSpreadsheets()
{
    context = new ClientContext(siteRoot);
    list = context.Web.Lists.GetByTitle("EventBudgets");

    CamlQuery query = new CamlQuery();
    query.ViewXml = "<View><Query><Where><Contains><FieldRef Name='FileLeafRef' />" +
        "<Value Type='Text'>Budget</Value></Contains></Where></Query><ViewFields>" +
        "<FieldRef Name='FileLeafRef' /></ViewFields></View>";

    docs = list.GetItems(query);
    context.Load(docs);
    context.ExecuteQueryAsync(QuerySucceded, QueryFailed);
}
```

■ **Note** Collaborative Application Markup Language, CAML for short, is an XML-based language used in a SharePoint environment for operations such as querying or defining elements. Many of the new APIs in 2010 build layers of abstraction on top of CAML but there are still times when you will need to use it. For a more detailed look at what it is and definitions of the schemas, see `http://msdn.microsoft.com/en-us/library/ms462365.aspx`.

As mentioned earlier, the architecture of Silverlight requires us to use a background thread for network operations, but once the call is complete we need to dispatch a call back to the UI thread. Listing 5-16 sets this up for us. The callback methods, `QuerySucceded` and `QueryFailed`, will be called by the background thread once the asynchronous call to `ExecuteQueryAsync` completes. Both of these methods will then dispatch a call to `QueryComplete,` which will execute back on the UI thread; `QueryComplete` will load the result of the query into the list box.

Listing 5-16. Callbacks Once the Query for the List of Spreadsheets is Complete

```
private void QuerySucceded(object sender, ClientRequestSucceededEventArgs args)
{
    UpdateUI updateUI = QueryComplete;
    this.Dispatcher.BeginInvoke(updateUI, true);
}

private void QueryFailed(object sender, ClientRequestFailedEventArgs args)
{
    UpdateUI updateUI = QueryComplete;
    this.Dispatcher.BeginInvoke(updateUI, false);
}

private void QueryComplete(bool success)
{
    // if success is true and we have some items returned in docs
    if (success && docs.Count > 0)
    {
        List<Workbook> workbooks = new List<Workbook>();
        foreach (ListItem li in docs)
        {
            workbooks.Add(new Workbook {
                Name = li["FileLeafRef"].ToString().Replace(".xlsx", ""),
                FileName = li["FileLeafRef"].ToString() });
        }
        workbookList.ItemsSource = workbooks;
        workbookList.SelectedIndex = 0;
    }
    else
        workbookList.Items.Clear();
}
```

Once we have the list of spreadsheets loaded, we want to let users browse the available chart images for the currently selected spreadsheet. To do this, we need to write some code to implement an event handler for the **SelectionChanged** event of the list box. Again we will be making an asynchronous call so we need to repeat the pattern of making a call and supplying a callback to be executed once the call returns. Listing 5-17 provides the event handler, **WorkbookSelected**, as well as the callback, **LoadChartsComplete**.

*Listing 5-17. An Event Handler and Callback for the List Box's **SelectionChanged** Event*

```
private void WorkbookSelected(object sender, SelectionChangedEventArgs e)
{
    workbook = ((Workbook)((ListBox)sender).SelectedItem);
    chart.Source = null;
    WebClient request = new WebClient();
    request.DownloadStringCompleted +=
        new DownloadStringCompletedEventHandler(LoadChartsComplete);
    request.DownloadStringAsync(new Uri(siteRoot +
        "_vti_bin/ExcelRest.aspx/EventBudgets/" + workbook.FileName + "/model/Charts"));
}

private void LoadChartsComplete(object sender, DownloadStringCompletedEventArgs e)
{
    var reader = XmlReader.Create(new StringReader(e.Result));
    var feed = SyndicationFeed.Load(reader);
    chartList.ItemsSource = feed.Items;
}
```

The last bits of code we need to add are the event handlers to support changing the large chart image when a user clicks on a thumbnail, and to show the workbook and comment form when a user clicks the button (Listing 5-18). The first, **ChartSelected**, is very straightforward. Here we simply set the source of the large image control to match the source of the currently selected thumbnail (notice both are the same image; we are just setting different dimensions). The **ViewWorkbook** method is a bit more interesting. What we are looking to accomplish here is to open the **EventBudgetComment.aspx** page loaded with the currently selected workbook, but we want to do this without losing the context of the page the chart browser is loaded in, so we take advantage of the dialog window framework built into SharePoint. But wait, the dialog is not part of the Silverlight Client OM. It is available only via JavaScript, so we need to use the **HtmlPage.Window** object from the **System.Windows.Browser** namespace to broker calls from Silverlight to the browser's JavaScript runtime.

Listing 5-18. Handling Click Events for the Thumbnails and the Button

```
private void ChartSelected(object sender, MouseButtonEventArgs e)
{
    chart.Source = ((Image)sender).Source;
}

private void ViewWorkbook(object sender, RoutedEventArgs ev)
{
    var options = HtmlPage.Window.CreateInstance("SP.UI.DialogOptions");
    options.SetProperty("showMaximized", true);
```

```
        options.SetProperty("url", siteRoot + "SitePages/EventBudgetComment.aspx?workbook=" +
            siteRoot + "EventBudgets/" + workbook.FileName);
        options.SetProperty("autoSize", false);
        options.SetProperty("title", workbook.Name);
        HtmlPage.Window.CreateInstance("SP.UI.ModalDialog.showModalDialog", options);
}
```

With our Silverlight application complete, we need to get it deployed into our SharePoint environment. There are multiple ways we could accomplish this, such as a custom feature or sandboxed solution, but we will opt for simplicity in this case. Follow the steps below to deploy your application and create a page to host it.

■ **Note** Chapter 14 includes an example that deploys a Silverlight application using a sandboxed solution.

---

1. If you haven't done so already, build your project to compile and generate the necessary output files. If you are using a default project configuration, you'll find the output directory at `[ProjectDirectory]\Bin\Degub`.

2. Copy the `ChartBrowser.xap` file from the output directory to the EventBudgets document library.

3. Back in the SharePoint site you are using for the solution, select New Page from the Site Actions menu, name your new page `ChartBrowser` and click Create.

4. Select the Insert tab of the ribbon and click the Web Part button. Select Media and Content as the category and Silverlight Web Part for the web part, click Add.

5. In the URL field of the Silverlight Web Part dialog type `http://[siteroot]/EventBudgets/ChartBrowser.xap` and click OK.

6. When the page reloads, edit the web part properties. Change the Height to be `600`, select the option for the width to adjust to fit the zone, and select None for the chrome type. Accept the rest of the default values, click Apply and then OK.

With the above steps complete, you should see a view similar to Figure 5-18. If you haven't done so already, now would be a good time to create some new budget files using the InfoPath form we started off this chapter with so you will have some spreadsheets in the list.

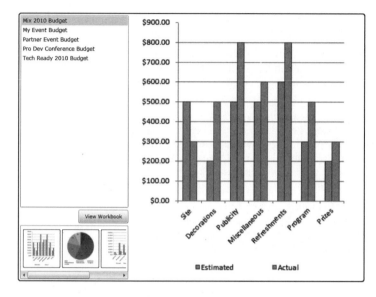

Figure 5-18. This Silverlight Chart Browser application

Important Lessons

The Event Budget process incorporated several key techniques worth highlighting as they could easily be reused in other projects.

InfoPath: The form we created for our example was very simple and focused specifically on the interfaces exposed by Excel Services. We hope you appreciate the power and simplicity of using InfoPath to create rich business forms tied into the enterprise without a lot of code.

Excel Services APIs: Excel is a big part of most organizations and the new ways we have to easily interact with our spreadsheets creates endless possibilities. Taking advantage of REST and Web Services is not limited to applications running within the context of SharePoint; these services can be utilized from any application.

SharePoint Client APIs: Learn them, use them, love them. SharePoint 2010 has greatly expanded our options for developing applications and we are no longer constrained to using server-side code running within SharePoint or available web services as our only options. It is now much easier to take advantage of the services offered by SharePoint and to more easily extend the capabilities of your custom applications.

Extension Points

While coding this example, we thought of several variations to the solution we didn't incorporate. Mostly, these were not included because they distracted from the overall objective of the solution. We call them out now as extension points since they may be applicable to a specific project you are working on.

> **Add workflow and integration:** Again, the form we created is very simple but could easily be extended. Looking specifically at the event process, creating a budget spreadsheet is only one piece of it. There would likely need to be approvals, integration with vendor systems to support logistics, and much more. The form is an excellent place to begin all the various steps in the process, and InfoPath makes this easy.

> **Generalize Chart Browser:** The Silverlight application could be refactored to support connecting to any document library to show charts from any spreadsheet. Nothing in the code is specific to event budget spreadsheets except for the location where we look for the files; the location could be set using the web part parameters.

Further Reading

- The following links are to resources that we think a reader interested in the material presented in this chapter would find useful: Excel Services 2010 Overview `http://blogs.msdn.com/excel/archive/2009/11/03/excel-services-2010-overview.aspx`

- Excel Services in SharePoint 2010 REST API Examples `http://blogs.msdn.com/excel/archive/2009/11/09/excel-services-in-sharepoint-2010-rest-api-examples.aspx`

- Excel REST API on Cum Grano Salis' blog `http://blogs.msdn.com/cumgranosalis/archive/tags/REST/default.aspx`

- Creating Silverlight User Interfaces for SharePoint 2010 Solutions `http://msdn.microsoft.com/en-us/sharepoint/ee513155.aspx`

■ ■ ■

CHAPTER 6

Merging SharePoint List Data into Word Documents

Organizations often have sets of document templates that are used throughout the enterprise. It can be a challenge to make sure that information workers are uniformly using the latest template and capturing the appropriate metadata everywhere the document templates are used. It is not unusual for some templates to share common data elements such as customer information or product details. Often authors, who are responsible for working with these templates, are retyping, cutting and pasting, or otherwise repetitively importing data elements into the appropriate places in the document. Furthermore, they may use a completely separate application to locate and maintain the data set. In this chapter, we will describe how, as a developer, you can construct a solution that uses a SharePoint site to enable users to merge list data into Microsoft Word documents.

Real-World Examples

Users have been looking for ways to automate data merge functionality since the beginning of word processing. It is, in essence, a different take on a mail merge. In this case, the data source is a SharePoint list. In more and more companies these days, workers are relying on SharePoint lists in place of local spreadsheets or Access databases. Users can create a custom list with custom fields using just a browser, making it easier than ever to build these repositories without relying on a developer. Add to this the fact that the list is Web-based and allows other users' to edit individual items, and the lure is undeniable. The scenario is so generic that it could apply to almost any organization in any industry. If the list involves customer contact information, the documents templates could be contracts, statements of work, and letters. If the list comprises task assignments, the document templates could be work orders, summary sheets, and status updates. If the list holds product information, the document templates could include order forms.

Solution Overview

For this solution, we will develop a feature that, when enabled in a site, provides the functionality to merge list-item data into specific organizational document templates. SharePoint already provides functionality similar to this, with quick parts that can bind areas of the document to its properties. However, this is limited to a document's properties, which means you can't pull in data from a separate SharePoint list, only from properties of the document in its library. In this solution, we will utilize a completely different list in the site. To provide some context for our work, we focused our efforts on building a solution that deals with an organization's customers. Once the feature has been enabled in a site, the solution will create a Customer Contacts list along with a Customer Documents document library. The document library will reference the organization's document templates, which will be configured as SharePoint content types. The Customer Contacts list will be enhanced with an additional action integrated into that list's ribbon interface, so that for a specific contact, a user may select to build a customer document. After the selection, the user will be directed to a custom application page that enables him to select which specific type of customer document he would like to be constructed with the contact's data. In this example, we will build a business fax template, a customer follow-up template, and a template to thank new customers. Once the user has selected a document type, the application page will merge the contact's data with the document using the Open XML file format, and store the resulting file in a site library.

This solution should be flexible enough to allow any site administrator to simply turn on this functionality for the site. For this reason, we have developed the solution as a SharePoint feature. Features are a way of packaging a set of customizations as a single unit that can be activated or deactivated. With Visual Studio 2010, features take just a little effort to set up, and they increase the reusability of the solution and ease deployment complexities. (See the section "Building the Customer Documents Feature Project" later in this chapter for more detail.)

Solution Walkthrough

This section details the major elements of the solution and the decisions that were made in coding it. The walkthrough will show you how to create content types for the organization's document templates. We will describe how to package your solution as a feature that can be enabled by any site administrator who desires the functionality. This includes how to set up a feature project in Visual Studio, the XML files used to define the feature's customizations, and how to deploy it. The walkthrough also includes the construction of a custom SharePoint application page. Finally, the contact data and the document come together through the use of custom XML parts and Microsoft Word 2010 content controls.

Creating Content Types

In the scenario for this solution, an organization has a set of document templates that are often used to communicate with customers. These document templates and their required metadata should be used uniformly throughout the enterprise. We want to define the settings for each document type once and have any site or even any library in the site collection be able to reference them. For this reason, we will explain how to define each as a SharePoint content type.

Content types allow organizations to reuse settings that apply to a particular category of content. These settings include metadata requirements, a template file, workflows, and policies. Once the content type is defined for the site collection, any library can be configured to support the content type. In SharePoint 2010, you can also set up publish-subscribe relationships for the content type definitions to be replicated across site collections. This technique is actually used in Chapter 11's solution, in case you are interested. Enabling a content type for a library results in an additional selection being added to the library's New menu, as shown in Figure 6-1.

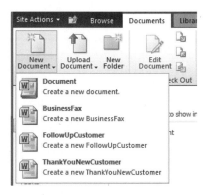

Figure 6-1. Content types in a library's New menu

Interestingly, the metadata columns associated with the library and the content type do not have to match. This allows users to upload different files of different content types with different metadata to the same document library. This flexibility breaks down the barriers that required administrators to create multiple libraries in older versions of SharePoint. It allows you to store different types of documents that should be grouped based on their user or security requirements. It also provides a single point of administration, as changes to the content type need to be made in only one place. Content types also support inheritance, where a derived type can reuse and extend its parent's settings.

To view the content types of a site collection, navigate to the Site Settings administration area from the top site in the collection. There you'll find the Site Content Types gallery. Figure 6-2 displays the gallery, including the Customer Metadata Model group and its content types, which you will create using the steps in the remainder of this section.

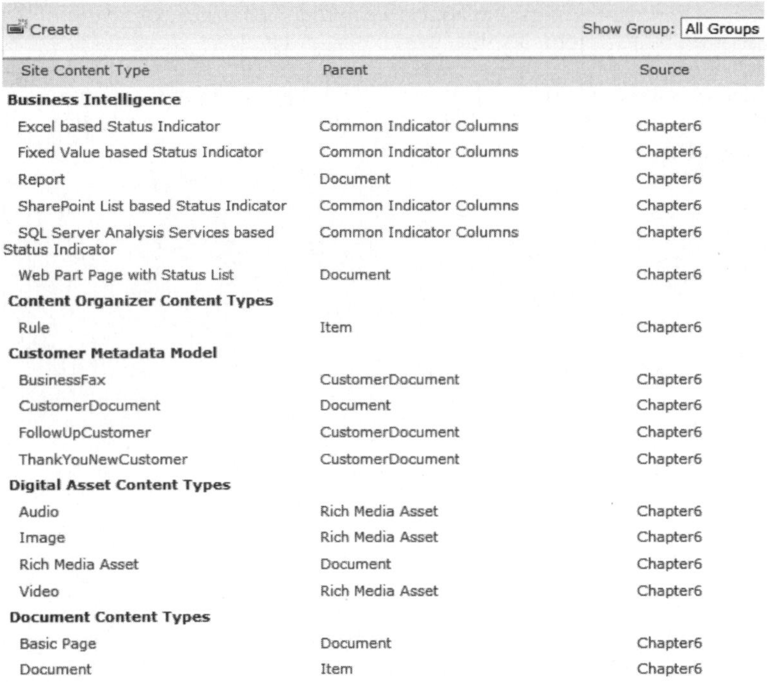

Site Content Type	Parent	Source
Business Intelligence		
Excel based Status Indicator	Common Indicator Columns	Chapter6
Fixed Value based Status Indicator	Common Indicator Columns	Chapter6
Report	Document	Chapter6
SharePoint List based Status Indicator	Common Indicator Columns	Chapter6
SQL Server Analysis Services based Status Indicator	Common Indicator Columns	Chapter6
Web Part Page with Status List	Document	Chapter6
Content Organizer Content Types		
Rule	Item	Chapter6
Customer Metadata Model		
BusinessFax	CustomerDocument	Chapter6
CustomerDocument	Document	Chapter6
FollowUpCustomer	CustomerDocument	Chapter6
ThankYouNewCustomer	CustomerDocument	Chapter6
Digital Asset Content Types		
Audio	Rich Media Asset	Chapter6
Image	Rich Media Asset	Chapter6
Rich Media Asset	Document	Chapter6
Video	Rich Media Asset	Chapter6
Document Content Types		
Basic Page	Document	Chapter6
Document	Item	Chapter6

Show Group: All Groups
📧 Create

Figure 6-2. *Site Content Type gallery page*

By browsing through some of the default content types, you can see that they include settings for columns, workflow, information panels, and information management policies. Each content type also has an associated template that can be set from its Advanced Settings page. The documents used in our example will be a business fax, a customer follow-up, and a thank-you letter for new customers. Though these document templates are different, they are all related by a common, overlapping core of metadata requirements for the organization. So in defining them, we will first create a content type called CustomerDocument that will contain all of the common settings and serve as a parent for the others. Follow these steps to create the CustomerDocument content type:

1. Click the **Create** toolbar button on the Site Content Type Gallery page.

2. Enter **CustomerDocument** as the content type name.

3. Since all of our types are documents, select **Document Content Types** and then **Document** to identify the parent content type.

4. Use the radio button to create a new group named **Customer Metadata Model** and click **OK**.

Notice that this content type automatically inherits the Name and Title columns due to its child relationship with the Document content type. All of these columns are SharePoint site columns. Like content types, site columns provide an element of reuse as they uniformly define a column for a site collection. For this reason, content types must use site columns. Follow these steps to extend the CustomerDocument content type to include a Company metadata column:

1. Since Company is a site column that already exists, select **Add from Existing Site Columns**.

2. Locate the Company site column in Core Contact and Calendar Columns.

3. Click the Add button.

4. Click OK.

5. Click on the Company column in the list and make it a required field.

6. Click OK.

Now repeat the content-type creation steps (the first numbered list) for the BusinessFax, FollowUpCustomer, and ThankYouNewCustomer types, except select the CustomerDocument content type as the parent. Notice that each gains the Company site column in its settings. Add a few different columns for each so you can explore how the library changes to accommodate the various schemas. Also, upload a Word 2010 document to serve as a template from the content type's Advanced Settings page. We will modify the templates later, but for now use the Business Fax Cover Sheet, Follow Up to Prospective Customer, and Thank You to New Customer templates from Microsoft Office Online. The Business Fax Cover Sheet template can be found in the Faxes group of Microsoft Office Online's templates and the other two are in the Letters group in the Business category. Make sure that when you save them, you choose to use the Office 2010 file format, resulting in a .docx file extension. You can also get these files in the code download for this chapter. The Word documents are stored in a folder named Extras.

To test your content types, you will want to associate them with a document library. This library must be in the same site collection, but not necessarily the same site. Pick any test document library and follow these steps to enable the content types:

1. Navigate to the library's Settings page using the Library Settings button in the Library tab of the ribbon.

2. Select Advanced Settings from the General Settings group.

3. Use the radio buttons to enable the management of content types.

4. Click OK.

5. The library's Settings page should have a new section called Content Types. Use the Add from Existing Content Types link to associate our content types: BusinessFax, FollowUpCustomer, and ThankYouNewCustomer. The result should look like Figure 6-3.

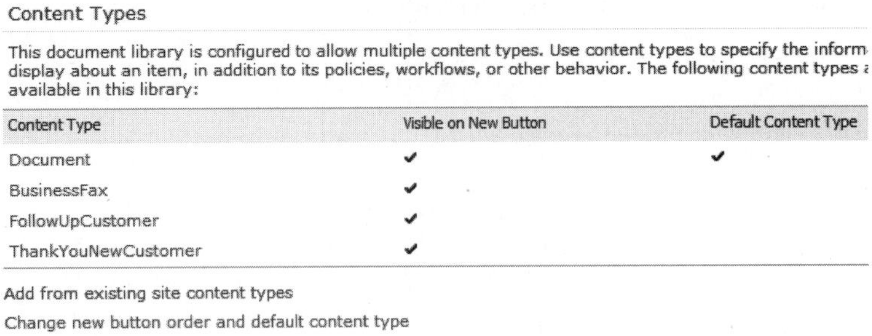

Content Types

This document library is configured to allow multiple content types. Use content types to specify the inform display about an item, in addition to its policies, workflows, or other behavior. The following content types a available in this library:

Content Type	Visible on New Button	Default Content Type
Document	✔	✔
BusinessFax	✔	
FollowUpCustomer	✔	
ThankYouNewCustomer	✔	

Add from existing site content types
Change new button order and default content type

Figure 6-3. A document library with content types listed

Now create at least one instance of each document type and save them to the document library. Do not enter any new content into the files, but complete the metadata entry form. Later we will use these documents to explore their XML structures, modify them to hold custom data, and upload them as new templates for the content types.

Building the CustomerDocuments Feature Project

Our solution will provide the organization with a set of elements that together enable any site in the site collection to maintain a list of customer contacts, a customer document library, and the ability to merge contact data into specific document templates. The important point here is that we want to provide multiple instances of this capability throughout the site collection. Some sites may want to leverage it while others may not. For this reason, we will package our solution as a SharePoint feature.

A *SharePoint feature* is a deployable unit that packages site customizations and custom code into a single component that an administrator can activate or deactivate. Features have a defined scope that dictates the breadth of their influence. A feature can be scoped to the entire server farm, a single web application, a site collection, or just a site (web). This scope determines the level of administrator needed to turn it on or off and the level at which its customizations are applied. Features can include customizations such as list templates, list instances, or custom menu items, and can be used to provision new files such as master-page templates, web part definitions, and web-content-management page layouts. Features can even run custom code in response to their activation or deactivation. Figure 6-4 displays the Manage Site Features administration page from the Site Settings of a team site we will use in this chapter.

Name		Status
Content Organizer		Activate
Create metadata based rules that move content submitted to this site to the correct library or folder.		
CustomerDocumentsFeature		Deactivate Active
Adds a custom action to contact list items to merge a contact item into a Word document		
E-mail Integration with Content Organizer		Activate
Enable a site's content organizer to accept and organize email messages. This feature should be used ony in a highly managed store, like a Records Center.		
Group Work Lists		Activate
Provides Calendars with added functionality for team and resource scheduling.		
Hold and eDiscovery		Activate
This feature is used to track external actions like litigations, investigations, or audits that require you to suspend the disposition of documents.		
Metadata Navigation and Filtering		Deactivate Active
Provides each list in the site with a settings pages for configuring that list to use metadata tree view hierarchies and filter controls to improve navigation and filtering of the contained items.		
Offline Synchronization for External Lists		Deactivate Active
Enables offline synchronization for external lists with Outlook and SharePoint Workspace.		

Figure 6-4. Site features of a team site

To understand the impact of a feature, explore what happens when you deactivate the Team Collaboration Lists feature. You will receive a warning; deactivate it. Turning off this feature removes your ability to create instances of most of the list types in your site. In fact, this option will not even show up in any creation dialog. If you reactivate the feature, the options return. In case you are wondering, deactivating this feature does not delete any existing lists that have already been created. But that was a choice by the developers who created this feature. You will have to decide what you want to happen when your feature is activated and deactivated on a site.

To create the feature, we will use a new SharePoint Empty Project in Visual Studio 2010. Name the project and solution **CustomerDocumentsFeature**. Use the following steps to create the project:

1. Open Visual Studio 2010 and start a new project.

2. In the Installed Templates tree, expand Visual C#. Expand SharePoint. Select the **2010** node for the SharePoint 2010 project types.

3. Using the drop-downs above the project types, make sure you are targeting the **.NET Framework 3.5**.

4. Select **Empty SharePoint Project** from the list of project types.

5. Name the project **CustomerDocumentsFeature** and leave the default choices of creating a new solution with the same name. Your completed dialog should look like Figure 6-5.

Figure 6-5. *Creating the CustomerDocumentsFeature project*

6. Click **OK**.

7. In the next SharePoint Customization dialog, choose the Deploy as a farm solution option, since our solution is really an enterprise one that would be built by developers, deployed into production by system administrators, and used across multiple site collections. Specify the URL of the site where you created the content types. For our environment it was `http://edhild3/sites/chapter6`.

Defining the Feature

Your project is currently just an empty SharePoint project and needs the definition of the feature that a site administrator will activate to add customizations to the site. Specifically, our customizations will result in the creation of a contact list called CustomerContacts and a document library named CustomerDocuments. We will make sure that the content types we just created are automatically attached to the document library. We will include a custom ribbon element for contact items that enables the user to indicate she would like to merge the selected contact with one of our document templates. Clicking this button will take the user to a custom applications page where we will perform the merge and return the resulting document. But let's not get too far ahead of ourselves. Fortunately, Visual Studio 2010 provides SharePoint developers with tools to define such a feature. Use the following steps to create the feature that will bundle all of these customizations.

1. Right-click on the Features node in Solution Explorer and choose to **Add Feature**. This will create a new SharePoint feature named Feature1 and open its Visual Studio designer.

2. Close the designer. Right-click on Feature1 and rename the feature to **CustomerDocumentsFeature**.

3. Now open the designer again. Make sure the Title of the feature is **CustomerDocumentsFeature**. Set the Description value to **Adds a custom action to contact list items to merge a contact item into a Word document**. Lastly, set the scope to **Web** as all of our customizations will be scoped to a particular SharePoint site.

The next part of this section will specify the customizations that we want to occur when our feature is activated. Each of these will be specified in an element manifest. An element manifest contains the settings of the customizations that the feature will contain. You can have any number of manifests, but the Visual Studio Project Items will add one for each type of item you add to the Visual Studio solution. Let's first focus on making our feature create the CustomerContacts list.

1. Right-click on the project and choose to Add a New Item.

2. In the Add New Item dialog, choose List Instance and name the item **CustomerContacts**.

3. The dialog will contact the site you selected when you created the Visual Studio solution, to see what list templates are available. It is important to realize that we are not creating the list in the site, but rather specifying that this feature should create such a list automatically when it is activated. Figure 6-6 shows the customization wizard with the settings for the title of the list (**CustomerContacts**), the list template type (**Contacts**), and the URL (**Lists/CustomerContacts**), as well as the option to have the list automatically placed on the quick launch navigation bar of the site.

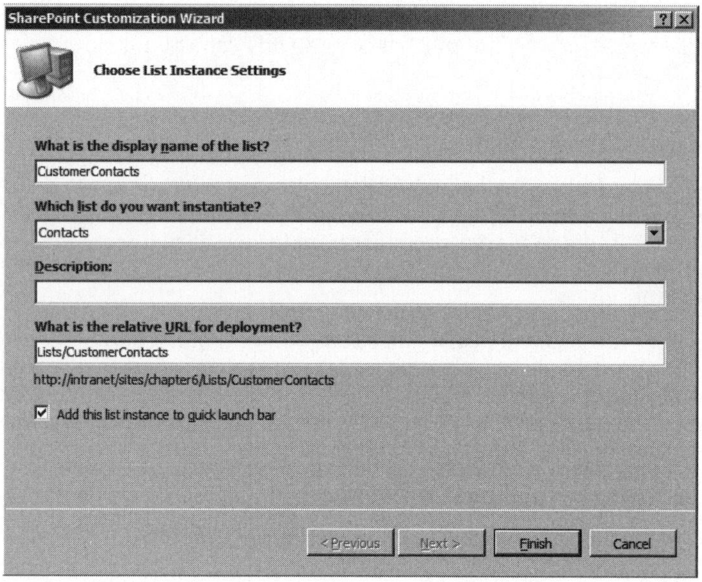

Figure 6-6. Adding the CustomerContact list instance to the feature

We will take a brief moment here to appreciate what Visual Studio is doing for us under the hood. Remember, the feature is the overarching umbrella that will reference each of our customizations. The feature is defined by an XML file feature.xml. Customizations are stored in element manifests usually named elements.xml. If you expand the CustomerContacts node, you can see this file and the XML that defines the customization shown in Listing 6-1.

Listing 6-1. Creating the Customer Contacts List

```
<Elements xmlns="http://schemas.microsoft.com/sharepoint/">
  <ListInstance Title="CustomerContacts"
                OnQuickLaunch="TRUE"
                TemplateType="105"
                FeatureId="00bfea71-7e6d-4186-9ba8-c047ac750105"
                Url="Lists/CustomerContacts"
                Description="">
  </ListInstance>
</Elements>
```

It is fairly straightforward to decode what is going on in the elements file. Listing 6-1 includes a ListInstance element that tells the feature that upon activation a new list should be added to the site. The element includes the title of the list, that the list should be on the quick launch navigation bar, and the desired URL. The TemplateType attribute equates to our choice that we wanted an instance of SharePoint's contacts list. The FeatureId GUID specifies the internal SharePoint feature where the contacts list definition is contained. It's a good thing that Visual Studio finds these GUIDs for us as part of the wizard. Otherwise, you'd have to hunt through the Features directory of the 14 hive

(C:\Program Files\Common Files\Microsoft Shared\Web Server Extensions\14\TEMPLATE\FEATURES) to find it in a `feature.xml` file.

Now repeat the same steps you used to create the CustomerContacts list instance for the CustomerDocuments document library. Be sure to name the library **CustomerDocuments**, set its URL to **Lists/CustomerDocuments**, and make sure you are creating an instance of the **Document Library** template.

Now let's turn our attention to adding a new button to the ribbon of contact items in our site. Like our other customizations, this too will be contained in its own element manifest. Unfortunately, there is no project item that will automatically write the XML necessary to get our button in the right spot. Instead, use the following steps to add an empty element manifest that we will code ourselves.

1. Right-click on the project and choose to **Add** a **New Item**.

2. In the Add New Item dialog, choose the Empty Item SharePoint project item template and name the item **CustomerDocumentsElements**.

Expand the node to find the element manifest file where we will place the XML markup to tell SharePoint to add a button for contact items in the site. The next few code listings will detail all the XML you'll need to place in the file. If you are not inclined to type all this in yourself, just grab the corresponding file from the code download. Listing 6-2 kicks off the element manifest by defining the custom action. The `Id` attribute is a string that uses a naming convention of specifying not only a name but also the location the button is to be placed. This doesn't actually determine location (we will see that later), but it's a good practice when naming your custom actions. In this case, we want the `BuildCustomerDocuments` action to make a customization to the actions group for list items. The `RegistrationType` attribute indicates an attachment type. In this case, the action is associated with a list. Other possible attachment types include `ContentType`, `FileType`, or `ProgId`. The `RegistrationId` attribute further clarifies the attachment by specifying the identifier of the list, item, or content type that the attachment is associated with. In this case, the value of 105 represents the list template ID matching this action with contact lists.

Listing 6-2. Defining the Build Customer Document custom action

```
<?xml version="1.0" encoding="utf-8"?>
<Elements xmlns="http://schemas.microsoft.com/sharepoint/">
  <CustomAction Id="Ribbon.ListItem.Actions.BuildCustomerDocuments"
                Location="CommandUI.Ribbon"
                RegistrationId="105"
                RegistrationType="List"
                Title="Build Customer Document">
```

The next section of the element manifest file defines the user interface extension and, in particular, the button we would like to place in the actions group for contact items (see Listing 6-3). Here the `Location` attribute of the `CommandUIDefinition` element is the real factor in determining where our ribbon customization will go. Notice that we are specifying that our extension should be added to the controls collection of the actions group for list items. You may wonder how we figured out the correct name. The good news here is that most of the out-of-the-box ribbon interface is stored in the `CMDUI.XML` file in the 14 hive. By default that file is located at `C:\Program Files\Common Files\Microsoft Shared\Web Server Extensions\14\TEMPLATE\GLOBAL\XML`. You can learn a lot from inspecting this file and the different type of techniques used to set up the interface. The rest of the user interface definition specifies our button, the images to use depending on the button's size, and a label. The sequence number determines the order the button will be placed within the group. `TemplateAlias` is a value that controls the layout of the graphic and label on the ribbon. We found this value by looking at the CMDUI.XML file for a similar layout where the label is directly below the image. Lastly, a command attribute specifies a specific handler that should be called when the user clicks the button. We will cover that in the next listing. Figure 6-7 shows what the end result will look like.

Listing 6-3. Defining the Build Customer Doc Button

```
<CommandUIExtension>
  <CommandUIDefinitions>
    <CommandUIDefinition
        Location="Ribbon.ListItem.Actions.Controls._children">
      <Button Id="Ribbon.ListItem.Actions.BuildCustomerDocumentsButton"
              Image16by16="/_layouts/images/DOC16.gif"
              Image32by32="/_layouts/images/DOC32.gif"
              LabelText="Build Customer Doc"
              Sequence="100"
              TemplateAlias="o1"
              Command="HelloCommand" />
    </CommandUIDefinition>
  </CommandUIDefinitions>
```

Figure 6-7. The deployed Build Customer Doc button

The last section of the element manifest file, shown in Listing 6-4, specifies the command handler that dictates what should happen when the user clicks the button. In this case, we want the user to be redirected to a custom application page named BuildCustomerDoc.aspx that we will add to the feature later. Fortunately, SharePoint's JavaScript libraries already have a GoToPage method defined for such a task. In addition to redirecting, we want to make sure we pass some key information to that custom application page. Mainly we want to pass the specific contact's identifier along with its list identifier as querystring parameters. Notice that the URL used in the XML has placeholder tokens that SharePoint will automatically fill in. There is a bit of Javscript work being done here to retrieve the identifier of the selected contact. In this solution, we only expect the user to select a single contact since that is all our documents are set up to support. We are also using the SiteUrl placeholder so that our custom application page can be surfaced regardless of what site the user happens to be on. The SelectedItemId placeholder tells our application page which contact item the user had selected before clicking the button. The ListId placeholder passes the identifier of the list containing the selected item. You can read up on more URL tokens and custom actions at http://msdn.microsoft.com/en-us/library/ms473643(office.14).aspx.

Listing 6-4. The Command Handler for the Build Customer Doc Button

```
    <CommandUIHandlers>
      <CommandUIHandler
        Command="HelloCommand"
        CommandAction="javascript:GoToPage('{SiteUrl}/_layouts/↵
            CustomerDocumentsFeature/BuildCustomerDoc.aspx?↵
            List={ListId}&amp;ID={SelectedItemId}');"/>
    </CommandUIHandlers>
  </CommandUIExtension>
 </CustomAction>
</Elements>
```

The last customization we want to include in this section is binding the content types we created earlier to the CustomerDocuments library. In this case, these content types are already defined in the site collection, so we are simply binding them to our library. If you wanted to see how you could include the content types in the feature itself, check out the solution in Chapter 14. Defining a binding can be done by adding the XML in Listing 6-5 to the CustomerDocuments elements file just after the definition of the `ListInstance` element.

Listing 6-5. Binding Content Types to the Document Library

```
<ContentTypeBinding
    ContentTypeId="0x010100AA8705BBBC554342BC1396AB7FB723B401"
    ListUrl="Lists/CustomerDocuments"
/>
<ContentTypeBinding
    ContentTypeId="0x010100AA8705BBBC554342BC1396AB7FB723B402"
    ListUrl="Lists/CustomerDocuments"
/>
<ContentTypeBinding
    ContentTypeId="0x010100AA8705BBBC554342BC1396AB7FB723B403"
    ListUrl="Lists/CustomerDocuments"
 />
```

This addition contains three `ContentTypeBinding` elements that are responsible for linking the content types we created earlier with the Customer Documents document library. Now the `ContentTypeIds` in Listing 6-5 will be specific to your environment since you created them in the earlier step. Each of these bindings maps to one of the CustomerDocument content types we created earlier: BusinessFax, FollowUpCustomer, and ThankYouNewCustomer. Looking at the `ContentTypeIds` in Listing 6-5, it is easy to tell that they all share a common parent. The telling sign is that the ID is exactly the same up to the last digit. In SharePoint, when a content type is derived from another type, it simply extends the ID by a few characters. In addition, the fact that each of these types begins with 0x0101 tells us that an ancestor of this type is the base Document content type. As Figure 6-8 shows, you can obtain the content type IDs in your environment by copying the ctype querystring parameter on the Site Content Type administration page. Use this technique to retrieve each of your `ContentTypeIds` and update the code in Listing 6-5 to match your environment.

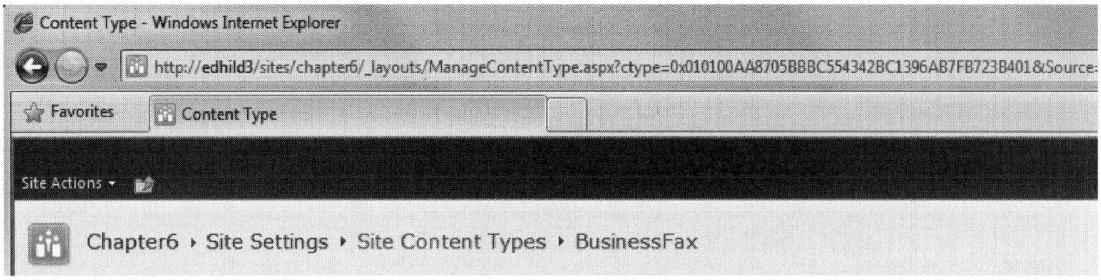

Figure 6-8. Obtaining the Content Type ID

Just to wrap up our behind-the-scenes thread, go back and pull up the designer for the CustomerDocumentsFeature feature. You'll notice that each of our element files are referenced as items in the feature. This designer interface is shown in Figure 6-9. If you click the Manifest button at the bottom of the designer, you'll see the `feature.xml` file that Visual Studio built for us.

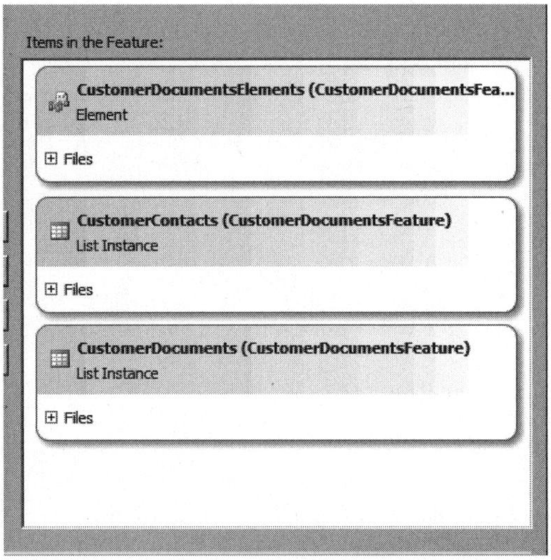

Figure 6-9. The feature in Visual Studio's Feature Designer

Deploying the Feature

Even though we are not completely done with the feature (it's missing the custom application page), you have enough that is worth deploying and testing on your team site. To deploy the feature, just right-click on the project and choose Deploy. This will package the solution up and place your files in the correct locations on the SharePoint server. It will also activate your feature, which should create the contacts list and document library, along with binding the content types and incorporating the new ribbon button. Take some time to click through and verify that all of these customizations are working. Of course, if you click the new button in the ribbon, you'll get an error. We will resolve that in just a bit. As a note, if you redeploy this project to the team site, you may see the dialog that is shown in Figure 6-10. Even though Visual Studio is deactivating the existing feature as part of the deployment, we have not written any code to actually delete the list and library instances. Clicking the Resolve Automatically button will perform those deletions for you as part of your debugging process, and you can have Visual Studio remember this choice by using the Do not prompt me again check box.

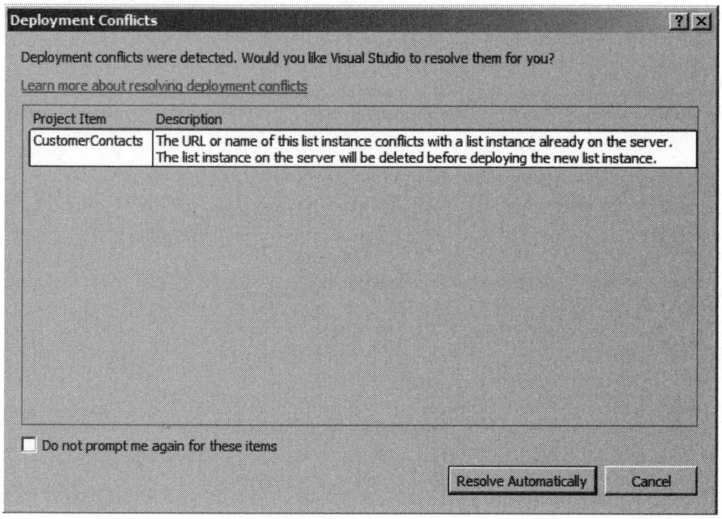

Figure 6-10. *Resolving deployment conflicts*

Building a Custom Application Page

When a user selects the Build Customer Document action from a contact item in the site, the solution will redirect the user to an application page that will show the document templates that are available from the Customer Documents document library. After the user makes a selection, the page will serialize the contact list item and place it in the Word document template as a custom XML part. The next section of this chapter goes into further detail about Microsoft Word's support for custom XML parts. We will focus on creating the page, laying out its controls, and the initial processing. Figure 6-11 depicts the end goal for `BuildCustomerDoc.aspx` (the Build Customer Documents page).

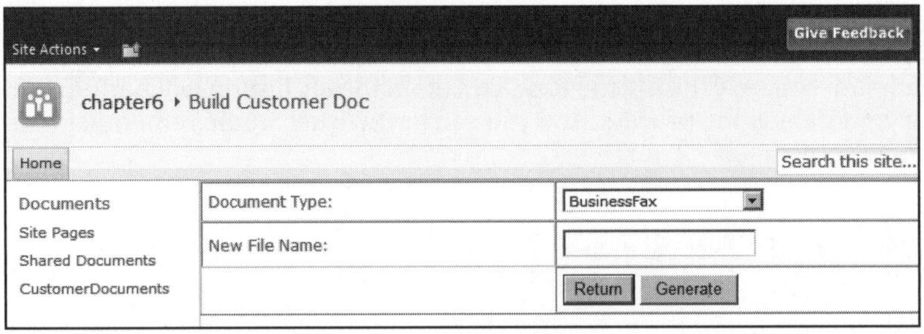

Figure 6-11. *The Build Customer Documents custom application page*

The Build Customer Documents page is termed an application page because it is not part of a site definition, but rather lives in SharePoint's Layouts directory. This means that the ASPX page can be accessed from the path of any site through the _layouts virtual folder. Application pages are ASP.NET pages that derive from a SharePoint class `LayoutsPageBase`. Fortunately, Visual Studio supports adding a custom application page as a project item. Use the following steps to get an empty application page into the CustomerDocumentsFeature project.

1. Right-click on the project and choose to **Add** a **New Item**.

2. In the Add New Item dialog, choose the Application Page project item template and name the item **BuildCustomerDoc.aspx**.

After the addition of the application page completes, you'll notice that a few things have changed in your project. First, a Layouts folder has been added. This is a SharePoint mapped folder, meaning that it has a corresponding location in the 14 hive. This is Visual Studio's way of organizing where things need to be deployed when it creates the deployment package. Within the Layouts folder, there is a folder that is the name of your project. This folder is created in the server's Layouts folder directly in an effort to avoid name collisions with other application pages that may have been created for different solutions. Lastly, the requested `BuildCustomerDoc.aspx` is in that folder. If you view the markup of the application page, you will see several content placeholders. The last two are just for the title, so place the text **Build Customer Doc** there. The focus of this section will be on the Main content placeholder, as that's where our user interface needs to be defined for the page. Instead of dragging all the controls yourself or retyping the markup of the server controls, copy and paste what you need from the code download—it's just a table with a drop-down a list control, a textbox, a label, and two buttons. The ASPX markup of the Main placeholder is shown in Listing 6-6.

Listing 6-6. *Content of the Build Customer Documents Application Page*

```
<table border="1" cellpadding="5" cellspacing="0"
       style="width:100%; font-size: 9pt" >
<tr>
    <td>Document Type:</td>
    <td><asp:DropDownList ID="lstContentTypes"  runat="server"
                          EnableViewState="true"/></td>
</tr>
```

```
<tr>
    <td>New File Name:</td>
    <td><asp:TextBox ID="txtFileName"  runat="server"
                     EnableViewState="true"/></td>
</tr>
<tr>
    <td></td>
    <td><asp:Button ID="btnCancel"  Text="Return" runat="server" /> 
        <asp:Button ID="btnOK" Text="Generate" runat="server" /></td>
</tr>
</table>
<asp:Label ID="lblMessage" runat="server" EnableViewState="true"
  Text="Your new Document has been saved to the CustomerDocuments library" />
```

This application page would be shown in response to a user clicking on the Build Customer Document action from any site that has the feature activated. For this reason, the page must first establish its context and get references to the site collection and the site from which it is being invoked. With these pieces of information, the application page can use the querystring parameters that were passed by the custom action to identify the contacts list the user was in when he selected the action, as well as the individual item he selected. Listing 6-7 includes the code for these initial operations, which you can find in the code-behind file `BuildCustomerDoc.aspx.cs`. We are not including every line of code in the text (like using statements), so please use the code download.

Listing 6-7. Initializations of the Application Page

```
SPSite siteCollection = null;
SPWeb webObj = null;
Guid listId = Guid.Empty;
int itemId = 0;
SPFolder customerDocLib = null;

protected void Page_Load(object sender, EventArgs e)
{
 try
 {
    siteCollection = SPContext.Current.Site;
    webObj = SPContext.Current.Web;
    listId = new Guid(Server.UrlDecode(Request.QueryString["List"]));
    itemId = int.Parse(Request.QueryString["ID"]);
    customerDocLib = webObj.GetFolder("Lists/CustomerDocuments");
```

During the page-load event, several of the server controls on the page are initialized. The label is hidden, the event handler for the Generate button is configured, and the Cancel button is set up to return the user to the previous page where the custom action was selected. The drop-down list is populated with the content types that are bound to the site's Customer Documents document library. We exclude the default Document content type since it is not a custom one that will support the contact's data as a custom XML part. Listing 6-8 includes the code necessary to set up the server controls.

Listing 6-8. Setting Up the Server Controls

```
lblMessage.Visible = false;
//build button event handler
btnOK.Click += new EventHandler(btnOK_Click);
if (! this.IsPostBack)
{
  string returnUrl = "javascript:GoToPage('{0}');return false;";
  this.btnCancel.OnClientClick = string.Format(returnUrl,
                                  Request.QueryString["Source"]);
  IList<SPContentType> contentTypes = customerDocLib.ContentTypeOrder;
  //populate the drop down
  int i = 0;
  foreach (SPContentType contType in contentTypes)
  {
    if (contType.Name != "Document")
    {
      ListItem item = new ListItem(contType.Name, i.ToString());
      lstContentTypes.Items.Add(item);
    }
    i++;
  }
}
```

Using a Custom XML Part in a Document Template

The custom application page will merge the selected contact item with the chosen document template. To facilitate this operation, we will leverage the fact that the document templates are Microsoft Word files saved using the new Open XML file format. As explained in Chapter 4, the Microsoft Office desktop tools have switched from their proprietary binary-formatted files to formats based on Open XML specifications. Now each file—whether spreadsheet, presentation, or document—is really a package of parts and items. Parts are pieces of content for the file, whereas items are metadata describing how the parts should be assembled and rendered. Most of these pieces are XML files, making it possible for them to be manipulated through code. You can gain insight into the structure of an Open XML–based file by replacing its file extension with .zip, since the file is really an ordinary Zip archive. We will use an instance of the business-fax template we created earlier. Make sure you are modifying a BusinessFax document that has been saved to the site's Customer Documents document library once before. This will help you understand how SharePoint uses the Open XML file formats, as well. Figure 6-12 shows the root of the archive for the Business Fax document.

Name ▲	Type
_rels	File Folder
customXml	File Folder
docProps	File Folder
word	File Folder
[Content_Types].xml	XML Document

Figure 6-12. Examining the archive of a Word document

The XML file in the root is named [Content_Types].xml and it stores content-type directives for all the parts that appear in the archive. A content type contains metadata about a particular part or groups of parts and, more importantly, contains a directive as to how the application should render that part. For example, Listing 6-9 shows just a few lines from the XML file, but clearly delineates how this file tells the rendering application which parts are images, styles, relationships, custom properties, and even the main document.

Listing 6-9. The Document's Content Types

```
<Override PartName="/customXml/itemProps1.xml"
    ContentType="application/vnd.openxmlformats-officedocument.↵
                customXmlProperties+xml" />
<Default Extension="wmf" ContentType="image/x-wmf" />
<Default Extension="rels" ContentType="application/vnd.openxmlformats-↵
                                package.relationships+xml" />
<Default Extension="xml" ContentType="application/xml" />
<Override PartName="/word/document.xml"
    ContentType="application/vnd.openxmlformats-officedocument.wordprocessingml.↵
                document.main+xml" />
<Override PartName="/word/styles.xml"
    ContentType="application/vnd.openxmlformats-officedocument.wordprocessingml.↵
                styles+xml" />
```

Pay particular attention to the first line of Listing 6-9. The Override element is describing the itemProps1.xml file as being something more than just any XML file inside the document package. In fact, itemProps1.xml is a file that contains the properties of a custom XML part. It describes item1.xml, which stores the actual custom XML data. All of the Office document types support having a custom XML folder that is capable of storing information. In fact, SharePoint itself creates three custom XML parts in Office files when they are uploaded into site libraries. These XML parts are for storing metadata values, the schema of the document information panel, and workflow information. Though all of the Office files can store custom XML, Microsoft Word offers the unique added benefit of having a set of content controls that can bind to the custom XML parts, displaying the data inline with the document. So open the BusinessFax document you created earlier and follow these steps to add content controls that we will bind to contact data:

1. Delete the text following the Fax Number: prompt.

2. Click on the Developer tab in the Microsoft Word ribbon. This tab may be hidden on your machine, but it can be enabled through the backstage. Click the **File** menu and then choose **Options**. In the left-hand navigation choose **Customize Ribbon**. Check the **Developer** group in the right-hand list and click **OK**.

3. Place your cursor after the colon (:) and click the plain-text content control button **Aa** in the Controls group.

4. Click the Properties button in the ribbon on the right-hand side of the Controls group.

5. Set the Title and Tag values to **FaxNumber**.

6. Click the check box to keep the content control from being deleted accidentally.

7. Click the check box to disable editing of the control's content. The end result should look like Figure 6-13.

Figure 6-13. Adding content controls to a document

Repeat the same steps to add a plain-text content control for the To field. Name the content control FullName. The document could have many more content controls, but these two are enough to illustrate the solution. In this example, we are relying on just the plain-text content control, but Microsoft Word does support others, such as picture, rich text, drop-down list, and a calendar control for dates. Next we will add an additional custom XML part with contact data, and bind these controls to specific parts of the XML data. It used to be that you had to do all this manually in the XML parts, which included creating several property files, specifying XPath queries for the controls, and repackaging everything back up. Fortunately, there is now a toolkit that does most of the heavy lifting for you: The Word Content Control Toolkit. Download this utility from `http://www.codeplex.com/dbe` and install it into your environment. Use the following steps to get the new custom XML part with contact data into the document and bindings to the content controls setup.

1. Launch the Word Content Control Toolkit.

2. Open the BusinessFax document you placed the content controls on.

3. In the bottom right-hand corner, click the **Create a new XML Part** link.

4. Click the **Edit View** tab in the right-hand pane and place the contents of Listing 6-10 in the text area. This is just a portion of the fields that SharePoint can give us about a contact, but it's enough to bind the controls we added to the BusinessFax template. Notice that we took the time to declare our own namespace: `http://www.sample.com/2006/schemas/contact/`. This will be useful in determining which custom XML part is ours when we perform the merge in the next section.

Listing 6-10. The Contact Custom XML Part

```xml
<?xml version="1.0"?>
<sc:Contact xmlns:sc="http://www.sample.com/2006/schemas/contact/">
  <sc:ID>1</sc:ID>
  <sc:Last_x0020_Name>hild</sc:Last_x0020_Name>
  <sc:First_x0020_Name>ed</sc:First_x0020_Name>
  <sc:Full_x0020_Name>ed hild</sc:Full_x0020_Name>
  <sc:E-mail_x0020_Address/>
  <sc:Company>sample inc</sc:Company>
  <sc:Fax_x0020_Number>333-333-333</sc:Fax_x0020_Number>
  <sc:Address/>
  <sc:City/>
  <sc:State_x002F_Province/>
  <sc:ZIP_x002F_Postal_x0020_Code/>
</sc:Contact>
```

5. Click the **Bind View** tab in the right-hand pane.

6. Click the **Full_x0020_Name** node. It will become highlighted as a result of the selection.

7. Now use the left mouse button and drag the highlighted node to the FullName content control listed in the left hand side of the tool. As you'll see, the toolkit will write the corresponding XPath expression for the control, which will bind it to this data element of our custom XML part.

8. Repeat the previous step for the FaxNumber node. The result should look like Figure 6-14.

9. Click the **Save** button to commit the new custom XML part and content control bindings to the document. If you open this file again in Microsoft Word, you should see that the data from the custom XML part is surfaced through the content controls. This modified file then needs to be re-uploaded as the document template for the BusinessFax content type.

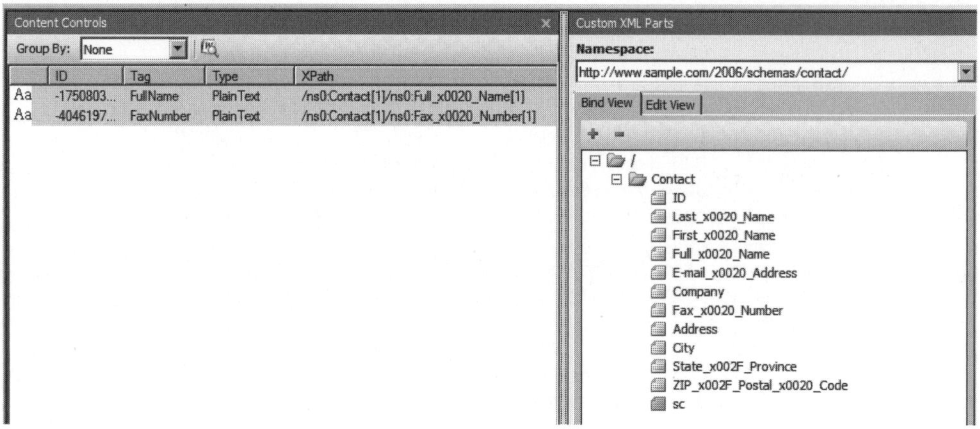

Figure 6-14. Binding content controls to the Custom XML part

Performing the Merge

The `BuildCustomerDoc.aspx` application page has the responsibility of serializing the contact list item and placing it in the custom XML part we created in the preceding section. All of this work happens when the user clicks the Generate button on the custom application page (shown in Figure 6-11) to generate the document. Before looking at the `OnClick` event handler, there are a few other assemblies we need to add references to:

- **WindowsBase**: This assembly gives us access to the `System.IO.Packaging` namespace, which is used to open up Office files that use the Open XML file format.

- **DocumentFormat.OpenXml**: This assembly is provided by the Open XML Format SDK 2.0. For this chapter we are using the March 2010 release, which you can download and install from: `http://msdn.microsoft.com/en-us/library/bb448854(office.14).aspx`. This assembly lets us manipulate the content of the presentation without having to write XML nodes directly. The SDK provides an object model that is an abstraction from the actual XML, making our code easier to read and write.

Be sure to grab the appropriate `using` statements for the code-behind from the code download. The button's `OnClick` event handler locates the document template for the selected content type and copies it to a memory stream. This way the copy can be modified without changing the content type's template. Listing 6-11 includes this code.

Listing 6-11. Copying the Content Type's Document Template

```
Stream docStream = new MemoryStream();
SPContentType contentType = customerDocLib.ContentTypeOrder[int.Parse↵
    (lstContentTypes.SelectedValue)];
SPFile templateFile = contentType.ResourceFolder.Files↵
    [contentType.DocumentTemplate];
Stream templateStream = templateFile.OpenBinaryStream();
BinaryReader reader = new BinaryReader(templateStream);
BinaryWriter writer = new BinaryWriter(docStream);
writer.Write(reader.ReadBytes((int)templateStream.Length));
writer.Flush();
reader.Close();
templateStream.Dispose();
```

The next step is to locate the custom XML part where the application page needs to place the content data. Unfortunately, this is not as easy as it may seem. We can't be guaranteed that the custom XML part we created earlier is still named `item4.xml` (which is what the Word Content Control named it). SharePoint may have reordered the parts when we uploaded the document to the system. Therefore, the code in Listing 6-12 opens the stream as a Word Document package and iterates through the custom XML parts, looking for the namespace (`http://www.sample.com/2006/schemas/contact/`) used to represent the contact data.

Listing 6-12. Finding the Contact Data Custom XML Part

```
//open .docx file in memory stream as package file
docStream.Position = 0;
WordprocessingDocument wordDoc = WordprocessingDocument.Open(docStream, true);
MainDocumentPart mainPart = wordDoc.MainDocumentPart;
//retrieve package part with XML data
XmlDocument xDoc = null;
CustomXmlPart customPart = null;
foreach(CustomXmlPart cp in mainPart.CustomXmlParts)
{
  xDoc = new XmlDocument();
  xDoc.Load(cp.GetStream());
  if (xDoc.DocumentElement.NamespaceURI ==
          "http://www.sample.com/2006/schemas/contact/")
  {
    customPart = cp;
    break;
  }
}
```

With the custom XML part located, the code continues. We first clear the custom XML part of any previous data (our sample data, for example) by calling the `RemoveAll()` method. The next step is to serialize the selected contact into an XML representation and store the result in the custom XML part. Listing 6-13 includes the code that performs this operation. Notice the use of the `XmlConvert` class to make sure that the column names are properly escaped for XML.

Listing 6-13. Serializing the Contact to the Custom XML Part

```
SPListItem contactItem = null;
contactItem = webObj.Lists[this.listId].GetItemById(this.itemId);
//serialize the contact item into this customXml part
XmlNode rootNode = xDoc.DocumentElement;
rootNode.RemoveAll();
foreach (SPField field in contactItem.Fields)
{
  XmlNode fieldNode = xDoc.CreateElement("sc",
                      XmlConvert.EncodeName(field.Title),
                      "http://www.sample.com/2006/schemas/contact/");
  if (contactItem[field.Id] != null)
  {
    XmlNode fieldVal = xDoc.CreateTextNode(contactItem[field.Id].ToString());
    fieldNode.AppendChild(fieldVal);
  }
  rootNode.AppendChild(fieldNode);
}
xDoc.Save(customPart.GetStream(FileMode.Create, FileAccess.Write));
```

At this point, the memory stream contains the properly constructed document with the selected content data injected into the custom XML part. The only remaining task is to save the modified file back to the CustomerDocuments library with the file name requested by the user. Listing 6-14 contains this code. Note that we are assuming the user gives us a unique name for the file. If he chooses an existing name, we will overwrite it, which would generate a new version of the file if versioning were turned on. You'd probably want to add more safety to this save operation in a production environment.

Listing 6-14. Saving the File Back to the Document Library

```
//deliver file to library
customerDocLib.Files.Add(txtFileName.Text, docStream);
lblMessage.Visible = true;
```

With the custom application page complete and the document templates updated with their content controls and custom XML parts, redeploy the feature. Place a contact in the Customer Contacts list and run the merge by selecting the Build Customer Document action. Choose the BusinessFax content type and generate the merged document.

Important Lessons

This chapter incorporated several key techniques that are worth highlighting as they can easily be reused in other projects.

> **Defining content types:** The solution detailed how to define the settings associated with a type of content for an organization. By creating a SharePoint content type, administrators have a single definition that can be reused uniformly throughout the site collection.

Developing a feature: The solution was packaged as a SharePoint feature. This enables any administrator in the site collection to activate or deactivate the functionality included in it. This technique increases the flexibility of the solution and centralizes the steps needed to deploy it.

Custom application page: The feature included a custom application page that was deployed to the server's Layouts directory. The page was created using the Visual Studio project item template and was integrated seamlessly to extend the site's functionality.

Open XML file format: The manipulation of the Microsoft Word documents on the server was made possible by the fact that the templates were stored using the Open XML file format. The format's support for custom XML parts enabled us to insert data into the file without requiring Word to be installed on the server. The Open XML Format SDK streamlined the code we needed to write in order to navigate and manipulate the file.

Microsoft Word content controls: Inserting the data into a custom XML part would have done little if it were not for Microsoft Word's content controls. These controls can be placed into a document and bound to the custom XML part through an XPath query. We automated this step using the Word Content Control Toolkit. Though we used them in a read-only manner in this chapter, if a user were able to change the value in the control, the control would update the custom XML part.

Extending SharePoint 2010's Ribbon: SharePoint 2010 enables you to declaratively extend its ribbon interface. In this solution, we added a new button for when the user is focused on a contact item in the site.

Extension Points

While coding this example, we thought of several variations to the solution that we didn't incorporate. Mostly, these were not included because they distracted from the overall objective of the solution. We call them out now as extension points since they may be applicable to a specific project you are working on.

Delete a list and a library on feature deactivation: The solution created the CustomerContacts list and CustomerDocuments library in the feature. You could use the FeatureDeactivating event of a feature receiver to find the CustomerDocuments library and CustomerContacts list and delete them. We don't see this as an automatic action every feature should take, since the user could very well lose some important data. Every feature is unique and you'll want to consider the cleanup activities carefully.

Set company property in the custom XML part: In our example, the contact data was serialized into the custom XML part. However, all of the content types used in the example expected a Company value to be specified as a metadata property since the Company site column was added to the parent content type. We also mentioned that SharePoint uses the custom XML parts for data, including the file's metadata. Use the same technique to set the Company property before it is saved to the library.

Add context sensitivity to the ribbon extension: In our example the ribbon button is enabled even if the user has yet to select a contact item. We included a link in the Further Reading section of this chapter that details how you can wire up some JavaScript events to enable and disable the button accordingly.

Configure the content types as a feature: In the solution, the content types are created by interacting with the site, but they could have been made a feature. They could not, however, be in the same feature as the rest of the solution since content types can't be declared inside a feature of web-level scope (usually site collection). You would need a completely separate feature. Of course, you would then want to set an activation dependency between them.

Further Reading

The following links are to resources we think a reader interested in the material presented in this chapter would find useful:

- Adding Custom Button to the SharePoint 2010 Ribbon `http://blogs.msdn.com/jfrost/archive/2009/11/06/adding-custom-button-to-the-sharepoint-2010-ribbon.aspx`

- Word Content Control Toolkit `http://www.codeplex.com/dbe`

- Creating a SharePoint 2010 Ribbon Extension - part 2 `http://www.wictorwilen.se/Post/Creating-a-SharePoint-2010-Ribbon-extension-part-2.aspx`

- Default Server Ribbon Customization Locations `http://msdn.microsoft.com/en-us/library/ee537543(office.14).aspx`

- Declarative Customization of the Ribbon `http://msdn.microsoft.com/en-us/library/ee534970(office.14).aspx`

- Brian Jones: Open XML Formats Blog `http://blogs.msdn.com/brian_jones/`

- Intro to Word XML Part 1: Simple Word Document `http://blogs.msdn.com/brian_jones/archive/2005/07/05/435772.aspx`

- Module 10: Creating Dialogs and Ribbon Controls for SharePoint 2010 video `http://msdn.microsoft.com/en-us/sharepoint/ee513157.aspx`

- OpenXMLDeveloper.org `http://openxmldeveloper.org/`

CHAPTER 7

■ ■ ■

Automating Document Assembly

Windows SharePoint Services provides an enhanced storage system that facilitates collaboration. This system improves upon old collaboration techniques of simply e-mailing documents back and forth or dropping them in a file share. Relying on e-mail is awkward, as team members are never sure they have the most up-to-date version of the document, and consolidating the changes becomes an ongoing, laborious task. File shares are also limited in that the files may be difficult to find, users have no idea if they are currently being edited by another team member, and versioning is reduced to Save As/Rename operations. In contrast, SharePoint's system of Web-enabled content databases provides a rich experience for the team working on the document. The environment provides check-in/check-out functionality, versioning, metadata, search, and an entire web site for storing lists of data related to the creation of the document.

However, even this system becomes strained in scenarios in which the team's documents are really collections of separate components. Frequently, these components are independent and different team members are responsible for different pieces. Under these circumstances, team members ideally should be able to submit their contributions whenever completed. Yet this work often takes place serially because the file in a SharePoint library can be checked out by only one user at a time. In this chapter, we will detail how, as a developer, you can enhance this experience to provide an automated method of document assembly. We will have a master document that a user may markup with requests for supplemental contributions by other team members. This will result in tasks being created in a SharePoint team site. Contributors can then attach their contributions to the task and when they mark it complete, we will merge their contribution back into the correct place of the master document.

Real-World Examples

The key identifier that makes this solution applicable to an organization is any process in which different team members work on specific sections of a document. Consulting firms often have a sales resource, a project manager, and a development lead working on distinct portions of a proposal. The sales resource focuses on background information on the company, case studies, and pricing. The project manager is responsible for documenting the project lifecycle, creating a high-level project plan, and detailing the change/review mechanisms. Meanwhile, the developer is taking the customer's functional requirements and outlining a proposed solution. You also typically have individual résumés that need to be collected from specific members of the organization. All of these pieces have to be put together to complete the proposal. This problem is rather generic and can be found across many different customer types. In the construction industry, different team members are often responsible for certain sections of a contract. Even in the military, different organizations or levels are tasked with completing specific sections of a deliverable, such as in a policy review from different functional areas of the organizational branch. By allowing the team to divide and conquer the work, the solution in this chapter enables an efficient process that reduces the amount of time and level of effort it takes to complete an entire document.

Solution Overview

To provide some context for our automated document assembly solution, we've focused on a scenario in which a sales person in an organization is constructing a proposal that requires updated résumés from key individuals in the company. We will give this sales person a tool that will help identify the correct people to include, as well as mark up the document with placeholders for their contributions. This tool will be a Visual Studio Tools for Office (VSTO) Microsoft Word 2010 template. By extending a Word template with VSTO, we will be able to add an actions pane specific to the document where we can place additional controls for the sales person to use. These controls will let the sales person search for individuals in the company, using functionality that leverages SharePoint 2010's search web service to look through the profile repository for matching individuals. (This is the same profile repository that surfaces in the enterprise's My Sites and People search functionality.) Once a desired person is found, the actions pane will enable the sales person to insert a placeholder for the employee's résumé and specify a due date by which it must be provided.

After the sales person has marked up the proposal document with résumé placeholders, she will save it to a Proposals document library in a SharePoint site. When the proposal lands in this library, several things will happen. First, we will leverage SharePoint 2010's Document ID service to assign a unique identifier to the document. We will use this in several ways—to allow us to easily find the file, but also in the body of the document, a practice in many enterprises that lets users relate a printed document back to its electronic counterpart.

Besides assigning the Document ID, we will also develop an event handler that will parse the document looking for the résumé placeholders. For each of these résumé requests, we will create a corresponding task in the SharePoint site. This task will be for the identified person, have the delivery date indicated by the sales person, and contain information so that we can relocate the document and specific placeholder in the proposal once the contribution has been submitted.

Our scenario then shifts from the sales person to the individual identified as needing to provide an updated résumé. This person will be notified that a new résumé has been requested. Completing the task involves attaching a Microsoft Word document containing the updated résumé, along with marking the task as complete. An event handler monitoring the task list will see that the task has been completed and merge the attachment into the correct location of the proposal document. This merge won't just be text; we will incorporate other embedded items such as pictures and smart art. It is important to realize that when we are working on the Word documents on the server, this is made possible by the Open XML file format. In both cases, we are able to perform these operations on the server—interacting with streams and XML documents. At no time are we automating Microsoft Word on the server. In fact, Microsoft Word doesn't even need to be installed on the server for this solution to work.

Lastly, it isn't really appropriate for our proposal VSTO solution to be the end result that we would send directly to a customer. This is because the document has references back to our custom VSTO assembly that would then require installation and trust outside of our enterprise. Therefore, we will enable the organization to convert the constructed proposal from Microsoft Word to PDF format. This conversion will be done on the server using SharePoint 2010's Word Automation Services.

Solution Walkthrough

The following section will detail the major elements of the solution and the decisions that were made in coding it. The walkthrough will show you how we set up the SharePoint site to support the proposals and their corresponding tasks. We will demonstrate how to turn on the Document ID service and how to take the default document library's Word template as a starting point to a Word 2010 template project in Visual Studio 2010. We will explain how content controls can be used to surface metadata properties of the file into the body of the document, as well as to how to add them dynamically as content placeholders. With the Visual Studio Tools for Office solution, we will show you how to build a document actions pane and how to have that pane interact with SharePoint's search web service. Our VSTO solution will also extend the backstage interface so that a user can easily check on the status of the tasks from the proposal document. When the proposal template tool is complete, we will demonstrate how to deploy it so it is available as the default document template of the site's document library.

We will also walk you through the creation of the two event handlers that will use the Open XML file format to operate on the proposal. The first event handler will be responsible for parsing the proposal and creating tasks for each résumé request. The second one will respond to a completed résumé submission, merging the contents of the résumé back into the proposal. The walkthrough will also show you how to provide a workflow that converts the final proposal from a Word format to PDF using SharePoint's Word Automation Services. As in most of our chapters in the book, not every line of code will be explained. Since there are so many moving pieces to this chapter, we want to focus on the major elements of the solution design. We highly recommend you download the accompanying code for this chapter from Apress's site in order to follow along and reuse some of the objects.

Setting up the SharePoint Site and Document ID Service

For the solution, you will need a site for building out the components. In our environment, we chose the root web of a site collection. Its URL is `http://edhild3/sites/sales`. It is this site that will contain the document library and task list we will discuss in just a bit. Within your SharePoint environment you will also need a Search center. Most enterprises have their search center deployed as part of their root intranet site collection or as a site collection unto itself. In our environment, the enterprise search center is located at `http://edhild3/search`. If you don't have a search center, take the time to create one. If you are going to add it to an existing site collection, just be sure to activate the SharePoint Server Publishing Infrastructure site collection feature before creating the search center.

You also need to make sure you have some individuals in the profile repository. In our environment, we have two accounts that we will request résumés from: northamerica\edhild and northamerica\chadwach. These accounts exist in Active Directory and have been granted access to the site where we will be creating the tasks and proposal. They also have profiles in the profile repository. You can have SharePoint import attributes from AD or simply go the User Profile Service Application and create the accounts there. If you have not seen this interface, use the following steps to navigate there to either create or confirm your user data. Of course, with the user data in place, make sure you perform a new search crawl and that you can actually find a person by performing a people search through your search center.

1. Open SharePoint's Central Administration site.

2. Under the Application Management heading, click **Manage service applications**.

3. Locate the User Profile Service Application and click it to highlight that application. Click the **Manage** button in the ribbon.

4. Under the People heading, click **Manage User Profiles**.

5. From here, you should be able to search through existing profiles. Clicking the **New Profile** button lets you to manually create profiles for your accounts. Be sure to define something worth searching for. For example, for Ed Hild we used the title of **Development Team Lead** with a description that he likes **Visual Basic and C#.**

Getting back to the sales site where we'll be developing the proposals solution, one of the first things we will want to do is turn on the Document ID service. If you go to the site's settings and look at the Site Collection's features, you'll find a Document ID Service feature that needs to be activated. You can see this option in Figure 7-1.

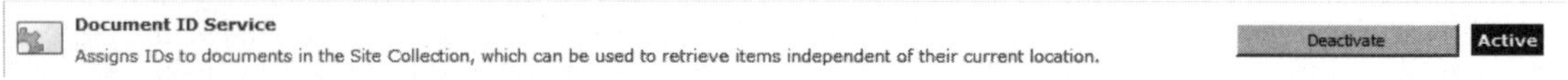

Document ID Service
Assigns IDs to documents in the Site Collection, which can be used to retrieve items independent of their current location.
Deactivate | Active

Figure 7-1. Activating the Document ID Service

Activating this feature extends the Document and Document Set content types with additional capability. Mainly, there is a new Document ID column that for each new file (or each new document set) will hold a unique value that can be used to retrieve the file through a static URL, regardless of where the file is located. You have some out-of-the-box influence on the format of these identifiers and even more if you want to code your own document ID provider. Once the Document ID Service has been turned on, the Site Collection settings will have a new option entitled Document ID Settings. Figure 7-2 shows some of the options there. Notice that you can determine what characters you want the identifiers to begin with.

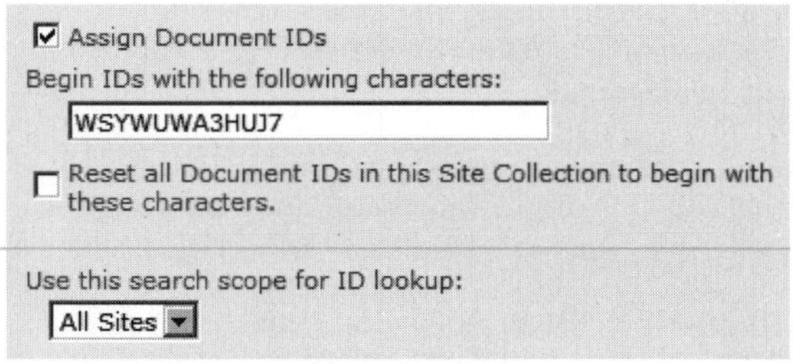

☑ Assign Document IDs
Begin IDs with the following characters:

WSYWUWA3HUJ7

☐ Reset all Document IDs in this Site Collection to begin with these characters.

Use this search scope for ID lookup:
All Sites ▼

Figure 7-2. Document ID settings

The word "begin" here is important as SharePoint will append an identifier for the list as well as the list item, leaving your complete identifiers to look something like: `WSYWUWA3HUJ7-1-12`. This means that the document could be retrieved through a static URL in the format of `http://edhild3/sites/sales/_layouts/DocIdRedir.aspx?ID=WSYWUWA3HUJ7-1-12`. The following URL gives you more detail on Document IDs, including what happens when you move or copy files: `http://msdn.microsoft.com/en-us/library/ee559302(office.14).aspx`.

Now in your development site, create a new document library called **Proposals**. To this library, add a new column named **ProposalID** that will hold a single line of text and make sure it is placed in the default view. You may be wondering why we would need a ProposalID when the Document ID Service has already added a Document ID column to the Document content type. The reason is that the Document ID column is a bit locked down internally within the product. For example, you won't actually see it in the definition of site columns or in use in the content types. It also is not available as a quick part in Microsoft Word, which is what we normally would use to get the identifier into the body of the document unless there's already a value assigned. This won't work with our approach of providing a template tool, since no Document ID would be present until the file is saved to the library and we don't want our sales person to have to know how to place quick parts onto a document. We will therefore use the ProposalID column for most of our work, and add a bit of code later to make sure its value stays in sync with the Document ID.

We will also need a tasks list. Create one in the site named **ResumeTasks**. Extend this list by adding **ProposalID** and **RequestID** columns. Both of these are single lines of text and present in the default view. The ProposalID in the task list will help us remember which proposal document the task is referring to. The RequestID column will contain a GUID value that matches a placeholder control inside the proposal document where the résumé content is to be placed.

Preparing the Document Template

Now let's turn our attention to the document template of the Proposals library; this will be the central part of the tool for the sales person working on the proposal. By default, each document library has a blank Word template that we can modify to represent a typical proposal. Use the following steps to open the document template so you can enter the boilerplate text along with a content control for the value of the ProposalID field.

1. Click on the **Proposals** library in the left-hand navigation of your site.

2. Open up the Library tab in the ribbon and click on the **Library Settings** button.

3. In the General Settings section, click **Advanced Settings**.

4. In the Document Template setting, click the **(Edit Template)** link. This will launch Microsoft Word so you can edit the template and save the changes back to the library.

We want to enter some boilerplate text, a control to hold the value of the ProposalID field, and a Résumés heading that will be the beginning of the section where the résumé contributions will be inserted. The boilerplate text can really be anything. Make sure the Résumés heading is the last paragraph in the document as we will use that as a marker when we write some code a bit later. Use the following steps to insert the control for the ProposalID field. The end result should look like Figure 7-3.

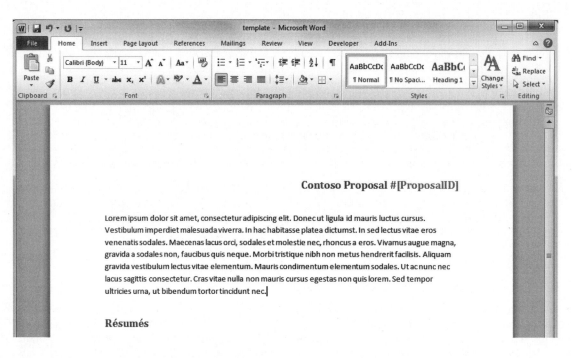

Figure 7-3. *Modifying the Proposal Document Template*

1. Place your cursor where you want the ProposalID field control to be placed and make sure you have any styles you'd like applied selected. In our example, the first line is right-aligned and uses the Heading 1 style.

2. Click the **Insert** tab in the ribbon.

3. In the Text group, click the down-arrow to access the options of the **Quick Parts** button. Quick Parts are already configured content controls in Microsoft Word that enable you to surface the file's data (in this case, properties) in the body of the document.

4. Choose the **Document Property** menu option.

5. Select **ProposalID**.

6. Now just click **Save** to commit your changes so this document becomes the template for the document library. You can test this out by going to the Proposals library and from the Document tab, choosing **New Document**.

This completes the non-code portion of preparing the document template. We now want to export the template from the SharePoint site so we can use it as the starting point for our Visual Studio solution in the next section. An easy way to export this file is to use SharePoint Designer. Simply open your site in SharePoint Designer and choose the **All Files** option in the Navigation menu. Browse to the Proposals library and open its **Forms** folder, where you'll see our `template.dotx` file. Select it and choose the **Export Files** button in the ribbon. Save the exported `template.dotx` file to your local Documents folder. Figure 7-4 shows this export option in SharePoint Designer.

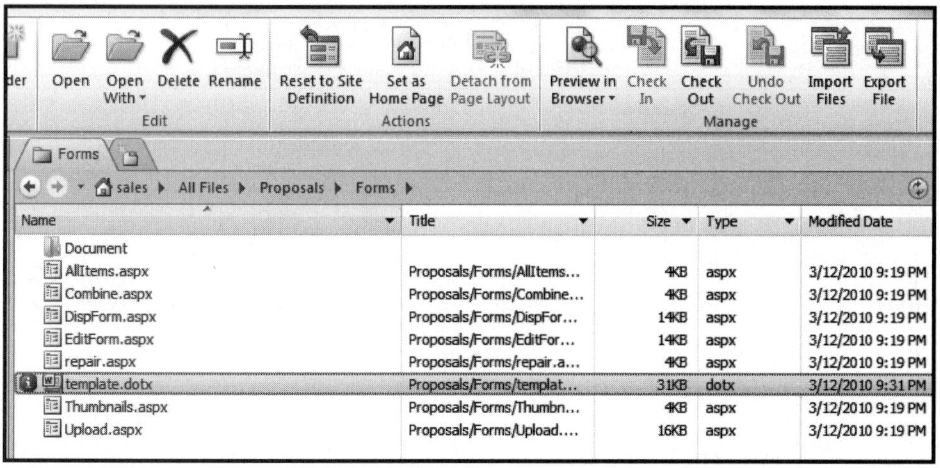

Figure 7-4. Exporting the Document Template using SharePoint Designer

Creating the Visual Studio Tools for Office Solution

In this section of the walkthrough, we will move over to Visual Studio and create a document-level Visual Studio Tools for Office project out of the Microsoft Word template. Start Visual Studio and choose to create a **New Project**. Under the C# language node, select Office and then 2010 to display the VSTO project templates.

From the listing of Visual Studio installed templates, select Word 2010 Template. Name the project **templateProject**. Leave the default option of creating a new solution and confirm that the .NET framework drop-down at the top of the dialog is set to .NET Framework 4. As we discussed in Chapter 4, there are several advantages to using version 4 of the framework for Office development, such as C# support for optional parameters. We want to make sure that these advantages are available to us. Your New Project dialog should look like Figure 7-5.

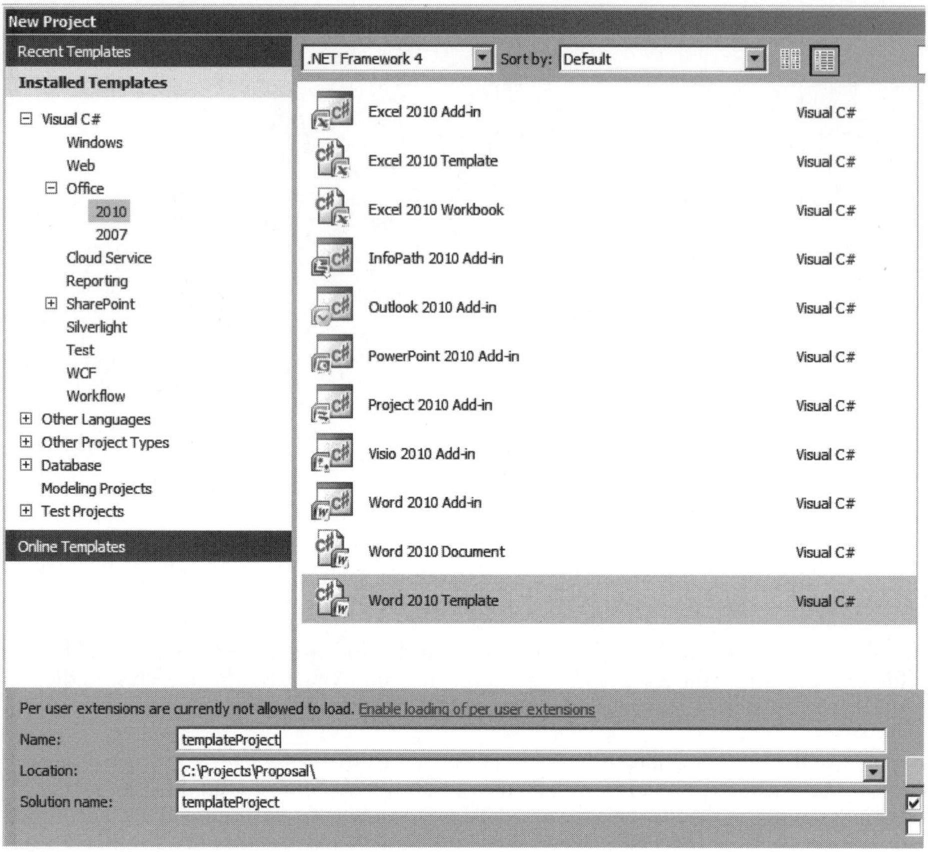

Figure 7-5. Creating the VSTO solution for the proposal template

Clicking OK starts a project wizard that asks if you wish to create a brand new Word template for the basis of the project or use a copy of an existing template. Choose **Copy an existing document** and browse to the `template.dotx` file that you exported from the site earlier.

When the new project is created, your solution will contain a few files by default. These are visible in the Visual Studio Solution Explorer window. You'll find a `template.dotx` node with a code file named `ThisDocument.cs`, which is the main entry point for document-level projects. This file is where developers can write code for events and where we will wire up our actions pane in the next section. You can go ahead and close the designer that is surfacing Microsoft Word. Our work in Visual Studio will supplement the work we have already done inside the document.

Before we get to coding away, let's take care of one other item at the project level. We will need a web service reference to the SharePoint search functionality since our document will be remote from the server (on the user's desktop) when it is being used. SharePoint 2010 contains a `search.asmx` web service that will be our entry point for issuing a remote search query and getting results. This search API remains unchanged from SharePoint 2007—good news for developers who built solutions leveraging it in the previous release. This also means that most of the references and examples you find describing this web service for SharePoint 2007 will be useful in building solutions for the 2010 version. You interact with

134

search.asmx using the ASP.NET 2.0 style of web services, so it will take us a few steps to get the appropriate reference into our Visual Studio 2010 project. Follow the steps below to set the web service reference.

1. Right-click on the templateProject and choose **Add Service Reference**.

2. Click the **Advanced** button in the bottom left-hand corner of the dialog.

3. Click the **Add Web Reference** button in the bottom left-hand corner of the dialog since we need to add an ASP.NET 2.0 asmx style reference.

4. Enter the URL for the search.asmx web service, which should be off the Search center you identified earlier in the chapter. In our environment the URL is http://edhild3/search/_vti_bin/search.asmx.

5. Click the green arrow.

6. Once you can see the operations of the web service in the window, name the service reference **SPQueryService** in the textbox to the right.

7. Click the **Add Reference** button. Your project structure in Visual Studio's Solution Explorer should look like Figure 7-6.

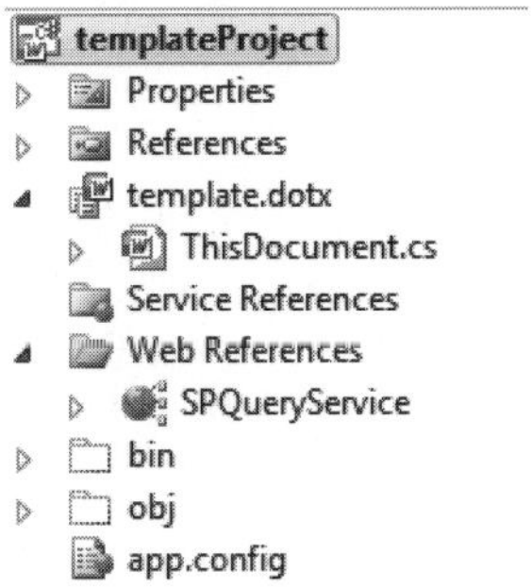

Figure 7-6. The templateProject solution structure

In the next few sections, we will walk through the major elements of the VSTO solution, which creates a tool out of the Microsoft Word proposal template. As in our other chapters, we won't detail every line of code so we highly recommend you download the code for this chapter from the Apress web site and follow along.

The Document Actions Pane

Most people are familiar with the task pane in Microsoft Office applications. In Microsoft Word, the Research pane is an example of a task pane that enables a user to search registered repositories for more information without having to leave the Word application. Task panes provide another surface (usually located to the right of the document) for a developer to build additional user interface elements that add capability to the Word application. While task panes are application-level and can be called on regardless of the document that is open, document actions panes present similar user interface options but are available only for a specific document or document template. This is exactly why we chose to create a document-level project in the last section. Our pane makes sense only if the user is working with the proposal template. You can create a custom document actions pane using a Windows Forms user control. Figure 7-7 shows the design surface of the ProposalPane user control.

Résumés

Use the dialog below to find employess whose résumés should be included in the response.

[Search]

☐ lstResults

Due Date: 4/20/2010 ▦▾

[Add]

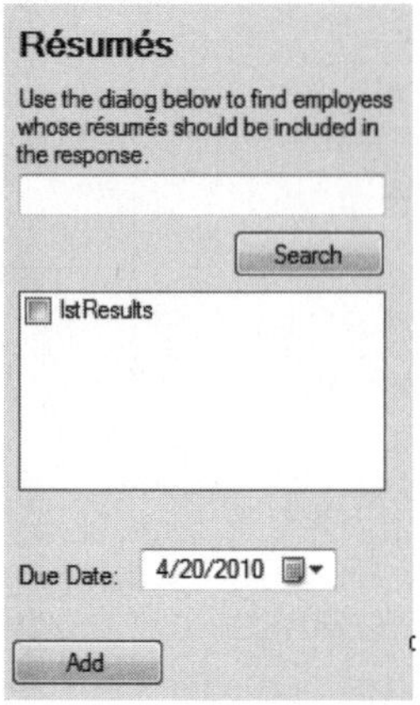

Figure 7-7. Designing the ProposalPane control

The ProposalPane user control contains some labels at the top for instructions. The `txtKeywords` textbox will enable the user to enter a search query that will perform the people search against the profile repository. The search button is responsible for executing the web service call and populating the CheckedListBox control below with results. Our sales person user can then select the desired individuals, choose a due date using the DateTimePicker control and click the Add button. This button will dynamically place a content control at the end of the document, below the Résumés heading, for each checked individual. The content of this control will specify whose résumé is requested along with the due date so we can create the correct tasks. With the user control created, the code in Listing 7-1 in the `ThisDocument` class loads it up as a document actions pane when our template is opened.

Listing 7-1. Adding the ProposalPane as a Document Actions Pane

```
private ProposalPane proposalPane = new ProposalPane();

private void ThisDocument_Startup(object sender, System.EventArgs e)
{
    this.ActionsPane.Controls.Add(proposalPane);
}
```

The next bit of code we want to draw attention to is the code that runs in response to the user clicking the Search button. The initial portion of this code is presented in Listing 7-2. First, the proxy for SharePoint's search web service is configured with the URL of the search center, the current user's credentials, and a timeout value of 20 seconds in case the server is too busy for our request. Next, a `queryPacketTemplate` string variable shows the structure of the XML envelope our query must be wrapped in that we pass to the web service. The most important attribute here is that the query type is set to MSSQLFT. There are two types of search queries we could submit through this API—a keyword style and a style that resembles SQL Select statements, which is the style we will use here. We won't delve into all of the options here and turn this into a reference on search query syntax; if this is an area of interest, you'll find some reference links in the Further Reading section at the end of this chapter.

Listing 7-2. Building the Search Request

```
private void btnSearch_Click(object sender, EventArgs e)
{
  SPQueryService.QueryService service = new SPQueryService.QueryService();
  service.Url = "http://edhild3/Search/_vti_bin/search.asmx";
  service.PreAuthenticate = true;
  service.Credentials = System.Net.CredentialCache.DefaultCredentials;
  service.Timeout = 20000; //wait 20 secs

  string queryPacketTemplate = "<?xml version=\"1.0\" encoding=\"utf-8\" ?>"
    + "<QueryPacket xmlns=\"urn:Microsoft.Search.Query\">"
    + "<Query domain=\"QDomain\"><SupportedFormats>"
    + "<Format>urn:Microsoft.Search.Response.Document.Document</Format>"
    + "</SupportedFormats>"
    + "<Context><QueryText language=\"en-US\" type=\"MSSQLFT\">"
    + "{0}</QueryText></Context>"
    + "</Query></QueryPacket>";
```

In the next section of code shown in Listing 7-3, you can see our actual SQL statement in the sqlQueryTemplate string variable where we ask for the PreferredName and AccountName of any person who has the user-entered keyword in any of the indexed properties of the profile repository. The next two lines simply package everything together as one XML string. You may wonder how we came to know about the PreferredName and AccountName properties. The answer to that lies in the User Profile Service Application you accessed earlier in this chapter. Using the Manage User Properties option in the service application takes you to a listing of the properties in the profile store. Note that the display name you see here is not always the internal property name. Edit the property to see its internal name. This listing of profile properties is shown in Figure 7-8.

Listing 7-3. The SQL Search Query

```
string sqlQueryTemplate = "SELECT PreferredName, AccountName FROM SCOPE() "
    + "WHERE \"Scope\" = 'People' AND CONTAINS(*,'{0}') ";

string enteredText = txtKeywords.Text.Replace(' ', '+');
string sqlQuery = string.Format(sqlQueryTemplate, enteredText);string queryXml =
string.Format(queryPacketTemplate, sqlQuery);
```

■ **Note** Pay particular attention to the fact that we are replacing any space character with a plus symbol. There are several characters the user can enter that would present a problem for our code. We are accounting for the spaces, but, for example, a query for a user with the last name of O'Brian would also be a problem because of the apostrophe. Use the links in the Further Reading portion of this document to get a fuller explanation of characters that cause problems and how you can handle for them.

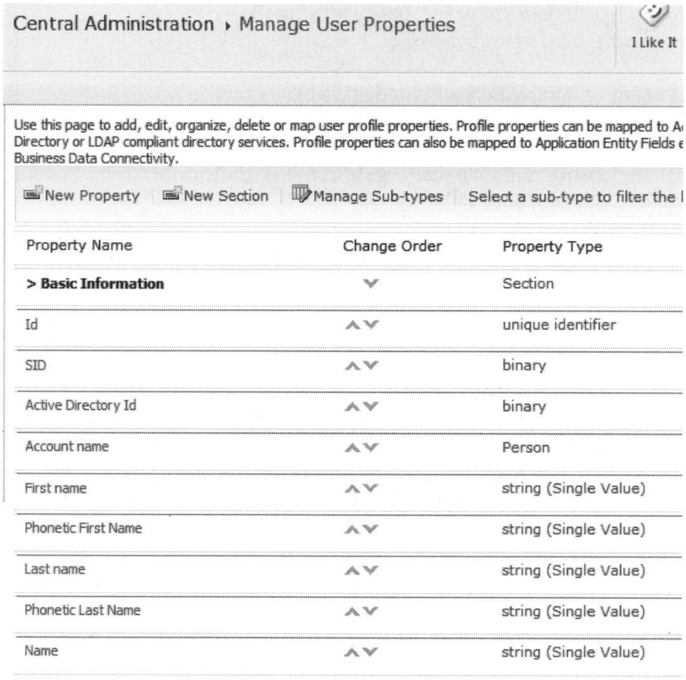

Central Administration › Manage User Properties   I Like It

Use this page to add, edit, organize, delete or map user profile properties. Profile properties can be mapped to A
Directory or LDAP compliant directory services. Profile properties can also be mapped to Application Entity Fields e
Business Data Connectivity.

New Property   New Section   Manage Sub-types   Select a sub-type to filter the l

Property Name	Change Order	Property Type
> **Basic Information**	⌄	Section
Id	⌃⌄	unique identifier
SID	⌃⌄	binary
Active Directory Id	⌃⌄	binary
Account name	⌃⌄	Person
First name	⌃⌄	string (Single Value)
Phonetic First Name	⌃⌄	string (Single Value)
Last name	⌃⌄	string (Single Value)
Phonetic Last Name	⌃⌄	string (Single Value)
Name	⌃⌄	string (Single Value)

Figure 7-8. Discovering profile properties

Before we look at the section of the search button's click event handler where we process the results, we wanted to call out a helper class we constructed simply to make placing the people in the results list easier. The `PersonResultItem` class we placed at the bottom of the code-behind of the user control is just a class that contains the returned `PreferredName` and `AccountName` information for a specific search result (see Listing 7-4). The reason we created the class was to be able to specify the `ToString()` method that will be used by the `CheckedListBox` for the display value of the item. In this case, we want the `PreferredName`, which is the display name for the account.

Listing 7-4. The PersonResultItem Helper Class for Reading Results

```
internal class PersonResultItem
{
  public string PreferredName { get; set; }
  public string AccountName { get; set; }
  public PersonResultItem(string preferredName, string accountName)
  {
    PreferredName = preferredName;
    AccountName = accountName;
  }
  public override string ToString()
  {
    return this.PreferredName;
  }
}
```

So the last piece of code for our Search button, shown in Listing 7-5, executes the query and adds the results to the list box. In this instance, we are using the `QueryEx` method of the search web service, which returns the results as a dataset with a table named `RelevantResults`. We are using a `WaitCursor` here to keep things simple; a more advanced approach would be to make an asynchronous web service call.

Listing 7-5. Executing the Query and Processing the Results

```
this.UseWaitCursor = true;
DataSet ds = service.QueryEx(queryXml);
DataTable tbl = ds.Tables["RelevantResults"];
lstResults.Items.Clear();
foreach (DataRow r in tbl.Rows)
{
  lstResults.Items.Add(new PersonResultItem(↩
      r["PreferredName"].ToString(),↩
      r["AccountName"].ToString()));
}
this.UseWaitCursor = false;
}
```

So far, our ProposalPane enables the sales person to perform a people search from within the Word template. Once the results have been gathered and the user selects which people to request résumés for, the control needs to place résumé requests into the document in the Résumés section. To accomplish this, the code in Listing 7-6 finds the Résumés section by knowing that it is the last paragraph in the document. For each selected individual, we insert a paragraph containing a rich-text content control. When this control is created, we name it with the string Resume along with a GUID so we can guarantee uniqueness. The control is titled **Resume Request** and the same GUID is placed in its tag property for us to retrieve later. This tag value allows us to tell the résumé requests apart and relate the corresponding tasks we need to create in the SharePoint site later. Lastly, we place some formatted text in the control so that it will fit the format of "Resume request for northamerica\edhild due by 4/20/2010". Figure 7-9 shows the end result running in Microsoft Word.

Listing 7-6. *Inserting Content Controls for Resume Requests*

```
foreach (PersonResultItem person in lstResults.SelectedItems)
{
  Microsoft.Office.Interop.Word.Paragraph last = ↵
    Globals.ThisDocument.Paragraphs[Globals.ThisDocument.Paragraphs.Count];
  last.Range.InsertParagraphAfter();

  Globals.ThisDocument.Paragraphs[Globals.ThisDocument.Paragraphs.Count]↵
    .Range.Select();
  Microsoft.Office.Tools.Word.RichTextContentControl ctl;
  Guid id = Guid.NewGuid();
  ctl = Globals.ThisDocument.Controls.AddRichTextContentControl(↵
    "Resume " + id.ToString());
  ctl.Title = "Resume Request";
  ctl.Tag = id.ToString();
  ctl.PlaceholderText = string.Format("Resume request for {0} due by {1}", ↵
    person.AccountName, dtDueDate.Value.ToShortDateString());
}
```

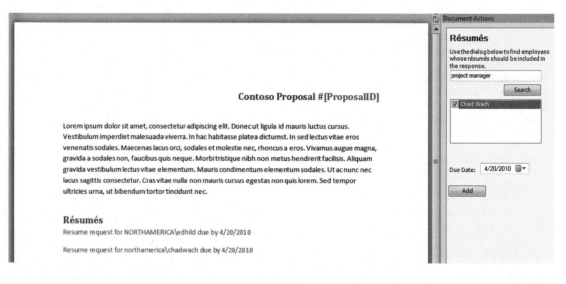

Figure 7-9. *Résumé request as dynamic content controls*

Extending Backstage

As described in Chapter 4, Microsoft Office 2010 provides a new extension point for developers called the *backstage*. This interface replaces the old-style, drop-down file menu, bringing a ribbon-like treatment to operations users will perform on their documents, or a way to present information about the document. The new interface opens up a lot of real-estate for providing useful information. Our solution will provide a click link to the SharePoint site's résumé tasks list, filtering the list for the tasks specific to the open proposal. We point out in the Extensions section of this chapter how you could make this much more elaborate by actually bringing the task details into this interface. The Further Reading section also includes links for more details about advanced options, and more controls you could utilize in the backstage environment.

To get started with our customization, add a new project item to the Visual Studio templateProject. Choose the Ribbon (XML) item template and name the file backstagecustomization.cs. As mentioned in Chapter 4, there is no designer for backstage customizations; however, these extensions leverage the same ribbon infrastructure as the ribbon items the user sees while authoring the document. When the new project item process completes, two files will have been added—an xml file and a class file. Both of these in concert will be used to build our backstage extension. Let's start with the XML file, which is shown in Listing 7-7.

Listing 7-7. *The Backstage Customization Ribbon XML*

```xml
<?xml version="1.0" encoding="UTF-8"?>
<customUI xmlns="http://schemas.microsoft.com/office/2009/07/customui"
          onLoad="Ribbon_Load">
  <backstage>
    <tab idMso="TabInfo">
      <firstColumn>
        <group id="ProposalInfoGroup"
               label="Proposal Information"
               helperText="Use the link provided to get details on resume
                           tasks for this proposal. Note that document must
                           be saved to SharePoint initially for this link to
                           work.">
          <topItems>
            <hyperlink id="taskLink" label="View tasks"
                       getTarget="GetHyperLink"/>
          </topItems>
        </group>
      </firstColumn>
    </tab>
  </backstage>
</customUI>
```

Notice that this ribbon XML uses a different namespace than the one that was added by default. In the backstage, the tabs are listed vertically on the left-hand side of the screen. By specifying the idMso of TabInfo, we are telling Word to place our customization on the out-of-the-box Info tab. We then define a new Group that will be placed in the first column of that tab. This group has a label, description, and an inner hyperlink control. The text for this hyperlink will always be "View Tasks", but the URL for the hyperlink will be dynamically determined using a ribbon callback technique. This is because we want the URL to filter the résumé tasks list for tasks specific to this proposal. Since this will be different for different proposals, we add a callback method into the backstagecustomization.cs file named GetHyperLink, which will return the correct URL string. Use the following URL for more details on building ribbon customizations and, in particular, for figuring out what controls can be loaded there and the method signature of callbacks for their properties: http://msdn.microsoft.com/en-us/library/ee691833(office.14).aspx. Listing 7-8 shows our GetHyperLink callback method.

Listing 7-8. The GetHyperLink Ribbon Callback

```
public string GetHyperLink(Office.IRibbonControl control)
{
  string url = "http://edhild3/sites/sales/Lists/ResumeTasks/AllItems.aspx";
  string filterTemplate = "?FilterField1=ProposalID&FilterValue1={0}";
  string id = Globals.ThisDocument.plainTextContentControl1.Text;
  if (id != string.Empty)
  {
    return url + string.Format(filterTemplate, id);
  }
  else
  {
    return url;
  }
}
```

The GetHyperLink method builds a URL to the résumé tasks list in the SharePoint site. Assuming the proposal has been saved to the site at least once, it will have a Document ID and therefore a ProposalID. We will show you later how to synchronize those values. If a ProposalID exists, we can access its value through the quick part content control that we added in the very beginning. We didn't name the control, so it is referenced here as plainTextContentControl1. Notice how we can filter the list for the user by specifying both the field to filter by as well as the filter value as query parameters in the URL. If this ProposalID content control does not have a value, we need our hyperlink to do something so we send the user to the résumé tasks default all items view.

Last but not least, we need to inform Word of our ribbon customization when the document-level project loads. This is accomplished with the code in Listing 7-9 which is placed in the ThisDocument.cs file. Figure 7-10 shows the end result of our customization alongside the versioning group on the Info tab.

Listing 7-9. Loading the Backstage Customization for the Document

```
protected override Microsoft.Office.Core.IRibbonExtensibility⏎
    CreateRibbonExtensibilityObject()
{
  return new backstagecustomization();
}
```

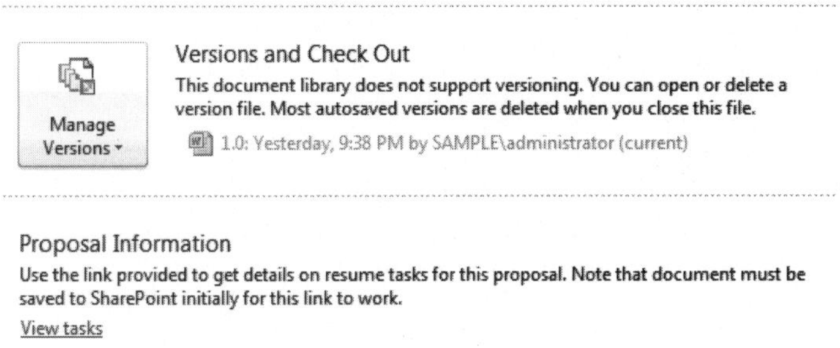

Versions and Check Out
This document library does not support versioning. You can open or delete a
version file. Most autosaved versions are deleted when you close this file.

Manage
Versions ▾

1.0: Yesterday, 9:38 PM by SAMPLE\administrator (current)

Proposal Information
Use the link provided to get details on resume tasks for this proposal. Note that document must be
saved to SharePoint initially for this link to work.

View tasks

Figure 7-10. The Proposal Information Backstage Customization

Deploying the Proposal Template Tool

Now that the proposal template tool is complete, we want to deploy it so that is available as the default template of the Proposals SharePoint library. Remember, though, since this is a document-level project, we are really talking about deploying the `template.dotx` file along with the assembly that has our VSTO customizations. Visual Studio Tools for Office solutions are usually deployed using ClickOnce, which means the user accesses the solution from a central location such as a web site or a file share. The solution installs the first time the user accesses the document, and then the application has the ability to reach back to this installation point to check for updates.

You may be skeptical about SharePoint as a deployment destination. SharePoint is not your typical web application and we really don't want assemblies treated as content in its databases. Storing the assembly outside of the content database is not a requirement, just more of a general practice. A more accurate description of what we are going to do is to deploy the solution through ClickOnce to a file share, but distribute the `template.dotx` file via SharePoint. This approach is valid since the template file maintains a reference to where its VSTO components were deployed. So our users will be able to access the document as they normally would and if it is the first time the file is accessed, it will reach back to the deployment file share to install the solution. This also increases the flexibility of the solution, as you could deploy the document to many different sites, but have a single point of maintenance for the code-behind assembly.

To get started, we need to first get our templateProject solution deployed. Right-click on the project and choose **Properties**. Within the Visual Studio dialog, as seen in Figure 7-11, select the **Publish** tab.

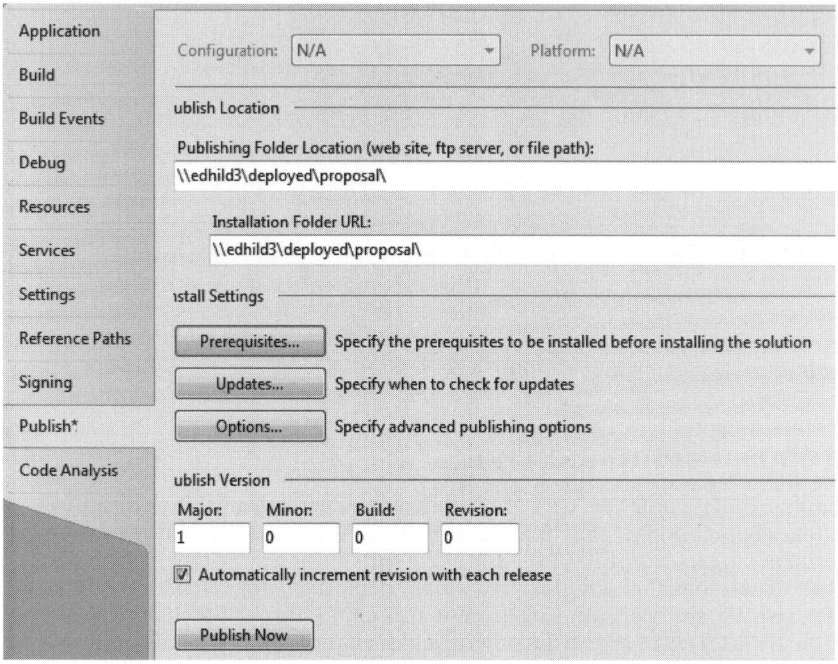

Figure 7-11. Publishing the VSTO Solution

Now ClickOnce deployment is a topic that goes far beyond the scope of this book, so we include some references for you to do more research in the Further Reading section of this chapter. For now, we will just explain enough to get this project integrated with your SharePoint environment. In Figure 7-11, notice that we have specified a file share for the publishing location and the installation folder. For our approach of using the SharePoint library to deploy the solution, these should be the same. Please make sure this is actually a valid path in your environment. You will likely also want to change the default Updates option. Clicking the Updates button lets you set the application to check for updates every time it is loaded. This is useful if you expect to still be doing some debugging. Finally, click the Publish Now button to publish the VSTO solution, `template.dotx` file, and other application settings information to the shared folder.

Remember when we used SharePoint Designer to export the library's template file so we could use it to create the Visual Studio project? Use the same technique now, but import the `template.dotx` file that was placed in the deployment shared folder.

Chances are you need to adjust the Trust Settings in Microsoft Word before it will even attempt to load the solution. There are many different ways to establish trust, such as by location or publisher (using a signing certificate). Since location is the easiest to set up in a development environment, we will take that approach. Launch Microsoft Word and use the following steps to set up the trust settings.

1. Launch a new instance of Microsoft Word.

2. Click the File menu and choose **Options**.

3. Click **Trust Center** in the left-hand navigation.

4. Click **Trust Center Settings** button.

5. Click **Trust Locations** in the left-hand navigation.

6. Check the checkbox at the bottom of the dialog to **Allow Trusted Locations on My Network**.

7. Click the **Add New Location** button.

8. Enter your deployment file share location (for our environment, this was `\\edhild3\deployed`). Choose the checkbox so that **Subfolders of this location are also trusted**.

9. Repeat the previous step for the SharePoint location where the `template.dotx` file is deployed. We simply added the root of the site collection `http://edhild3/sites/sales` and selected to trust all the subfolders.

10. Click **OK** twice.

Depending on your environment, you may also want to disable opening the document in Protected View. This is also done in the Trust Center settings of Microsoft Word. You should now be able to go to the SharePoint site and choose **New Document**, which will retrieve the template. Since this is the first time you are launching the customization from its deployment location, the installer for the customization will be launched. You will only see this step the first time. Subsequent requests simply check for updates. Your proposal template should now load along with your document actions pane.

■ **Note** A few issues have surfaced in our development environment, making us have to run the setup.exe in the deployment folder as an additional step. From a clean client machine, this doesn't appear to be a problem, but just in case you are using a single virtual machine as both server and client, we thought it worth mentioning. Again, please look to the Further Reading section of the chapter if you want more ClickOnce and SharePoint deployment details.

Using SPMetal

In the next two sections of this chapter we'll focus on the event handlers that will respond to proposal documents being stored in the library and the résumé task requests being completed. Since we will be writing code against the lists in our SharePoint site, we will take a moment to generate a helper class to streamline the amount of code we need to write. SPMetal is a command line tool that generates code that is an alternative to the SharePoint object model. By default, the tool is located at `C:\Program Files\Common Files\Microsoft Shared\Web Server Extensions\14\BIN`. Simply point it at a SharePoint team site and the resulting code file will contain strongly-typed entity classes for all of the site's lists and libraries as they are configured at the moment in time that you run the tool. This code is often easier to use than the SharePoint object model equivalents. The best example of this is querying the list for a specific item. Using the SharePoint object model, you could issue a query for specific items of a list using an XML-formatted CAML query such as the one in Listing 7-10. Notice that the query is just in the form of a string with no IntelliSense provided for structure, field names, or possible values.

Listing 7-10. Querying for Specific List Items using CAML

```
SPList list = m_web.Lists["ResumeTasks"];
SPQuery query = New SPQuery();
query.Query = "<Where><Eq><FieldRef Name='ProposalID'/><Value
                        Type='Text'>12345</Value></Eq></Where>";
SPListItemCollection items = list.GetItems(query);
```

Instead, the entity classes created by SPMetal support LINQ. So the query in Listing 7-10 becomes less code to write, even easier to understand, and definitely less prone to spelling a field or value incorrectly. Listing 7-11 shows the transformed query, which also gets only the collection of the title fields we're interested in.

Listing 7-11. Query for Specific List Items using SPMetal and Linq

```
using (EntitiesDataContext dc = new EntitiesDataContext(webUrl))
{
  var q = from resumetask in dc.ResumeTasks
          where resumetask.ProposalID == "12345"
          select resumetask.Title;
```

A developer would typically use SPMetal during the coding phase, running the tool and adding the generated file into the Visual Studio project. To run the tool, launch a command window and type a command similar to `SPMetal /web:http://edhild3/sites/sales /code:ProposalEntities.cs /language:csharp`. In this command we have specified three parameters. The first, *web*, specifies the site you'd like to use as the source. The generated code file will contain classes for working against a similarly structured site. In this case, we chose our team site where we are building the solution. The second parameter, *code*, specifies the name of the file you want the generated code to be placed in. This file will be placed in the same directory as the SPMetal tool. Once you have it, copy it and add it to the Visual Studio project we will create in the next section. The last parameter, *language*, specifies the .NET language you'd like the generated code to be in. There are many more parameters to this file and if you are going to be spending a lot of time coding against SharePoint data sources, we recommend spending some time to get to know all of its options. We have added a link in the Further Reading section of this chapter.

■ **Note** It is important to realize that this code runs in the context of the developer running the command unless another user is specified as a parameter. Since SharePoint security trims what a user has access to, make sure the user running this tool actually has access to the data you are planning to code against.

The Proposal Document Event Handler

In this next section of the walkthrough, we will add a new Visual Studio SharePoint project to the solution that will contain the event handlers that run in response to both the proposal being saved to the document library as well as a user completing her résumé task. With Visual Studio select to add a new project to the current solution. Under the C# language node, select SharePoint and then 2010 to display the SharePoint 2010 project templates.

From the listing of Visual Studio installed templates, select EventReceiver. Name the project **ProposalEvents**. Leave the default option of creating a new solution and confirm that the .NET framework drop-down at the top of the dialog is set to .NET Framework 3.5. Your New Project dialog should look like Figure 7-12.

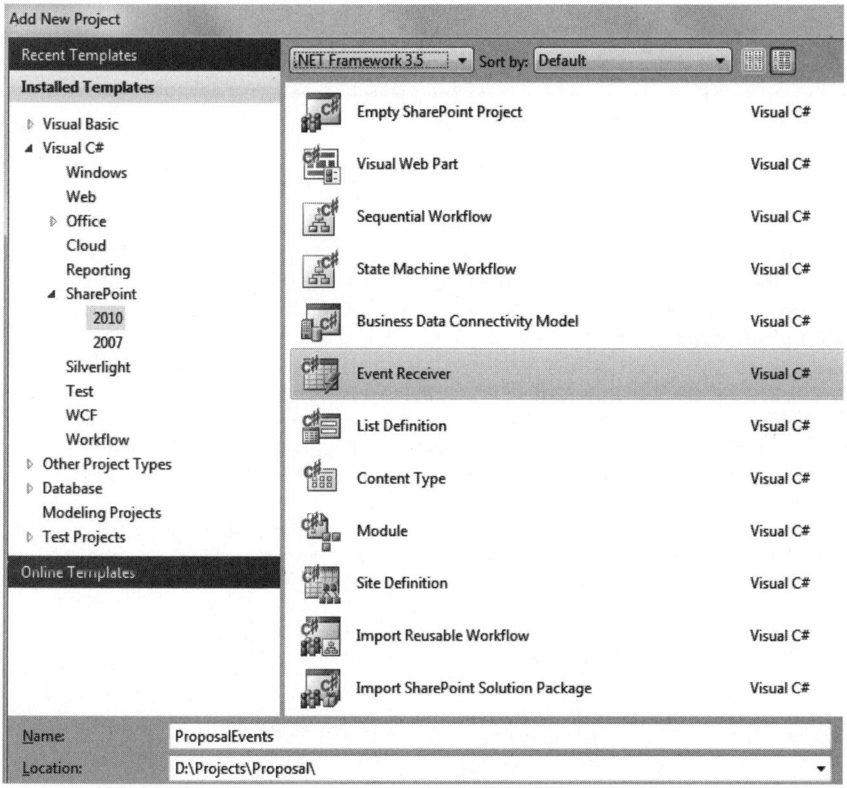

Figure 7-12. Creating the ProposalEvents Solution

Clicking OK will start the SharePoint Customization Wizard, which will ask a few questions about the solution you are going to build. The first dialog in this wizard asks for the SharePoint site you want Visual Studio to deploy to when you debug your code. Stick with the same site you used earlier in the chapter, `http://edhild3/sites/sales`.

You are also asked whether your solution is a farm or sandboxed solution. This alludes to security restrictions that will be placed on your solution and whether it is a part of the enterprise (farm) or a customization for a specific site collection (sandboxed). Since our code will be operating on files using Open XML, it falls outside the typical restrictions of sandboxed solutions, so choose the **farm level** option. The wizard's next screen asks how to bind your event handler. We will be starting with the code

147

that generates the résumé tasks when the proposal is saved. In this case, we want to bind it to a List, so choose **List Item Events**. We then get to pick a particular list type—choose **Document Library**.

■ **Note** You might be curious why we are not asked to specifically pick the Proposals document library. This is because, declaratively, we can only bind an event handler to a list type or content type. So our event handler will actually run in response to this action for any document library in the site. If you wanted to scope this down to a specific list or library, you would write code in a feature receiver so that upon activation, the feature binds the specific list and event handler. Another option would be to define the proposals as their own content type and bind the receiver that way. This approach is an Extension Point for the chapter.

Lastly, we get to select which events we wish to respond to. You will notice that most of these events either have "is being" or "was" in their description. This refers to whether you want your event handler to be called synchronously with the action or asynchronously after it has taken place. Since the generation of résumé tasks can happen after the document is saved, select both the **An item was added** and **An item was updated** options. Click **Finish**.

Once the new project is created, your solution will already have a few files by default, including an event receiver named `EventReceiver1`. Right-click and rename this to **ProposalDocumentReceiver**. When you expand this node, you will see an `Elements.xml` file, which has the registration information that this SharePoint customization is an event handler, the class that contains the code that should be run, and the events it is responding to. The class `EventReceiver1.cs` already has the `ItemAdded` and `ItemUpdated` events stubbed out for you.

Before jumping into the actual code that will parse the document and create the résumé tasks, let's get a few other things out of the way. First, don't forget to add the `ProposalEntities` class we created with SPMetal earlier. Also, there are a few assemblies we need to add references to:

- **WindowsBase**: This assembly gives us access to the System.IO.Packaging namespace, which is used to open up Office files that use the Open XML file format.

- **DocumentFormat.OpenXml**: This assembly is provided by the Open XML Format SDK 2.0. For this chapter we are using the March 2010 release, which you can download and install from: `http://msdn.microsoft.com/en-us/office/bb265236.aspx`. DocumentFormat.OpenXml allows us to manipulate the content of the presentation without having to write XML nodes directly. The SDK provides an object model that is an abstraction from the actual XML, making our code easier to read and write.

- **Microsoft.SharePoint.Linq**: This assembly is included in the SharePoint install, though you may have to browse to it when adding the reference. Its default location is `C:\Program Files\Common Files\Microsoft Shared\Web Server Extensions\14\ISAPI\Microsoft.SharePoint.Linq.dll`. Microsoft.SharePoint.Linq allows us to query the list for specific items using LINQ instead of the old CAML used in previous versions of SharePoint. It is used by the SPMetal class we generated earlier.

Now that the appropriate references have been added, you can add the **using** statements into the event receiver code file we will be modifying. These statements are the key namespaces we will use in the code, and they keep us from having to fully qualify their class names. If you notice that the namespaces are not resolving, you may have missed adding a reference to an assembly. Listing 7-12 details the **using** statements that need to be added to the code-behind file of the class **EventReceiver1.cs**.

Listing 7-12. Using Statements

```
using DocumentFormat.OpenXml.Wordprocessing;
using DocumentFormat.OpenXml;
using DocumentFormat.OpenXml.Packaging;
using System.Linq;
using System.Collections.Generic;
using System.Text;
using System.IO;
```

The code in the **ItemAdded** and **ItemUpdated** methods is almost identical. Looking at Listing 7-13, you see that we first make sure it is the Proposals library that we are working with. Had you bound the event handler with a content type or through a feature receiver, this would not have been necessary. We then retrieve a reference to the file and web we are working with and call the method where most of the work will happen—**ProcessFile**.

Listing 7-13. Handling the ItemAdded Event for the Proposal Library

```
public override void ItemAdded(SPItemEventProperties properties)
{
  if (properties.List.Title != "Proposals") return;
  SPFile file = properties.ListItem.File;
  SPWeb web = properties.ListItem.Web;
  ProcessFile(file, web);
  base.ItemAdded(properties);
}
```

The **ProcessFile** method begins by addressing the fact that we really want the Document ID to be synchronized with our ProposalID field. You might think that, ideally, this should have happened as part of a synchronous event; however, the Document ID field simply isn't available for you to retrieve at that moment. Therefore, we have to perform this action in the after event, being very careful that we don't cause any events to run again as part of the change, or trigger the creation of any new versions. Listing 7-14 contains this part of the **ProcessFile** method. We determined this property's internal name by attaching Visual Studio's debugger and looking at the properties collection.

Listing 7-14. Syncing the ProposalID and Document ID fields

```
if (!file.Name.EndsWith(".docx")) return;
this.EventFiringEnabled = false;
file.Item.Properties["ProposalID"] = file.Properties["_dlc_DocId"].ToString();
file.Item.SystemUpdate(false);
this.EventFiringEnabled = true;
```

Listing 7-14 starts by confirming that we are operating on a Microsoft Word document that has been saved using the Open XML file format. Using the `EventFiringEnabled` property allows us to make sure that this update of properties will not cause any new events to be raised. Notice that instead of updating the file, we are focused on the file's SharePoint item. This is because we are not changing the file itself, just its metadata. Using the `SystemUpdate` method with a false parameter tells the system not to create a new version as a result of the update. It is important to realize that we are only updating the property of the proposal document and not its body. This property will be retrieved by Microsoft Word upon opening and then displayed in our content control, but if the property isn't saved again, its value isn't really part of the document. This isn't much of an issue in this solution as we expect our sales person would still be working on the file as the résumés are coming in, but we wanted to make sure you clearly got the action that was being performed here.

The next portion of the `ProcessFile` method is going to tackle finding those content controls we placed under the Résumés heading so that we can create the correct tasks. The fact that we have saved this document using the Open XML file format allows us to perform this action without having to have Microsoft Word on the server. As explained in Chapter 4, the Microsoft Office desktop tools have switched from proprietary binary-formatted files to formats based on Open XML specifications. Now each file—whether it be a spreadsheet, presentation, or document—is really a package of parts and items. Parts are pieces of content for the file, whereas items are metadata describing how the parts should be assembled and rendered. Most of these pieces are XML files, making it possible for them to be manipulated through code. You can gain insight into the structure of an Open XML–based file by replacing its file extension with .zip, since the file is really an ordinary Zip archive. Figure 7-13 shows the root of the archive for a test proposal document.

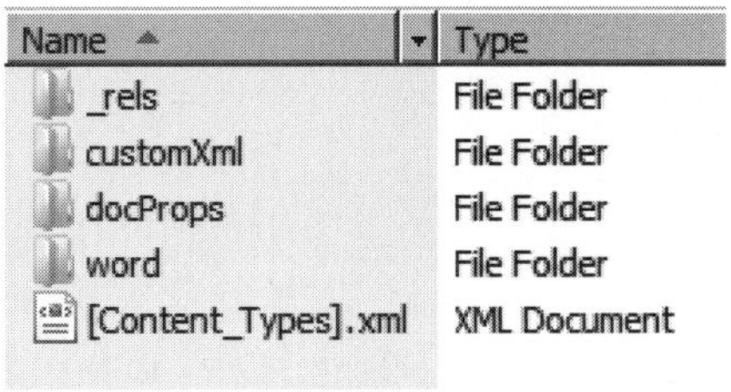

Figure 7-13. Examining the archive of a Word document

The XML file in the root is named `[Content_Types].xml` and it stores content-type directives for all the parts that appear in the archive. A content type contains metadata about a particular part or groups of parts and, more importantly, contains a directive about how the application should render that part. For example, Listing 7-15 shows just a few lines from the file, but clearly delineates how the file tells the rendering application which parts are styles, relationships, settings, and even the main document.

Listing 7-15. The Document's Content Types

```
<Default Extension="rels" ContentType="application/vnd.openxmlformats-↵
    package.relationships+xml"/>
<Default Extension="xml" ContentType="application/xml"/>
<Override PartName="/word/document.xml" ContentType="application/vnd.↵
    openxmlformats-officedocument.wordprocessingml.document.main+xml"/>
```

```
<Override PartName="/word/settings.xml" ContentType="application/vnd.↵
   openxmlformats-officedocument.wordprocessingml.settings+xml"/>
<Override PartName="/word/styles.xml" ContentType="application/vnd.↵
   openxmlformats-officedocument.wordprocessingml.styles+xml"/>
```

Pay particular attention to the Override element for the part named **/word/document.xml**. This file contains the document's contents, and by inspecting it we can see the impact of tagging the document with the custom schema elements. Figure 7-14 shows the **document.xml** file in Visual Studio. We have collapsed a few of the XML nodes to focus in on one of the résumé request controls.

```
      <w:t>Résumés</w:t>
    </w:r>
  </w:p>
  <w:sdt>
    <w:sdtPr>
      <w:alias w:val="Resume Request"/>
      <w:tag w:val="f0116752-a5c8-4936-8566-44d08a231e31"/>
      <w:id w:val="1732124448"/>
      <w:placeholder>
        <w:docPart w:val="95AE5564C16E4459A363747CDE5F3560"/>
      </w:placeholder>
      <w:showingPlcHdr/>
    </w:sdtPr>
    <w:sdtContent>
      <w:p w14:paraId="3BF2D2DC" w14:textId="77777777" w:rsidR="00074F9C" w:rs
        <w:r w:rsidRPr="00E365EA">
          <w:rPr>
            <w:rStyle w:val="PlaceholderText"/>
          </w:rPr>
          <w:t>Resume request for NORTHAMERICA\edhild due by 4/21/2010</w:t>
        </w:r>
      </w:p>
    </w:sdtContent>
  </w:sdt>
```

Figure 7-14. An Open XML Look at the Resume Request Content Control

Notice that the entire portion of the control we are interested in is wrapped with an **sdt** (structured document tag) element, which is how the text content control is persisted in XML. There are a series of properties (sdtPr), which includes our name of the control (alias) as well as our tag. Later on, the actual content of the control is specified; this includes a paragraph containing our formatted text indicating whose résumé we want and the due date.

Now the good news is that if all this XML is making your eyes glaze over, help is on the way. Remember that the Open XML Format SDK we installed earlier is going to provide an object model that moves us up a layer from manipulating this XML directly. In addition, we will get LINQ support to make finding these nodes in the document relatively painless.

Moving back to the **ProcessFile** method, the code in Listing 7-16 opens the proposal document as a stream and uses the Open XML classes to declare a Word-processing document, letting us find the main document part. By using the alias property in the XML, we use a LINQ query to generate the list of résumé request controls. This LINQ query is looking for SdtBlocks within the document that have an alias property with the value of "Resume Request".

151

Listing 7-16. Finding the Resume Requests in the Proposal

```
using (Stream stream = file.OpenBinaryStream())
{
  using (WordprocessingDocument wpDoc = WordprocessingDocument.Open(stream, true))
  {
    MainDocumentPart docPart = wpDoc.MainDocumentPart;
    DocumentFormat.OpenXml.Wordprocessing.Document doc = docPart.Document;
    //find all resume requests
    string alias = "Resume Request";
    List<SdtBlock> requests = new List<SdtBlock>();
    requests = (from w in doc.Descendants<SdtBlock>()
                where w.Descendants<SdtAlias>().FirstOrDefault() != null &&
                w.Descendants<SdtAlias>().FirstOrDefault().Val.Value == alias
                select w).ToList();
```

Once we have the list of controls, we then want to enumerate through them. For each one, we need to retrieve the GUID that was the unique identifier we put in the tag property of the control. We will use this as a `RequestID` for the tasks so we can tell if we already created a corresponding task in the résumé tasks list. The code in Listing 7-17 retrieves the tag property, then uses the SPMetal-generated `ProposalEntitiesDataContext` to look for any list items in the task list that may have that `RequestID`.

Listing 7-17. Looking to See if a Resume Task Already Exists

```
foreach (SdtBlock request in requests)
{
 //get the tag for this request
 string tag = request.GetFirstChild<SdtProperties>().GetFirstChild<Tag>().Val.Value;

//is there a task list item with that GUID as a RequestID field
using (ProposalEntitiesDataContext dc = new ProposalEntitiesDataContext(web.Url))
{
  var resumeTasks = dc.GetList<Item>("ResumeTasks").Cast<ResumeTasksTask>();
  var foundTasks = from task in resumeTasks
                   where task.RequestID == tag
                   select task;
  if (foundTasks == null || foundTasks.Count<ResumeTasksTask>() == 0)
  {
```

If we don't find a task with the corresponding `RequestID`, then this is the first time we are seeing it in the proposal document and a task should be created. The code in Listing 7-18 creates a new task item, sets its properties, and persists it back to the `ResumeTasks` list. We perform some string manipulation to parse the text of the control in order to set the task properties appropriately. Notice that to resolve the user accounts, we simply look at the `AllUsers` collection of the web. This means that the users must have visited the site or been explicitly granted permission in order for this code to work. There are several different ways to try to resolve user accounts. Chapter 11 provides alternatives if you are interested.

Listing 7-18. Creating a Resume Task

```
SPList resumeTaskList = web.Lists["ResumeTasks"];
SPListItem newTask = resumeTaskList.Items.Add();
newTask["Title"] = "Your resume is requested";
newTask["Body"] = "Please attach your latest resume for inclusion in a proposal";
//parse current content for assigned person and date
string instruction = request.GetFirstChild<SdtContentBlock>().↵
   GetFirstChild<Paragraph>().GetFirstChild<Run>().GetFirstChild<Text>().Text;
// Resume request for sample\administrator due by 12/12/2009
string account = instruction.Substring(19, instruction.IndexOf(" ", 19) - 19);
string dateDue = instruction.Substring(instruction.LastIndexOf(" ") + 1,
   instruction.Length - instruction.LastIndexOf(" ") - 1);
SPUser person = web.AllUsers[account];
newTask["AssignedTo"] = person;
newTask["DueDate"] = dateDue;
newTask["ProposalID"] = file.Properties["_dlc_DocId"].ToString();
newTask["RequestID"] = tag;
//save the task
newTask.Update();
}
}
}
```

You have completed enough now to go ahead and deploy the ProposalEvents project. You can just right-click on the project and choose Deploy. Or, just running the project will deploy the feature to your site, activate it, and attach the debugger. Remember that your code will run for a brief period after a proposal has been successfully saved to the site. Be sure to check for résumé tasks as well as the setting of the ProposalID. Figure 7-15 shows the ResumeTasks list for the two requests we made in a test run.

🗋	Your resume is requested ☒ NEW	Ed Hild	Completed	(2) Normal	1/5/2010	100 %	WSYWUWA3HUJ7-3-3	6aa9494d-46e4-4735-b454-ccb99fb412a1
🗋	Your resume is requested ☒ NEW	Chad Wach	Completed	(2) Normal	1/6/2010	100 %	WSYWUWA3HUJ7-3-3	fd361e5a-e5f2-453e-aff5-703feb8b38e2

Figure 7-15. Generated Resume Tasks

The Résumé Tasks Event Handler

Using what you learned in the previous section. Add an additional SharePoint 2010 event receiver to the ProposalEvents project named **ProposalTaskReceiver**. You can do this through the add new item option of the project. This event handler will be tied to the ItemUpdated event of task lists in the site. We only need the updated event this time since our earlier code is responsible for adding the task. We now need to respond when the user completes the task and attaches a résumé in the form of an Open XML-based Word document. Since much of code is concerned with checking to make sure the task is related to a proposal, the task is complete, and there is indeed a Word attachment, we won't include every line of code here. Again, please download the accompanying code for this chapter so you can follow along.

The code in Listing 7-19 starts the heavy lifting by retrieving the attached résumé as a stream and then uses the ProposalID field to query the Proposals library for the corresponding proposal document.

Listing 7-19. Retrieve the Attachment and Find the Proposal Document

```
//retrieve attachment
string resumeAttachment = String.Empty;
resumeAttachment = properties.ListItem.Attachments.UrlPrefix +
                   properties.ListItem.Attachments[0];
SPFile resumeFile = properties.Web.GetFile(resumeAttachment);
//make sure it is a word document
if (resumeAttachment.EndsWith(".docx"))
{
  //get the proposal document
  SPFile proposalFile = null;
  using (ProposalEntitiesDataContext dc = new ProposalEntitiesDataContext(↵
    properties.WebUrl))
  {
    Microsoft.SharePoint.Linq.EntityList<ProposalsDocument> proposals =
        dc.GetList<ProposalsDocument>("Proposals");
    var found = from doc in proposals.ToList()
                where doc.DocumentIDValue ==
                      properties.ListItem["ProposalID"].ToString()
                select doc.Name;
    string name = found.First<String>();
    proposalFile = properties.Web.Folders["Proposals"].Files[name];
  }
```

Next, the method opens the proposal document as a stream and uses the Open XML Format SDK classes to access the main document part. The LINQ query shown in Listing 7-20 is then used to find the résumé request using the alias and the tag property, which needs to match the RequestID field of the task.

Listing 7-20. Finding the Corresponding Resume Request Control in the Proposal

```
//find the resume request
string alias = "Resume Request";
List<SdtBlock> requests = new List<SdtBlock>();
requests = (from w in doc.Descendants<SdtBlock>()
            where w.Descendants<SdtAlias>().FirstOrDefault() != null &&
            w.Descendants<SdtAlias>().FirstOrDefault().Val.Value == alias &&
            w.Descendants<Tag>().FirstOrDefault() != null &&
            w.Descendants<Tag>().FirstOrDefault().Val.Value ==
                properties.ListItem["RequestID"].ToString()
            select w).ToList();
```

Once we have found the correct location for the résumé, we prepare for the insertion by creating an `AltChunk`. An `AltChunk` in Word is a way of inserting additional content without having the merge all the XML yourself. This is even more time-saving when you consider that the posted résumé might contain embedded object like images, smart art, and so forth that would only be referred to using relationships in the document part's XML. `AltChunks` do all the hard work for you. As you can see in Listing 7-21, we create a new `AltChunk` with a unique name, feed it the résumé using the résumé's stream, and then remove the request content control we had as a placeholder. This is the line of code that calls the `Remove` method. Since the résumé has been provided, there is no need to keep the placeholder around that told us of the request. The last two lines simply commit the changes we have made back to the stream of the proposal document.

Listing 7-21. Inserting the Résumé into the Proposal

```
//build the addition
string chunkId = String.Format("AltChunkId{0}", properties.ListItemId.ToString());
AlternativeFormatImportPart chunk = docPart.AddAlternativeFormatImportPart↵
   (AlternativeFormatImportPartType.WordprocessingML, chunkId);
chunk.FeedData(resumeFile.OpenBinaryStream());
AltChunk altChunk = new AltChunk();
altChunk.Id = chunkId;
SdtBlock newBlock = new SdtBlock();
newBlock.AppendChild(altChunk);
requests[0].InsertBeforeSelf(newBlock);
//remove the request content control
requests[0].Remove();
//save the result
doc.Save();
wpDoc.Close();
```

Finally, we need to save the modified stream back to document in the proposals library. There is a bit of an issue in that the document could be locked while we are trying to make this change. The possibilities are: no lock at all, a shared lock, or an exclusive lock. An exclusive lock is placed on the file if a user has explicitly checked it out. A shared lock occurs if, say, the sales person still has the proposal open in Microsoft Word, but hasn't checked out the file. The reason for the shared lock is that Microsoft Word actually supports co-authoring. This is new functionality to the 2010 stack that allows multiple users to work on a Word document at the same time and, as they save back to the library, they pick up each other's changes. In this scenario, co-authoring is not really happening with another user, but rather with our code running on the server. It is worth pointing out that in a production system, you should probably code this portion as a workflow so you can set a timer and retry if there is an exclusive lock. This chapter is complex enough already, though, so let's go with the assumption that are sales people are trained not to check out proposals exclusively. (See Listing 7-22.) Redeploy the ProposalEvents project. Figure 7-16 shows a résumé merged back into the proposal.

Listing 7-22. Saving the Changed Proposal Document

```
if (proposalFile.LockType != SPFile.SPLockType.Exclusive)
{
  proposalFile.CreateSharedAccessRequest();
  proposalFile.SaveBinary(stream);
  proposalFile.RemoveSharedAccessRequest();
}
```

Contoso Proposal #WSYWUWA3HUJ7-5-1

Lorem ipsum dolor sit amet, consectetur adipiscing elit. Donec ut ligula id mauris luctus cursus. Vestibulum imperdiet malesuada viverra. In hac habitasse platea dictumst. In sed lectus vitae eros venenatis sodales. Maecenas lacus orci, sodales et molestie nec, rhoncus a eros. Vivamus augue magna, gravida a sodales non, faucibus quis neque. Morbi tristique nibh non metus hendrerit facilisis. Aliquam gravida vestibulum lectus vitae elementum. Mauris condimentum elementum sodales. Ut ac nunc nec lacus sagittis consectetur. Cras vitae nulla non mauris cursus egestas non quis lorem. Sed tempor ultricies urna, ut bibendum tortor tincidunt nec.

Résumés

Ed Hild is a Technology Architect at the Microsoft Technology Center in Reston, VA specializing in Portal and Collaboration solutions. At the MTC, he meets daily with both commercial- and public-sector customers to discuss business requirements and map them to the Microsoft platform. He helps customers understand product features, best practices, and necessary customizations for them to realize SharePoint's full potential. Ed has previously presented at Microsoft Dev Days, Tech Ed, and Microsoft SharePoint Conference events as well as many local area user groups. He published an advanced SharePoint developer book through Apress entitled: Pro SharePoint Solution Development and was included in the MSPress Microsoft Office SharePoint Server 2007 Best Practices book. Ed's previous experiences include a high school teacher, government contractor, Microsoft Certified Trainer and lead developer at a Microsoft partner.

Figure 7-16. The Merged Proposal Document

Incorporating Word Automation Services

Since our scenario involves sending this constructed proposal to a customer, we have to address the fact that it isn't appropriate to send the Word document because of its relationship to the VSTO solution. Even if we could strip away the assembly, it is not a given that the destination customer has the ability to read our Open XML-formatted file. Though it's possible to detach a VSTO customization (http://msdn.microsoft.com/en-us/library/bb772099(VS.100).aspx), it requires some more code and only solves half of the problem. Instead, we are going to use this opportunity to build a SharePoint workflow that leverages the new SharePoint 2010 Word Automation Services to create a PDF version of the document. Word Automation Services is server-side functionality that solves a key problem for enterprises related to doing bulk format conversions of files. Basically think of the ability to perform Save As operations on Word documents to other formats. This SharePoint Service is able to do this on sets of files, and to do it as a background process so it will not have a significant impact on the server. This is, of course, without having the Microsoft Word desktop application installed. We do need to write some code, however, to schedule our proposal document for conversion, and in this solution we have decided to encapsulate this functionality in a workflow. The choice of a workflow is a bit arbitrary, but looking at the big picture, this conversion would likely be the last step of a human-oriented approval process. We will add this workflow project to the solution that contained our other projects earlier. So right-click on the solution and choose to add a new project. Under the C# language node, select SharePoint and then 2010 to display the SharePoint 2010 project templates. From the list of Visual Studio installed templates, select the Sequential Workflow template. Name the project **PublishToPDF**. Your New Project dialog should look like Figure 7-17.

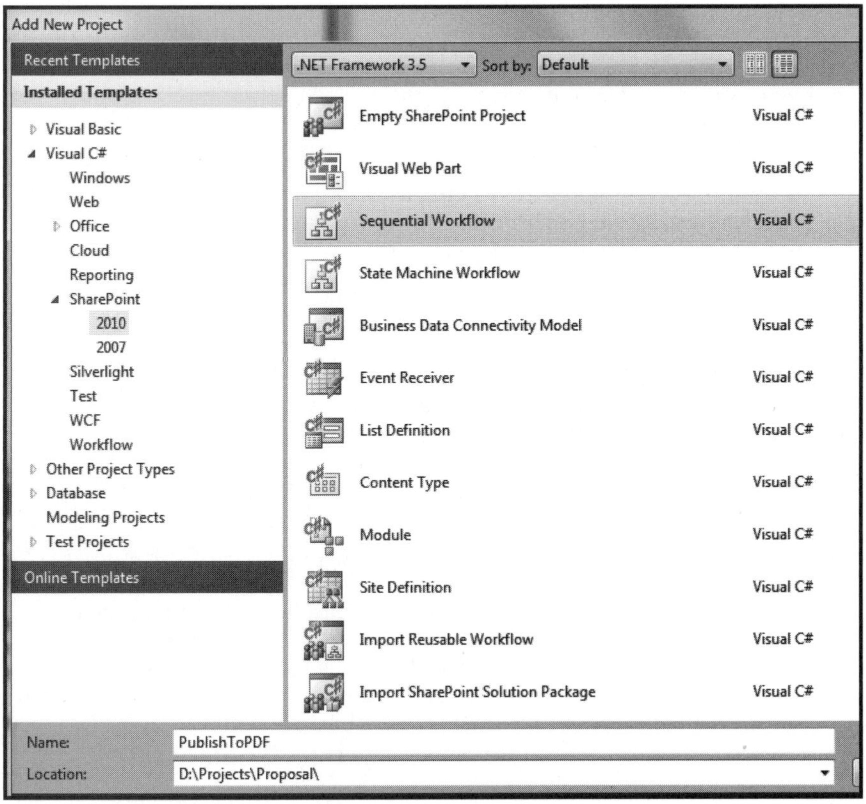

Figure 7-17. Creating the PublishToPDF workflow project

Clicking OK will start the SharePoint Customization Wizard. Specify the SharePoint site we have been working with (such as `http://edhild3/sites/sales`) and select a farm-level solution. Name the workflow **PublishToPDF** and, since this workflow will be operating on our proposal documents, select a List Workflow. The next screen configures the association of the workflow with the library. Be sure in the first drop-down to choose **Proposals**. The defaults for the other settings are fine. Since we are focused on building the solution in a development environment, on the next dialog, choose to allow the workflow only to be manually started. Click **Finish** and Visual Studio will add the project to the solution.

Once the new project is created, the solution will already have a few files by default. The `Workflow1` node will be the focus of most of our attention. Workflows in Visual Studio are really a function of Windows Workflow Foundation and are presented in Visual Studio with a flow-chart type of design experience. There are entire books on Windows Workflow Foundation and, in fact, SharePoint-specific workflows so we will only provide enough information to complete the necessary tasks here. Chapter 11 has a larger focus on workflows and goes into much more detail.

Before jumping into the actual code that communicates with Word Automation Services, let's get a few other things out of the way. There are a few assemblies we need to add references to:

- **Microsoft.Office.Word.Server**: This assembly gives us access Word Automation Services functionality. By default, it is located at `C:\Program Files\Common Files\Microsoft Shared\Web Server Extensions\14\ISAPI`. You may receive a warning about a version of the .NET Framework and the System.Web.DataVisualization. Just continue adding the reference; we will take care of that warning with the next few references.

- **System.Web**: This assembly is part of the .NET Framework and should show up in the .NET tab of the references dialog. Be sure to choose the version from the 2.0 framework. The runtime version should be version 2.0.50727.

- **System.Web.DataVisualization**: Be careful adding this reference as we do not need the version of this assembly that ships as part of version 4.0 of the .NET Framework. Instead, we need to look for the one tied to version 3.5. It may be listed in your .NET Add Reference tab. If it is not, the good news is that this was part of the prerequisites for your SharePoint installation as it is required for the Chart controls. You should be able to find this assembly at `C:\Program Files (x86)\Microsoft Chart Controls\Assemblies`. You only need `System.Web.DataVisualization.dll,` not the additional Design assembly.

Now that the appropriate references have been added, you can add the `using` statement for Word Automation Services into the code-behind file of Workflow1. This statement is: `using Word = Microsoft.Office.Word.Server;`

Figure 7-18 shows the design surface of the workflow you need to build. Basically, there are only two shapes that need to be added. A code activity shape will contain our code for communicating to the Word Automation Services functionality. You can find this shape in the Visual Studio toolbox under the Windows Workflow v3.0 heading. The second shape is SharePoint-specific. It is a LogToHistoryListActivity shape and can be found in the toolbox under the SharePoint Workflow heading. This shape allows us to record entries in the history list of the SharePoint site as a form of audit trail. If you look at the example in the code download, you'll see that this shape has a History Description property that we set to "**Document submitted for conversion**" in order to inform users that their request was received and recorded.

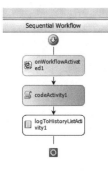

Figure 7-18. The PublishToPDF Workflow

Double-clicking on the code activity will create an event handler for the code in Listing 7-23. The code begins by building a URL for the proposal document that we would like converted. A new conversion job object is then configured with a name, user context, and the source and destination file names. You might wonder how the service knows that we want a PDF file. The conversion job can automatically determine the output format by looking at the destination URL, which in our case ends in ".pdf". You can gain finer control over the conversion using a ConversionJobSettings object as described at `http://msdn.microsoft.com/en-us/library/microsoft.office.word.server.conversions.conversionjobsettings_properties(office.14).aspx` . Lastly, the conversion job is started, which requires us to run as the system account since the current user may not have enough permission to kick it off. Go ahead and deploy your workflow and manually start it on a test proposal.

Listing 7-23. Code to Schedule Conversion using Word Automation Services

```
private void codeActivity1_ExecuteCode(object sender, EventArgs e)
{
  string file = workflowProperties.WebUrl + "/" + workflowProperties.ItemUrl;
  //schedule the conversion
  Word.Conversions.ConversionJob conversionJob = new ↵
      Word.Conversions.ConversionJob("Word Automation Services");
  conversionJob.Name = "Proposal Conversion";
  //run under the user that ran the workflow
  conversionJob.UserToken = workflowProperties.OriginatorUser.UserToken;
  conversionJob.AddFile(file, file.Replace(".docx", ".pdf"));
  SPSecurity.RunWithElevatedPrivileges(delegate { conversionJob.Start(); });
}
```

It is important to realize that when this workflow completes, all we have done is successfully scheduled a task that informs Word Automation Services that it has work to do. In fact, you can go ahead and deploy the project and run the workflow on a proposal document. Don't be surprised that the workflow will report a completed status without a new PDF file showing up in your document library. This is because Word Automation Services runs on a schedule (default every 15 minutes) and won't create that PDF until its next execution time. This feature is to help keep this functionality from overwhelming server resources; however, it really impacts demonstrations. The good news is that you can manually tell this timer job to run. Use the following steps to make the job run on demand and you should get your PDF file. You could also do this via code or Windows PowerShell commands. Of course make sure you have Adobe Acrobat Reader installed if you want to open it.

1. Open SharePoint 2010's Central Administration.

2. Under the Monitoring heading, click **Check job status**.

3. Click Job **Definitions** in the left-hand navigation.

4. Locate the Word Automation Services Timer Job which may require you to page through the listing of jobs since they are in alphabetical order. Click the name of the timer job.

5. Click the **Run Now** button to force this service to process your conversion request.

6. You should be able to see this job execute by looking at either the Running Jobs or Job History portions of this administration tool. When it is complete, you should have the PDF file shown in Figure 7-19.

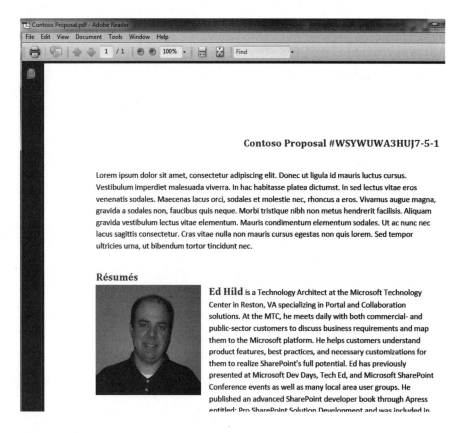

Figure 7-19. PDF version of the proposal

Important Lessons

This proposal document-assembly solution incorporated several key techniques that are worth highlighting as they can easily be reused in other projects.

Content controls in the body of a document: Content controls are a Microsoft Word feature that allow you to promote data into the body of the document. In this case, we used quick parts, which are already configured content controls for metadata properties of the document.

VSTO document-level project: In this solution we extended the document library's Microsoft Word template file with custom functionality that turned the document into a tool for building proposals. Since our extensions only make sense for the specific template, we created the solution as a document-level project. The extensions included a document actions pane as well as new backstage functionality.

Event handlers that process the document using Open XML: In this solution, we needed to parse the document on the server to look for résumé request controls whenever the document was saved or modified. SharePoint event handlers enabled us to respond to these events, and the Open XML SDK eased the task of querying through the XML of the file.

SPMetal: This solution used the SPMetal tool to construct entity classes for working with SharePoint site data. By using these classes, we were able to make LINQ-style queries on SharePoint lists and refer to fields of list items with IntelliSense. This resulted in fewer lines of code that were less error-prone.

Merging document chunks into a central document: This solution needed to be able to take résumés and inject them into the proposal document. This work had to be done on the server. We were able to use the AltChunks technique to streamline the necessary Open XML notation to perform the merge.

Scheduling document conversions with Word Automation Services: SharePoint 2010 has a new service that can perform scheduled conversions of Microsoft Word documents. In this solution we used a workflow as the scheduling mechanism.

Extension Points

While coding this example, we thought of several variations to the solution that we didn't incorporate. Mostly, these were not included because they distracted from the overall objective of the solution. We call them out now as extension points since they may be applicable to a specific project you are working on.

Convert the résumé task event handler into the workflow: In our example, we just created another event handler for merging the résumé into the proposal document since we had just taken a large part of the chapter to teach you the details of event handlers. The only issue is that the proposal document could potentially be exclusively locked by a user. You would need a way of waiting and retrying to get a successful shared lock. Changing this part of the solution into a workflow would be a way to accomplish this.

Make the people-search web service call asynchronous: Currently, the actions pane only uses a wait cursor as the method to inform the user that work is being performed. Also, all of the work is being performed on the same thread. A better approach would be to use the async version of the web service call and specify a delegate that should be called when the call is complete.

Incorporate BCS quick parts from an external list: You may well have some sort of CRM database whose data would be part of this proposal. You can use the business connectivity services functionality of SharePoint to register this repository and create an external list in the SharePoint site. By adding external data columns as metadata properties of the Proposals library, you would gain quick parts for embedding the external customer data into the document. Chapter 10 contains a good starting point for building this extension.

Further Reading

Here are a number of links to resources we think you'll find useful:

- How to Query Search using the Web Service `http://www.dotnetmafia.com/blogs/ dotnettipoftheday/archive/2008/07/17/how-to-query-search-using-the-web-service.aspx`

- Using SharePoint Web Services `http://www.obacentral.com/en/Learn/ Recommended%20Reading/Using%20SharePoint%20Web%20Services.pdf`

- Adding References for Word Automation Services `http://msdn.microsoft.com/ en-us/library/ee559644(office.14).aspx`

- VSTO Deployment via SharePoint `http://www.craigbailey.net/vsto-deployment-via-sharepoint/`

- Word Automation Services `http://msdn.microsoft.com/en-us/library/ ee558278(office.14).aspx`

- Brian Jones: Open XML Formats Blog `http://blogs.msdn.com/brian_jones/`

- Intro to Word XML `http://blogs.msdn.com/brian_jones/archive/2005/ 07/05/435772.aspx`

- SPMetal `http://msdn.microsoft.com/en-us/library/ee538255(office.14).aspx`

- OpenXMLDeveloper.org `http://openxmldeveloper.org/`

- Introduction to the Office 2010 Backstage View for Developers `http://msdn. microsoft.com/en-us/library/ee691833(office.14).aspx`

- Customizing the Office 2010 Backstage View for Developers `http://msdn.microsoft.com/en-us/library/ee815851(office.14).aspx`

- How to Use altChunk for Document Assembly `http://blogs.msdn.com/ericwhite/archive/2008/10/27/how-to-use-altchunk-for-document-assembly.aspx`

■ ■ ■

CHAPTER 8

Extending PowerPoint to Build a Presentation Based on Site Content

Windows SharePoint Services (WSS) provides the enterprise with easily creatable workspaces where information can be collected and shared among users working toward a common goal. This goal could be many different things—preparation for an event, execution of a business process, or even creating materials for a project. Often, organizations build presentations as an output of this collaboration or for routinely reporting on the status of the team. Microsoft PowerPoint gives users a powerful canvas for constructing presentations. Too often, however, information workers expend too much effort and time to locate, duplicate, and organize information into the presentation. Moreover, the presentation's authors are likely retyping, cutting and pasting, or otherwise manually importing content. Not only are we looking to reduce this effort, we also want to increase its accuracy. So for this chapter, we will detail how, as a developer, you can extend PowerPoint to provide a tool that is capable of building out slides populated with content stored in a SharePoint site.

Real-World Examples

Just about any time you have a chain of command in an organization, people farther down are collecting, summarizing, and reporting up. Not surprisingly, this happens often in the military. Each of our branches spends a considerable amount of resources aggregating information from outside content repositories and applications to construct briefings for higher officers. It is not unheard of for a team to get an extremely early start every day to gather the information required for a commander's briefing. These efforts are far too manual today, requiring authors to dig through old e-mails in organizational mailboxes, search file shares, and copy data from the user interfaces of multiple applications. The commercial world is not too different in this regard. Just look at any company that has projects and managers responsible for them. They're equally mired in the manual creation of presentations, whether to report the status of a project internally or to present to the customer.

Solution Overview

We will extend Microsoft PowerPoint to create a tool that lets presentation authors import data from a SharePoint site. To provide some context for our solution, we have focused our efforts on building a briefing presentation made of imported items that reside in a typical meeting workspace. When the custom import tool is launched, it will examine a user-supplied site to see if it contains an objectives list, a list of agenda items, or any slide libraries. The objectives and agenda lists are a part of the default template for meeting workspaces in SharePoint. In this sample, we added slide libraries because it is not too farfetched to think that users who are a part of this collaboration may have built slides of their own that should be included in the briefing output. Once the site has been examined, the custom import tool will walk the user through a wizard process, offering to build slides for the content it finds in the site. Note that this tool will provide more functionality than the out-of-the-box slide library integration, enabling the creation of slides for list data.

This application should be flexible enough to support the construction of slides in any presentation the author may be working on. To meet this requirement, the solution will be an application-level add-in. As an add-in, this tool will always be available from within PowerPoint. To provide a launching point, the tool will add controls to the Microsoft Office Ribbon interface. From the Ribbon, the author will be able to start the tool, which presents itself as a custom task pane. This pane presents the user with the wizard experience of steps and prompts, building slides as instructed in the current presentation.

As the wizard executes, it asks the user if she wishes to have a presentation slide built for the content it finds on the site. If the user chooses to build a slide for the objectives, the add-in will query the SharePoint site for the objectives list items and place them in a new slide as a bulleted list. If the user chooses to build a slide with the agenda, the add-in will query the SharePoint site for the agenda list items and place them in a new slide displayed within a table. In addition, the add-in will populate the Notes page of the slide with additional details, such as owner of the agenda item or any notes contained in the SharePoint site. Lastly, the add-in will display a list of links to slide libraries it finds on the site. Each link will open the library in the browser so the user can select slides to import into her presentation using the slide library import process.

Solution Walkthrough

Now we will detail the major elements of the solution and the decisions that were made in coding it. The walkthrough will show you how to get started with Visual Studio to create the Briefing PowerPoint add-in. We will take a look at how you can use Visual Studio Tools for Office (VSTO) to extend the Office Ribbon interface, and we'll examine the wizard process so you can see how we simplified coding an experience where the user moves through a series of steps, each representing a specific function with its own interface and actions. We will then explain the work that goes into building each of the PowerPoint slides for our briefing. This work includes creating new slides, placing content as a bulleted list, inserting and populating a table, placing content on a slide's notes page, and linking in the SharePoint slide libraries.

Creating the Project

Using Visual Studio to build a PowerPoint add-in project is made very straightforward by VSTO's project types. Simply start Visual Studio and select to create a new project. Under the C# language node, select Office and then 2010 to display the VSTO project templates.

From the list of Visual Studio installed templates, select PowerPoint 2010 Add-in. Name the project BuildBriefing. Leave the default option of creating a new solution and confirm that the .NET framework drop-down at the top of the dialog is set to .NET Framework 4. As discussed in Chapter 4, there are several advantages to using version 4 of the framework for Office development, such as C# support for optional parameters. We want to make sure these advantages are available to us. Your New Project dialog should look like Figure 8-1.

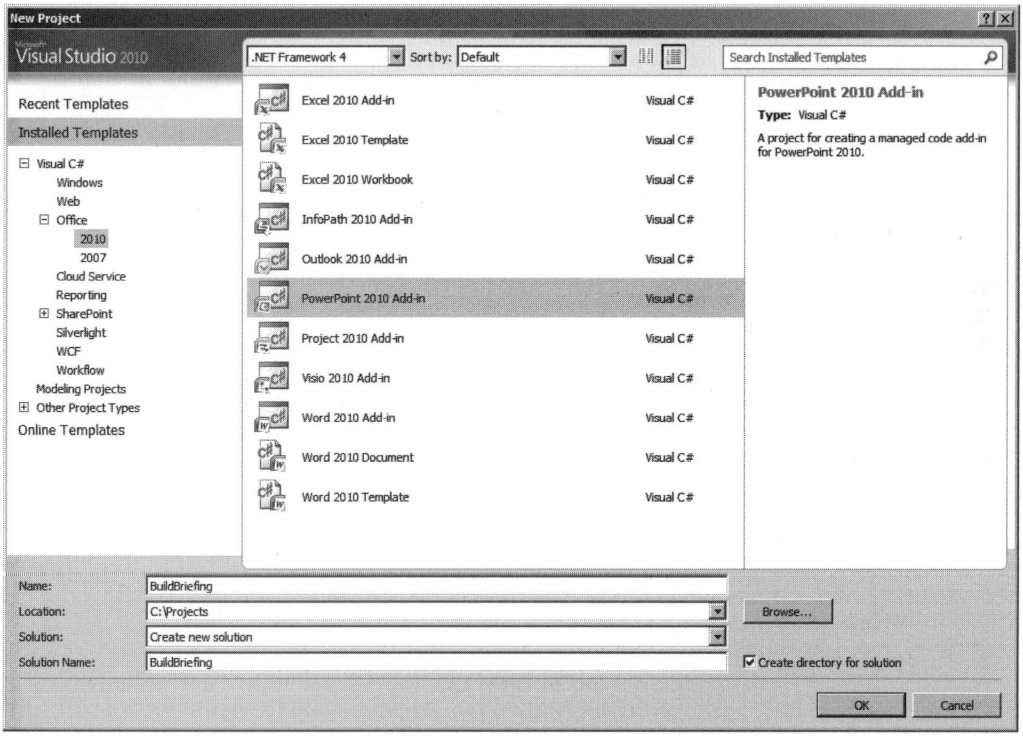

Figure 8-1. Creating a PowerPoint Add-in project

Once the new project is created, your solution will already have a few files by default, which are visible in the Solution Explorer window of Visual Studio. There will be a PowerPoint node that you can expand to see a code file named `ThisAddIn.cs`. This file is the main entry point for add-ins. It is where developers can write code for events at the add-in's application-level scope. Common events include items like Startup and Shutdown.

It is important to understand that this PowerPoint add-in will not have access to the same SharePoint assemblies that make up the server-side object model. This is because the add-in will run within the PowerPoint application on a user's desktop, and therefore remote to the SharePoint server. As you will see a bit later, SharePoint 2010 provides a client-side library to assist with communication. The communication between our add-in and the SharePoint server will be over HTTP. However, the current setting of the project will prevent us from leveraging code that references the `System.Web` assembly. Let's remove this restriction by changing the Target Framework setting for the project so that the client-side library will be permitted. Follow these instructions:

1. Right-click on the BuildBriefing project and choose Properties.

2. On the Application tab, locate the Target Framework selection dialog.

3. Change this setting from .NET Framework 4 Client Profile to .NET Framework 4.

4. Click Yes in the confirmation dialog.

Now we can add the references to the SharePoint 2010 client-side library and runtime for .NET applications. As discussed in Chapter 3, SharePoint 2010 provides several different types of client-side libraries, enabling communication from solutions not running on the server. For this project, add the `Microsoft.SharePoint.Client` and `Microsoft.SharePoint.Client.Runtime` assemblies to the project. These assemblies may be on your .NET tab of the Add Reference dialog. If not, you can find them in the `C:\Program Files\Common Files\Microsoft Shared\Web Server Extensions\14\ISAPI` folder in a default installation.

Customizing the Ribbon

First we need a way for the user to launch the Briefing application from within PowerPoint. To provide this starting point, we will focus our attention on the user interface of the Microsoft Office 2010 system—the Ribbon. The Ribbon interface occupies the top portion of most of the Office applications and presents a different experience from the layered menus and toolbars of Office releases before 2007. This interface is simpler, improving the organization of commands and providing a more graphical representation of options. One of its primary goals is to surface functionality that users desired but didn't know was there because of how buried or obscure many menu items were.

In earlier versions of Office, developers spent significant effort writing code utilizing the `CommandBars` object to create new buttons, extend menus, hide existing options, and make other user interface customizations. By using compiled code to make these changes, developers found themselves writing lengthy code for a relatively simple result. Moreover, the code was typically not portable from project to project and couldn't be reused across different Office applications. So, in addition to providing an enhanced experience for the end user, the Ribbon interface offers the developer an improved programming model for manipulating it.

The biggest difference in the Ribbon programming model is that customizations to the user interface are defined using XML, not compiled code. Through a custom XML file, a developer can manipulate the Ribbon interface, controlling its tabs, groups, and controls, and adding new elements as well as hiding default ones. Since the customizations are stored in an XML file, they are easier to reuse in different projects and different Office applications. Typically, an add-in also includes a class that implements the proper interfaces to serve up the XML markup to the Office application, as well as code for callbacks. These callbacks are code that will run in response to the user interacting with the Ribbon. You might think you are in for writing a ton of code to get your add-in, XML file, and class to align properly. Fortunately, with the VSTO 2010 release, you have the option of simply ignoring this plumbing and using a ribbon designer to make your customizations. As you will see, though, you still have the option of reverting to the traditional XML-only/non-designer approach that is sometimes necessary with more advanced changes, such as customizations to context menus or backstage (discussed in Chapter 4).

Before getting started with the Briefing project, let's take a look at the desired end-state of our ribbon customizations. Figure 8-2 shows that the Briefing add-in has customized the Office Ribbon to include new items on the Add-Ins tab. On this tab there is a SharePoint group with a toggle button control that displays Briefing with a custom graphic. When the user presses this button, the application displays a custom task pane to walk her through the wizard process.

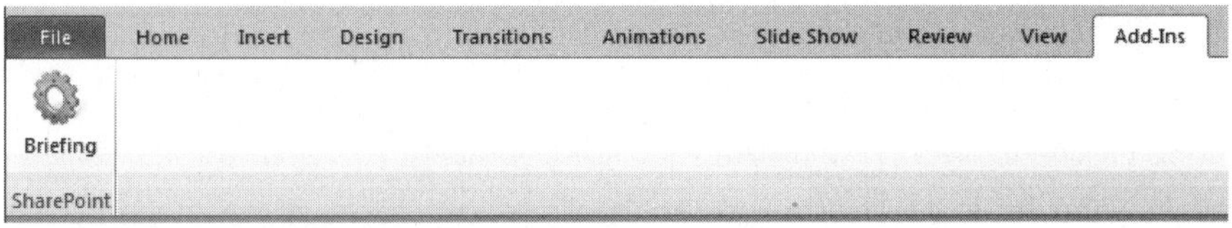

Figure 8-2. The customized ribbon interface

To implement this in your Briefing project, first add a new item. From the Add New Item dialog, select the Office installed templates node and choose Ribbon (Visual Designer). Notice the other option to build your ribbon customization through the XML method discussed earlier. Leave the name `Ribbon1.cs` and click Add. When the designer opens within Visual Studio, it will default to placing your customization on the PowerPoint built-in Add-Ins tab. We will use this tab, but you could choose to create your own. Right-click in the grey area of the ribbon next to the Add-Ins tab and you will see the commands to add or remove tabs. For now, just click on the group control, `group1`, and you will be able to change its label property to `SharePoint`. From the toolbox, double-click the `ToggleButton` control to add our button to the group. A `ToggleButton` is similar to regular Windows forms buttons except that it remains in an on or off (pressed or not pressed) state rather than reacting as to a single click. Change the following properties of the button:

- Set the toggle button's `ControlSize` property to `RibbonControlSizeLarge`.

- Use the images property to add the icon. Clicking the "..." button will open a dialog that lets you import an image into this add-in's resource file. For our solution, we used a gear image from the Visual Studio graphics library. If you installed the graphics library, it is a zip file whose default location is `C:\Program Files (x86)\Microsoft Visual Studio 10.0\Common7\VS2010ImageLibrary\1033`. After you open the file, you can find this graphic in the `Objects\png_format\WinVista` folder.

- Set the toggle button's `Label` property to **Briefing**.

- Set the toggle button's `ScreenTip` to **Import SharePoint items to create a briefing**. This text will appear when the user hovers over the button.

- Make sure the `ShowImage` property is set to True so your gear graphic displays.

Now the toggle button needs to actually do something. With the ribbon designer, adding this activity is the same as with most controls in Visual Studio. Double-click the toggle button to create a click event handler in the code-behind file. This code will take on the responsibility of hiding or showing the custom task pane interface to the user. We will match the pressed state of the button with whether or not the task pane should be visible. The complete event handler is shown in Listing 8-1.

Listing 8-1. The toggle button's click event handler

```
private void toggleButton1_Click(object sender, RibbonControlEventArgs e)
{
    Globals.ThisAddIn.ctp.Visible = toggleButton1.Checked;
}
```

Now this code will not resolve since we have not defined the custom task pane **ctp** object in the **ThisAddIn** class. In VSTO projects, a task pane can simply be a Windows Forms user control. Add one to the project—we named ours **ucTaskPane**. You can also use Windows Presentation Foundation (WPF) user controls, which are often useful to respond to resizing of a task pane or Office application. Listing 8-2 shows the code in the **ThisAddin.cs** file that loads our task pane during the add-in's startup event.

Listing 8-2. Creating the custom task pane

```
public CustomTaskPane ctp;

private void ThisAddIn_Startup(object sender, System.EventArgs e)
{
  ctp = Globals.ThisAddIn.CustomTaskPanes.Add(new ucTaskPane(), "Custom Briefing");
  ctp.DockPosition = Office.MsoCTPDockPosition.msoCTPDockPositionRight;
  ctp.Width = 250;
}
```

With the ribbon customization, task pane user control, and startup code, you should be able to test your solution. Running the project will launch PowerPoint. Find your customizations to the Ribbon and see how the toggle button controls the visibility of the task pane.

Architecture of the Task Pane and Wizard Step User Controls

The Briefing add-in presents its user interface through a custom task pane that loads to the right-hand side of PowerPoint's application window. The wizard experience for the user is a series of steps. The necessary logic and actions for each of these steps is wrapped into a single user control. Here is the primary goal of each step.

1. Receive the URL of the SharePoint site and examine its contents.

2. Build a presentation slide for the items in the objectives list.

3. Build a presentation slide for the items in the agenda list.

4. Display a list of slide libraries so the user can import presentation slides from the site.

5. Display a conclusion message.

The user may not actually need to do each of these five steps. Based on the examination of the site entered in step 1, it may be appropriate for the wizard to skip certain subsequent steps. For example, if the site does not contain any slide libraries, the user should not even be exposed to step 4. For this reason, our architecture compartmentalizes each of the steps into its own user control. A step user control is responsible for displaying an interface, gathering input from the user, doing its work, and reporting back. The task-pane control serves as a controller, with the responsibility of orchestrating the step controls and collecting the information they report back that may be necessary further down the process. This approach is known as the Model-View-Controller (MVC) pattern. You can read more about this pattern at `http://msdn.microsoft.com/en-us/library/ms978748.aspx`.

To provide uniformity to the step user controls, we defined an object interface with some common elements that each control must implement. This makes it easier for our task-pane controller to interact with them since it can be guaranteed that the elements of the interface are a part of the step control. Listing 8-3 details the contents of the interface.

Listing 8-3. The IStep interface

```
interface IStep
{
  ucTaskPane ParentPane
  {
    get;
  }
  event EventHandler Completed;
  void WorkComplete();
  void Start();
}
```

The `IStep` interface requires that each step user control have the following:

- A read-only property that provides a reference to the task pane.

- An event named `Completed` that will be used to inform the task pane that a particular step has done its work and the task pane should move on.

- A `WorkComplete()` method where the `Completed` event will be fired.

- A `Start()` method that will be called by the task pane, telling the step control that it is its turn in the process.

The task pane controller is a user control but with very little interface. For the most part, it is simply a container that will orchestrate the step controls presenting themselves to the user. The only control placed on the step control at design time is a StatusStrip control with a label for displaying status messages while the step controls do their work. The step controls are loaded during runtime. In the code-behind file for `ucTaskPane`, you will see an instance of each of the `Stepn` controls loaded into an array named `steps` (where *n* represents the sequence number) in its controls collection. Since these are loaded from code, each has a default visibility property of false and is associated with a `wizard_Completed` event handler. In the task pane's load event, the first step control is told to start.

Most of the remaining code in the task pane is dedicated either to orchestrating the hiding or showing of step controls or to collecting information from the work they do. At this point, we recommend you grab the code download from the Apress web site and follow along as we will not be listing every line of code in this chapter. The text here will focus on the most interesting sections of code that warrant explanation and leave some of the mundane but necessary code lines (such as declaring variables) for you to view in the download. Listing 8-4 details the critical elements of the step orchestration process.

Listing 8-4. Task pane orchestration of steps

```
private IStep[] steps = new wizardSteps.IStep[] {new step1(),
       new step2(), new step3(), new step4(), new step5() };

private int currentStep = 1;

void wizard_Completed(object sender, EventArgs e)
{
  if (currentStep < steps.length) this.MoveToNextStep();
}

private void MoveToNextStep()
{
  this.Controls[currentStep].Visible = false;
  currentStep++;
  IStep step = (IStep) this.Controls[currentStep];
  step.Start();
}
```

The `currentStep` variable from Listing 8-4 is the task pane's internal cursor that keeps track of which step is being shown to the user. The `wizard_Completed` event handler is a code block that runs when any of the steps have finished their work. Notice that when the controls are loaded into the task pane, each of them is matched with the same event handler. Since the code we are going to run in response is the same for each step, there is no reason to have an event handler code block for each of them individually. The `MoveNextStep()` procedure performs the orchestration. It first hides the control that is currently being displayed. The `currentStep` is used here since the `Controls` collection is zero-based and the `StatusStrip` we added earlier is at position 0. The `MoveToNextStep()` routine then finds the next control. We convert the control to the IStep interface it implements. This gets us access to the `Start()` method. You may be wondering with this code how we account for a step needing to be skipped. The answer is that the `Start()` method of each of the step controls first determines whether it has work to do before showing itself. Listing 8-5 is a representative `Start()` method from step 2.

Listing 8-5. A Sample Step Control Start() Method

```
public void Start()
{
 //get reference to the custom task pane
 taskpane = (ucTaskPane)this.Parent;
 if (ParentPane.HasObjectivesList)
 {
   //show this step
   this.Visible = true;
 }
 else
 {
   //skip over this step
   this.WorkComplete();
 }
}
```

The task pane control also maintains some information obtained from a step control that will be used later on in the process. This includes the URL of the SharePoint site the user entered, whether or not it had any of the lists it could build content from, as well as a collection of information about the slide libraries contained in the site.

The step1 User Control: Examining the Site

The first step control is responsible for examining the SharePoint site specified by the URL the user entered. For our example, we simply created a meeting workspace to act as a test environment and populated it with content. Specifically, the control is looking to see if the site contains a list named Objectives, a list named Agenda, and information on any slide libraries. The Objectives and Agenda lists are there by default, but you will have to create at least one slide library if you want to see that piece in action. Take the following steps to add a slide library to your site:

1. Navigate to your basic meeting workspace site.

2. From the Site Actions menu, choose the View All Site Content link.

3. Click the Create button.

4. Use the Libraries filter and click the Slide Library object. Click the Create button.

5. Enter a name for the slide library. As an example, enter **Meeting Slides**.

6. Since we want the slide library to be the same across all instances of this meeting (if, for example, it had a recurring schedule), choose the Yes radio button in the Change items into a series question.

7. Leave the Versioning radio button at No and click Create.

8. You will be redirected to a page that displays the library's items.

9. Now you will want to have a sample PowerPoint 2010 presentation to upload here. Any presentation with a few slides will do. Save the presentation locally before you publish the slides. Then, from the backstage interface, which is accessible by clicking the File button, choose Save and Send. Select Publish Slides and click the Publish Slides button.

10. This walks you through a wizard that publishes your PowerPoint presentation to the SharePoint site. Be sure to select the checkboxes of the slides you want sent to the site. Click Browse to locate the destination. You will need to specify the URL of your meeting workspace and then select the slide library you created earlier. In our environment, this was `http://edhild3/sites/meeting1`. When finished, the library should contain an item for every slide in your presentation. The slide library breaks apart your presentation into individual slides, which would allow different users to work on different slides at the same time. Be sure to wait for the Publish Slides progress bar located at the bottom of the PowerPoint application window to complete before moving on.

The step control is designed to first ask the user for the URL of the meeting workspace. When the user clicks the Next button, the step control goes to work. To discover information about the lists and libraries contained in the site, the Briefing application will rely on the SharePoint client-side .NET managed API. This API is one of several new libraries to ease the developer experience for building applications that need to talk to SharePoint and are not running on the actual SharePoint server. There are three new client-side APIs: .NET managed, Silverlight, and ECMAScript. Since the PowerPoint add-in is managed code, we will use the corresponding client-side .NET managed API. These new libraries are meant to reduce the complexity that developers often encountered when using the web services provided by SharePoint 2007. Those web services usually did not match the object model hierarchy found in server-side code and often the responses were simply XML fragments that had to be parsed. This meant that a developer could not take the skills and knowledge obtained from writing server code to the client. With the client-side APIs of SharePoint 2010, this problem is solved since these libraries present the same object-model hierarchy. There are subtle differences around data retrieval. Let's start with Listing 8-6, which establishes the client-side context and retrieves the lists that exist within the meeting workspace.

Listing 8-6. Retrieving the site's lists and libraries

```
private void btnNext_Click(object sender, EventArgs e)
{
  this.btnNext.Enabled = false;
  this.ParentPane.Message = "Examining Site";
  this.UseWaitCursor = true;

  this.ParentPane.SiteUrl = this.txtSiteUrl.Text;
  //establish client context for accessing SharePoint content
 using (SPClient.ClientContext ctx = new
                SPClient.ClientContext(this.ParentPane.SiteUrl))
    {
      SPClient.Web web = ctx.Web;
      SPClient.ListCollection coll = web.Lists;
      ctx.Load(coll);
      //gather default properties about all lists in the site
      ctx.ExecuteQuery();
```

The first two lines of code make the user aware that the application is doing some work. We disable the button to keep users from pressing it multiple times, change the cursor, and display a meaningful message in the status strip of the task pane. The next section is all about getting information on the lists that exist in the meeting workspace. Much like code you would write on the server-side, the first step is to establish a context. On the server this would be a `SPContext` object, but in the .NET managed client-side API, the equivalent is a `ClientContext` object. Just like its server-side counterpart, the context is established by passing in the URL of the site you will be examining. Since this code isn't running on the server, the client-side APIs are much more explicit about when the server will be queried to retrieve data. In fact, if you set a breakpoint at the beginning of the `btnNext_Click` event handler and debug this code, you'll notice that `web.Lists` is actually empty until after the context's `ExecuteQuery` method is called. With the client-side API, you must specify what it is you want retrieved, and then an execute method retrieves it. In this example, we are only passing in that we would like info on the `Lists` collection of the meeting workspace. Since we didn't provide any more detail, the resulting `ListCollection` object will be populated with the lists that exist and their default properties, but not any list items. Once that has been done, the method continues with the code in Listing 8-7, which shows how you can use a LINQ query to see if the site contains an Agenda list. The same technique is used for finding the Objectives list.

Listing 8-7. Looking for the list named Agenda

```
var q1 = from list in coll
         where list.Title == "Agenda"
         select list;
if (q1 != null) this.ParentPane.HasAgendaList = true;
```

Looking for libraries that are actually slide libraries is just as easy. In this case, we can't go by the title of the library since the libraries could be named anything. Fortunately, all slide libraries are based on the same template, which has an ID of 2100. This ID was found by digging through the out-of-the-box features of the SharePoint environment, located at `C:\Program Files\Common Files\Microsoft Shared\Web Server Extensions\14\TEMPLATE\FEATURES`. If you locate the SlideLibrary folder, you'll find a `SlideLibrary.xml` element file that defines the list template and its ID of 2100. So Listing 8-8 shows how to locate these libraries in the SharePoint meeting workspace site.

Listing 8-8. Looking for slide libraries

```
var q3 = from list in coll
         where list.BaseTemplate == 2100
         select list;
if (q3 != null)
{
   this.ParentPane.HasSlideLibrary = true;
```

For slide libraries, our application is going to need more information than simply the fact that there are some in the site. We would like to have URLs and names for these libraries so we can provide links directly to them in the task pane. So the remainder of this method iterates through the libraries, capturing this information in a **struct** helper class called **LibraryItem**. As Listing 8-9 shows, we have to do a little manipulation to make sure we are capturing a full URL that our client application can use.

Listing 8-9. Recording URLs and names for slide libraries

```
Uri link = new Uri(this.ParentPane.SiteUrl);
foreach (SPClient.List list in coll)
{
  if (list.BaseTemplate == 2100)
  {
    LibraryItem slideLibrary = new LibraryItem();
    slideLibrary.Name = list.Title;
    if (link.Port == 80 || link.Port == 443)
    {
      slideLibrary.Url = link.Scheme + "://" + link.Host + list.DefaultViewUrl;
    }
    else
    {
```

```
        slideLibrary.Url = link.Scheme + "://" + link.Host + ":" +
                          link.Port + list.DefaultViewUrl;
    }
    this.ParentPane.SlideLibraries.Add(slideLibrary);
}
```

Now the control has completed its examination of the site and informed the task pane of the information it found. As you can see in the code download, this control then wraps up its work in the same manner as the others. It sets a status message for the task pane and calls the `WorkComplete()` method. From there, the step control raises its `Completed` event so the task pane can take control and move the processes along to the next step.

The step2 User Control: Building Objectives

The step2 user control is responsible for building a presentation slide containing the content in the SharePoint site's Objectives list. The task pane will shift control over to this step by calling its `Start` method. In this method, the control checks to see if the Briefing add-in had previously found an Objectives list on the user's site. If so, the step exposes its user interface to the user. If not, the control simply calls `WorkComplete` to raise its `Completed` event, skipping itself and moving on to the next step in the process. Assuming the user interface is displayed, the user is presented with two options. The first is for the application to build a presentation slide containing a bulleted list of the objectives items from the site. The second is to simply skip this feature and move onto the next step.

If the user chooses to have an objectives slide built, the add-in again uses the SharePoint client-side .NET managed API. This time, we are interested in getting all the items in the Objectives list. The process is the same as before—we tell the API what we would like retrieved and then call the context's `ExecuteQuery` method. Notice how the code in Listing 8-10 specifies that we want the Objectives list along with a Collaborative Application Markup Language (CAML) query. CAML queries are not new to SharePoint developers. They involve writing what look like SQL select statements in an XML-based string format. However, you won't see that in Listing 8-10, because the client-side object model has a CamlQuery class that makes it easier to write these queries, especially when all you want is all of the default properties of all the items.

Listing 8-10. Requesting items in the Objectives list

```
SPClient.Web web = ctx.Web;
SPClient.ListCollection coll = web.Lists;
SPClient.List objectivesList = coll.GetByTitle("Objectives");
SPClient.CamlQuery query = SPClient.CamlQuery.CreateAllItemsQuery();
SPClient.ListItemCollection items = objectivesList.GetItems(query);
ctx.Load(items);
ctx.ExecuteQuery();
```

At this point, the `objectivesList` object contains each individual objective from the site and we are ready to build our PowerPoint slide in the user's presentation. Listing 8-11 details how the new slide is added and how the Objectives are populated as a bulleted list.

Listing 8-11. Requesting Items in the Objectives List

```
PowerPoint.Slide slide;
PowerPoint.Presentation presentation;
presentation = Globals.ThisAddIn.Application.ActivePresentation;
PowerPoint.CustomLayout layout = presentation.SlideMaster.CustomLayouts↵
                  [PowerPoint.PpSlideLayout.ppLayoutText];
slide = presentation.Slides.AddSlide(presentation.Slides.Count+1,layout);
slide.Shapes.Title.TextFrame.TextRange.Text = "Objectives";

StringBuilder sBuilder = new StringBuilder();
foreach (SPClient.ListItem item in items)
{
  sBuilder.Append((string)item.FieldValues["Objective"]);
  sBuilder.Append("\n");
}
slide.Shapes[2].TextFrame.TextRange.Text = sBuilder.ToString().TrimEnd('\n');
Globals.ThisAddIn.Application.ActiveWindow.View.GotoSlide(slide.SlideIndex);
```

To construct the slide, the code obtains a reference to the user's active presentation and uses its slide collection's **AddSlide** method. The **AddSlide** method takes two parameters: the index where the new slide should be placed and the layout the slide should use. The line before this shows how to grab the particular layout you want using the **SlideMaster**'s **CustomLayouts** collection. In this case, we want the slide to be at the end of the presentation, and the layout should be the one that has only a title and textbox. With the slide created, the content is placed on it by accessing its various shapes. Because of our layout selection, there are two shapes that need our attention. The first is at index one and it represents the title of the slide. This shape is easily accessed by the **Title** property of the slide's shapes collection, which is set to the literal string "Objectives". The second shape, at index two, is populated using a **StringBuilder**. The text of the **StringBuilder** is the text of each objective, separated by a carriage return (\n). Placing the carriage return character is what gives us each objective as a bullet item. Of course, we do need to clean up the carriage return after the last item. The last line of Listing 8-11 directs PowerPoint to make our new slide the current one. The end result is shown in Figure 8-3.

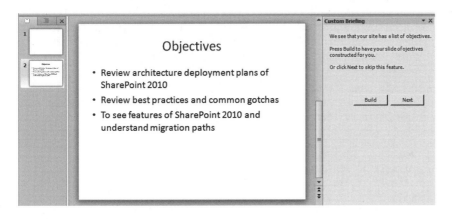

Figure 8-3. The contructed Objectives slide

The step3 User Control: Building Agenda Items

The step3 user control is not much different from step2. In its **Start** method, it also decides whether or not to show itself. Assuming the site has an Agenda list and the user chooses to build a presentation slide, step3's Next button-click event handler again uses the SharePoint client-side .NET managed API. This time the control queries for all of the items in the Agenda list.

Instead of simply building another bulleted list, this slide ambitiously presents the agenda items in a PowerPoint table, while also providing more detailed content in the Notes portion of the slide. To get the slide setup for a table, the layout used in the **AddSlide** method is still the one that has only a title and a content area. But this time, we then find the corresponding placeholder of the large content area in order to use its size and position for the placement of our table. The table is added by accessing the slide's **Shapes** collection and calling its **AddTable** method. This method expects several parameters: the number of rows, which in this case in the number of agenda list items, the number of columns, and position information (top, left, width, and height). In this example, we will populate the table with two columns of information: the time and title of the agenda item. Finally, the width of each column is set appropriately and the **FirstRow** property is set to False since our table will not have any column headings. Listing 8-12 presents this code segment.

Listing 8-12. Adding a Table to the Presentation's Slide

```
slide = presentation.Slides.AddSlide(presentation.Slides.Count+1,layout);
slide.Shapes.Title.TextFrame.TextRange.Text = "Agenda";

PowerPoint.Shape placeholderTable = slide.Shapes.Placeholders[2];
PowerPoint.Shape tblAgenda = slide.Shapes.AddTable(items.Count, 2,↵
                placeholderTable.Left, placeholderTable.Top,↵
                placeholderTable.Width, placeholderTable.Height);

tblAgenda.Table.Columns[1].Width = 200;
tblAgenda.Table.Columns[2].Width = 400;
tblAgenda.Table.FirstRow = false;
```

With the table on the slide, our attention focuses on the processing of agenda items. As with objectives, we will cycle through a collection built using each item we retrieved from the query. With this information we will not only place content into the table, we will also keep a running **StringBuilder** that will be used to write text to the Notes portion of the slide. Listing 8-13 details this processing where content is placed in the table and there is some additional processing of the Notes field.

Listing 8-13. Processing the agenda items

```
StringBuilder notesText = new StringBuilder();
for (int i = 1; i<=items.Count; i++)
{
  string time = (string) items[i-1].FieldValues["Time"];
  string title = (string) items[i-1].FieldValues["Title"];
  string owner = (string) items[i-1].FieldValues["Owner"];
  string notes = string.Empty;
//we need to make another request to get the notes field stripped of HTML markup
  SPClient.FieldStringValues values = items[i-1].FieldValuesAsText;
  ctx.Load(values);
```

```
ctx.ExecuteQuery();
if (values["Notes"] != null && values["Notes"] != string.Empty)
{
  notesText.Append(string.Format("({0}): {1}", owner, values["Notes"]));
  notesText.Append("\n");
}

tblAgenda.Table.Cell(i,1).Shape.TextFrame2.TextRange.Text = time;
tblAgenda.Table.Cell(i, 2).Shape.TextFrame2.TextRange.Text = title;
}
slide.NotesPage.Shapes.Placeholders[2].TextFrame2.TextRange.Text = ↵
        notesText.ToString();
```

If you look carefully at Listing 8-13, you will see another use of the context's `ExecuteQuery` method. This might seem odd since we told you earlier that we retrieved all the default fields of the list. The reason for this is that the Notes field is a bit different from the others we have been working with. In SharePoint, this field is one that is allowed to support rich text formatting. Therefore, its default values contain HTML markup within a `<div>` tag. This HTML would make no sense and a lot of noise in our Notes section of the slide, so this query is actually asking the server to clean this up and give us the field's value without HTML. If any text remains after the HTML is removed, it is added to the `StringBuilder`, which is used in the last line of Listing 8-13 to populate the placeholder in the slide's `NotesPage`.

The result of our efforts is a slide that presents the time and title of each agenda item in a nicely formatted table. In addition, more detailed content is added to the Notes portion of the slide to help the presenter deliver the material. Figure 8-4 shows a sample result.

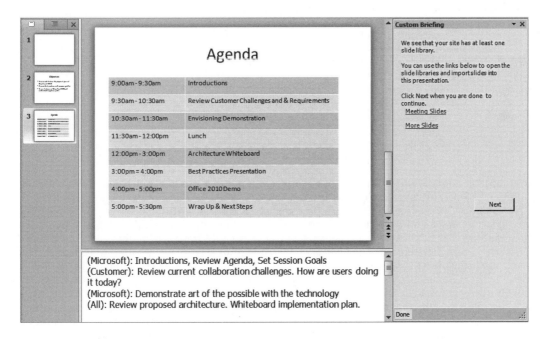

Figure 8-4. Complete Agenda presentation slide

The step4 User Control: Integration with Slide Libraries

The step4 user control is responsible for informing the user of the slide libraries that exist on the SharePoint site. A slide library is a SharePoint library type that allows users to work on individual slides. This granularity enables a great collaboration experience as users can work on just their portion while others simultaneously edit theirs. The slide library also promotes slide reuse as the slides can be imported into other decks. Our assumption with this example is that the meeting workspace has at least one slide library that includes existing slides to be imported into the presentation.

Like the other steps, step4 checks to see if at least one slide library was discovered previously and only shows itself if that was the case. In addition, this control's Start method includes a call to the ListSlideLibraryLinks method. This method will populate a panel with LinkLabel controls for each of the slide libraries discovered on the site. The experience we are going for is that the Briefing application's task pane will provide links that open the user's browser directly to the chosen slide library. From there, the user can select the desired slides and import them into the presentation. Listing 8-14 details the construction of the LinkLabel controls.

Listing 8-14. Building LinkLabel controls for slide libraries

```
private void ListSlideLibraryLinks()
{
  pnlLinks.Controls.Clear();
  LinkLabel[] linkControls = new LinkLabel[ParentPane.SlideLibraries.Count];
  for (int i=0; i<this.ParentPane.SlideLibraries.Count; i++)
  {
    linkControls[i] = new LinkLabel();
    linkControls[i].Location = new Point(5, 25 * i);
    linkControls[i].LinkClicked +=new ↵
            LinkLabelLinkClickedEventHandler(step4_LinkClicked);
    linkControls[i].LinkBehavior = LinkBehavior.AlwaysUnderline;
    LibraryItem item = (LibraryItem) ParentPane.SlideLibraries[i];
    linkControls[i].Text = item.Name;
    LinkLabel.Link link = linkControls[i].Links.Add(0, item.Name.Length);
    link.LinkData = item.Url;
  }
  pnlLinks.Controls.AddRange(linkControls);
}
```

In Listing 8-14, linkControls is an array of LinkLabels containing enough controls for the number of slide libraries previously discovered. Within the loop, a new LinkLabel control is created for each slide library. The LinkLabel's Location property specifies the horizontal and vertical placement of the control. Since we will be creating a number of these controls, the vertical position is a calculation based on the iteration of the loop. The next line of code sets up an event hander for LinkLabel so that we can run code in response to the user clicking on it. The LinkLabel's LinkBehavior is set to always present its text as underlined, and the actual text value is set to be the name of the slide library. In addition to these properties, the LinkLabel control needs to have a link created within it that specifies which portion of its text should be the active link. In this case, we want the link to be the entire length of the slide library's name. We also place the URL that the browser should open to as LinkData that will be retrieved in our event handler. Figure 8-5 shows what this step looks like in the task pane, which shows two slide libraries in the meeting workspace.

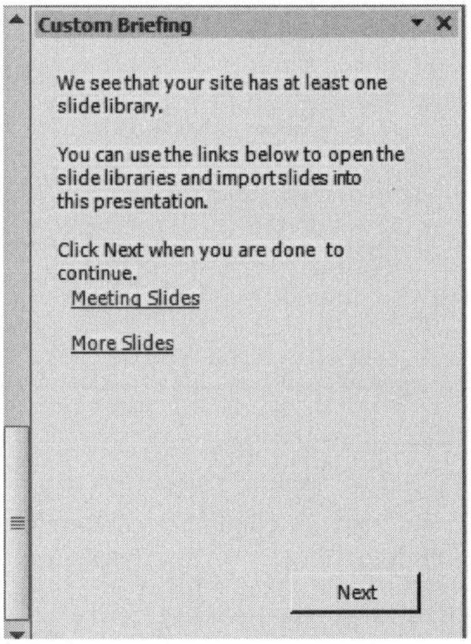

Figure 8-5. Displaying links to slide libraries

When the user clicks on one of the LinkLabels, our event handler responds by opening the browser and directing the user to the URL of the slide library. This event handler launches the browser automatically by using the System.Diagnostics namespace and starting a process with the URL as a parameter. This opens the browser to the location we specify. The URL of the slide library is obtained by accessing the LinkData of the event argument. Listing 8-15 shows this event handler's code.

Listing 8-15. Launching the browser to a selected slide library

```
void step4_LinkClicked(object sender, LinkLabelLinkClickedEventArgs e)
{
  System.Diagnostics.Process.Start(e.Link.LinkData.ToString());
}
```

Once in the browser, the user will be able to use out-of-the-box functionality to select slides and import them into the current presentation. To perform this operation, the user must select the checkboxes next to the slides he wants to import and click the Copy Slide to Presentation button. The user is then asked if he want to send it to a new or open presentation. This is shown in Figure 8-6.

Figure 8-6. Importing slides from a slide library

Select the open presentation option to have the slides imported into the presentation you have been constructing. Notice there is also an option to receive notifications if the slide in the site were to change after this import has occurred. This is the "Tell me when this slide changes" option. If selected, the slide will be imported/copied into the current presentation, but with a pointer back to the site. Each time the user opens the presentation, PowerPoint will check to see if the source slide has been modified since the import. If so, the user will be alerted and asked if he wishes to update the presentation. This is a powerful feature that enhances the reuse of content within the organization.

Though there is a step5 user control, this is the last step where presentation slides are constructed. The last step user control simply informs the user that he has completed the Briefing application and that he can close the task pane by clicking the button in the Ribbon interface.

Important Lessons

The PowerPoint Briefing application incorporated several key techniques that are worth highlighting as they could easily be reused in other projects.

Launching the task pane from the Ribbon interface: The Briefing add-in utilized VSTO's Ribbon support to add a toggle button to launch and close its task pane. This integrated the custom application into the common Office experience.

Creating a wizard-like experience in the task pane: To complete the process of building slides based on site content, the Briefing add-in leads the user through a series of steps. This application designates the task pane as a controller of the process and gives it the responsibility of orchestrating the step controls. Other projects you construct with a similar experience can benefit from the architecture used in this solution. Specifically, this Briefing add-in streamlined the amount of code that needed to be written by defining a common interface for all step controls and encapsulating each step's functionality into its respective control. The task pane then became trivial to code as it only moves the user from step to step, storing any necessary data during the process.

Discovering a site's lists and libraries: One of the main interaction points this application has with SharePoint is to query the site to discover what lists and libraries it contained. This was accomplished through SharePoint's client-side .NET managed API. This API followed the pattern of establishing a client-side context object, specifying the data to be gathered, and then executing the query.

Retrieving a particular list's items: The other interaction point with SharePoint is when the Briefing add-in requests all the items of a specific list. This was used to obtain the content of both the Objectives and Agenda lists. Again, the application accomplished this through SharePoint's client-side .NET managed API.

Extension Points

While coding this example, we thought of several variations to the solution that we didn't incorporate. Mostly, they were not included because they distracted from the overall objective of the solution. We call them out now as extension points since they may be applicable to a project you are working on.

Include check boxes to allow a user to select which items to import: In our example, the user was only presented with the options to build the slide with all of the objectives or to skip them entirely. There could be a rather elegant third option in which the Briefing add-in could query to get the items and display them in the task pane with check boxes. The user could then select which of the objective or agenda items should be placed into the new slide. Coding this option would be very similar to the technique used to build the collection of LinkLabels in step 4.

Add an update operation: Currently, the Briefing add-in simply creates new slides in the open presentation. Other than the built-in notifications for slide libraries, it does not have an update operation. An update may allow for the application to check if the lists have changed and incorporate those changes into existing slides. For this to be successful, the application would first need to store the URL that was initially used to construct the slides. This URL could be stored in a custom property of the PowerPoint application or simply in a Notes page of one of the slides. Assuming that the titles of the slides had not changed, the add-in could iterate through to find the right slide, use the stored URL to get the new items, and repopulate the necessary shapes.

Publish to a PowerPoint Broadcast Site: SharePoint 2010 includes a PowerPoint broadcast site that allows users to simultaneously view a delivery of the presentation through the PowerPoint web application. The last step in the wizard process could allow the user to specify his enterprise's PowerPoint broadcast site and then deliver the presentation there while setting the appropriate permissions.

Add an Excel Services Chart: SharePoint 2010 provides a REST interface for retrieving items from an Excel spreadsheet that has been published to Excel Services. Having a REST interface means that a properly formatted URL would be all that is necessary to retrieve chart from the spreadsheet as an image. Given this easy mode of access, you could create a slide that has an image shape with such a URL. Chapters 5 and 10 contain more information on Excel Services.

Further Reading

If you found the material presented in this chapter interesting, we think you'll find the following resources helpful as well.

- *CODE Magazine* article on interacting with PowerPoint from managed code http://www.code-magazine.com/Article.aspx?quickid=0607151

- Video on how to create an add-in for Microsoft PowerPoint http://msdn. microsoft.com/en-us/vsto/bb964496.aspx

- MSDN's Ribbon Overview http://msdn.microsoft.com/en-us/library/ bb386097(VS.100).aspx

- SharePoint's Managed Client Object Model http://msdn.microsoft.com/ en-us/library/ee537247(office.14).aspx

- Data Retrieval Overview http://msdn.microsoft.com/en-us/library/ ee539350(v=office.14).aspx

- Introducing Broadcast Slide Show http://blogs.msdn.com/powerpoint/archive/ 2009/10/09/introducing-broadcast-slide-show.aspx

- PowerPoint FAQ http://pptfaq.com

CHAPTER 9

■ ■ ■

Building a Presentation Server-Side within a Web Part

As we noted in Chapter 8, information workers who collaborate to prepare for an event, execute a business process, create materials for a project, or for any number of other reasons, generally need to present the output of their collaboration or simply report on the team's status. Very often nowadays, these workers will collaborate via a SharePoint site, and they'll typically use Microsoft PowerPoint as the canvas on which to construct their presentations. As in the previous chapter, we will try to reduce the amount of work it takes for these users to put a presentation together. In this chapter we will assume that the organization has a preconstructed template for presentations of a particular type and that building the presentation is a repeatable process of putting site content on slides. Our goal is to completely automate the construction of a presentation by combining site content with the existing presentation template. This construction takes place server-side via a custom web part that leverages the Microsoft Office XML file formats.

Real-World Examples

This problem is very similar to the one presented in Chapter 8, and therefore applies to the same types of customers. Any time someone is responsible for reporting on the status or state of a project or process, you will find users constructing briefings. We see this all the time, with military, government, and commercial customers alike. Each type of a process has a specific PowerPoint template and each briefing involves a user or team of users gathering the necessary information to populate the template with content. This requires the team to dig through old e-mails in organizational mailboxes, search file shares, or even copy data from the user interfaces of other applications. The result is a waste of productivity and an increase in the chance of an error when transferring the information into the PowerPoint presentation.

Solution Overview

The biggest difference between this solution and the one in the previous chapter is the level of automation. In Chapter 8 we built a Microsoft PowerPoint add-in that was capable of pulling SharePoint site content and building corresponding slides in the user's presentation. That approach facilitates presentation creation by providing the user with a tool. For this solution, we add the assumption that the organization has a PowerPoint file that serves as a template. This template is used over and over, with the only difference being the site content that is placed in it. To provide some context for our solution, we have focused our efforts on building a presentation whose slides contain items from a SharePoint site's Issues list. The Issues list in our site is an instance of the Issue Tracking list type. An Issue Tracking list is useful when users want to manage a set of tasks or problems. Each issue can be categorized, assigned, and prioritized. The resulting presentation should contain a title slide along with a slide for each of the issue categories. In our sample site, all of the issues are things that might be action items when a team is setting up a software application in a datacenter. They include items like the following:

- Install a backup device
- Optimize IIS
- Install service packs

Each of the items in the site's Issues list is categorized as Hardware, Software, or Other. These categories will be the titles of the main slides in the presentation we're creating. Note that in this solution we are dynamically populating slides with data. This is different from the out-of-the-box slide library functionality of SharePoint that promotes the reuse of slides across presentations.

In this chapter's solution we shift the work from a tool on the user's desktop to the SharePoint server. Since no human interaction is necessary, the work of merging the issues into the slides will be accomplished entirely server-side. The user will simply invoke the process by clicking a button in a custom web part. Of course, a web part isn't the only option you could use to provide an invocation point. Another good choice would be a custom action from the list or a list item. Since those techniques were used in previous chapters, though, we'll take the web part approach to show you some new things along the way. Our web part will execute the merger by opening up the PowerPoint presentation that serves as the template, placing content on the slides, and saving the new presentation back to a site document library. In the past, this type of solution would have caused developers to install Microsoft PowerPoint on the server and automate it through its primary interop assemblies, but such a solution is neither scalable nor recommended by Microsoft. Thankfully, Microsoft Office 2010 presents developers with another option, one that derives from the fact that the Office applications rely on an open XML file format. So our web part will be able to modify the presentation template simply by manipulating the XML at key places.

As the web part executes, it will retrieve its settings information to discover the file name of the presentation template and the name of the document library it is stored in. With the template, the web part will then iterate through the deck, using each slide's title to determine the work that should be used to populate the slide with content. For the title slide, the web part will place the name of the team site, the account name of the user who clicked the button, and a timestamp. The second slide will be a bulleted list of the titles of the hardware issues. The software issues will be placed on the next slide, in a table displaying the title of the issue, who it is assigned to, and its priority. The last slide will be a bulleted list of the Other category's issues. When the construction is complete, the web part will store the presentation as a new file in the same document library as the template. This file will be named according to a web-part setting.

Solution Walkthrough

The following section will detail the major elements of the solution and the decisions we made in coding it. The walkthrough will show you how to get started with Visual Studio 2010 to create the web part, as well as to deploy and debug it. We will introduce you to the new Visual Web Part project item and show you how it will save you time over the code-only approaches of the past. Since this web part could take more time than a normal page load to process its data, we will show you how to make this work happen without a full page load using an asynchronous, AJAX-style postback. We will detail how you can use the new SPMetal utility to generate helper classes to streamline the way you access site data from code. These site data queries will not be the CAML-based queries you may have written in previous versions of SharePoint, but rather simpler LINQ-based queries. We will also show you some of the tools provided in the Open XML Format SDK 2.0 that will make it easy for you to write the code necessary to modify the presentation—without having to resort to direct XML manipulation. You'll also see how to manipulate the presentation slides, placing content in specific shapes, as bullet lists, and even as a table.

Setting Up the Team Site and Content

Our example relies on an Issue Tracking list named Issues in a WSS team site. So from either a new or existing team site, use the following steps to create the list:

1. Click All Site Content in the left navigation control of the team site.

2. Click the Create button in the toolbar.

3. In the tracking category, select the Issue Tracking list type.

4. Name the list **Issues** and click Create. It is important that you follow the naming convention here since in this implementation the list name is static.

With the list created, there is an additional step to configure the categories to use our desired vocabulary of Hardware, Software, and Other. The Issues list should now be in the left-hand navigation of the team site. Use the following steps to modify the list's categories:

1. Click on its link to display the list.

2. Click the List tab in the Ribbon toolbar. Click the List Settings button in the Settings section.

3. In the Columns section, click on Category.

4. The choices are defined halfway down the page in a list box. Change the items to **Hardware**, **Software**, and **Other**. Place each string on a separate line.

5. Click OK.

For this example, it is useful to add the Category column to the default view so you can easily check that the items are being placed on the correct slide. From the List Settings page, perform the following steps:

1. Locate the Views section and click on the All Issues view.

2. Click the check box next to the Category column and set its position to 3.

3. Click OK.

You are now ready to enter some content for this solution. Be sure to choose a variety of items for each category. Changing the Assigned To and Priority values for the Software issues will be reflected in that slide's table. When complete, your list's contents should look something like Figure 9-1.

Issue ID	Category	Title	Assigned To	Issue Status	Priority	Due Date
1	Software	DNS Name resolution error on Server A 🗑 NEW	Ed Hild	Active	(2) Normal	12/3/2009 12:00 AM
2	Hardware	Memory Read Error on Dim on Server 2 🗑 NEW	Ed Hild	Active	(1) High	12/1/2009 12:00 AM
3	Other	Customer feedback changing scope 🗑 NEW	Ed Hild	Active	(2) Normal	12/1/2009 12:00 AM
4	Hardware	Install backup device 🗑 NEW	Ed Hild	Resolved	(2) Normal	11/30/2009 12:00 AM
5	Software	Optimize IIS 🗑 NEW	Ed Hild	Closed	(3) Low	12/1/2009 12:00 AM
6	Hardware	Setup external storage array 🗑 NEW	Ed Hild	Active	(1) High	12/3/2009 12:00 AM
7	Software	Install service packs 🗑 NEW	Ed Hild	Active	(2) Normal	12/2/2009 12:00 AM

Figure 9-1. The contents of the Issues list

Creating the Presentation Template

In addition to the Issues content, this solution will also need a Microsoft PowerPoint 2010 file to use as a template. This is a presentation made up of the slides and design that we desire, but no content. You can either use the steps here to create one yourself or grab the template file from the code download for this chapter. To create the PowerPoint presentation, apply your favorite visual design, and use the remaining details of this section to build the template slides.

■ **Note** These instructions include literal text strings in boldface that you should be placing on slides. Place the words that appear in boldface italics into the presentation.

For this solution there will be four slides in the template:

Slide 1 uses the default Title Slide layout. Place the text *#Site Title#* in the text box designated to contain the presentation's title. Our web part will replace this text with the name of the WSS team site during its processing. In the Sub-Title textbox, place two lines of text. For the first one, simply write *#Author#* and for the second, place the word *#Timestamp#*. Be sure you are pressing the Enter key from one line of text to the other, creating two paragraphs. We will use this information during the merge process when we insert the account name of the user, as well as a timestamp instead of these placeholders.

Slide 2 uses the Title and Content layout. Place the text **Hardware Issues** in the text box designated to contain the presentation's title. In the content area, place a single bullet with the text *#Content#*.

Slide 3 also uses the Title and Content layout. Place the text **Software Issues** in the text box designated to contain the presentation's title. Click the icon that represents a table to insert one into the content area. For the dimensions of the table, specify one row and three columns. Basically, all we want to do is enter the column headings; the web part will take care of putting the rows into the table for each of the issues in the Software category. For the column headings, use **Title**, **Assigned To**, and **Priority**. The resulting slide should look something like Figure 9-2, depending on what design you applied to the presentation.

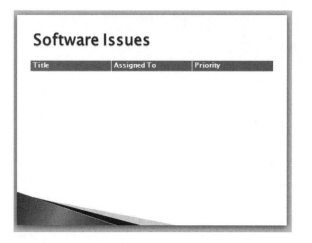

Figure 9-2. The presentation template's Software Issues slide

Slide 4 uses the Title and Content layout. Place the text *Other* in the text box designated to contain the presentation's title. In the content area, place a single bullet with the text *#Content#*.

Now save this presentation as `template.pptx` in the Shared Documents library of the site where you created the Issues list. Be sure the "save as" type you are using is PowerPoint Presentation (that's where the pptx file extension comes from). This is important, as this file format type uses the Open XML standards, enabling us to open and modify the file without using the PowerPoint application.

Creating the Project and Defining the SharePoint Feature

As described in Chapter 3, with the 2010 releases Microsoft made major steps in helping developers become more productive in building customizations for SharePoint with Visual Studio. For this example, we will start with an empty SharePoint 2010 project so we can help you become familiar with all the new tools and functionality. Use the following steps to create the DynamicPowerPoint Visual Studio 2010 project:

1. Open Visual Studio 2010 and start a new project.

2. In the Installed Templates tree, expand Visual C#, then expand SharePoint. Select the 2010 node for the SharePoint 2010 project types.

3. Using the drop-downs above the project types, make sure you are targeting the .NET Framework 3.5.

4. Select Empty SharePoint Project from the list of project types.

5. Name the project **DynamicPowerPoint** and leave the default choice of creating a new solution with the same name. Your completed dialog should look like Figure 9-3.

Figure 9-3. Creating the DynamicPowerPoint project

6. Click OK.

7. In the next SharePoint Customization dialog, choose the Deploy as a farm solution option, since our solution is really an enterprise one that would be built by developers, deployed into production by system administrators, and used across multiple site collections. And specify the URL of the site where you created the Issues list. For our environment it is `http://edhild3/sites/dynppt`.

Now that you have a project, let's take a look at some of the new tools you have been given for SharePoint development. The most exciting are the Feature Designer and the Package Explorer. As described in Chapter 3, these powerful additions to SharePoint Visual Studio development let developers visualize and work with complex XML configuration files without completely hiding the XML from you. Both of these are wrappers that will help us easily get our SharePoint customization deployed into the environment. A SharePoint package is a single file (`.wsp`) that contains all the bits the customization relies on. This includes images, assemblies, aspx pages, and so forth, along with a manifest file that tells SharePoint where they all should be physically placed. The package compartmentalizes its customizations into one or more features that can be turned on or off by administrators. The required level of administrator depends on the scope of the feature: web, site collection, web application, or farm. Activating the feature applies the customizations. For this example, our solution will just contain one feature. Use the following steps to set it up:

1. Right-click on the Features node in Solution Explorer and choose Add Feature.

2. Expand the Features node in the solution.

3. Right-click on the feature named Feature1 and choose Rename. Type **Main** as the new name for the feature. Notice that Visual Studio renames the dependent files.

4. Right-click the Main feature node and choose View Designer. Now we can set some of the properties of this feature.

5. Specify the title: **DynamicPowerPoint WebPart Feature**

6. Specify the description: **Enables a web part that builds a presentation from site content**.

7. Set the Scope to Site. This value really means site collection, which is the appropriate scope for the customization since it will contain a web part that needs to be placed in the site collection's web part gallery. It also means that a user will need to be a site collection administrator to activate the feature.

8. Just to see the option, click on the Manifest button at the bottom of the designer. By choosing the Edit Options you can overwrite the generated XML.

9. Add the XML attribute `Description="t"` into the definition of the feature, right after the XML namespace declaration. See in the Preview pane above how this change overwrites the description you entered in the designer. Don't leave this change in, but we wanted to show you that you can edit the XML manually if you are used to doing that from SharePoint 2007 work.

10. Go back to the Design view and click Save in the Visual Studio toolbar to commit your changes.

Adding the Visual Web Part

We will now focus on adding a web part to our project. In previous versions of SharePoint, building a web part was much like coding an ASP.NET server control—the experience was a code-only approach. If you wanted to add a label or button to the web part, you had to declare one and add it to the Controls collection of the web part. This was a disappointment for most developers as they had become accustomed to the drag-and-drop experience of creating ASP.NET pages. With SharePoint 2010 and Visual Studio 2010, developers now have a Visual Web Part project item. Use the following steps to add the web part to the current project.

1. Right-click on the DynamicPowerPoint project and choose Add ➤ New Item.

2. Make sure the Installed Templates tree is set to display SharePoint 2010 project items. Select the Visual Web Part template.

3. Specify the name: **DynPPTWP**. Once the item has been added, expand the DynPPTWP node. Your Solution Explorer window should look like Figure 9-4.

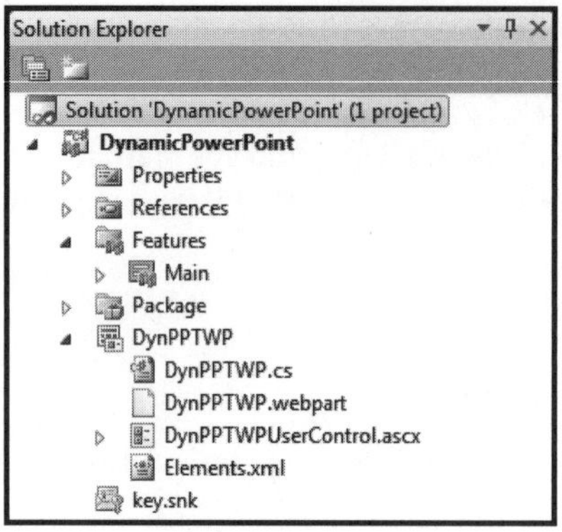

Figure 9-4. The added DynPPTWP Visual Web Part

Each of these files begs some explanation. First, the `DynPPTWP` class is the actual web part. It is the only thing here that is derived from the `WebPart` base class. At the moment, this class is really just a wrapper that loads up the `DynPPTWPUserControl`. However, as we will see in a bit, if you need to do anything that is web-part-specific such as adding custom web part properties, you will be modifying this file. The `DynPPTWP.webpart` file is an XML description file that SharePoint will use as a descriptor for the web part. Open it up and use Listing 9-1 to fill in the `Title` and `Description` that will be shown to users when they are viewing the web part in SharePoint's gallery.

Listing 9-1. Setting Web Part Metadata

```
<properties>
 <property name="Title" type="string">Dynamic PowerPoint Web Part</property>
 <property name="Description" type="string">Automates the creation of a
                             presentation from site content</property>
</properties>
```

The `DynPPTWPUserControl` file is a user control that supports a visual designer and it has a corresponding code-behind file. This user control will be the place where we build the user interface and the code that runs in response to user interaction. Lastly, the `Elements.xml` file is being used behind the scenes so that our web part is now part of our feature. Open it up and you can see the XML that pushes the `DynPPTWP.webpart` file up into the site collection's web part gallery. Our web part will be placed into a category that is specified using the Group property. Set the value of this property to **Contoso Web Parts**. Now go back to the Feature Designer and look at the Main feature. You'll see this web part has been added as an item.

Before jumping into the actual code we will use to query the SharePoint site and modify the presentation, let's get a few other things out of the way. First, there are some other assemblies we need to add references to:

- **WindowsBase**: This assembly will give us access to the `System.IO.Packaging` namespace, which is used to open Office files that use the Open XML file format.

- **DocumentFormat.OpenXml**: This assembly is provided by the Open XML Format SDK 2.0. For this chapter we are using the March 2010 release, which you can download and install from: `http://msdn.microsoft.com/en-us/library/bb448854(office.14).aspx`. This assembly lets us manipulate the content of the presentation without having to write XML nodes directly. The SDK provides an object model that is an abstraction from the actual XML, making our code easier to read and write.

- **System.Drawing**: This assembly contains some of the basic objects we will be adding to the presentation, such as a table.

- **Microsoft.SharePoint.Linq**: This assembly is included in the SharePoint install. It should be in the .NET tab of the Add References dialog. If not, you can browse to it when adding the reference. Its default location is `C:\Program Files\Common Files\Microsoft Shared\Web Server Extensions\14\ISAPI\Microsoft.SharePoint.Linq.dll`. This assembly will allow us to query the list for specific items using LINQ as opposed to the old CAML used in previous versions of SharePoint.

- **System.Web.Extensions**: Since our web part may take some time to put the presentation together, we don't want to make our end-user sit through a whole page refresh. This assembly gives us access to the ASP.NET Ajax controls so our web part can do its work without impacting the rest of page.

Now that the appropriate references have been added, you can add the using statements into the code files we will be modifying. These statements are the key namespaces we will use in the code and keep us from having to fully qualify their class names. If you notice that the namespaces are not resolving, you may have missed adding a reference to an assembly. Listing 9-2 details the using statements that need to be added to the code-behind file of the user control, `DynPPTWPUserControl.ascx.cs`.

Listing 9-2. The using statements

```
using Microsoft.SharePoint;
using Microsoft.SharePoint.WebControls;
using System.IO;
using DocumentFormat.OpenXml.Presentation;
using DocumentFormat.OpenXml.Packaging;
using Drawing = DocumentFormat.OpenXml.Drawing;
using System.Linq;
using System.Text;
```

When a user places this web part on a SharePoint page, she is creating a specific instance. She could, in fact, place many instances of the same web part on the same page. A fundamental feature of web parts is that each instance maintains its specific configuration or settings data. There are some common settings, such as width, height, visibility, border, and so forth that our web part will get for free, but our code must account for any specific configuration information that we want during execution. For this solution, we have identified three different pieces of information that we want an author to be able to input into a specific instance of our web part (but the values will be shared among all site visitors). These three settings are the name of the library that's storing our files, the name of the presentation template file, and the name that should be used when saving the generated file. Listing 9-3 shows how a web part property can be coded to hold a setting value. Since this code is web-part-specific, it resides in the DynPPTWP.cs file.

Listing 9-3. A web part property

```
[WebBrowsable(true), Personalizable(PersonalizationScope.Shared)]
public string LibraryName { get; set; }
```

In Listing 9-3, an auto-implemented property called LibraryName is declared. The important items here that are different from any other C# class are the attributes preceding the property: WebBrowsable and Personalizable. The WebBrowsable attribute describes this property as one that should be displayed in the administrative settings interface that is shown when the web part is configured. This interface is shown in Figure 9-5.

Figure 9-5. Entering a web part's configuration settings

The Personalizable attribute has a parameter whose value is either PersonalizationScope.Shared or PersonalizationScope.User. This scope dictates whether the value stored applied to all users (Shared) or can be set differently for different users (User). The User setting is handy when you want to allow each site visitor to customize the setting in his own version of the page.

It is important to realize that in this text, we are calling out some of the significant code elements, patterns, and best practices, but not printing and explaining every single line of code. Declaring the other two web part properties, for example, is done in exactly the same way as the one we described here, so printing those code listings would be a bit redundant. We highly recommend that you have the code available from the code download as you go through the remainder of this chapter, so we can focus your attention on the really interesting code pieces. The only other line of code, besides properties, in the web part class is the declaration of an `m_errormessage` string variable. We will use this to capture the message for any error our code encounters.

Building the Web Part User Interface

The page refresh in the browser has long been the bane of developers building rich internet applications. In the past, a user filling out a very long form on the web might have had to persevere through lengthy wait times as the change of a drop-down list or click of a button could require a postback, resulting in the whole page re-rendering. For this reason, the mid to late 1990's had a burst of activity bent on finding an effective way to have this roundtrip to the server happen asynchronously, with only a portion of the page having to be redrawn. Once browser standards caught up with developers, AJAX (asynchronous JavaScript and XML) became a popular implementation choice as a solution. Much of the SharePoint 2010 interface takes advantage of these techniques, and since our web part may take a bit of time to merge its data into PowerPoint, we will need this asynchronous behavior as well. Fortunately, ASP.NET provides a few controls that will handle all the plumbing for us. Figure 9-6 shows the layout of controls of the `DynPPTWPUserControl` in the Visual Studio designer.

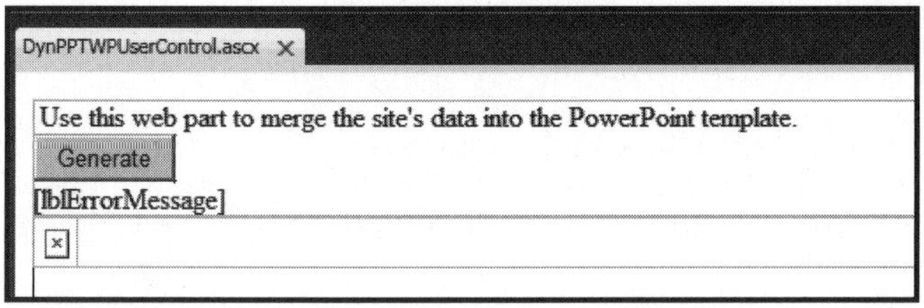

Figure 9-6. *Layout of controls for the web part interface*

The outer two containers, which look like table borders, are actually the AJAX controls that will give us the asynchronous behavior. The first container is an `UpdatePanel`. You can find this control in the AJAX Extensions group of the Visual Studio Toolbox. By using an update panel, we will be able to redraw its contents without having to refresh the entire page. The second container is an `UpdateProgress` control that will display during the processing of the server roundtrip. This control gives us the ability to provide a visual cue to the user that our web part is doing its work, and then the control will disappear when the redraw is complete. Make sure the `AssociatedUpdatePanel` property of this `UpdateProgress` control is set to `UpdatePanel1`. This property defines the relationship between the `UpdatePanel` and `UpdateProgress` controls. Though we are only using one of each, you could have many if you needed to redraw different portions of your web part independently.

Within the `UpdatePanel`, we have placed two label controls and a button control. The label controls are named `lblInstructions` and `lblErrorMessage`. The `lblInstructions` control is used to inform users of the actions they need to perform. This will start with some text telling them what clicking the button will do. Later, this label will inform the user where the resulting presentation was stored. The `lblErrorMessage` control is set to display no text, and will only be visible if there is an error message to display. In a production environment, it is usually bad form to display detailed error messages to your users that give them some insight into the logic of the web part. For example, telling a user the name of a database server, connection string, or stored procedure called may disclose too much information. Usually you would log this information so that it could be investigated, then display a more user-friendly error message. We chose to display the detailed messages here because it is useful for developers while building their code. Lastly, the button is named `btnGenerate`. When the user clicks this button, we begin the process of getting the SharePoint list data and putting it in the presentation. Go ahead and double-click this button in the designer to create the event handler in the code-behind file.

Within the `UpdateProgress` control, we've added an image control named `Image1`. This image control will be an animated gif that displays a progress bar. The reason Figure 9-6 shows this as a broken image is that the `ImageUrl` property will only be valid once it is being used in a SharePoint site. Since our web part may be used in lots of different sites and even site collections, the image must be placed in an area that is uniformly accessible. With a SharePoint solution, this means adding it into a special images folder that is always accessible through a virtual directory named `_layouts`. To add this special folder location to your Visual Studio Project, right-click on your DynamicPowerPoint project and choose Add ➤ SharePoint "Images" Mapped Folder. Notice that Visual Studio adds an Images folder to your solution with a subfolder that is named the same as your solution. Anything you add to the Images folder will be automatically specified in the package manifest to be deployed to the appropriate place on your servers. The reason for the subfolder is to help prevent any file name collisions that may occur with multiple projects. For the actual image, we chose an animated progress bar called `status_anim.gif` that came in the graphics library of Visual Studio. You can also just get this file from our code download. Once the file has been added, the `ImageUrl` property of the `Image1` control should be set to `"_layouts/images/DynamicPowerPoint/status_anim.gif"`.

Believe it or not, we are done laying out the user interface. We do not need to write any fancy DHTML or JavaScript code to get the asynchronous behavior; simply using these ASP.NET AJAX controls in our design will give us the desired result. We can now work on the code-behind file of the user control without any worry about whether our code used AJAX or not.

Overview of Office XML Formats, SDK Tool, and PresentationML

The web part is going to merge the contents of the Issues list into the slides, leveraging the fact that our presentation template was saved using the Open XML file format. As explained in Chapter 4, starting with Microsoft Office 2007, Microsoft switched from its proprietary binary-formatted files to formats based on Open XML specifications. Now each file—whether it be a spreadsheet, presentation, or document—is really a package of parts and items. *Parts* are pieces of content for the file whereas *items* are metadata describing how the parts should be assembled and rendered. Most of these pieces are XML files, making it possible for them to be manipulated through code. You can gain insight into the structure of an Open XML–based file by replacing its file extension with `.zip` since the file is really an ordinary Zip archive. Figure 9-7 shows the root of the archive for the PowerPoint presentation we built earlier.

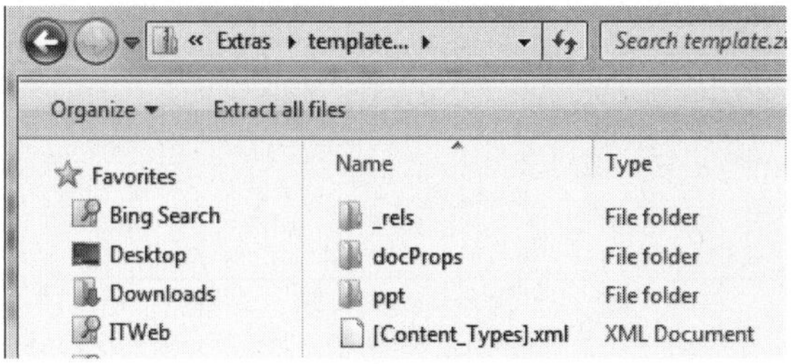

Figure 9-7. Examing the archive of a PowerPoint presentation

The XML file in the root is named `[Content_Types].xml` and it stores content-type directives for all the parts that appear in the archive. A content type contains metadata about a particular part or groups of parts and, more importantly, contains a directive for how the application should render that part. For example, Listing 9-4 shows just a few lines from the file, but clearly delineates how this file tells the rendering application which parts are slides, images, note pages, and so forth.

Listing 9-4. A presentation's content types

```
<Override PartName="/ppt/slides/slide1.xml"
  ContentType="application/vnd.openxmlformats-
  officedocument.presentationml.slide+xml" />
<Default Extension="jpeg"
  ContentType="image/jpeg" />
<Override PartName="/ppt/notesSlides/notesSlide1.xml"
  ContentType="application/vnd.openxmlformats-
  officedocument.presentationml.notesSlide+xml" />
```

PresentationML (Presentation Markup Language) is the Open XML syntax for PowerPoint presentations. It is one of the easier Open XML file formats to understand, as presentations have an obvious composition. A presentation is made up of slides. Each slide has a collection of shapes, which in turn hold content. Picture a PowerPoint slide that contains a title at the top and a bulleted list below. Such a slide contains two rectangle shapes. The first rectangle contains the user-entered title and the second one contains paragraphs of text formatted to be displayed as a bulleted list. Exploring the files located in the presentation's archive will help you understand how PowerPoint assembles these elements.

Begin with `presentation.xml,` which is located in the **ppt** folder of the archive. Opening this file in Internet Explorer will display XML similar to that in Figure 9-8.

```
<?xml version="1.0" encoding="UTF-8" standalone="yes" ?>
- <p:presentation xmlns:a="http://schemas.openxmlformats.org/drawingml/2006/main"
    xmlns:r="http://schemas.openxmlformats.org/officeDocument/2006/relationships"
    xmlns:p="http://schemas.openxmlformats.org/presentationml/2006/main"
    saveSubsetFonts="1">
- <p:sldMasterIdLst>
    <p:sldMasterId id="2147483660" r:id="rId2" />
  </p:sldMasterIdLst>
- <p:sldIdLst>
    <p:sldId id="256" r:id="rId3" />
    <p:sldId id="257" r:id="rId4" />
    <p:sldId id="258" r:id="rId5" />
    <p:sldId id="259" r:id="rId6" />
  </p:sldIdLst>
  <p:sldSz cx="9144000" cy="6858000" type="screen4x3" />
  <p:notesSz cx="6858000" cy="9144000" />
+ <p:defaultTextStyle>
</p:presentation>
```

Figure 9-8. The presentation.xml file

The `presentation.xml` file contains the list of slides (`<p:sldLst>`), references to the slide and notes masters, as well as the sizes of the slides (`<p:sldSz>`) and notes pages (`<p:notesSz>`). The sequence of the slide nodes is important, as the rendering application will display them in the order they are listed here. Notice that each slide node, as well as the master nodes, has an `r:id` attribute. This identifier is a key to a specific relationship that will tell the rendering application where the part for this item is located. The relationship information for this presentation is stored in `presentation.xml.rels` file in the `ppt\_rels` folder of the archive. Listing 9-5 is the XML node in this file that tells the application that the first slide's content is stored in `slide1.xml`.

Listing 9-5. Example of a presentation relationship

```
<Relationship
Id="rId3" Type="http://schemas.openxmlformats.org/officeDocument/↵
  2006/relationships/slide" Target="slides/slide1.xml"
/>
```

Following the relationship links, you can see that the contents of the slides are stored in the `ppt\slides` folder of the archive. In our example, this directory contains four XML files; one for each of our slides in the presentation we created to act as the template. Now the good news is that if all this XML is making your eyes glass over, there are some tools to help. Remember that the Open XML Format SDK we installed earlier is going to provide an object model that moves us up a layer from manipulating this XML directly. It also comes with an optional tool download named the Open XML SDK 2.0 Productivity Tool for Microsoft Office that contains several useful actions. Once installed, this tool is located at C:\Program Files (x86)\Open XML SDK\V2.0\tool by default. We will focus on two actions this tool provides: the ability to compare Open XML files and the ability to generate code that creates Open XML files. The ability to compare Open XML files is often useful when you want to view, say, the template file you are working with alongside the generated presentation file after your code has run. It also helps with graphically highlighting the changes so you can understand just what XML is different between the two files. For example, Figure 9-9 uses this tool to highlight the Hardware Slide in our template to a file that has the bulleted list we want.

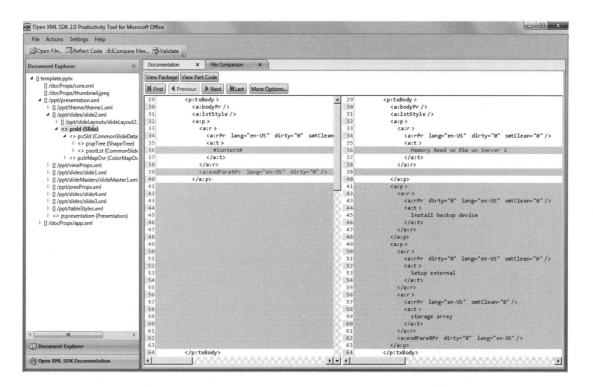

Figure 9-9. Using the compare files action of the Open XML SDK tool

Another action supported by this tool we will call out is the ability to reflect code. This action is a code generator. Once you open an Open XML-based file, you can browse the structure of the file. Selecting a specific item shows you the XML for that portion of the file, as well as a generated function in C# for creating that part of the file. This will be used repeatedly in our code that manipulates the slides. For example, Figure 9-10 shows this tool being used to create a function that creates a paragraph node for a bulleted list.

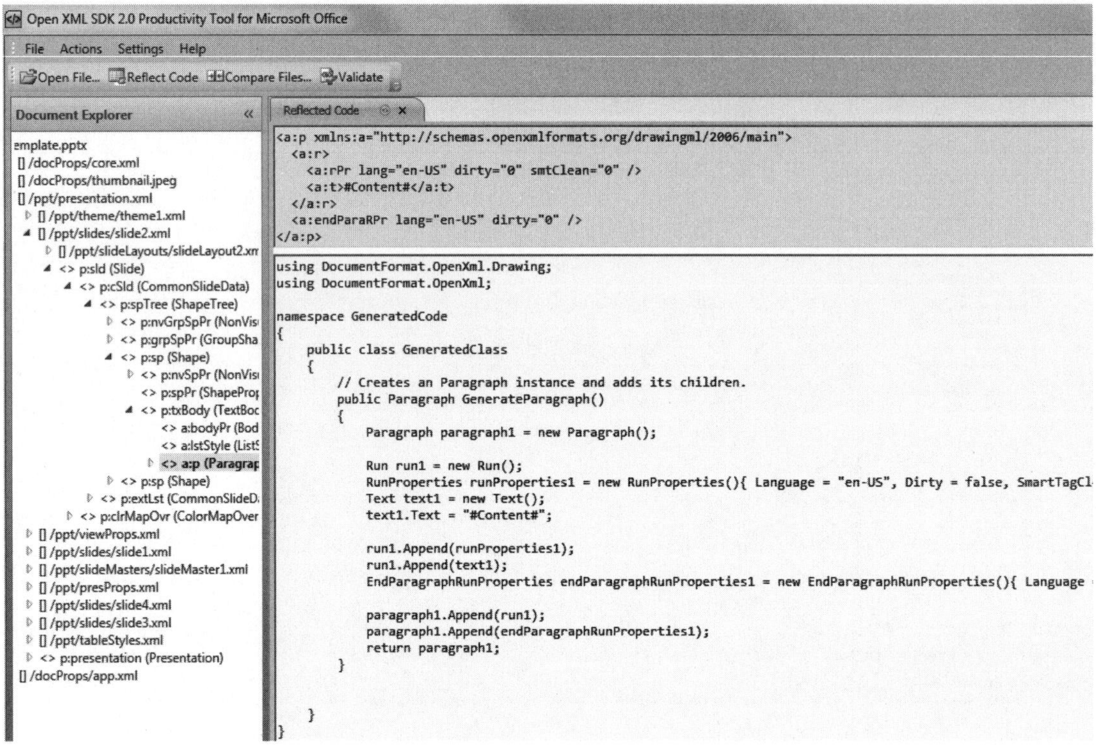

Figure 9-10. Using the reflect code action of the Open XML SDK tool

The SPMetal Tool

SPMetal is a command line tool that generates code that is an alternative to the SharePoint object model. By default, the tool is located at `C:\Program Files\Common Files\Microsoft Shared\Web Server Extensions\14\BIN.` Simply point it at a SharePoint team site and the resulting code file will contain strongly typed entity classes for all of the site's lists and libraries as they are configured at that moment in time. This code is often easier to use than the SharePoint object model equivalents. The best example of this is actually the main task our web part will perform—querying for data. Using the SharePoint object model, you could issue a query for specific items of a list using an XML-formatted CAML query such as the one in Listing 9-6. Notice that the query is just in the form of a string with no IntelliSense provided for structure, field names, or possible values.

Listing 9-6. Querying for specific list items using CAML

```
SPList list = m_web.Lists["Issues"];
SPQuery query = New SPQuery();
query.Query = "<Where><Eq><FieldRef Name='Category'/><Value
                      Type='CHOICE'>Hardware</Value></Eq></Where>";
SPListItemCollection items = list.GetItems(query);
```

Instead, the entity classes created by SPMetal support LINQ. So the query in Listing 9-6 becomes less code to write, even easier to understand, and definitely less prone to spelling a field or value incorrectly. The transformed query, which also gets only the collection of title fields we are interested, in is Listing 9-7.

Listing 9-7. Query for specific list items using SPMetal and LINQ

```
using (EntitiesDataContext dc = new EntitiesDataContext(webUrl))
{
  var q = from issue in dc.Issues
          where issue.Category == Category.Hardware
          select issue.Title;
```

A developer would typically use SPMetal during the coding phase, running the tool and adding the resulting file to his Visual Studio project. To run the tool, launch a command window and type a command similar to SPMetal /web:http://edhild3/sites/dynppt /code:Entities.cs /language:csharp. In this command we have specified three parameters. The first, *web*, specifies the site to use as the source. The generated code file will contain classes for working against a similarly structured site. In this case, we chose our team site where we created the Issues list. The second parameter, *code*, specifies the name for the file you want the generated code to be placed in. This file will be placed in the same directory as the SPMetal tool. Once you have it, copy and add it to your solution. The last parameter, *language*, specifies the .NET language you want the generated code to be in. There are many more parameters to this file and if you are going to be doing a lot of coding against SharePoint data sources, we recommend spending some time to get to know all of its options. We have added a link in the Further Reading section of this chapter.

■ **Note** It is important to realize that this code runs in the context of the developer running the command unless another user is specified as a parameter. Since SharePoint security trims the data to which a user has access, make sure the user running this tool actually has access to the data you are planning to code against.

Once the file was generated, there were a few things we cleaned up before we used it in the web part. First, SPMetal does not dig deep enough to determine the actual possible values for some of the choice fields. It simply creates an enumeration with the default values. So, for example, Listing 9-8 shows the modified Category enumeration which is the choice field in our Issues list. It is important that these are in the same order as you defined in the category field of the list. We also corrected the values for Priority so that they would show up as High, Medium, and Low in the presentation slide.

Listing 9-8. Correcting the Category enumeration

```
public enum Category : int {
  None = 0,
  Invalid = 1,
  [Microsoft.SharePoint.Linq.ChoiceAttribute(Value="Hardware")]
  Hardware = 2,
  [Microsoft.SharePoint.Linq.ChoiceAttribute(Value="Software")]
```

```
    Software = 4,
    [Microsoft.SharePoint.Linq.ChoiceAttribute(Value="Other")]
    Other = 8,
}
```

Iterating through the Template

To get the web part to place content into the template, we will go back to the Generate button on the user control and the button's click event handler. Here we will add code to open the presentation template and iterate through its slides. We will be placing a lot more code into this user control in this section. If you get overwhelmed, please download the code for this chapter from the Source Code section of http://apress.com. Each slide's title will control what content gets placed there. When this process is complete, the web part will save the modified file back to the site's document library. Listing 9-9 details the button-click event handler.

Listing 9-9. Opening the presentation template and saving the new file

```
protected void btnGenerate_Click(object sender, EventArgs e)
{
  Stream templateStream = null;
  try
  {
    m_web = SPControl.GetContextWeb(this.Context);
    SPFolder sharedDocs = m_web.GetFolder(parentWebPart.LibraryName);
    SPFile templateFile = sharedDocs.Files[parentWebPart.TemplateName];
    templateStream = templateFile.OpenBinaryStream();
    this.ProcessSlides(templateStream);
    sharedDocs.Files.Add(parentWebPart.FileName, templateStream, true);
    this.btnGenerate.Visible = false;
    lblInstructions.Text = String.Format("The presentation has been created ↩
          as {0} in the {1} library", parentWebPart.FileName, ↩
          parentWebPart.LibraryName);
  }
  catch (Exception ex)
  {
    parentWebPart.m_errorMessage = ex.Message;
  }
}
```

The first line of the Try block enables the control to get a reference to the particular SharePoint web it is being invoked from. Since this web part could be reused on many different sites in a deployment, the web part must identify its container so it can find the list, library, and files it needs to complete its task. Notice the use of the properties for retrieving the library and the presentation template file. These properties have the values that were specified in the settings interface for the web part. This layer of abstraction adds flexibility to the solution, instead of our having to hard-code these values. Once the template file has been located, it is opened as a stream and passed to a processing routine. This processing will include iterating over the collection of slides and placing content on them. When this is complete, the modified stream is saved back to the document library as a new file with the provided filename.

The outermost layer of the presentation template's processing involves iterating through the collection of slides and examining their titles. Instead of having to write this entire block of code ourselves, we can use Microsoft-provided code that includes common tasks when working with Open XML-formatted files. You can obtain the code at http://msdn.microsoft.com/en-us/library/cc850843(office.14).aspx. These examples include two functions we used grab titles from each of the slides: GetSlideTitle() and IsTitleShape(). With these added as helper functions, the ProcessSlides method determines the work necessary for each slide using the code in Listing 9-10. Notice the use of the Open XML Format SDK gives us objects like PresentationDocument, PresentationPart, and Presentation so we don't have to navigate the XML of the package directly.

Listing 9-10. Constructing content selectively based on slide title

```
public void ProcessSlides(Stream fileStream)
{
  PresentationDocument presDoc = PresentationDocument.Open(fileStream, true);
  PresentationPart presPart = presDoc.PresentationPart;
  Presentation presentation = presPart.Presentation;
  if (presentation.SlideIdList != null)
  {
    //get the title of each slide in the slide order
    foreach (SlideId slideId in presentation.SlideIdList.Elements<SlideId>())
    {
      SlidePart slidePart = (SlidePart)
              presPart.GetPartById(slideId.RelationshipId.ToString());
      //get the slide's title
      string title = GetSlideTitle(slidePart);
      switch (title)
      {
        case "#Site Title#":
           BuildTitleSlide(slidePart, m_web.Title);
           break;
        case "Hardware Issues":
           BuildHardwareSlide(slidePart, m_web.Url);
           break;
        case "Software Issues":
           BuildSoftwareSlide(slidePart, m_web.Url);
           break;
        case "Other":
           BuildOtherSlide(slidePart, m_web.Url);
           break;
      }
      slidePart.Slide.Save();
    }
  }
}
```

Building the Title Slide

The first slide of the presentation is the title slide. For content, we will place the name of the team site in the title shape, as well as the current user name and date in the subtitle shape. Merging the content into this presentation slide is rather easy since the template has placeholder content and existing paragraphs that the code simply needs to replace. The BuildTitleSlide() method will first use a LINQ query to find all the shapes in the slide. For each shape it finds, it will look through its properties to find a PlaceholderShape which will tell us the type of shape it is (Title, CenteredTitle, or SubTitle). In either the Title or CenteredTitle cases, we will replace the contents of the shape's paragraph with the title of the SharePoint site. Remember the SubTitle has two paragraphs, one for the name of the user who clicked the Generate button in the web part, and the other for the current date. Listing 9-11 details this method.

Listing 9-11. Building the title slide

```
private void BuildTitleSlide(SlidePart slidePart, string siteTitle)
{
  var shapes = from shape in slidePart.Slide.Descendants<Shape>()
               select shape;
  foreach (Shape shape in shapes)
  {
    PlaceholderShape placeholderShape = shape.NonVisualShapeProperties.↵
      ApplicationNonVisualDrawingProperties.GetFirstChild<PlaceholderShape>();
    if (placeholderShape != null && placeholderShape.Type != null && ↵
      placeholderShape.Type.HasValue)
    {
      Drawing.Paragraph paragraph = null;
      Drawing.Text text = null;
      switch (placeholderShape.Type.Value)
      {
        case PlaceholderValues.Title:
          paragraph = shape.TextBody.Descendants<Drawing.Paragraph>().First();
          text = paragraph.Descendants<Drawing.Text>().First();
          text.Text = siteTitle;
          break;
        case PlaceholderValues.CenteredTitle:
          paragraph = shape.TextBody.Descendants<Drawing.Paragraph>().First();
          text = paragraph.Descendants<Drawing.Text>().First();
          text.Text = siteTitle;
          break;
        case PlaceholderValues.SubTitle:
          paragraph = shape.TextBody.Descendants<Drawing.Paragraph>().First();
          Drawing.Text authortext = ↵
               paragraph.Descendants<Drawing.Text>().First();
          authortext.Text = this.Context.User.Identity.Name;
          paragraph = shape.TextBody.Descendants<Drawing.Paragraph>()↵
               .ElementAt(1);
          Drawing.Text timestamptext = paragraph.Descendants<Drawing.Text>()↵
               .First();
          timestamptext.Text = DateTime.Today.ToShortDateString();
          break;
      }
    }
  }
}
```

The result of this work is a presentation whose title slide has the name of the team site, the user name of the person who generated the presentation, and the date the presentation was created. Figure 9-11 shows this slide in the resulting PowerPoint presentation file.

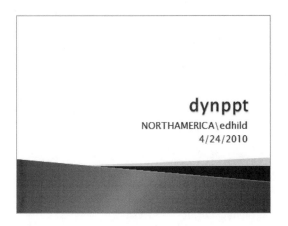

Figure 9-11. The completed title slide

Building the Slide for Hardware Issues

The second slide is to contain a listing of the hardware-issue items. In the presentation template, this slide contains only two shapes. The first shape is a rectangle that already has one bullet item (paragraph). This is where the titles of the hardware issues are to be placed as bulleted items. The second is for the title of the slide. This is already populated and will not have to be modified. How did we figure these out? Open up the template in the Open XML SDK 2.0 Productivity Tool for Microsoft Office and explore the shape tree. The `BuildHardwareSlide` method first establishes an `EntitesDataContext` using the SPMetal-generated code from before. This context tells the generated code exactly which site we want to be operating against. The method uses a LINQ query using the Open XML Document Format SDK classes to find the necessary paragraph and then remove any existing bullet items. Then another LINQ query returns all the title fields of the items in the Issues list that have a category value of Hardware. Since we only need the title field values for this slide, the LINQ query gets them for us as a set of strings. We simply enumerate the returned titles and add a paragraph for each one, which will have the result of creating a bullet item. The `GenerateParagraph` method used here was one we generated using the reflect code action of the productivity tool so we wouldn't have to mess with all the details of the necessary XML attributes. Finally, PresentationML requires that the last bullet paragraph has an `EndParagraphRunProperties` child element. The complete method is in Listing 9-12.

Listing 9-12. Building the Hardware Issues slide

```
private void BuildHardwareSlide(SlidePart slidePart, string webUrl)
{
  try
  {
    using (EntitiesDataContext dc = new EntitiesDataContext(webUrl))
    {
      var texts = from text in slidePart.Slide.Descendants<TextBody>()
                  select text;
      texts.First().RemoveAllChildren();
      var q = from issue in dc.Issues
              where issue.Category == Category.Hardware
              select issue.Title;

      texts.First().AppendChild(new Drawing.BodyProperties());
      texts.First().AppendChild(new Drawing.ListStyle());
      foreach (string title in q)
      {
          texts.First().AppendChild(this.GenerateParagraph(title));
      }
      texts.First().LastChild.AppendChild( new Drawing.↵
            EndParagraphRunProperties(){ Language = "en-US" });
    }
  }
  catch (Exception ex)
  {
      parentWebPart.m_errorMessage = ex.Message;
  }
}
```

Figure 9-12 shows the Hardware Issues slide in the resulting PowerPoint presentation file.

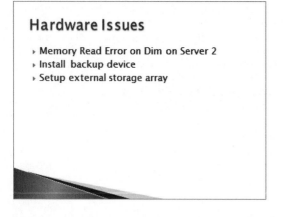

Figure 9-12. The completed Hardware Issues slide

■ **Note** The techniques used in building the Hardware Issues slide are also used to build the presentation's fourth slide, containing the Other category's issues.

Building the Slide for Software Issues

The third slide is to contain a table of the software issues. In the presentation template, we placed the slide's title as well as a three-column table containing only column headings. The first column will contain the title of the issue items. The second column will contain the name of the user whom the item is assigned to, and the last column will contain the item's priority. The BuildSoftwareSlide method uses a LINQ query to find the first empty table. Then, using the same technique we used to retrieve hardware items, a LINQ query locates the issues categorized as Software. This time we want several fields for each item, so we select the list item itself, which is of type IssuesIssue. With the content retrieved, we enumerate through each item, constructing and adding a new row to the table. This code is detailed in Listing 9-13. Notice how the SPMetal entity classes give us a nice way to access specific issue list item fields.

Listing 9-13. Building the Software Issues slide

```
private void BuildSoftwareSlide(SlidePart slidePart, string webUrl)
{
  try
  {
    var tables = from table in slidePart.Slide.Descendants<Drawing.Table>()
                 select table;
    using (EntitiesDataContext dc = new EntitiesDataContext(webUrl))
    {
      var q = from issue in dc.Issues
              where issue.Category == Category.Software
              select issue;
      foreach (IssuesIssue item in q)
      {
        //add a row to the table
        Drawing.TableRow tr = new Drawing.TableRow();
        tr.Height = 370840;
        tr.Append(CreateTableCell(item.Title.ToString()));
        tr.Append(CreateTableCell(item.AssignedTo.ToString()));
        tr.Append(CreateTableCell(item.Priority.Value.ToString()));
        tables.First().Append(tr);
      }
    }
  }
  catch (Exception ex)
  {
    parentWebPart.m_errorMessage = ex.Message;
  }
}
```

Table rows in PresentationML are not very different from those in HTML. Each table row contains table cells, which in turn contain paragraphs of text. In Listing 9-13, we had a table with rows, but there was a call to the CreateTableCell function that was responsible for the actual cell. Again, this is a good place for the productivity tool to come to the rescue and write this code for you. Listing 9-14 contains the code we wrote for the BuildTableCell function.

Listing 9-14. Adding a cell to the slide's table

```
public Drawing.TableCell GenerateTableCell(string text)
{
    Drawing.TableCell tableCell1 = new Drawing.TableCell();

    Drawing.TextBody textBody1 = new Drawing.TextBody();
    Drawing.BodyProperties bodyProperties1 = new Drawing.BodyProperties();
    Drawing.ListStyle listStyle1 = new Drawing.ListStyle();

    Drawing.Paragraph paragraph1 = new Drawing.Paragraph();
    Drawing.Run run1 = new Drawing.Run();
    Drawing.RunProperties runProperties1 = new Drawing.RunProperties()
            { Language = "en-US", Dirty = false, SmartTagClean = false };
    Drawing.Text text1 = new Drawing.Text();
    text1.Text = text;

    run1.Append(runProperties1);
    run1.Append(text1);
    Drawing.EndParagraphRunProperties endParagraphRunProperties1 =
            new Drawing.EndParagraphRunProperties() { Language = "en-US", Dirty = false };

    paragraph1.Append(run1);
    paragraph1.Append(endParagraphRunProperties1);

    textBody1.Append(bodyProperties1);
    textBody1.Append(listStyle1);
    textBody1.Append(paragraph1);
    Drawing.TableCellProperties tableCellProperties1 = new Drawing.TableCellProperties();

    tableCell1.Append(textBody1);
    tableCell1.Append(tableCellProperties1);
    return tableCell1;
}
```

Figure 9-13 shows the Software Issues slide in the resulting PowerPoint presentation file.

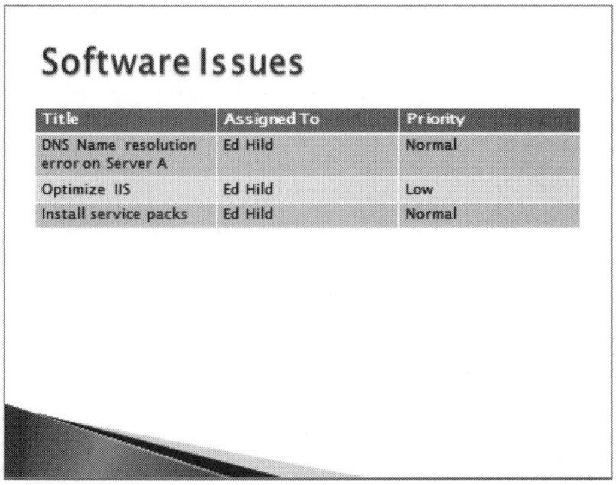

Figure 9-13. The completed Software Issues slide

Deploying and Debugging the Web Part

A typical developer spends just about as much time deploying and debugging as actually writing code. In fact, after years of development, we are pleasantly surprised when something works the first time and spend more time digging just to make sure it wasn't a coincidence. In previous versions of SharePoint and Visual Studio, there was a mountain's worth of manual steps to get code into an environment and the Visual Studio debugger attached to the right worker process, even if the environment was local for the developer. In the 2007 wave of technologies, it seemed every developer had her own set of batch files or help tools to try to ease this burden. Thankfully, with SharePoint 2010 and Visual Studio 2010, it can be as easy as pressing F5. We'll spend just a moment showing you how to make sure this is set up correctly and the steps it would take to debug this web part.

First, you need to make this Visual Studio project aware of the SharePoint site you'd like to test your web part in. By specifying this setting, you are telling Visual Studio which SharePoint farm your solution should be deployed to and which site collection this web part feature should be activated in. Believe it or not, you already told Visual Studio this location when you first created the project. You can confirm this setting by selecting the DynamicPowerPoint solution in Solution Explorer and looking at its `SiteUrl` property.

Right-clicking on your solution in Solution Explorer will bring up the variety of build options. Choosing Build will simply compile your code and create the package without pushing it to SharePoint. Deploy will build and then take the SharePoint package, deploy it to your farm, and activate the features. The Clean option is to remove your solution and its bits from the SharePoint environment. Figure 9-14 shows these options.

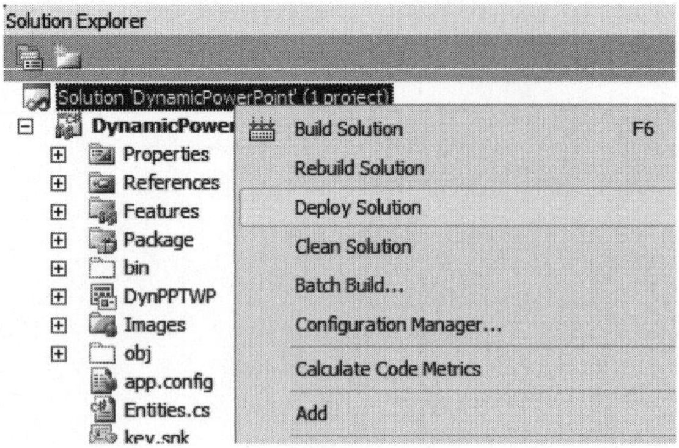

Figure 9-14. The SharePoint solution's build options

Go ahead, build and deploy your solution. Interestingly, pressing F5 would have done this and attached Visual Studio to the correct IIS worker process, but you would have one small problem. Your web part is not actually on the page. Your feature was activated, which places the web part in the gallery, but it isn't on the web part page. Usually you only have to do this once and then pressing F5 will be all that is necessary. Use the following steps to add your web part to the page:

1. Go to the default page in your site with the Issues list. Click the Page tab to bring up the Ribbon.

2. Click the Edit button in the toolbar. You should see the Editing Tools tabs appear (Format Text and Insert).

3. Make sure you have an editable area of the page selected, such as just below the listing of documents in the Shared Documents library. Click the Insert tab on the Ribbon.

4. Click the Web Part button.

5. Choose the Contoso Web Parts category. Remember when we set this in the web part's `Elements.xml` file?

6. Make sure the Dynamic PowerPoint Web Part is selected. Use the right-most column's drop-down to choose which zone the web part should be added to and then click Add. Figure 9-15 shows these options in the editor.

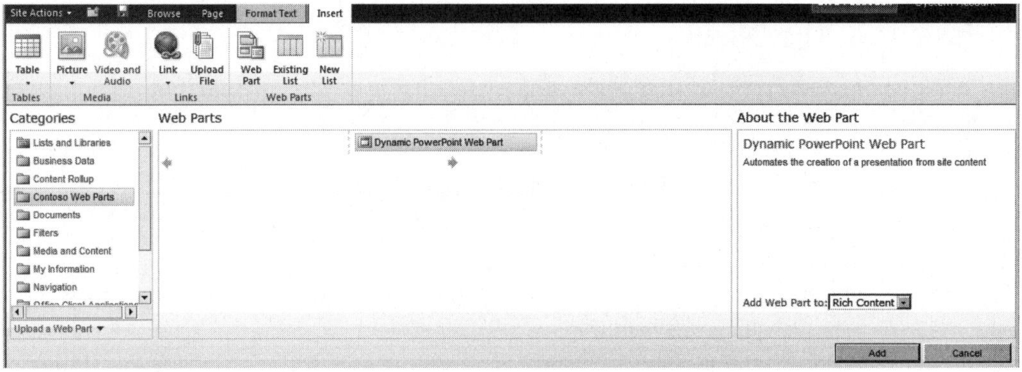

Figure 9-15. Adding the Web Part to the Page

By the way, do not forget that by adding the web part to the page you are really creating just a specific instance. This web part still needs to have its properties set so that it knows which file to use as a template, what the generated presentation filename should be, and when document library contains these files. You can specify these settings by choosing the Edit Web Part option from the menu accessible from the down-arrow in the upper-right hand corner of the web part.

Important Lessons

The DynamicPowerPoint web part incorporates several key techniques that are worth highlighting, as they could easily be reused in other projects.

Web-part construction including configuration settings. This solution detailed the steps necessary to build, deploy, and debug your own SharePoint web part using the Visual Web Part project template. The web part uses an AJAX-style user interface. Many of the values this web part needs for processing—such as the template file name, document library, and file name for the created file—were implemented as configuration settings rather than being hard-coded. This increases the flexibility of the web part, as these values could change from site to site.

The Open XML Format SDK. The Open XML Format SDK gave us a set of classes that made it easier to work with Open XML-based files. We didn't have to get into the weeds of the actual XML; instead the classes allowed us to query for specific objects and would write the necessary XML for us. This SDK also has a useful tool. We used the Open XML SDK 2.0 Productivity Tool for Microsoft Office to compare files and to generate code we could use in our solution.

SPMetal. This solution used the SPMetal tool to construct entity classes for working with SharePoint site data. By using these classes, we were able to make LINQ-style queries on SharePoint lists and refer to fields of list items with IntelliSense. This resulted in fewer lines of code that were less error-prone.

Extension Points

While coding this example, we thought of several variations to the solution that we didn't incorporate because it distracted from the overall objective of the solution. We call them out now as extension points since they may be applicable to a specific project you are working on.

Place content on the Notes pages. Explore how PresentationML records the Notes pages for slides. Start by generating a sample Open XML–formatted presentation with some slide content and notes. Rename the file so you can explore the package and its parts. Use the relationship items to navigate to the notes page parts. Compare what you find here to the structure in productivity tool. Practice placing notes programmatically for a presentation slide.

PowerPoint Broadcast. PowerPoint Broadcasts are a new feature in SharePoint 2010 that allows simultaneous users to participate in the delivery of a presentation without traditional web conferencing software. Create a site collection using the PowerPoint Broadcast Site template, then publish your presentation there and invite other users. They will all be able to see the slides as you deliver them.

Further Reading

If you found the material in this chapter interesting, you may find the resources pointed to by following links useful as well:

- Brian Jones: Open Xml Formats Blog `http://blogs.msdn.com/brian_jones/`

- Introduction to PresentationML `http://blogs.msdn.com/brian_jones/archive/2006/04/11/573529.aspx`

- Getting Started Building Web Parts in SharePoint 2010 `http://msdn.microsoft.com/en-us/sharepoint/ee513148.aspx`

- Visual Studio 2010 Tools for SharePoint Development `http://msdn.microsoft.com/en-us/magazine/ee309510.aspx`

- What's New in the Open XML SDK 2.0 for Microsoft Office `http://msdn.microsoft.com/en-us/library/cc471858(office.14).aspx`

- SPMetal `http://msdn.microsoft.com/en-us/library/ee538255(office.14).aspx`

- OpenXMLDeveloper.org `http://openxmldeveloper.org/`

CHAPTER 10

■ ■ ■

Surfacing Line-of-Business Data in Outlook

It is rare to find an organization with seamlessly integrated data that is uniformly used by the organization's business applications. More common is a set of siloed tools that duplicate data islands with no obvious authoritative source. Information workers in this type of environment often jump in and out of such tools, copying and pasting data from one screen to the next to accomplish their tasks. With SharePoint, the organization is introducing enterprise portals and collaboration workspaces into this environment—and without careful planning, they are increasing the risk of redundant data. SharePoint lists often need to relate to values whose source is an external application. In this chapter, we will detail how as a developer you can register an external application so that its data is available in SharePoint, rather than expecting your end users to duplicate data in yet another system. This will be accomplished using SharePoint 2010's Business Connectivity Services (BCS).

But you were expecting this to be a chapter on Outlook, right? Integrating SharePoint with the external application is only the beginning. Shouldn't this effort be reusable by other applications? Microsoft Outlook is capable of maintaining lots of different types of objects— messages, contacts, tasks, notes, and so forth. These objects often need to relate to the data that is usually locked in your external applications. Therefore, this chapter will also show you not only how to connect an external database to SharePoint, but also how to make its data available offline in Outlook. We will also extend Outlook's functionality so users can see visualizations of the data in the external system from the Outlook interface and create follow-up tasks in a SharePoint site.

Real-World Examples

Almost every organization has classic integration problems with their data repositories whose values need to be a part of other applications. Obvious examples include a database of customers or products. Other repositories may describe units of the organization, such as divisions, departments, and teams. Having this data referenceable is useful for task-oriented processes, project-management plans, and lists of issues.

Organizations also routinely extend Outlook forms in solutions. Often, they want to use Outlook as a tool to construct messages that require more metadata than the average e-mail. Such data is usually required to enforce routing logic, security, or retention policies. Customer relationship management systems (CRM) are also built on the fundamental principle of extending the basic message, contact, meeting, or task with more data about its context.

213

Solution Overview

Data in a line-of-business system tends to be siloed to its particular application. However, within an organization this data must often be available to users who may never even open the application. This is especially true for data elements that are referenced often. To provide some context, in this chapter we will simulate a line-of-business CRM system implemented as a simplified database of customer and order information.

The first goal of this solution is to detail how SharePoint 2010's Business Connectivity Services and SharePoint Designer enable the integration of line-of-business applications. The Business Connectivity Services functionality is an evolution of the Business Data Catalog (BDC) feature that first appeared in SharePoint 2007. In the 2010 release, BCS provides new functionality as well as a dramatically improved toolset. We will use SharePoint Designer to quickly define our external system, letting the designer generate all the necessary steps for performing the normal operations of read, write, list, and delete. We will then choose how this data should be interpreted by the Microsoft Office client application (Outlook) and create an external list in a SharePoint site. This list will be a SharePoint entry point into the data and, unlike the BDC of old, we can modify the list items and have the changes reflected in the original data store.

With the external list created, we will connect the list to Outlook 2010. This will invoke an integration point between the SharePoint server and the Office client, in that the server creates a dynamic solution package and registers it in Outlook. The solution then works with the BCS client functionality of Office to control the synchronization process between server and client. Once the solution is completed, the customers in our CRM database will appear as contacts in Outlook, with the columns of SQL data mapped to Outlook contact properties.

But why stop there? Not only do we want to present our database records in Outlook, we want to provide our end users with a way to visualize order information and act on the data they are seeing. Therefore, this solution will also include an Outlook form region that will add new functionality to the Outlook contact form. The extension will provide two key features. The first is a chart that shows the total sales by month for the customer in a specified year. This chart will be created in an Excel 2010 spreadsheet that will be published through SharePoint's Excel Services. The Outlook form region will be able to specify parameters for the chart and receive an image rendering of it through a URL using Excel Services' REST API.

The second feature of the Outlook form region will enable the end user to create a new follow-up action. The feature will consist of a few fields on the form region that when submitted create a task in a SharePoint site, thus enabling a team of users to be notified of the request and appropriate action to be taken. In coding this piece, we will use SharePoint's new client-side API for managed .NET applications.

Solution Walkthrough

Now let's look at the major elements of the solution and the decisions that were made in coding it. We'll show you how to use SharePoint Designer to connect an external database to SharePoint and render it in an external list, then describe how to connect this list to Outlook so users can see the customer records as Outlook contacts. We will detail how to use Microsoft Excel and Excel Services to render a visualization of the order information in the CRM database. Using Visual Studio, we will build an Outlook add-in and Outlook form region that extends the functionality of the Outlook contact form to provide the desired capabilities. Lastly, we will enable the user to issue follow-up items from the form region that result in SharePoint tasks being created. As with most of the chapters in this book, not every line of code will be explained. Since there are so many moving pieces to this solution, we want to focus on the major elements. We highly recommend you download the accompanying code for this chapter from Apress's site in order to follow along and to use some of the objects there.

The Sample LOB Database

For our sample LOB application, we will use a SQL Server 2008 database named CRMSample. This database stores a list of the organization's customers and some orders that have been placed by them. The cardinality of the relationship between customers and orders is one to many, which means that a single customer could have multiple orders. Figure 10-1 shows the Customer and Order tables of the database.

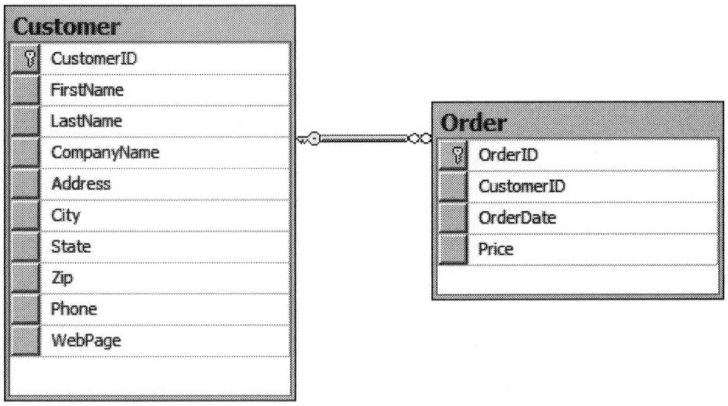

Figure 10-1. The CRMSample Database

To set up the database in your environment, copy the MDF and LDF files of the CRMSample database to your SQL Server. If you did a default install, SQL Server 2008 uses the following path to store these database files: `C:\Program Files\Microsoft SQL Server\MSSQL.10.MSSQLSERVER\MSSQL\Data`. Once the files are in place, right-click on the Databases node of Management Studio's Object Explorer and select Attach. In the dialog, click Add and locate the `CRMSample.mdf` file. The default options are fine. Your dialog should look like Figure 10-2. Click OK; the Object Explorer will refresh to include the CRMSample database. (If you need more help attaching databases in SQL Server 2008, use the steps at `http://msdn2.microsoft.com/en-us/library/ms190209.aspx`.)

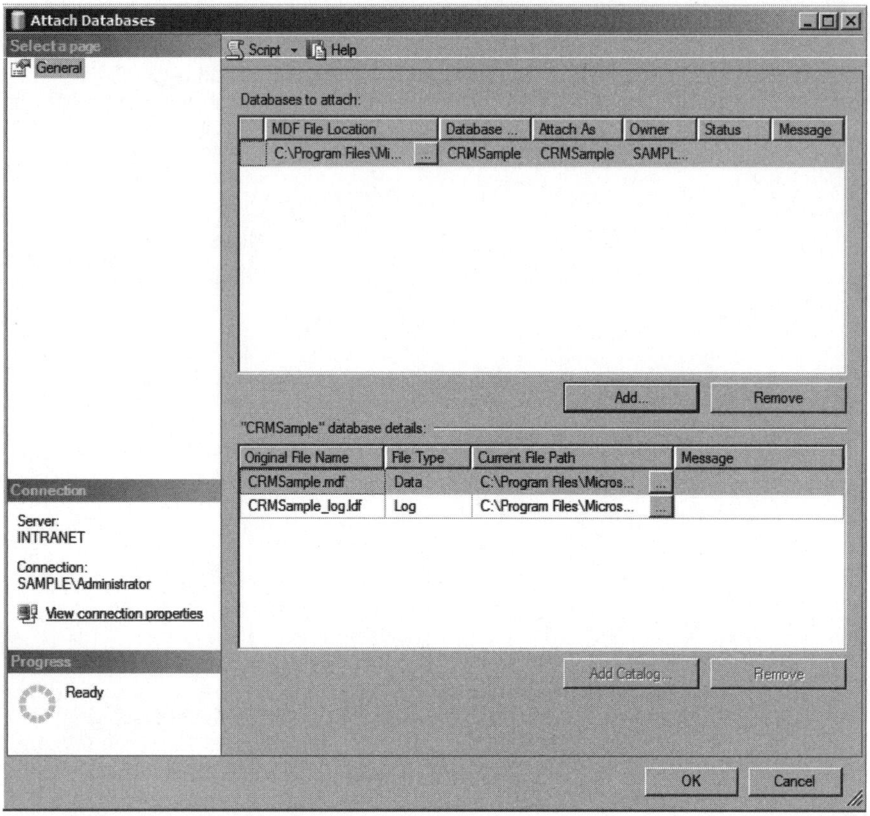

Figure 10-2. Attaching the CRMSample database

While you are in SQL Server's Management Studio, it's a good idea to confirm that the server's security settings will support our integration strategy. There are several options for controlling security when tying an application to SharePoint, which we will elaborate on later in this chapter. In this solution, we will rely on a model in which BCS impersonates the end user's account information when talking to SQL Server. Since both SharePoint and SQL Server are on the same machine in our environment, this will not require any configuration other than making sure the user accounts have rights to the SQL Server database either explicitly or through group membership. Later we will discuss the impact of this choice and also show a different model for Excel Services where we use a service account to communicate with SQL Server regardless of the end user account. For now, make sure your users have access to read and modify the data in this database and that an Active Directory (AD) service account (preferably one of the SharePoint 2010 managed accounts you created when setting up the environment) also has access.

Creating the External Content Type with SharePoint Designer

BCS provides a framework to integrate external applications into SharePoint so that sites can surface data stored there. SharePoint Designer supports connections to external data through a WCF web service, custom .NET class, or directly to a SQL Server database.

■ **Note** You can also create BCS models using Visual Studio 2010, an approach that provides more flexibility in the types of systems you can integrate with. But the rapid development time of SharePoint Designer is so compelling that we decided to focus on it in this chapter.

There are several supported integration scenarios, including surfacing the external application as an external list where the data appears to the user as if it were in a SharePoint list. You can also use the external data in web parts as well as for columns of lists and libraries. BCS also allows you to hook the application into SharePoint's search so it can be crawled by the search service and displayed as search-result items. All of these scenarios are supported without a developer having to introduce new compiled code into the environment. This is an important advantage, as in earlier versions of SharePoint developers sometimes built their own web parts, controls, or protocol handlers to accomplish these tasks. Regardless of the project type, each required custom code to be written, tested, deployed, and maintained. With BCS, you can focus on describing the application, detailing how to connect to the external application as well as its different entities, relationships, and methods. In addition, new to Office 2010, is the ability for Office clients to synchronize this data to a local cache so that it is usable in the Office clients. It is this functionality we will use to have the customer data rendered as Outlook contacts.

Start by creating a SharePoint site as a host for the integration solution. This can be a normal site using the normal SharePoint Team Site template. In our environment, this site was located at `http://edhild3/sites/crm`. Once the site has been created, open it in SharePoint Designer 2010. Just click **Open Site** and specify your team site's URL.

If you're familiar with SharePoint Designer 2007, you will notice that the interface of the 2010 release has been dramatically changed. Like the rest of the Office applications, SharePoint Designer 2010 now uses the ribbon interface to make actions easier to find. A new Site Objects navigation on the left-hand side of the tool simplifies finding the right starting point to perform certain types of work. This navigation replaces the folder structure of the site, which required you to understand cryptic folder names in order to know where items such as master pages and content types were located. You can still access the structure of the site by clicking the All Files folder at the bottom of the Site Objects menu.

Since our goal is to integrate the SharePoint site with the external CRMSample database, click on the External Content Types node in Site Objects. The first time you access this it may take a few seconds to resolve. If this is a brand new site, you shouldn't have any types defined, so just click the **External Content Type** button in the New group of the ribbon. This will take you to a Summary View of the external content type. We want to first focus our attention on the External Content Type Information group of controls in the top-left portion of the screen. It is here that you can enter the basic information about the content type. Use the steps below and when you are finished, the page should look like Figure 10-3.

1. Specify **Customer** as the name of the content type.

2. Specify **Customer** as the display name of the content type.

3. Change the Office Item Type drop-down to **Contact**. This is the setting that lets Outlook treat the customer database records as Outlook contacts.

4. Change the Office Sync for External List drop-down to **Enabled**. Otherwise, Outlook will not be able to take the content offline.

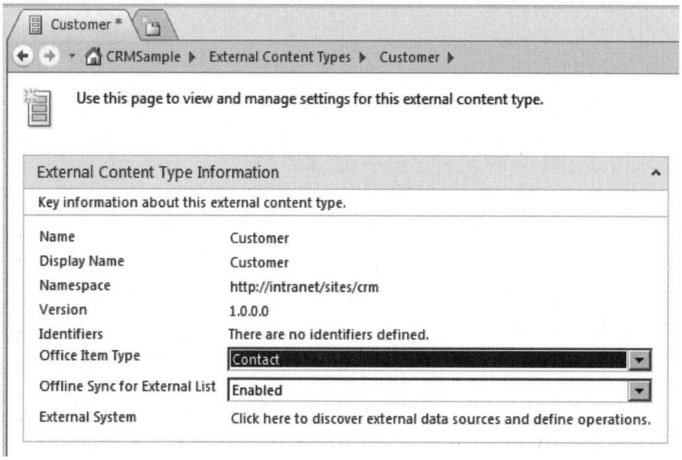

Figure 10-3. Defining the Customer external content type

Now we need to use SharePoint Designer on the external system we wish to pair with this external content type definition. On the ribbon, click the **Operations Design View** button in the Ribbon to go to the area where you can define your SQL Server connection and the content you want to interact with. Use the following steps to establish the connection to the Customer table of the CRMSample database:

1. Click the **Add Connection** button at the top of the Operations Design View.

2. Choose **SQL Server** in the External Data Source Type Selection dialog.

3. Specify the SQL Server connection properties. In our environment, the SQL Server is on the same machine as SharePoint. Even so you need to make sure you provide a name that both the SharePoint Server and a potential client can resolve. We entered **edhild3**. The name of the database is **CRMSample**. And for security, select the option to **Connect with User's Identity**. You can see these options in Figure 10-4.

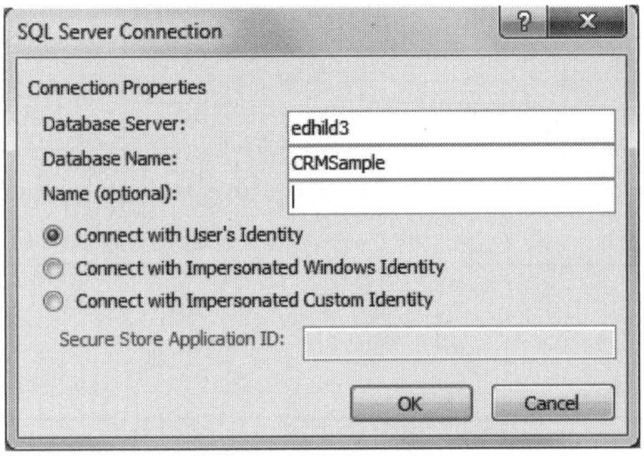

Figure 10-4. Defining the SQL Server connection

■ **Note** As mentioned earlier, this solution takes advantage of the fact that our SQL Server and SharePoint Server are the same machine. If your users are using Windows authentication and your CRMSample database is on a remote server, your users would have to authenticate using Kerberos instead of NTLM to make sure their credentials could make it to the remote SQL Server. If you don't care about your users' credentials being used to access the SQL Server or you need to have alternate credentials for users, the last two options allow you to rely on the Secure Store Service of SharePoint 2010 to configure the account to be used. We will use this technique in setting up Excel Services later, and you can read more about it at `http://msdn.microsoft.com/en-us/library/ms566523(office.14).aspx`

---

4. In the SQL Server Connection dialog, click **OK**.

5. In the Data Source Explorer area, expand the **CRMSample** database node and then the **Tables** node so you can find the Customer table.

6. Right-click on the Customer table and choose **Create All Operations** from the context menu.

Our next step in connecting the Customer table to SharePoint involves giving SharePoint Designer enough information to generate the operations it will use to interact with the data store, including reading, editing, listing, and deleting customers. You won't have to write any SQL statements. You simply supply the wizard that opened when you chose Create All Operations with the appropriate information. Use the following steps to complete the All operations wizard:

1. Click **Next** to enter the Parameters configuration screen.

2. All of the columns of the table will be used as parameters, but you need to configure how the Office client applications will treat the data in each column. Use Table 10-1 to set properties for each parameter. Figure 10-5 shows the CompanyName field settings.

Table 10-1. Configuring the Customer Operation Parameters

Data Source Element	Office Property Setting	Notes
CustomerID	Custom Property	Make sure Map to Identifier is checked
FirstName	First Name	
LastName	Last Name	
CompanyName	Company Name	Select Show In Picker checkbox
Address	Business Address Street	
City	Business Address City	
State	Business Address State	
Zip	Business Address Postal Code	
Phone	Business Telephone Number	
WebPage	Business Home Page	

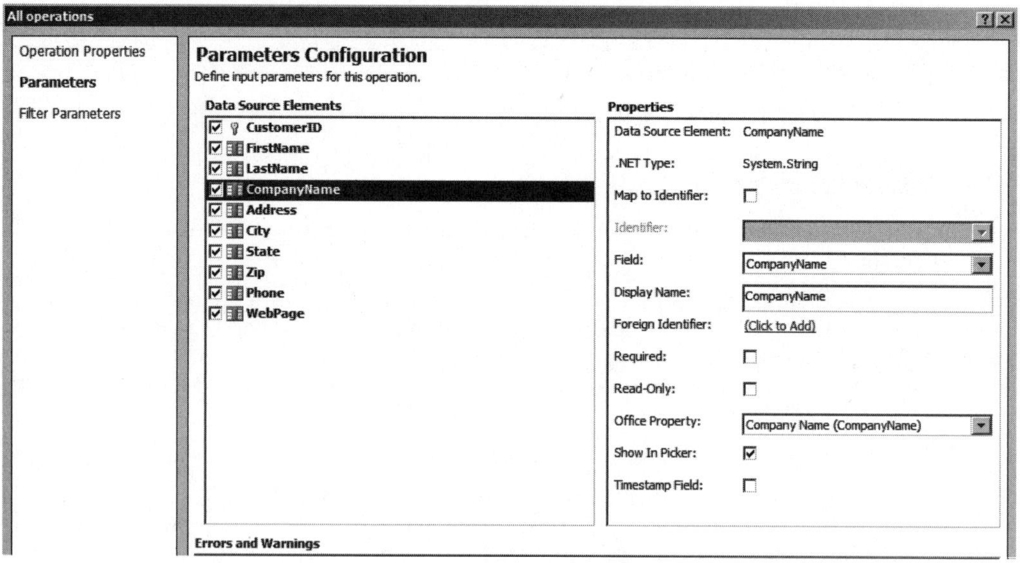

Figure 10-5. Configuring the CompanyName parameter for operations

3. Click **Next**.

4. You will see a warning at the bottom of the wizard recommending that you add a Limit Filter for this type to help prevent reading extremely large datasets that may cause a bottleneck in your system. Click the **Add Filter Parameter** button.

5. Click the (**Click to Add**) hyperlink on the right-hand side of the screen next to the Filter label.

6. In the Filter Configuration dialog, set the filter type to **Limit** and click **OK**.

7. Optional: Underneath the Filter link you clicked earlier, use the Default Value setting to set a limit on the number of records that should be returned. You can simply type that number over the <<None>> text. In our environment, we set it to **3000**, but obviously there are a lot of factors that should go into this setting, such as the power of your servers, your network, and the number of records you expect in the table.

8. Click **Finish**.

9. Click **Save** in the Quick Access Toolbar area (just above the File menu of SharePoint Designer) to save your changes to the Customer external content type.

Now that you have defined the external content type and given SharePoint Designer information about the data, you can create an external list in the SharePoint site. This external list will appear to end users as any other SharePoint list, but it is really an interface to the data in your external system. SharePoint will automatically build the forms necessary for users to view, edit, delete, and even add new customers to the CRMSample database. SharePoint Designer will create the external list in the same SharePoint site you opened at the beginning of this chapter. Click the Create Lists and Form button on the ribbon, and use Figure 10-6 to complete the resulting dialog. Here you specify the name of the list to create and the operation that should be used to read an item. For this example we won't create a custom InfoPath form for interacting with the data, though we will discuss it as a possible extension point at the end of the chapter.

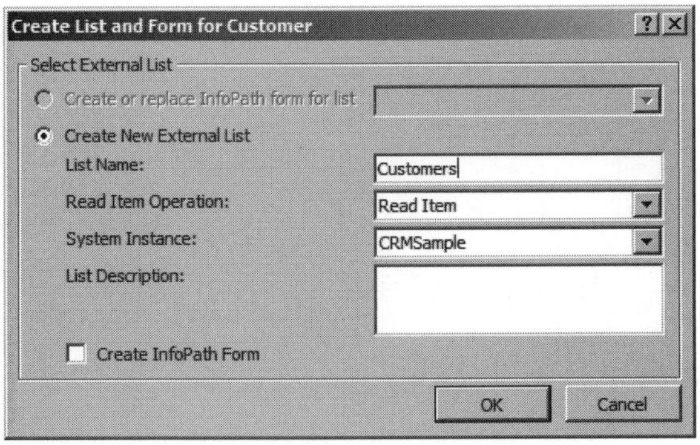

Figure 10-6. Creating the Customers external list in the SharePoint site

After you click OK, SharePoint Designer will create the external list in the SharePoint site. We are now done with SharePoint Designer. There is one additional configuration option you may have to set before jumping to the list in your site. Mainly, you will need to confirm the security settings of the BDC Service Application in your SharePoint farm. Use the following steps to set up security settings for the Customer external content type.

1. From Central Administration, click the **Manage service applications** link in the Application Management group.

2. Highlight the Business Data Connectivity Service application and click **Manage** in the Ribbon.

3. Click the checkbox next to the Customer external content type and click the Set Object Permissions button in the Ribbon.

4. Enter an account or group for the users who should have access to the external content type and click the **Add** button. You can then define specific permissions for these users. In our development environment, we simply granted ourselves all of the permissions. Make sure the checkbox for these permissions to apply to all the methods of the external content type is checked.

5. Your Set Object Permissions dialog should look like Figure 10-7. Click **OK**.

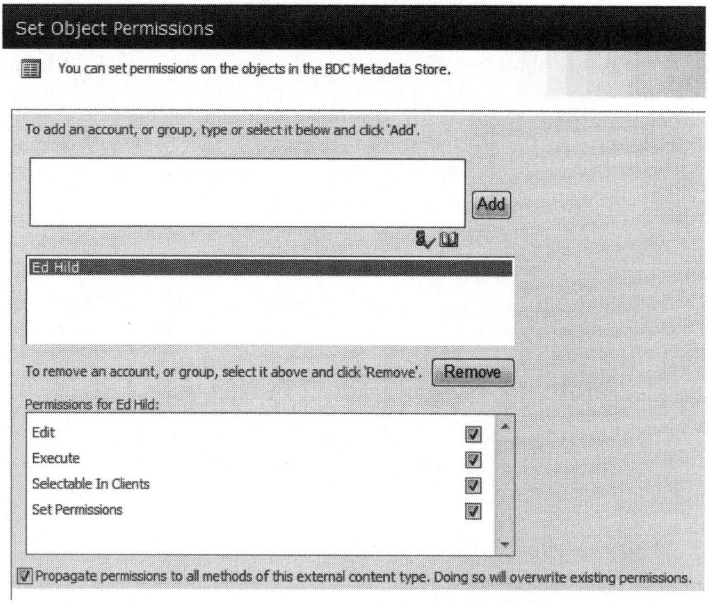

Figure 10-7. Setting permissions on the external content type

Now navigate back to your development team site and play around with some edits in both in the external list and directly in the SQL database. Figure 10-8 shows the Customers external list in the SharePoint site.

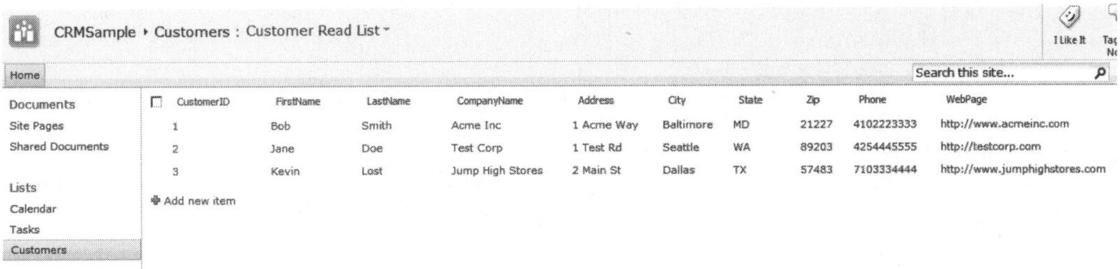

Figure 10-8. The Customers external list

Connecting the External List to Outlook

In the previous section we focused on connecting the external database into SharePoint and creating an external list in a SharePoint site. With this complete, our users can interact with the data in the SharePoint site and the corresponding changes are made to the CRMSample database. Now we will extend the reach of this data onto the desktop, to Outlook. Use the following steps to connect the external list to Outlook:

1. While viewing the items on the Customers external list, click the **List** tab on the ribbon.

2. Click the **Connect to Outlook** button in the Connect & Export group.

3. SharePoint will generate a dynamic solution package to register this list with the BCS client functionality. Click **Install** when you are asked to install the Office customization as shown in Figure 10-9. Note that the warning about the "Unknown Publisher" results from SharePoint using self-signed certificates to sign the packages. An administrator in a production environment can change this to use a specific certificate that is trusted by the client machines, or else a trust with the BCS signing certificate must be established.

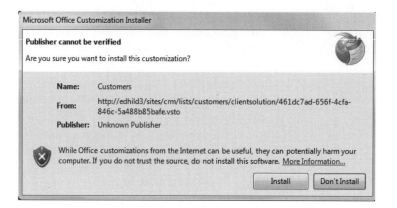

Figure 10-9. Installing the Office customization

4. When you are informed that the installation has been successful, open up Microsoft Outlook. You should see a new heading below your Outlook Tasks navigation button entitled SharePoint External Lists, with your Customers list underneath as in Figure 10-10. There may be a delay before you actually see the customer contacts in Outlook as it may take a while for the first synchronization to complete.

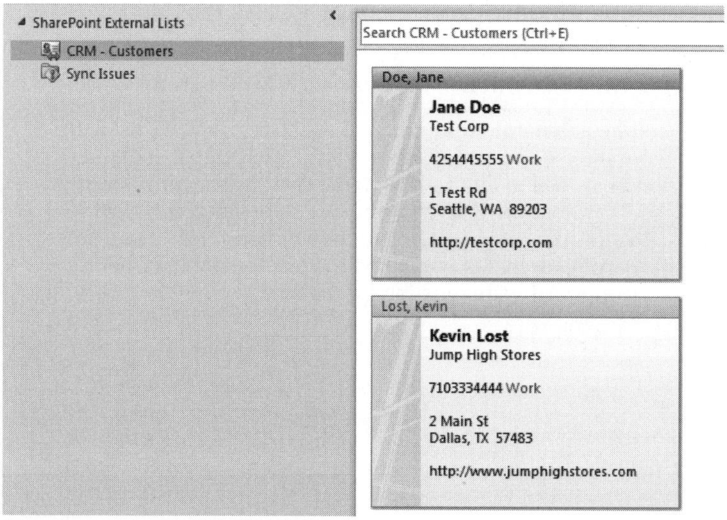

Figure 10-10. External content types in Outlook

Remember that when we defined the parameters of our external content type, we were very explicit in mapping each data value to a known Office property. As shown in Figure 10-11, Outlook honored these settings and when you open a particular Customer contact, each of the parameters is placed on the contact form as you would expect.

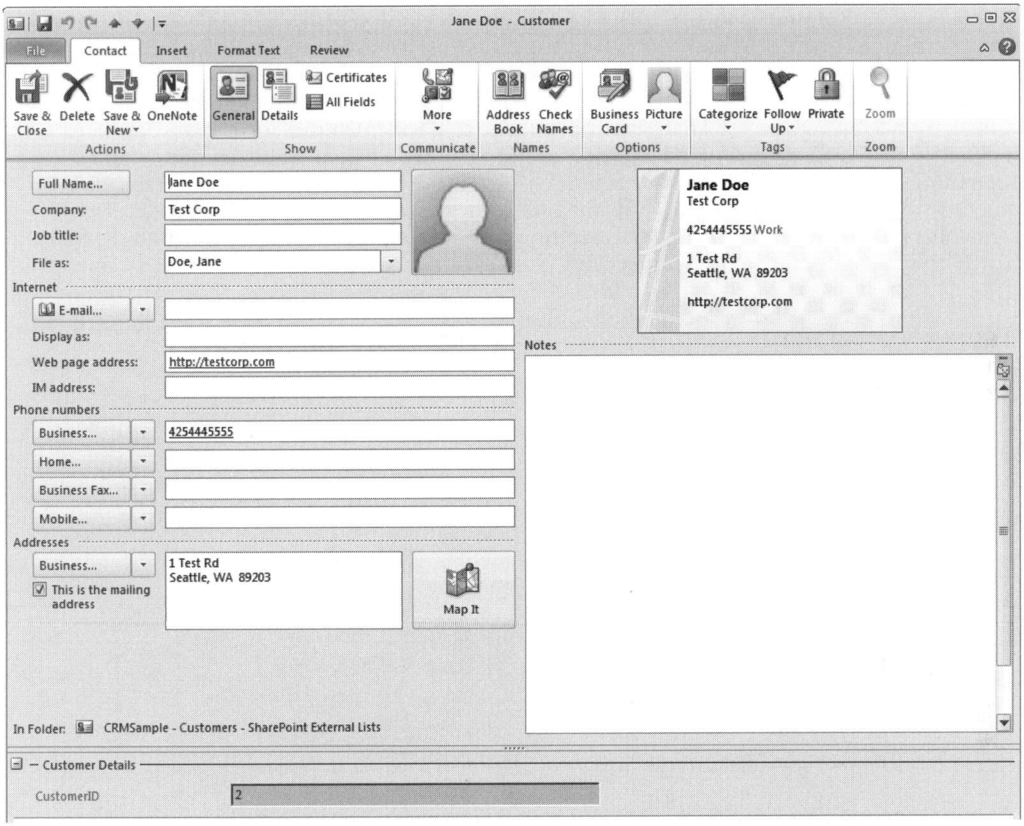

Figure 10-11. Viewing customer data in Outlook

Just as you played a bit to get a feel for making edits in the SharePoint external list and the database, now take some time to gain experience with the Customers in Outlook. You can edit, delete, and even create new customers. Just note that external lists in Outlook have their own method of synchronization. They do not update during a Send/Receive action as you might expect. There is an internal timer that determines the synchronization schedule. You can force a sync, however, by right-clicking on the Customers external list node where Outlook displays its folders and selecting **Sync Now**.

As this point, we already have a very interesting solution and we have not written one line of code. To review, we took external data that lived in a line-of-business application's SQL database and connected it to SharePoint through SharePoint's Business Connectivity Services. With that done, we could get an offline copy in Outlook. Since our data is most like Outlook contacts, we mapped each field to a corresponding Office contact property. After the synchronization, our external data can be maintained as Outlook contacts.

Visualizing Customer Order Data using Excel

One of the goals for our solution is to give a user a visual representation of a customer's total dollar value of orders by month for a given calendar year. To accomplish this, we will use SharePoint's Excel Services to build a parameterized spreadsheet containing a chart we can display in Outlook. But before we get into Excel and the chart, we need to take care of a few items in the environment to make this approach possible. First, we need a SQL Server Analysis Services cube that will enable us to slice the data across different dimensions. The code download for this chapter includes a Visual Studio solution named CRMSampleCube. Open this project on your SQL Server using the SQL Server Business Intelligence Development Studio tool. Note that for SQL Server 2008, this tool is Visual Studio 2008-based. We will review elements of this solution, confirm that its settings are correct, and deploy it to Analysis Services. Figure 10-12 shows the structure of this project.

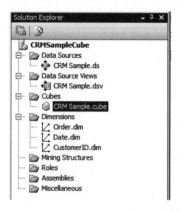

Figure 10-12. The CRMSampleCube project

The first node in this project is the data source, connecting this solution to the transactional CRMSample database. Right-click on the `CRM Sample.ds` node and choose **View Designer**. Confirm that the connection string is valid for your environment. If it's not, correct it. If you are doing everything on a single machine, using "." (without the quotes) instead of the server name is adequate. The second node, CRM Sample.dsv is the data source view that lets you see all artifacts you'll be building your cube on. Viewing this in the designer shows you that we are focusing on the Orders table from the CRMSample database. In the Dimensions group, you can see the three ways we want to analyze our data. The first dimension is Order, which is based on the primary key of the table OrderID and uniquely defines each row. The second dimension, Date, lets you slice the data by an element of time, such as year, month, or day. The CustomerID dimension allows you to group the data by customer for analysis. Update the cube by right-clicking on it and choosing **Process**. Your analysis solution should now be deployed to your SQL Server.

■ **Note** The Customer dimension is based only on the CustomerID since that's all that is necessary for the visualization we are going to build. If you prefer, you could add the Customer table to the cube and build the dimension from the company's name. Just be sure to make corresponding change to the Excel spreadsheet we will create later.

With the OLAP cube created, we will now configure Excel Services. Remember when we discussed the security options related to accessing the CRMSample database through BCS? We need to specify how we want security to be handled as the user interacts with the Excel spreadsheet that has to access to our Analysis Services cube. With BCS, we showed you how you can have the user's identity pass all the way through to the data source. This time, we will incorporate another technique relying on a single account to access the cube, no matter which user is interacting with the spreadsheet. This approach is useful when you don't need individual identity information or configuration at the back-end and you want all users to be treated equally. Getting this to work with Excel Services is going to involve configuring security settings both on the server and on the Excel workbook itself. On the server, we will configure an application account in the Secure Store Service and tell Excel Services to use this when no other security configuration preferences have been set in the workbook. Use the following steps to configure the Secure Store Service:

1. From Central Administration, click **Application Management**.

2. In the Service Applications group, click **Manage service applications**.

3. Find the Secure Store Service Application node. Click to select it and click the **Manage** button in the ribbon.

■ **Note** If you have not set up this shared service application, you will be required to generate a new key before creating the new application detailed below. Just click the Generate New Key button in the ribbon and specify a pass phrase.

---

4. Click **New** in the ribbon to create a new application entry in the Secure Store Service.

5. Enter the following Application Settings:

   Target Application ID: **Excel Services Unmanaged Acct**

   Display Name: **Unmanaged Acct**

   Contact Email: **edhild@microsoft.com**

   Target Application Type: **Group** (since we want all users to use the same account)

6. Click **Next**.

7. Click **Next** in the fields dialog, as the only two pieces of information we need are the user name and password.

8. For membership settings, specify an Active Directory group that will administer these settings. We chose **northamerica\edhild**. Also, specify which users will be members and leverage the application account. We used **northamerica\Domain Users**.

9. Click **OK**.

10. When the screen refreshes, you should be back at the list of applications defined in the Secure Store Service. Select the Excel Services Unmanaged Acct you just created, and choose **Set** in the Credentials group of the ribbon. This lets you specify the user name and password to use to connect to the Analysis Service cube, regardless of which user is using the spreadsheet.

11. Specify the user name and password of the account you'd like the system to use. It is OK to use one of your SharePoint service accounts here. Click **OK**.

Now that we have an account defined in the Secure Store Service, we must tell Excel Services to use this information when no other security preferences have been specified. This approach is called specifying the Unmanaged Account. Use the following steps to complete this task:

1. From Central Administration, click **Application Management**.

2. In the Service Applications group, click **Manage service applications**.

3. Find the Excel Services Application node. Click to select it and click the **Manage** button in the ribbon.

4. Click **Global Settings**.

5. At the end of this page, there is a set of settings specific to external data. There will be a textbox allowing you to specify the Application ID in the Secure Store Service that Excel Services should use as an unmanaged account. Enter the ID of **Excel Services Unmanaged Acct**.

6. Click **OK**.

We can now focus on the spreadsheet. Grab the spreadsheet named `CRMSales.xlsx` from the code download. We won't cover how to build this from scratch, but instead explain its key components. First, let's finish the security discussion by looking at the security configuration of the data connection in the workbook. You can find the CRMSampleCube connection through the ribbon by clicking on the Data tab and then the Connections button. Choose to display the properties of the connection, and on the Definition tab you'll see an Authentication Settings button. Click it to show the dialog in Figure 10-13. The setting of None means that Excel Services will use the Unmanaged Account configuration to talk to the data source.

Figure 10-13. Excel Services Authentication Settings in the Workbook

Now look at the top of Sheet1 of the spreadsheet, where you'll see two named ranges (cells B1 and B2) that serve as parameters for the spreadsheet. These ranges are named CustomerID and CalYear. As these values change, so do the values in the table and the chart. We have formatted these cells as Text (make sure these cells have a green corner to them) since we will use their values to build some strings that will serve as filtering expressions as we query the cube. You can see these expressions being built on Sheet2. These expressions will be used as parameters to cube queries and therefore they are built using the values of the named ranges. Listing 10-1 shows a few of these expressions for CustomerID 2 and CalYear 2008.

■ **Note** You might wonder why we are not simply using an Excel PivotTable in this solution. As you will see in a bit, we are planning to access the chart through the REST API of Excel Services, and you can't set the filters of an Excel PivotTable through the REST API, only named ranges. This approach is a work-around to that limitation.

Listing 10-1. Dynamic Expressions for Querying the Cube

```
[CustomerID].[2]
[Date].[Month].[January 2008]
[Date].[Month].[February 2008]
[Date].[Month].[March 2008]
[Date].[Month].[April 2008]
```

Now turn your attention back to Sheet1 and look at the table. It is here where these expressions will be used. The first column is simply the months of the year. The second column uses Excel's CUBEVALUE function to query the cube for specific data. Here is the function call for the month of January.

```
=CUBEVALUE("CRMSampleCube","[Measures].[Price]", Sheet2!A1, Sheet2!A2)
```

The parameters to this call specify the name of the cube, the metric (data point) we would like returned, and the two expressions we saw earlier slice the data. These expressions specify the particular customer (CustomerID 2) and the timeframe (January 2008) we want to consider.

From here, the chart is simply a column chart based on the data in the table. You can see that it is sensitive to the values in the named ranges by changing the customer or the calendar year. Note that the database in the code download only has order data for customers 1 and 2 for years 2008 and 2009. Use the following steps to publish this spreadsheet to the SharePoint site you used to create the external list:

1. From Excel's File menu, choose **Save & Send**.

2. Choose **Save to SharePoint**.

3. Click the **Publish Options** button at the top-right of the screen. These options allow you to choose to show only specific items in the workbook. Select the chart (named Chart 3). This choice is shown in Figure 10-14.

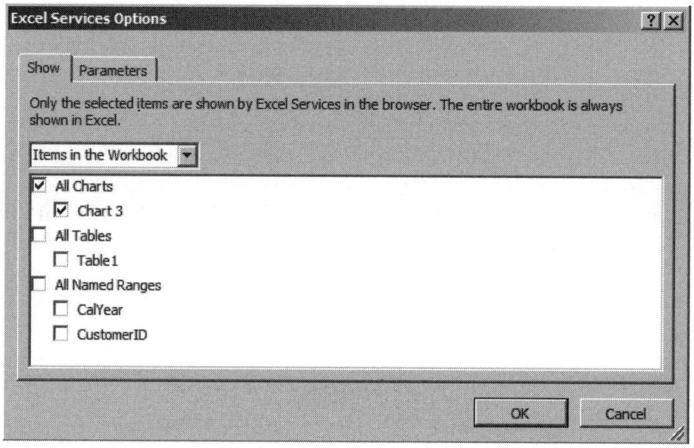

Figure 10-14. Selecting workbook items to publish to Excel Services

4. On the Parameters tab, make sure CalYear and CustomerID have been specified as parameters.

5. Click **OK**.

6. Click the **Save As** button to save the file to the Shared Documents library of your team site using `CRMSales.xlsx` as the file name. For us the URL is: `http://edhild3/sites/CRM/Shared Documents/CRMSales.xlsx`. You can also confirm the publish options on the Save As dialog.

7. Click **Save**.

This will publish your spreadsheet to the SharePoint server. It should open automatically into the Excel Service web interface. The parameters of CustomerID and CalYear should appear in a pane to the right of the chart. Just as in the Excel client, changing these values and clicking **Apply** will redraw the chart. You can get back to this interface by choosing the View In Browser option in your `CRMSales.xlsx` file in the Shared Documents library.

We are almost finished. Our desired visualization has been created in Excel and published to Excel Services. We can even change the parameters interactively in the browser and get the different charts we want. However, this browser interface isn't the ideal experience to bring into the Outlook client. When we extend the Outlook form (in the next section), we already know which customer we want selected and shouldn't need to change it; the user would simply open up a different customer contact. Fortunately, Excel Services in SharePoint 2010 provides another means for us to specify the parameters for the spreadsheet and get the chart we want. This alternative is called the REST API and it involves simply specifying a properly formatted URL that will return the corresponding chart as a PNG image. We could have used a web service to interact with Excel Services, but that would require a bit more code to be written, and the REST API gives us exactly what we need. Here is the URL you can use to request an image of the chart for CustomerID 1 and CalYear 2008.

```
http://edhild3/sites/crm/_vti_bin/ExcelRest.aspx/Shared%20Documents/↵
  CRMSales.xlsx/model/charts('Chart%203')↵
  ?Ranges('CalYear')=2008&Ranges('CustomerID')=1
```

Note that this should all be one line and is wrapped here just to fit in the text.

As you can see, the URL points to the spreadsheet asking for the chart object named Chart 3 while specifying input values for the two named ranges. You can put this URL in the browser now to test it. We will use it in the next section as we integrate this chart into Outlook. Figure 10-15 shows the resulting chart image. (You can find more Excel Services REST API examples at `http://msdn.microsoft.com/en-us/library/ee556820(office.14).aspx`.)

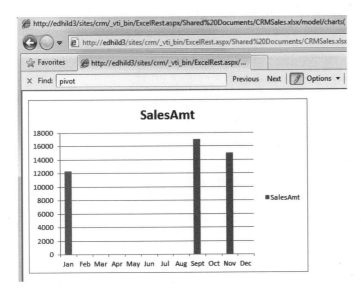

Figure 10-15. Using Excel Services' REST API to produce a chart

Extending the Outlook Contact Form

Users of Outlook interact with several different types of objects, including messages, contacts, tasks, and events. Each of these objects is presented in an Outlook form. It seems as if from the very beginning organizations have wanted to customize, extend, and inject code into these forms. This is largely due to Outlook's prominent place in the work lives of users. Many users leave it open all day, checking messages and maintaining their calendar. Before Outlook 2007, developers who wanted to customize an Outlook form usually found themselves redesigning the entire form, even when all they wanted to do was add a few fields. In older versions of Outlook, these custom forms were deployed centrally on the Exchange server. Developers also had a difficult time injecting their own code or script into their forms. Outlook 2007 introduced a new concept called Form Regions, which brought managed code to Outlook form development, and this continues in Outlook 2010.

An Outlook 2010 form-region solution is made up of two main elements. The first is the form region itself, which contains the layout of the form and its controls. The second is an Outlook add-in that hosts the form region. To build your form region, you can either use the Form Region Designer in Visual Studio 2010 or construct the form region in Outlook and store it as an Outlook Form Storage (OFS) file. We will use the Form Region Designer in this solution.

There are four types of form regions, which are distinguished by the way they interact with the existing Outlook form.

- *Separate:* Adds the form region as a new page in an Outlook form.

- *Adjoining:* Appends the form region to the bottom of an Outlook form's default page.

- *Replacement:* Adds the form region as a new page that replaces the default page of an Outlook form.

- *Replace-all:* Replaces the whole Outlook form with the form region.

Because we still want the customer information to display in the default contact form, we will choose to create our custom user interface as a separate form region type. This will place a new button in the ribbon that displays the new form region page. Use the following steps to create the Outlook form region add-in project and the form region item that will extend the contact form:

1. From Visual Studio 2010's New Project dialog, display the Office 2010 C# project types and select the Outlook 2010 add-in template.

2. Name the project and solution **CRMExtension**.

3. Make sure the **.NET Framework 4** is selected and click **OK**.

4. Right-click on your project in Solution Explorer and choose **Add -> New Item**.

5. Select Office to filter the item templates and select **OutlookFormRegion**. Name this item **CustomerDetails.cs** and click **Add**.

6. Choose the **Design a new form region** option and click **Next**.

7. Select **Separate** and click **Next**.

8. Name the form region **CustomerDetails** and click **Next**.

9. Select **Contact** to associate this form region with the default contact form. Make sure no other message classes are selected and click **Finish**.

Remember our design goals? We aim to extend the contact form for our customer records in Outlook so that the user can see the chart we built earlier and issue follow-up items that will be tasks in the SharePoint site. Again, we recommend grabbing this solution from the code download so you won't have to worry about identifying the value of every property of every control. So that we don't lose site of the overall goal, Figure 10-16 shows the completed solution running in Outlook.

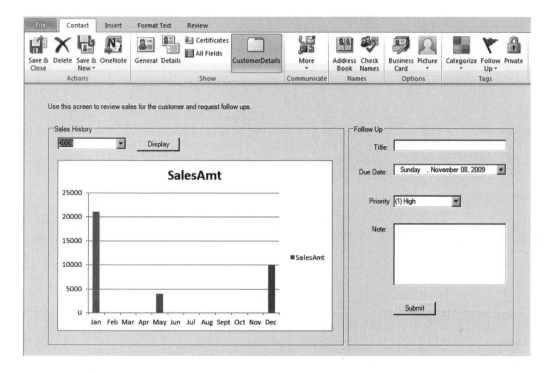

Figure 10-16. The CustomerDetails Outlook form region

If you dig through the code in the download, you'll see that in the form region's FormRegionShowing event handler, the form region is making sure that the contact that it is operating on is indeed a customer. To make this check, we look for the CustomerID parameter that was passed to Outlook as a custom property. This code is in Listing 10-2.

Listing 10-2. The FormRegionShowing Event Handler

```
private void CustomerDetails_FormRegionShowing(object sender, System.EventArgs e)
{
  Outlook.ContactItem item = (Outlook.ContactItem)this.OutlookItem;
  if (item.UserProperties["CustomerID::5"] != null)
  {
    lstYear.Items.Clear();
    int currentYear = DateTime.Today.Year;
```

```
    for (int i = 0; i < 5; i++)
    {
      lstYear.Items.Add(currentYear - i);
    }
    lstYear.SelectedIndex = 0;
    lstPriority.SelectedIndex = 0;
  }
  else
  {
    lblMessage.Text = "This contact is not a CRM customer.";
    groupBox1.Enabled = false;
    groupBox2.Enabled = false;
  }
}
```

You'll notice that we are accessing the CustomerID property using the string `CustomerID::5`. This was the key that Outlook assigned to our custom property. You may wonder how we discovered it. Simply click the All Fields button in the Show group of one of your customer contacts and you can see this property, as in Figure 10-17. In the FormRegionShowing event we also initialize the year drop-down to display the current year and the four previous.

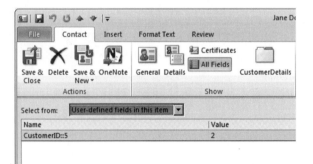

Figure 10-17. Finding keys for custom properties

If you look at the left side of the form region (in Figure 10-16), you see that we have integrated the chart from Excel Services. To get the image on the form region, we first created a Windows Presentation Foundation (WPF) user control named chart.xaml that has a single image control on its design surface. We chose to use WPF because its image control has no problem rendering a graphic from a URL source. In the code-behind of this file, we added one method, shown in Listing 10-3, which sets the source of the image to a specified URL.

Listing 10-3. Using the WPF Image Control

```
public void SetImage(string Url)
{
  image1.Source = new BitmapImage(new Uri(Url));
}
```

Now when the user selects a calendar year and clicks the display button, the code in Listing 10-4 takes over to generate a properly formatted URL to use in the WPF control. Since this may take a few seconds to render, we disable the display button while this code is running so the user doesn't just continue to click it. The slowest response will be when your Outlook form region loads for the first time and the spreadsheet is examined for the first time.

Listing 10-4. Retrieving the Selected Chart from Excel Services

```
private void btnDisplay_Click(object sender, EventArgs e)
{
 btnDisplay.Enabled = false;
 Outlook.ContactItem item = (Outlook.ContactItem)this.OutlookItem;
 int customerID = (int)item.UserProperties["CustomerID::5"].Value;
 int year = (int) lstYear.SelectedItem;
 string url = string.Format(@"http://edhild3/sites/crm/_vti_bin/ExcelRest.aspx/↵
    Shared%20Documents/CRMSales.xlsx/model/charts('Chart%203')↵
    ?Ranges('CalYear')={0}&Ranges('CustomerID')={1}", year, customerID);
 chart1.SetImage(url);
 btnDisplay.Enabled = true;
}
```

■ **Note** You may want to control Excel Services' behavior as to whether or not a call through the REST API causes a refresh of the data in the spreadsheet. You can find this option in the configuration of the Trusted File Location in the Excel Services service application in Central Administration.

The right-hand side of our Outlook form region enables the user to specify a follow-up action if required. The result that we want from this portion of the form region is that the data the user enters here should be used to create a task in the SharePoint site that hosts our Customers external list. This list just an out-of-the-box tasks list named FollowUps with an additional text column named Customer.

It is important to understand that this Outlook add-in and form region will not have access to the same SharePoint assemblies that make up the server-side object model. This is because the add-in will run within the Outlook application on a user's desktop, and therefore remote to the SharePoint server. As you will see a bit later, SharePoint 2010 provides a client-side library to assist us with the communication. This communication between our add-in and the SharePoint server will be over HTTP. However, the current setting of the project will prevent us from leveraging code that references the System.Web assembly. Let's remove this restriction by changing the Target Framework setting for the project. Follow these instructions to change the Target Framework setting on the project so that the client-side library will be permitted:

1. Right-click on the project and choose **Properties**.

2. On the Application tab, locate the Target Framework selection dialog.

3. Change this setting from **.NET Framework 4 Client Profile** to **.NET Framework 4**.

4. Click **Yes** in the confirmation dialog.

Now we can add the references to the SharePoint 2010 client-side library and runtime for .NET applications. As was discussed in Chapter 3, SharePoint 2010 provides several different types of client-side libraries, enabling communication from solutions not running on the server. For this project, add the **Microsoft.SharePoint.Client** and **Microsoft.SharePoint.Client.Runtime** assemblies to the project. These assemblies may show up on the .NET tab of the Add References dialog or you can find them in the `C:\Program Files\Common Files\Microsoft Shared\Web Server Extensions\14\ISAPI` folder in a default installation.

With this change in place, our Outlook form region can now take advantage of the SharePoint client API for managed applications. The code in Listing 10-5 establishes a client context for the desired SharePoint site, creates a new task item, and sets the item's fields to match our Outlook form region. The ExecuteQuery call at the end submits this request to the SharePoint server.

Listing 10-5. Using the SharePoint Client API to Add FollowUp Tasks

```
private void btnSubmit_Click(object sender, EventArgs e)
{
  btnSubmit.Enabled = false;
  using (ClientContext context = new ClientContext("http://edhild3/sites/crm"))
  {
    List oList = context.Web.Lists.GetByTitle("FollowUps");
    ListItemCreationInformation itemCreateInfo = new ListItemCreationInformation();
    ListItem oListItem = oList.AddItem(itemCreateInfo);
    oListItem["Title"] = txtTitle.Text;
    oListItem["DueDate"] = dpDueDate.Value.ToShortDateString();
    Outlook.ContactItem item = (Outlook.ContactItem)this.OutlookItem;
    oListItem["Customer"] = item.CompanyName;

    oListItem["Priority"] = lstPriority.SelectedItem.ToString();
    oListItem["Body"] = txtNote.Text;

    oListItem.Update();
    context.ExecuteQuery();

    MessageBox.Show("Follow up submitted");
    btnSubmit.Enabled = true;
  }
}
```

Important Lessons

This CRM extension application incorporated several key techniques that are worth highlighting as they can easily be reused in other projects.

Leveraging SharePoint Designer 2010 to connect external data to SharePoint BCS: SharePoint Designer 2010 provided us with a wizard-based, rapid toolset to project our database into SharePoint as an external list. It generated the methods for interacting with the data and enabled us to control how those values would be interpreted by the Office clients.

Connecting an external list to Outlook: Since our data was contact-like, it made sense to extend our use of BCS to the user's desktop in the form of Outlook contacts. There was no need to write additional code. SharePoint created the customization for Outlook dynamically, and once it was installed our users had a synchronized view of the data in their Outlook client.

Visualizing data with Excel Services: In this solution, we used Excel Services for much more than just rendering spreadsheets or web parts on a SharePoint site. We were able to use the Excel Services' REST API to request the chart object in the spreadsheet as an image to use in our custom application. This meant that we didn't need to have a copy of the data ourselves, or code any fancy web services, or use any complex chart controls in our Outlook form region.

Extending Outlook with form regions: This solution extended the functionality of the default contact form to provide the user with additional information and the ability to act on it. This was accomplished without making the user leave the contact form or open another application or browser.

Extension Points

While coding this example, we thought of several variations to the solution that we didn't incorporate. Mostly, these were not included because they distracted from the overall objective of the solution. We call them out now as extension points since they may be applicable to a specific project you're working on.

Create a custom InfoPath form for the external list: In our example, we just used the default interface for external lists. SharePoint supports customization of this form using InfoPath. With the custom form, you could add advanced validation or even look up information in other systems if necessary.

Take more data offline: Currently, the only data available offline to the user is the customer contacts in Outlook. You could incorporate Order information into the BCS so that it too is available offline, but then you wouldn't have access to Excel Services to render the chart. The chart control from the Microsoft Chart Controls for Microsoft .NET Framework 3.5 may be an alternative. You could also take the FollowUps list offline by connecting it to Outlook. Because it is not an external list, however, it would behave differently than the Customers.

Add workflow for FollowUps: You can add a workflow so that action is taken when new follow-up items are posted to the SharePoint site. You could do some sort of lookup on the Customer to determine which user is the relationship manager for that account and send out an e-mail notifying that user that a certain sales representative had asked her to look into something regarding the account.

Further Reading

The following links are to resources that we think a reader interested in the material presented in this chapter would find useful:

- Creating Outlook Form Regions `http://msdn.microsoft.com/en-us/library/bb386301(VS.100).aspx`

- SQL Server 2008 Analysis Services Resources `http://www.microsoft.com/sqlserver/2008/en/us/analysis-services.aspx`

- Plan Excel Services Authentication `http://technet.microsoft.com/en-us/library/ee662541(office.14).aspx`

- How to Use Excel's CUBEVALUE function `http://www.ehow.com/how_2248736_use-excels-cubevalue-function.html`

- Excel Services in SharePoint 2010 REST API Syntax `http://blogs.msdn.com/excel/archive/2009/11/05/excel-services-in-sharepoint-2010-rest-api-syntax.aspx`

- Client Object Model `http://msdn.microsoft.com/en-us/library/ee537247(office.14).aspx`

- Data Retrieval Overview `http://msdn.microsoft.com/en-us/library/ee539350(v=office.14).aspx`

- How to: Create an External Content Type Based on a SQL Server Table `http://msdn.microsoft.com/en-us/library/ee557243(v=office.14).aspx`

- Microsoft Business Connectivity Services `http://msdn.microsoft.com/en-us/library/ee556826(v=office.14).aspx`

- Accessing Excel Services' REST API `http://msdn.microsoft.com/en-us/library/ee556820(office.14).aspx`

CHAPTER 11

Site Provisioning Workflows

SharePoint owes a lot of its momentum in the marketplace to the way it empowers end users. Users can post documents, customize pages, launch workflows, and create lists without requiring the intervention of IT staff. One of the more powerful features is the ability to create sites and site collections. Given this power, a user can choose a title, select a location for the site, specify a description, and choose a site template. However, many organizations struggle with exactly how much power to give users and how much of the environment IT should take responsibility for. This balance can determine whether an organization ends up with a SharePoint environment that grows out of control or becomes a frustration point due to lack of responsiveness from IT. This topic is the focus of a lot of the governance material and discussion that started with the SharePoint 2007 release. One way to ease this is with workflows that take such issues into account. In this chapter, we will show you how as a developer you can enable site collection administrators to incorporate workflow processes into how IT responds to requests for new sites. We will also show you how Visio, SharePoint Designer, and Visual Studio all come together in SharePoint workflows.

Real-World Examples

Lots of organizations we have met with have expressed an interest in how to still empower users, but also add approval points, an audit trail, and some order to the decision-making process. Imagine a consulting firm that is creating an extranet where each site collection represents a customer. Within this site collection, subsites are created for each project the consulting firm takes on for that customer. While the site collections are created by an internal IT process, ideally the managers of projects for that customer should be able to self-provision their subsites to share their work. Though this permission can certainly be granted, the organization, and therefore IT, would likely want some constraints. A project manager, for instance, might be restricted to always choosing a specific site template designed for this extranet. She might not have a choice in the URL for the site; it could be a requirement that the URL be based on the project number. Concerns also usually arise about how long the site may be active and the percentage of quota space it will take from the rest of the site collection.

Solution Overview

To provide some context for our solution, we've decided to focus on a story line where a rather SharePoint-savvy department gets the idea to automate the site creation decision-making process within its department site collection. The department starts with a Visio flow diagram depicting the desired paths, approvals, and decision points, then turns the diagram over to a worker skilled with SharePoint Designer. Before any workflow can be created, the first observation is that SharePoint Designer does not provide a workflow action for creating sites. This department and the organization's development staff come together and the development team agrees to build a new workflow activity for site creation. With this in hand, the department goes back to SharePoint Designer to create the workflow, using the Visio diagram to visualize the status of a processing workflow.

In this solution, we will start in Visio by roughing out the decision-making process. Within this diagram, we will use the new SharePoint workflow-specific shapes, which will enable us to later import the diagram into SharePoint Designer to build the skeleton of the workflow. We will then shift gears to the development team where we will build a new workflow activity and a web application-level feature for deploying it. We will dive deep into SharePoint Designer, building out the workflow, in the process making some improvements in the decision paths that were proposed as part of the Visio diagram. The solution will conclude with the publishing of the workflow, which will update the Visio diagram and use it to visualize the workflow's status.

Solution Walkthrough

This section describes the major elements of the solution and the decisions that were made in coding it. The walkthrough will show you how to create the Visio diagram and explain the desired decision paths. We will go into detail about how to code a custom workflow activity that will support its use in SharePoint Designer. This will include how to templatize the workflow activity so that the SharePoint Designer user can supply input parameters during the workflow design process. We will then show you how you can leverage a web application-level SharePoint feature to get the activity's files in place, as well as the necessary `web.config` changes. We will then walk you through the workflow creation in SharePoint Designer, which will include steps to configure conditions, actions, workflow variables, calculations, and email, as well as how to gather additional information from downstream approvers. Finally, we will publish the workflow for testing in a site collection, and in the process use the Visio diagram for visualizing the status of a workflow instance.

Proposing the Workflow Using Visio

With the SharePoint 2010 release, Microsoft Visio plays an increased role for organizations. In this chapter, we will first use Visio to plan a SharePoint workflow. This is done with a set of new shapes that represent the set of conditions and actions you typically find in a SharePoint-specific workflow. As a benefit, you can import such a diagram into SharePoint Designer to jump-start the building of the workflow. In addition, SharePoint Portal Server 2010 introduces Visio Services, which lets us process a Visio diagram on the server, connect it to data, and use the diagram to produce an interactive visualization for the user. In this chapter, we will use Visio Services to show the state and path of a specific site request as it goes through the decision points. However, visualizing workflows is not the only use of Visio Services. For more information about how you can leverage this feature, take a look at the solution in Chapter 13.

For this solution, you can either take the time to follow the detail here about how to create the diagram, or simply grab it from the code download on the Apress web site. To get started, launch Microsoft Visio 2010. Visio will launch in the backstage interface, asking you what type of diagram you want to create. From the Template Categories area, select **Flowchart**. From this group, select the **Microsoft SharePoint Workflow** template, specify US units, and click **Create**.

When Visio opens to your empty drawing, you'll notice several categories of shapes in the toolbox. The default group is called Quick Shapes, which holds some of the more commonly used shapes in SharePoint workflows. However, let's take a moment to look through the entire toolset. The easiest group of shapes to understand is the SharePoint Workflow Terminators shown in Figure 11-1. These shapes simply depict where the workflow starts and stops. It is important to realize that you are limited to sequential workflows that move from step to step as they are being processed, as opposed to event-based state machines. Most workflow diagrams will have one start and one terminate shape.

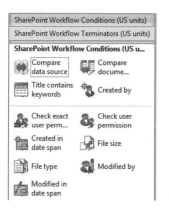

Figure 11-1. SharePoint Workflow Terminators shapes in Visio

The SharePoint Workflow Conditions group, shown in Figure 11-2, includes shapes that enable you to branch your decision process when some conditions are met. The shapes here allow you to check to see if the item the workflow is operating on is created by a specific user, is a certain type of file, is of a certain file size, or has a title with a certain keyword, plus several more. The generic Compare data source shape lets you pick some target you'll compare against and is a commonly used shape in workflows.

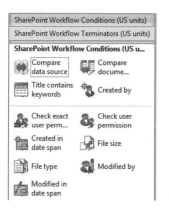

Figure 11-2. SharePoint Workflow Conditions shapes in Visio

The SharePoint Workflow Actions group, partially shown in Figure 11-3, includes shapes that enable you to have the workflow perform an action. This is a rather large set, so Figure 11-3 shows only the first few shapes in the group. These shapes represent the work your workflow is going to do. Does it need to send emails to notify certain users? Does it need to ask a user for approval or gather additional information? Do you need the workflow to copy, update, edit, or create a SharePoint list item? The Log to history list shape is popular as it allows your workflow to leave behind an audit trail.

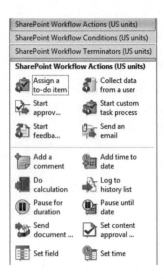

Figure 11-3. SharePoint Workflow Actions shapes in Visio

In our story line, the department itself uses Visio to outline the proposed decision-making process in order to govern the site creation process. It is important to realize that this flowchart is really an outline of how a business user might depict the process. As we'll see later, when a developer or IT-savvy user begins constructing the workflow, they often find other steps that need to be added or efficiencies that can be used to remove duplications in logic or process. Figure 11-4 shows a diagram of the decision-making process we will be working with.

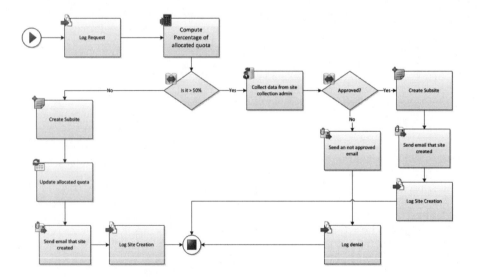

Figure 11-4. The Visio diagram for the site creation process

The department's diagram begins with the Start terminator and kicks off by first auditing that a request for a new site was received. This is done using the Log to history list shape. The next shape shows that the decision-making process will depend on how much of the department's site collection quota has been allocated. As we'll see later, the department will simply keep a running total in a separate SharePoint list. We will stick with this type of record-keeping solution. However, as we discuss in the Extension Points section of this chapter, this information could be obtained through SharePoint's API.

The next condition is a Compare data source shape that will divert the path based on whether or not the department has reached a 50 percent threshold in its allocations. If it has not, the left-most branch of the diagram executes. This includes the following shapes:

- A Comment shape, which you can find in the Workflow Actions group, for the creation of the site (since this will be the custom activity we will code later).

- An Update list item shape to increase the running total for the quota

- A Send an email to notify the requestor that the site has been provisioned

- A Log to history list to record the result of the workflow

If the department has already accounted for 50 percent of its site collection quota, approval of the site collection administrator is required. The first shape in this path is the Collect data from a user shape, which results in a task and form being created to decide whether this request should be approved. The Compare data source shape after this enables us to determine the result of the approval. If the request is not approved, the shapes in the middle column execute, including the Send an email and Log to history shapes to record the denial. If the request is approved by the site collection administrator, the shapes in the right-most column, which are similar to those in the first column, execute. Note that you can't simply draw a line from the approved shape to the first column. SharePoint workflow flowcharts impose limits that you also see enforced in SharePoint Designer. In particular, your workflow must be sequential and can't backtrack or jump to a previous step. You can verify that you haven't broken these rules by clicking the Check Diagram button in the Process tab of Visio's ribbon. You should always do this before using the diagram in SharePoint Designer.

To wrap up, you should definitely save your work. In addition to creating a Visio (.vsd) file, we also need to export the diagram into a format that SharePoint Designer can read. In the same Process ribbon tab, you'll see an Export button. Name the file `ProposedSiteCreationExport.vwi` and remember the location you saved it to.

Building the Custom Workflow Activity

As described in Chapter 3, with the 2010 releases Microsoft took major steps to help developers be more productive in building customizations for SharePoint with Visual Studio. For this example, we will start with an empty SharePoint 2010 solution and project so we can help you become familiar with all the new tools and functionality. This SharePoint project is going to be more of a deployment vehicle to get our custom workflow activity into the environment. The activity itself will be another project that we will add in just a bit. Use the following steps to create the SiteProvisionFeature Visual Studio 2010 project:

1. Open Visual Studio 2010 and start a new project.

2. In the Installed Templates tree, expand Visual C#. Expand SharePoint and select the **2010** node for the SharePoint 2010 project types.

3. Using the drop-downs above the project types, make sure you are targeting the **.NET Framework 3.5**.

4. Select **Empty SharePoint Project** from the list of project types.

5. Name the project **SiteProvisionFeature** and leave the default choices of creating a new solution with the same name. Your completed dialog should look like Figure 11-5.

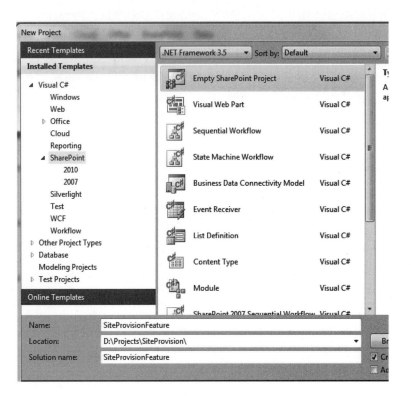

Figure 11-5. Creating the Visual Studio solution

6. Click **OK**.

7. In the next SharePoint Customization dialog, choose the Deploy as a farm solution option, since our solution will be registering the workflow activity at the web-application level. Specify the URL of a site where you will later test the workflow. For our environment it was `http://edhild3/sites/workflow`.

You can't add a custom workflow activity directly to the SharePoint project. This is because workflow activities are really a Windows Workflow Foundation feature and can have a much broader scope than living in a SharePoint host. Workflow activities also have their own Visual Studio project type, so you need to add another project to the solution. This time choose the Workflow node and select the Workflow Activity Library template. Verify you are still targeting the .NET Framework 3.5 and name this project **SiteProvisionActivity**. This is the project we will focus on here, and come back to the SharePoint project in the next section.

Before jumping into the actual code of the workflow activity, let's get a few other things out of the way. First, there are a few other assemblies we need to add references to: `Microsoft.SharePoint.dll` and `Microsoft.SharePoint.WorkflowActions.dll`. These should be in the .NET tab of the Add References dialog. If not, their default location is `C:\Program Files\Common Files\Microsoft Shared\Web Server Extensions\14\ISAPI`. We also want to rename the `Activity1.cs` default workflow activity file that Visual Studio placed in the project for you. Just right-click and choose to rename it to `ProvisionActivity.cs`. We also want the `using` statements shown in Listing 11-1. Most of these are so we can interact with the SharePoint site our workflow is running within. To add them, just right-click on the file and choose to view the code of the workflow activity.

Listing 11-1. Using Statements for the Custom Workflow Activity

```
using Microsoft.SharePoint;
using Microsoft.SharePoint.Workflow;
using Microsoft.SharePoint.WorkflowActions;
using Microsoft.SharePoint.Navigation;
using System.Diagnostics;
```

We also need to change the base class for this workflow activity. By default, the base class is `SequenceActivity`. It needs to be changed to just `Activity`. The main difference here is that we don't need our custom activity to contain other activities. It will be a black box performing the single operation of creating a subsite under the site where the workflow is executing. The code in Listing 11-2 shows the modified class declaration.

Listing 11-2. Changing the Base Class of the Workflow Activity

```
namespace SiteProvisionActivity
{
    public partial class ProvisionActivity : Activity
    {
        public ProvisionActivity()
        {
            InitializeComponent();
        }
```

When our workflow activity is used in SharePoint Designer, we want the builder of the workflow to be able to pass in values for the site creation process. Builders should be able to specify the title of the site, the URL it should have, a site description, the site template to use, a language locale identifier, whether or not the site should inherit permissions, and if it should overwrite a site that already exists. These are all parameters to the method of creating a new site in a site collection. Again, we wouldn't want to hard-code any of these, so they need to be variables that get passed into the workflow. To accomplish this, we will declare a set of dependency properties. You might not have seen dependency properties before. They are very similar to normal class properties. The difference is that these properties leverage a framework included in the .NET Framework 3.0 that enables them to support enhanced features such as change notifications, validation, and value resolution. Both Windows Presentation Foundation and Windows Workflow Foundation take advantage of this framework, though they use it slightly differently. You can read more about dependency properties using the links provided in the Further Reading section of this chapter. We won't show every property here in the text; we'll just focus on some important traits. You can get the whole set in the code download for this chapter. Listing 11-3 includes a string dependency property for the title of the site.

Listing 11-3. The SiteTitle Dependency Property

```
public static DependencyProperty SiteTitleProperty =
        DependencyProperty.Register("SiteTitle", typeof(string),
                              typeof(ProvisionActivity));
[Description("SiteTitle")]
[Category("Site Provision Actions")]
[Browsable(true)]
[DesignerSerializationVisibility(DesignerSerializationVisibility.Visible)]
public string SiteTitle
{
  get
  {
    return ((string)(base.GetValue(ProvisionActivity.SiteTitleProperty)));
  }
  set
  {
    base.SetValue(ProvisionActivity.SiteTitleProperty, value);
  }
}
```

■ **Note** With it taking a whole block of code to declare a dependency property, you might think you are in for a lot of typing. The good news is that Visual Studio includes a code snippet to write the skeleton for you. Just type **wdp** where you want the property and TAB twice. Then just customize the inserted code with your property-specific name and data type.

In addition to the parameters we want to include to create the desired site, there is one other dependency property we want to add, named **__ContextProperty**. By placing this property in our custom workflow activity, our workflow code can access the context of the host it is running in. This lets our activity know in which site collection it should create the new site. Without the context, we would have to make our workflow builder pass in the URL of the site collection as well. This approach makes more sense since it implies that the site collection for the new site is the same as the one where the workflow is running. The code in Listing 11-4 shows this dependency property.

Listing 11-4. Declaring the __Context Dependency Property

```
public static DependencyProperty __ContextProperty =
     DependencyProperty.Register("__Context", typeof(WorkflowContext),
                              typeof(ProvisionActivity));
[Description("Context")]
[ValidationOption(ValidationOption.Required)]
[Browsable(true)]
[DesignerSerializationVisibility(DesignerSerializationVisibility.Visible)]
public WorkflowContext __Context
{
```

```
get
{
   return ((WorkflowContext)(base.GetValue(ProvisionActivity.__ContextProperty)));
}
set
{
   base.SetValue(ProvisionActivity.__ContextProperty, value);
}
}
```

All of the real action happens in the Execute method of the custom workflow activity. This code is shown in Listing 11-5. With all the buildup, this may seem a bit anticlimactic. Through the context dependency property we just defined, the workflow discovers the site collection and web it is running within. In our story line, this would be the root web of the department's site collection. We then create a new subsite by adding a new entry. The Add method used here leverages all of the other dependency properties declared in the workflow activity. Should any error occur, we capture the exception in the Event Log. Finally, we return an **ActivityExecutionStatus** object to signal that our activity has completed its work.

Listing 11-5. The Workflow Activity's Execute Method

```
protected override ActivityExecutionStatus Execute(ActivityExecutionContext
                                                    executionContext)
{
  try
  {
    using (SPSite sourceSite = new SPSite(this.__Context.Web.Site.ID))
    {
      using (SPWeb currentWeb = sourceSite.AllWebs[this.__Context.Web.ID])
      {
        SPWeb newWeb = currentWeb.Webs.Add(SiteUrl, SiteTitle, SiteDescription,
                       LocaleID, SiteTemplate, bool.Parse(UseUniquePermissions),
                       bool.Parse(ConvertIfThere));
      }
    }
  }
  catch (Exception ex)
  {
    EventLog.WriteEntry("ProvisionActivity", ex.ToString());
  }
  return ActivityExecutionStatus.Closed;
}
```

■ **Note** If you are locking down the permissions for users who may be using this workflow, you may want to wrap the site creation code in a RunWithElevatedPriveledges delegate. You can read more about this here: `http://msdn.microsoft.com/en-us/library/microsoft.sharepoint.spsecurity.` `runwithelevatedprivileges(office.14).aspx.`

Since this workflow activity's assembly will be deployed to the GAC by the SharePoint feature we will describe in the next section, you will need to configure it to have a strong name. Use the following steps to complete that configuration:

1. Right-click on the **SiteProvisionActivity** project and select **Properties**.

2. Click on the **Signing** tab and check the checkbox to Sign the assembly.

3. Select **New** from the drop-down under the Choose a strong name key file instruction.

4. Name the file **key**. Clear the checkbox to protect the key file with a password and click **OK**.

5. Click **Save** and **Build** your project.

Deploying the Activity through a SharePoint Feature

Now we are going to go back to the SharePointFeature project we created earlier and use it to deploy the custom workflow activity. For our workflow activity to work within SharePoint Portal Server and be available for SharePoint Designer workflows, we have to deploy the assembly to the Global Assembly Cache and make sure it is registered in the web application's `web.config` file as a safe control and authorized type. We also need to publish an .ACTIONS XML file. This file is read by SharePoint Designer to construct the user interface for the activity while the workflow is being built.

For several deployment steps we will need to know the strong name of our assembly that contains the workflow activity. Strong names are a lot like fully qualified domain names. They include all of the details necessary to uniquely identify the assembly. In our environment, the strong name of the workflow activity's assembly is `SiteProvisionActivity, Version=1.0.0.0, Culture=neutral,` `PublicKeyToken= d5c639ac57ef5dbf`. The strong name is made up of the name of the assembly itself, the version number, the culture, and the assembly's public key token. This token was given when you signed the assembly with the key file. Use the following steps to retrieve your assembly's public key token which you will need in later steps. Be sure to copy it to the clipboard or Notepad for later use.

1. From your start menu, open the **Visual Studio Command Prompt (2010)**. You'll find it in the Visual Studio Tools folder within the Microsoft Visual Studio 2010 folder.

2. Navigate to your workflow activity's project folder and locate the DLL, which should be in the Debug folder of the Bin directory.

3. Use the **sn.exe** command to output the public key token. This command should take the form `sn.exe -T SiteProvisionActivity.dll`. If your command window is in QuickEdit mode, you can highlight and right-click to copy the value to the clipboard.

Let's first start with the .ACTIONS file. This file will be read by SharePoint Designer as it discovers what workflow activities have been published to the SharePoint server. SharePoint Designer looks for these files in a specific location. To reference this location in our project, we'll add a mapped folder, which will tell Visual Studio where the file should be published so it can act accordingly when building the solution package. To do this, right-click on the SharePointFeature project and choose Add SharePoint Mapped Folder. You should see a dialog like the one in Figure 11-6, allowing you to select the `Template\1033\Workflow` folder from the 14-hive.

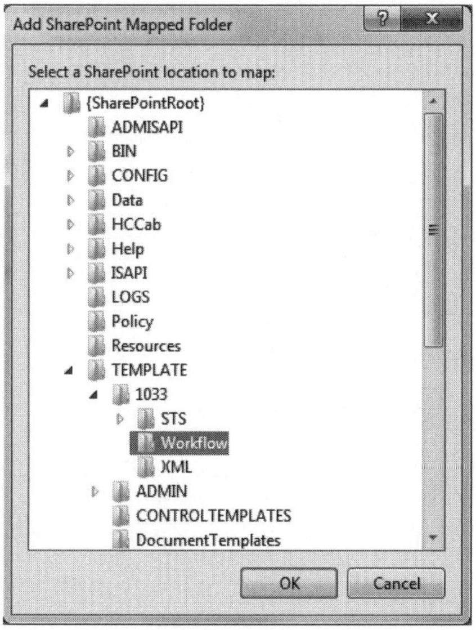

Figure 11-6. *Adding the Mapped Workflow Folder*

With the Workflow mapped folder in your project, now add an XML file to it named `ProvisionActivity.ACTIONS`. If you like, you can just grab it from the code download. This file defines the action for SharePoint Designer, specifies how the activity should be rendered in the SharePoint Designer workflow builder, and details the activities parameters. Listing 11-6 contains the initial part of this file, which defines the action. Be sure to use *your* public key token value instead of the one in the listing.

Listing 11-6. Defining the Action in an .ACTIONS file

```
<WorkflowInfo>
  <Actions Sequential="then" Parallel="and">
    <Action Name="Create SubSite" ClassName="SiteProvisionActivity.ProvisionActivity"
            Assembly="SiteProvisionActivity, Version=1.0.0.0, Culture=neutral, ↵
                      PublicKeyToken=<YourPublicKeyToken>"
            AppliesTo="all" Category="Site Provision Actions">
```

The next section of this file controls how the activity will be rendered in SharePoint Designer as the user builds the workflow. This really comes down to a human-readable sentence with placeholders for the various parameters that can be passed into the activity. As shown in Listing 11-7, the sentence is specified as an attribute of the `RuleDesigner` element. Within the string, we can add placeholders that represent the parameters. Within the `RuleDesigner` element, we can further define binding rules that tell SharePoint Designer how to display the placeholder and what parameter it corresponds to. In some cases we simply give the user a textbox, but notice that with the `UseUniquePermissions` and `ConvertIfThere` parameters, we can provide drop-down choices.

Listing 11-7. The Rule Designer Portion of the .ACTIONS file

```
<RuleDesigner Sentence="Create site named %1 at the URL %2 described as %3. ↵
  Use template %4 with locale %5. %6 use unique Permissions. %7 convert if ↵
  the site exists.">
 <FieldBind Field="SiteTitle" DesignerType="TextArea" Id="1"/>
 <FieldBind Field="SiteUrl" DesignerType="TextArea" Id="2"/>
 <FieldBind Field="SiteDescription" DesignerType="TextArea" Id="3"/>
 <FieldBind Field="SiteTemplate" DesignerType="TextArea" Id="4"/>
 <FieldBind Field="LocaleID" DesignerType="TextArea" Id="5"/>
 <FieldBind Field="UseUniquePermissions" DesignerType="Dropdown"
            Text="choose"  Id="6">
   <Option Name="Do" Value="True"/>
   <Option Name="Do not" Value="False"/>
 </FieldBind>
 <FieldBind Field="ConvertIfThere" DesignerType="Dropdown"
            Text="choose"  Id="7">
   <Option Name="Do" Value="True"/>
   <Option Name="Do not" Value="False"/>
 </FieldBind>
 </RuleDesigner>
```

The last portion of this file is shown in Listing 11-8 and includes the definition of the parameters for our activity. Notice that this list includes the `__Context` parameter. There is no need for it to be presented to the user through the `RuleDesigner` we defined earlier. We also use this section to define an initial default value for the `LocaleID` parameter.

Listing 11-8. The Parameters Portion of the .ACTIONS file

```
<Parameters>
  <Parameter Name="__Context" Type="Microsoft.SharePoint.WorkflowActions.↵
    WorkflowContext, Microsoft.SharePoint.WorkflowActions" Direction="In"/>
  <Parameter Name="SiteTitle" Type="System.String, mscorlib" Direction="In" />
  <Parameter Name="SiteUrl" Type="System.String, mscorlib" Direction="In" />
  <Parameter Name="SiteDescription" Type="System.String, mscorlib" Direction="In" />
  <Parameter Name="SiteTemplate" Type="System.String, mscorlib" Direction="In" />
  <Parameter Name="LocaleID" Type="System.UInt32, mscorlib" Direction="In"
            InitialValue="1033" />
  <Parameter Name="UseUniquePermissions" Type="System.String, mscorlib"
            Direction="In" />
  <Parameter Name="ConvertIfThere" Type="System.String, mscorlib" Direction="In" />
</Parameters>
</Action>
</Actions>
</WorkflowInfo>
```

Another task we must perform with this deployment-focused feature is to have it deploy our custom workflow activity's assembly to the Global Assembly Cache. To accomplish this, we will use the Package Designer. If you expand the Package node of your project in Visual Studio's Solution Explorer, you'll see a `Package.package` element. Double-click it to open the designer for the package. This tool allows us to control the SharePoint solution's manifest, which SharePoint will use during deployment to place the files in their correct locations. Since our assembly is not part of this project, we have to use the advanced functionality of the designer. Use the following steps to have this feature deploy our workflow activity assembly.

1. With the Package Designer interface open, click the **Advanced** button near the bottom of the designer.

2. Click the Add button.

3. Choose the option to Add Assembly from Project Output.

4. Choose the SiteProvisionActivity project from the drop-down for Source Project.

5. Make sure the Deployment Target is set to **Global Assembly Cache**. Do not close the dialog yet.

As it turns out, the Package Designer can also accomplish one of our other tasks—registering the class as a Safe Control in the web application where our feature will be activated. Add a new item to the Safe Controls section of this dialog and use Table 11-1 to complete the entry. Make sure you use your public key token value. Click **OK** when you are finished.

Table 11-1. Registering the Workflow Activity as a Safe Control

Property	Value
Namespace	SiteProvisionActivity
Type Name	*
Assembly Name	SiteProvisionActivity, Version=1.0.0.0, Culture=neutral, PublicKeyToken=<YourPublicKeyToken>
Safe	Checked
Safe Against Script	Checked

To complete this SharePoint project, we also need to make a change to the `web.config` file to register our workflow activity assembly as an authorized type. Authorized types are validated during the compilation step of a workflow, whereas a Safe Control entry simply confirms that the class or control is safe for invocation from a SharePoint ASPX page. The Package Designer does not perform this function. Instead, we will include a web-application-scoped feature that will make this modification when the feature is activated. Note that we are going to make these changes using code so we don't need developers or IT professionals trying to paste content into the `web.config` file directly. Use the following steps to add the feature to the SharePointFeature project.

1. Right-click on the Features node of the SiteProvisionFeature project and select **Add Feature**.

2. Right-click on the Feature1 node that was added and select Rename. Enter **SiteProvisionFeature** as the name.

3. Open the Feature Designer and change the scope of the feature to **Web Application**.

This new feature is not going to deploy any SharePoint customizations. Instead, we will simply use it to make the necessary `web.config` file change when the feature is activated in a web application. To be able to write code in response to the activation, we need to add an event receiver for the feature. You can do this by right-clicking on the SiteProvisionFeature node and choosing **Add Event Receiver**. This adds a new **SiteProvisionFeature.EventReceiver.cs** file within the node. Here is where we can place code that will run in response to one of the feature's events, such as activated, deactivating, installed, or uninstalling. Open the code file. Before dealing with the code in the FeatureActivated event, you will need to add one `using` statement: `using Microsoft.SharePoint.Administration;`

The change is made to the configuration file through the `SPWebConfigModification` class, which allows you to define a new entry for the `web.config` file. In addition, SharePoint will be able to tell you the set of modifications that were made in this manner, enabling you to find and remove them should it be necessary—like when your feature is deactivated or uninstalled. In this scenario, we want to use this technique to add an `authorizedType` entry.

■ **Note** You should not use this technique for making SafeControl changes. As we saw earlier, the Package Designer facilitates those changes.

The code in Listing 11-9 shows the declaration of the necessary modification. The `Owner` property is particularly important as it is the field you typically examine when looking for modifications to remove. To assist SharePoint in finding this modification for removal, the Name property is actually an XPath query that will uniquely identify the line that we want removed. The `Path` property specifies where in the `web.config` file the entry is to be placed. Make sure in the `Value` property that you are using the strong name of your assembly with the correct public key token.

Listing 11-9. Changing the `web.config` File upon Feature Activation

```
public override void FeatureActivated(SPFeatureReceiverProperties properties)
{
    SPWebApplication currentWebApp = (SPWebApplication)properties.Feature.Parent;
    SPWebConfigModification configMod = new SPWebConfigModification();
    configMod.Name = "authorizedType[@Assembly='SiteProvisionActivity, Version=1.0.0.0, ↵
Culture=neutral,PublicKeyToken=<YourPublicKeyToken>'][@Namespace='SiteProvisionActivity']↵
            [@TypeName='*'][@Authorized='True']";

    configMod.Owner = "SiteProvisionFeature";
    configMod.Path =
"configuration/System.Workflow.ComponentModel.WorkflowCompiler/authorizedTypes";
    configMod.Type = SPWebConfigModification.SPWebConfigModificationType.EnsureChildNode;
    configMod.Value - @"<authorizedType Assembly='SiteProvisionActivity, Version=1.0.0.0, ↵
            Culture=neutral, PublicKeyToken=<YourPublicKeyToken>' ↵
            Namespace='SiteProvisionActivity' TypeName='*' Authorized='True' />";
    currentWebApp.WebConfigModifications.Add(configMod);
    currentWebApp.Update();
    currentWebApp.WebService.ApplyWebConfigModifications();
}
```

Likewise, we will want to remove this `web.config` file change whenever the feature is deactivated for the web application. This can also be done in the feature's event receiver in the FeatureDeactivating event. The code in Listing 11-10 loops through the modifications that have been committed in this manner in the past looking for any modification that is owned by SiteProvisionFeature. Once those modifications have been found, they are removed and committed to the web application and farm.

Listing 11-10. Changing the `web.config` File when the feature is deactivating

```
public override void FeatureDeactivating(SPFeatureReceiverProperties properties)
{
    SPWebApplication currentWebApp = (SPWebApplication)properties.Feature.Parent;
    Collection<SPWebConfigModification> modificationCollection =
currentWebApp.WebConfigModifications;
    Collection<SPWebConfigModification> removeCollection = new
Collection<SPWebConfigModification>();

    int count = modificationCollection.Count;
    for (int i = 0; i < count; i++)
    {
        SPWebConfigModification modification = modificationCollection[i];
        if (modification.Owner == "SiteProvisionFeature")
        {
            // collect modifications to delete
            removeCollection.Add(modification);
        }
    }

    // now delete the modifications from the web application
    if (removeCollection.Count > 0)
    {
        foreach (SPWebConfigModification modificationItem in removeCollection)
        {
            currentWebApp.WebConfigModifications.Remove(modificationItem);
        }

        // Commit modification removals to the specified web application
        currentWebApp.Update();
        // Push modifications through the farm
        currentWebApp.WebService.ApplyWebConfigModifications();
    }
}
```

This is the last change we will make in this feature, so you can build and deploy your project. You can look at the `web.config` files for the new entries. You can also confirm that the feature has been activated by looking at your web application's features in Central Administration, as shown in Figure 11-7. If you want to know more about using the **SPWebModification** class, you can find more information at `http://msdn.microsoft.com/en-us/library/microsoft.sharepoint.administration.spwebconfigmodification(office.14).aspx`.

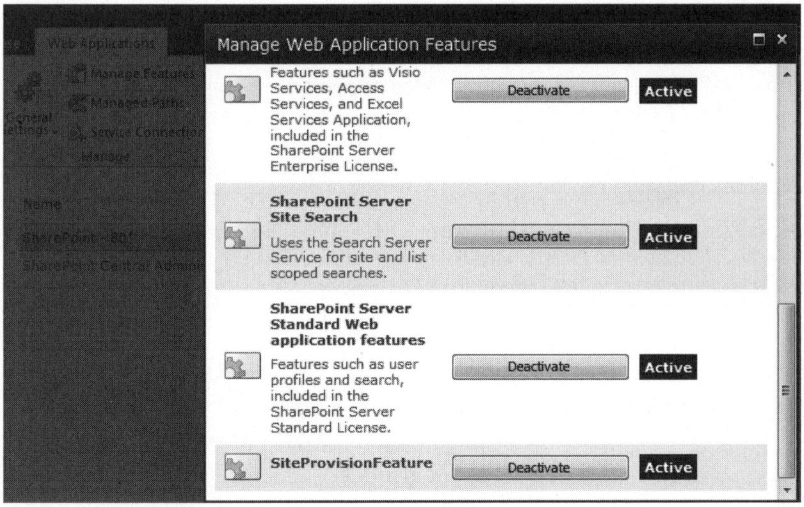

Figure 11-7. Viewing the web application's features

Preparing the SharePoint Site

There are a few things we want to do to prepare the SharePoint environment for building the workflow. According to our story line, we really want the developers involved as little as possible, yet we would also like the solution to be reusable in case this solution evolves into a best practice within the organization. So, for this chapter, we will define a SiteRequest content type that our workflow will operate on. This content type will be placed within a SharePoint Content Type Hub. A content type hub is a new SharePoint 2010 feature that enables the reuse of a content type throughout a SharePoint environment. In SharePoint 2007, content types were locked to site collections. By placing the content type in a hub, it will be published to other site collections in any web applications that use the same Managed Metadata Service Application. Another approach would have been to have a SharePoint developer wrap such a content type into a SharePoint feature. In fact, that technique is used in Chapter 14. A content type hub is really nothing but a site collection with that feature turned on. In our environment, the hub was the site collection at the root of the web application. Use the following steps to turn on this functionality.

1. Go to the site you want to be the content type hub (`http://edhild3` in our environment) and go to its **Site Settings**.

2. In the Site Collection Administration group, click the Site collection features link.

3. Activate the Content Type Syndication Hub feature.

4. Return to the Site Settings screen. You should notice new links for Content type publishing and the Content type service application error log. In fact, if you now look at the content types, there is a new Manage publishing option for this content type link. You can use this to control publishing as well to see its publishing history.

In addition to setting up the hub, you must also configure the Managed Metadata Service Application to push and pull content types. To configure these settings, follow these steps:

1. From Central Administration, click the **Manage Service Applications** link in the Application Management group.

2. Click just to the right of the Managed Metadata Service item to highlight it and choose Properties in the ribbon.

3. Scroll down to the bottom of the dialog and enter the URL of the site collection you selected as the hub and click the check box to report syndication errors. Figure 11-8 shows this option after it has been set.

Figure 11-8. Setting the Content Type Hub URL

4. Click OK and return to the list of service applications. Select the Managed Metadata Service proxy, which is the connection item directly below the row you selected earlier.

5. Click **Properties** in the ribbon. Check the **Consumes content types from the Content Type Gallery** option. All of the check boxes should be checked as in Figure 11-9.

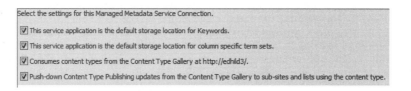

Figure 11-9. Configuring the Managed Metadata Service Connection

This completes the configuration of the content type hub and the managed metadata service application. So now when you define a content type in the hub site collection, that content type will be replicated out to other site collections in web applications that use the same managed metadata service. Note that this does not happen immediately. There are two timer jobs that manage the syndication process: Content Type Hub and Content Type Subscriber. If you want your content types to syndicate after you create them, run these two jobs from Central Administration in that order.

Within the content type hub you created, define a new content type named SiteRequest. The parent type for this should be the Item content type, which you can find in the List Content Types group. Use Table 11-2 to define the columns of SiteRequest.

Table 11-2. The SiteRequest Content Type

Column Name	Data Type	Notes
Title	Single line of text	Inherited from the Item content type
SiteDescription	Multiple lines of text	New site column. Optional. Plain Text
Reason	Multiple lines of text	New site column. Optional. Plain Text
End Date	Date and Time	Existing site column. Optional
SizeMB	Number	New site column. Optional. Zero decimal places

Now let's look at the site where you will test the provisioning workflow. In our environment, this is `http://edhild3/sites/workflow`. Make sure that the SiteRequest content type has been replicated from the content type hub. We will setup two lists that the workflow will interact with, one to store the site requests, and the other for the site collection administrator to keep a running total of the amount of quota that has been allocated. Use the following steps to create the Site Requests list:

1. From within your site collection to test the workflow, click All Site Content in the left-hand navigation.

2. Click Create.

3. Choose the Custom List template and specify the name of the list to be Site Requests. Click Create.

4. Click List Settings in the ribbon of the Site Requests list.

5. Click Advanced settings.

6. Click the radio button to Allow management of content types. Click OK.

7. In the Content Types area of List Settings, choose to Add from existing site content types.

8. Add your SiteRequest content type and click OK.

9. Click the **Item** content type in the Content Types area. Choose to **Delete this content type** so that it is no longer associated with the Site Requests list.

The second list will also be a custom list, named Quota Management. We will use this list to help the site collection administrator keep track of the amount of space she has allocated. For this test, let's assume the site collection is brand-new with a 100GB quota (102400 MB). From the List Settings area, add two new Number columns named Quota and Allocated, each with zero decimal places. Once you have created the list, add just one new item. This item will be a record-keeping place for the department to keep track of how much of its quota has already been used. For the new item, specify the values in Table 11-3.

Table 11-3. The Quota Management List Item

Column	Value
Title	Current
Quota	102400
Allocated	0

Building the Workflow with SharePoint Designer

In our story line, we are now back in the department as a user who is not a developer, but is tasked with taking the new site provisioning workflow activity and implementing the process roughed out in the Visio diagram. To accomplish the task, we will rely heavily on SharePoint Designer 2010. Launch SharePoint Designer and open the site where you created the lists in the previous section. In the left-hand navigation, click Workflows. You will notice an option in the ribbon to Import from Visio. This is a powerful option that lets us jump-start the workflow creation process by importing the flowchart created in the beginning of this chapter. Click the button and choose the exported (.vwi) version of that Visio document. Name the workflow **SiteRequestsWorkflow** and select the Reusable Workflow option that will operate on any item of SiteRequest content type. By choosing reusable workflow here, we are indicating that we may well use this workflow in other sites and site collections. Therefore, SharePoint Designer will not embed list identifiers into the workflow, making it more portable. Your settings should look like Figure 11-10. Click Finish.

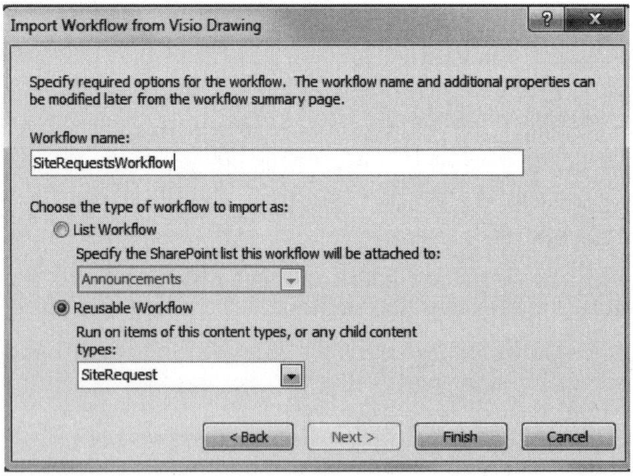

Figure 11-10. Importing the Visio Diagram into SharePoint Designer

After the import completes, you'll see that the flow that was depicted in Visio is now roughed out in the SharePoint Designer workflow editor. Workflows in SharePoint Designer are basically sequential flows of conditions and actions. The possible building blocks of these workflows are available through the Condition and Action buttons of the ribbon. Take some type to scroll through each of these to get familiar with the set. Notice in the set of actions that there is a new Site Provision Actions group with a Create SubSite action, as shown in Figure 11-11. This is the custom workflow activity we built in Visual Studio earlier in the chapter.

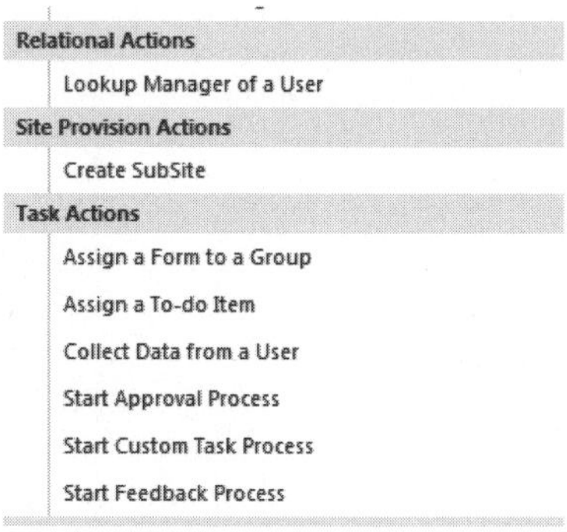

Relational Actions
Lookup Manager of a User
Site Provision Actions
Create SubSite
Task Actions
Assign a Form to a Group
Assign a To-do Item
Collect Data from a User
Start Approval Process
Start Custom Task Process
Start Feedback Process

Figure 11-11. SharePoint Designer's Site Provision Actions Group

The first step we want to take in the workflow is to log in the history list that the workflow has started. Click the **this message** link in the action and then the ellipses button. For the text areas of many items you'll find in a workflow (task descriptions, email, history list items, etc.), SharePoint Designer lets you templatize the string that will be used. This means that when building the workflow, you can use placeholders that will be filled in with the actual values when the workflow is executing. You can find the set of possible lookups by using the Add or Change Lookup button at the bottom of this tool. Figure 11-12 shows an appropriate message that includes placeholders for the name of the site and the person who made the request. In both cases, we are using the current item for the lookup since these values are a stored in the Site Requests list.

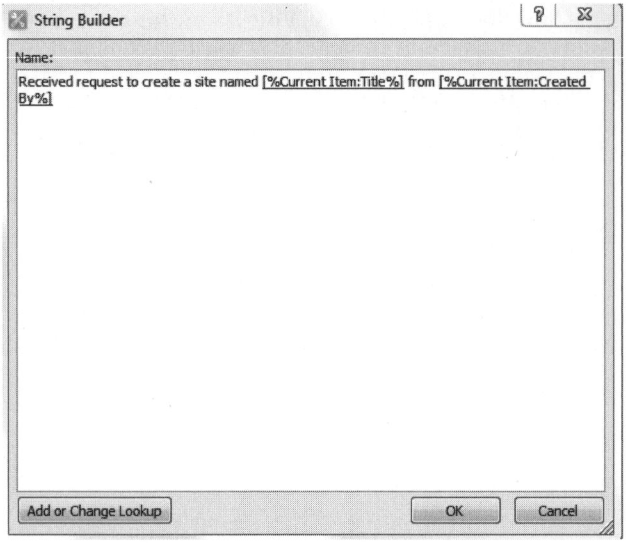

Figure 11-12. SharePoint Designer's String Builder tool

The next item imported by our Visio diagram informs us that we should be performing a calculation. The intent of this calculation is to determine how much of the quota space the site collection administrator has already allocated. This is where the Quota Management list comes in handy. However, we need to add some actions to store the quota and currently allocated values in variables before we can perform the calculation. As this indicates, we can deviate from the Visio diagram; in fact, this is a common occurrence. Often when using the structures provided by SharePoint Designer, the builder of the workflow will see ways to add to or even streamline the process.

Here we'll use two of the Set Workflow Variable actions to retrieve the Quota and Allocated columns from the Quota Management list. These should be placed just before the calculation step. In each case, declare a new variable of Number data type. When specifying the value, click the function button. You can then choose the Quota Management list as the source and the corresponding column as the field. When retrieving an item from a list, we do need to specify a filter as to which item we want. In this case, specify that we will filter for an item whose Title field has the value Current. Figure 11-13 shows these settings for the Quota workflow variable.

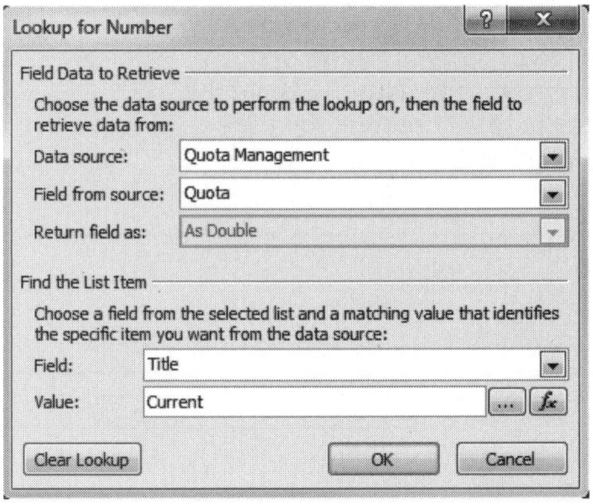

Figure 11-13. Retrieving a value from the Quota Management list

With these values retrieved, we can perform the calculation depicted in the Visio diagram. For the calculation, we want to divide the Allocated workflow variable by the Quota workflow variable and store the result in the variable PercentageUsed, which is also of type Number. The beginning of your workflow should now look like Figure 11-14.

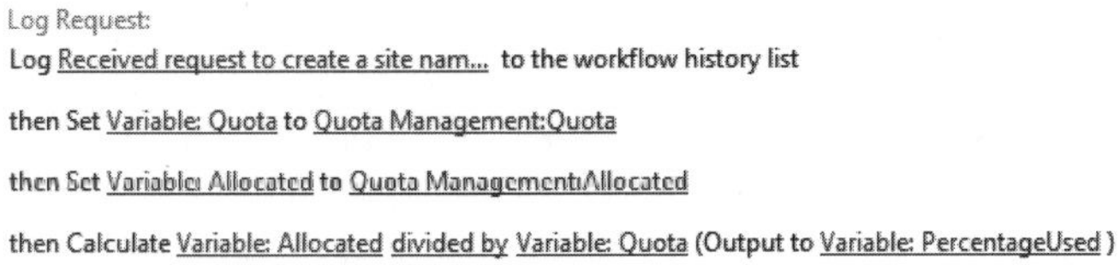

Log Request:
Log Received request to create a site nam... to the workflow history list

then Set Variable: Quota to Quota Management:Quota

then Set Variable: Allocated to Quota Management:Allocated

then Calculate Variable: Allocated divided by Variable: Quota (Output to Variable: PercentageUsed)

Figure 11-14. Beginning of the SiteRequestsWorkflow

The next portion of the workflow brings us to a decision point as to whether we should ask the site collection administrator for approval. For the If condition, check to see if the value of the PercentageUsed variable is greater than or equal to 0.5. This represents the 50 percent value in the Visio diagram.

Collecting data from a user is a very common step for SharePoint workflows and is accomplished by defining a task that is saved to the workflow's task list. This task is assigned to a user and captures the required additional data. SharePoint Designer provides a wizard for defining this task and the data we want to capture. We can then specify who we want to collect it from. Click the **data** hyperlink in the action to start the wizard. The following steps should be used to complete it.

1. Click **Next**.

2. Specify the Name of the task to be **SiteRequestTask**. Enter the description **Site request requires approval**. Click Next.

3. The next step of the wizard lets you specify the data you'd like to collect from the user. In this case, we want to know if the user gives us a thumb up or down as to whether we should create the site. Click the Add button. Give this field the name **IsApproved** and the description **Should this site be created**. Set the information type to Yes/No (check box). Your dialog should look like Figure 11-15. Click Next.

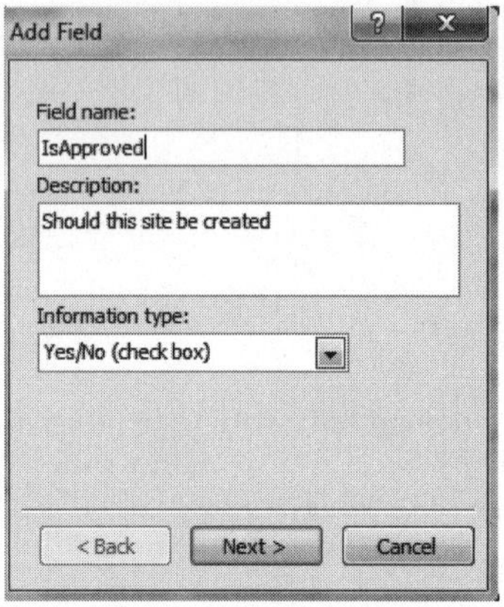

Figure 11-15. Specifying data to collect from a user in the workflow

4. Set the default value to **No** so it will not be checked on the form. Click **Finish** twice.

Now use the **this user** hyperlink. This dialog lets you specify the user or group this task should be assigned to. The site collection administrator could enter his name or email address. In this case, we used the People/Groups from SharePoint Site option to search for the site's Owners group.

To complete this action, define a variable to store the list item ID of the task. We named ours **taskId**. It is important to realize that you do not get the value the user entered as part of this action. This is because it may take the assigned user some time to complete the task. So to get the actual value, we need to set a workflow variable to pull it out of the task list. We named this variable **RequestApproved** and set its data type to be **Boolean**. Getting the correct value out of the task we assigned to the user is a bit tricky so be careful and follow these steps closely.

1. Click the value hyperlink and then the **fx** button.

2. For the Data source, choose the Association: Task List option. This represents the task list the workflow is configured to use.

3. For the Field from source setting, choose IsApproved.

4. Again, when choosing an item from a list, we need to specify how we want to select the specific item in that list. In this case, set the Field setting to be ID.

5. Remember that the ID of the task item we want to retrieve is stored in the **taskId** workflow variable. To retrieve this, click the fx button for the Value setting.

6. Choose Workflow variables and Parameters for the Data source.

7. Choose the taskId variable and set the Return field as setting to Item Id since it is storing the list item identifier of the task. Click OK. Your dialog should look like Figure 11-16. Click OK again to close the dialog.

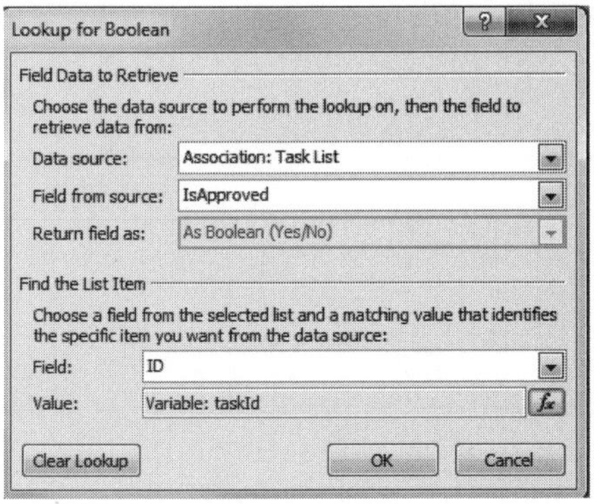

Figure 11-16. Retrieving the IsApproved value from the workflow task

Moving on to the next condition in the workflow, we want to test if the **RequestApproved** variable has been set to Yes. But before we jump into the steps of creating the site, sending emails, etc., notice that this block of actions is really the same as the set at the end of the workflow that runs if the administrator hasn't allocated at least 50 percent of the quota. In fact, the only difference is updating the running quota, which is something that was accidentally left out of the first block of site creation actions. It is easier to see this in the workflow designer than the Visio diagram, and in fact we can streamline our steps by only having to configure the site creation actions once. So instead of performing all the actions laid out in this initial set, we will just use a variable to test whether we need to do them later. You can delete the actions that are currently there using the drop-down menu that appears when you select the action. We created a new Boolean variable named **CreateSite** and used it in the remaining flow markup that was imported from Visio. This portion of the workflow should look like Figure 11-17.

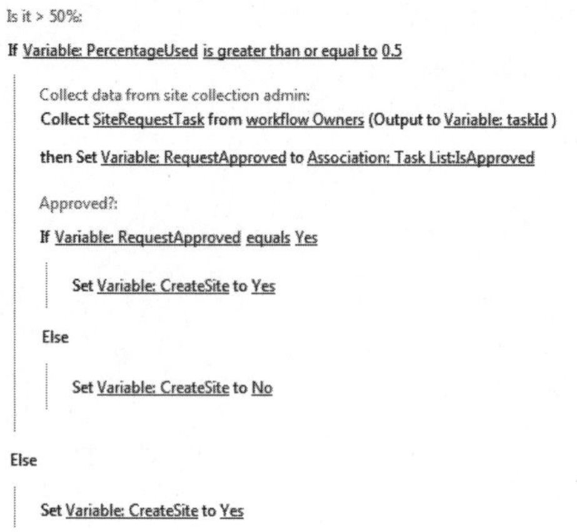

Is it > 50%:

If <u>Variable: PercentageUsed</u> <u>is greater than or equal to</u> <u>0.5</u>

    Collect data from site collection admin:

    Collect <u>SiteRequestTask</u> from <u>workflow Owners</u> (Output to <u>Variable: taskId</u>)

    then Set <u>Variable: RequestApproved</u> to <u>Association: Task List:IsApproved</u>

    Approved?:

    If <u>Variable: RequestApproved</u> <u>equals</u> <u>Yes</u>

        Set <u>Variable: CreateSite</u> to <u>Yes</u>

    Else

        Set <u>Variable: CreateSite</u> to <u>No</u>

Else

    Set <u>Variable: CreateSite</u> to <u>Yes</u>

Figure 11-17. Determining if the site should be created

Now we'll add an additional If condition below the portion in Figure 11-17. From the Condition button on the ribbon, select the option to add an **If any value equals any value** shape. We will use this to compare the `CreateSite` workflow variable. If the value is Yes, we will perform the actions to create the site, update the running total of quota allocated, log the action, and email the user. Clicking the Else-If button in the ribbon gives you an area to lay out the controls for the other possibility—a denial. This area will have a log shape along with a corresponding email.

Focusing on the success scenario, the first shape we'll add is the Create SubSite action. Use the current item's title for the name of the site and its URL. Use the SiteDescription field for the description. Specify the string STS#0 as the site template. This string corresponds to the out-of-the-box SharePoint team site template. Leave the locale set to 1033. Specify to not use unique permissions and to not convert if the site exists.

The next shape in the success scenario will update the `Allocated` workflow variable to include the amount for this requested site. Use the **Do Calculation** action and set the calculation to be the Allocated workflow variable plus the current item's SizeMB field. This field represents the amount of quota the user is requesting for the new site. Store the result in the `Allocated` workflow variable.

The next step is to update the Quota Management list with the new value. This can be accomplished with the **Update List Item** action. Choose the Quota Management list as the one to update. Add the value assignment that sets the Allocated field to the value of the `Allocated` workflow variable. Just like earlier, filter on the Title field for a value of Current to specify which item should be updated. This dialog should look like Figure 11-18.

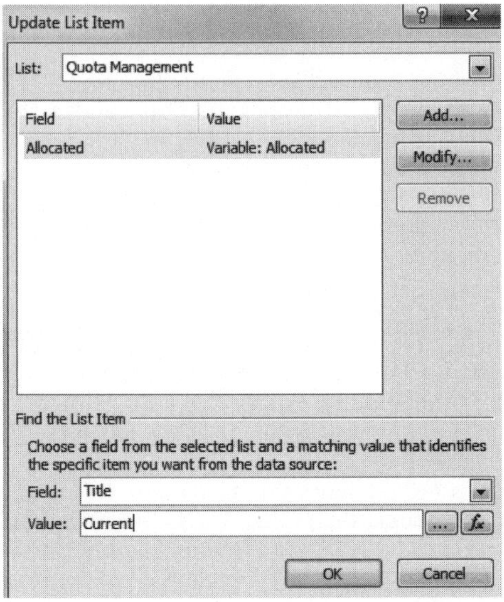

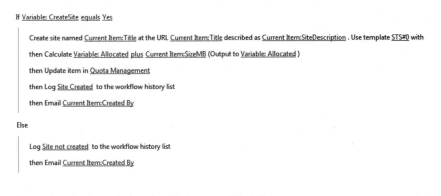

Figure 11-18. Updating the allocated amount in the Quota Management list

Finish up the success scenario by adding a Log to history list action and a Send an email action. Use these to record that the site was created and inform the requesting user that it is ready to use. Both are similar to steps done earlier so we won't detail them. For the email, you can select User who created current item as the recipient. Likewise, the denial scenario also includes both log and email actions. Figure 11-19 shows most of this section of the workflow. The Create SubSite action is so long it cuts off the edge of the screen. Go ahead and click Save in the ribbon to save your workflow.

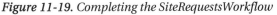

If <u>Variable: CreateSite</u> equals <u>Yes</u>

    Create site named <u>Current Item:Title</u> at the URL <u>Current Item:Title</u> described as <u>Current Item:SiteDescription</u> . Use template <u>STS#0</u> with

    then Calculate <u>Variable: Allocated</u> <u>plus</u> <u>Current Item:SizeMB</u> (Output to <u>Variable: Allocated</u>)

    then Update item in <u>Quota Management</u>

    then Log <u>Site Created</u> to the workflow history list

    then Email <u>Current Item:Created By</u>

Else

    Log <u>Site not created</u> to the workflow history list

    then Email <u>Current Item:Created By</u>

Figure 11-19. Completing the SiteRequestsWorkflow

Exporting the Updated Visio Diagram

Just a couple more steps before we test the workflow. If you still have the workflow editor open in SharePoint Designer, use the breadcrumb navigation and click on the name of the workflow. This takes you to some general settings and information about the workflow. Considering our story line, it would probably be appropriate for the workflow builder to go back to the team to show what has been done. The good news is that the team would not have to know how to interpret the SharePoint Designer workflow editor. We can use the Export to Visio button to generate another Visio Workflow Interchange File that could be loaded into Visio, graphically showing the team the workflow process that was built. Remember, it won't be exactly the rough flow that was sent in since we made a few changes along the way.

We can also use the Visio diagram as a visualization on the SharePoint site to show users exactly the process the workflow has taken for their site request. This leverages the fact that SharePoint Portal Server 2010 includes Visio Services. To have the workflow provide this functionality, simply check the Show workflow visualization on status page check box in the Settings group. Now click the Publish button in the ribbon, which will make your workflow available in the test site.

We also want to build an association with the SiteRequest content type. From the ribbon, click the Associate to Content Type button, then choose SiteRequest. This association is what binds the Workflow to a specific task and history list. In the web page that launches, click OK.

Testing the Solution

It is now time to test your complete site provisioning workflow. Go to your Site Requests list and create a new item. Remember the value you specify for SizeMB as this should be the updated Allocated value once the workflow completes. Right now our Allocated value is zero so this site should be created without administrator intervention. Once the item has been created, use the Workflows button to launch the SiteRequestsWorkflow. In a production environment, there would be no reason to show the user a screen where they simply click Start. The workflow could be configured to start automatically, in which case this screen would never be seen. Start the workflow. You should see that it finished without requiring a task to be completed by a user. Clicking the Completed link will take you to the workflow status screen. Notice how the Visio diagram is used to show the path the workflow took and that the history list is populated with the correct entries. This is also shown in Figure 11-20, though we had to zoom out to see the whole diagram.

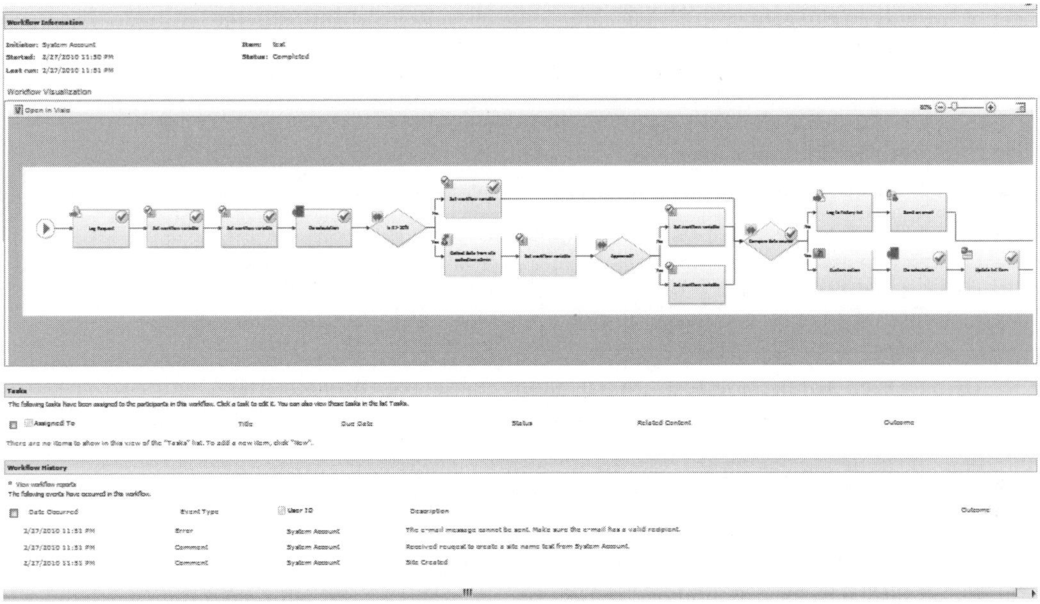

Figure 11-20. The workflow status page

Also confirm that the Allocated column of the Quota Management list was updated. You can edit this item and artificially up the allocated amount so that the other path through the workflow will trigger (a number greater than 51200). Adding another test item should result in the workflow pausing In Progress until the site collection administrator approves or declines the task. When you complete the task, SharePoint renders the form with the IsApproved field we defined in the SharePoint Designer wizard. This is shown in Figure 11-21.

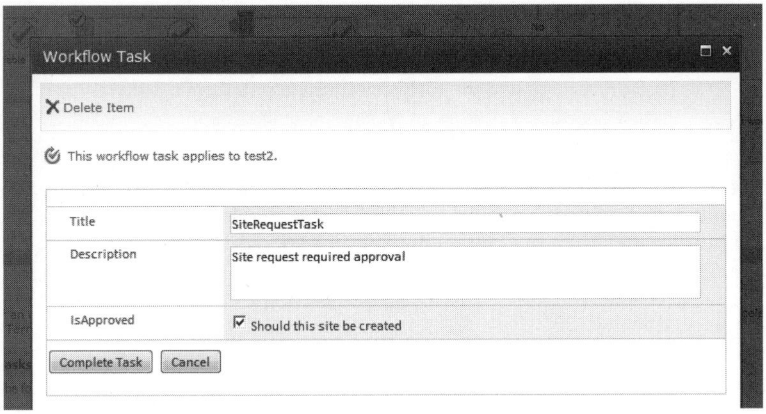

Figure 11-21. The custom workflow task

You may wonder where your sites actually are. If you click All Site Content in the left-hand navigation of the site, you can see the sites at the bottom of the list.

Important Lessons

This chapter incorporated several key techniques that are worth highlighting as they could easily be reused in other projects.

Creating a Custom Workflow Activity: The solution detailed how you can create a new building block for SharePoint workflows that also supports the SharePoint Designer workflow editor. This enables developers to extend the set of tools their power users have in SharePoint Designer.

Using a Web Application Feature to Change the Web.Config file: The solution used a SharePoint feature scoped at the web application level to not only deploy the workflow activity, but also to make a custom configuration change to the `web.config` file. This technique could be used for other such changes, such as appSettings entries for certain customizations.

Using Visio to Mock up a SharePoint Workflow: In this solution, we demonstrated that Visio 2010 includes SharePoint-specific workflow shapes that make it a prime candidate for mock-ups. These shapes also jump-start the workflow construction process as their flow can be imported into SharePoint Designer.

The SharePoint Designer Workflow Editor: This editor has been dramatically improved from the 2007 version and is a tool that developers as well as end users will leverage for workflows. It provides a rapid workflow design experience that enables you to control the decision flow, create tasks for users, send emails, and interact with the SharePoint site. Moreover, the ability to export your workflows provides an opportunity for reuse that was not present in earlier releases.

Using Visio to Visualize the Workflow: In this solution, we showed you that you can use Visio Services to enhance the workflow status page with a depiction of where the user is in the process.

Extension Points

While coding this example, we thought of several variations to the solution that we didn't incorporate. Mostly, these were not included because they distracted from the overall objective of the solution. We call them out now as extension points since they may be applicable to a specific project you are working on.

Include an option to add the site to navigation controls: In our solution, the site does indeed get created in the site collection, but the average end user might never know it is there. This is because our custom workflow activity did not include any options or code to add this site into the navigation structure of the site collection.

Base the workflow on the actual quota: In our solution, we used a list to keep track of the quota for the site collection and the amount allocated. You could change the workflow to use the site collection's actual quota, which is available through the object model, and use a property bag of the root web site to store the amount allocated. Of course, you would have to create additional workflow activities if you wanted these values to be available in SharePoint Designer.

Reuse the workflow: In the solution we created a reusable workflow, but didn't leverage it anywhere else. In SharePoint Designer, you can use the Save as Template button in the ribbon to export the workflow. This will persist the workflow to a SharePoint solution file (wsp) that you can reuse to create other solutions in the future. You will get a warning that this workflow contains lookups to other lists; this is because of our Quota Management list. Click OK, which saves it to Site Assets. You could then import the wsp file into a Visual Studio to create a SharePoint feature that included the workflow, its association, the quota management list, and its data. When performing this action, do not use the Import Reusable Workflow Visual Studio template, but rather the one that lets you import any wsp solution. This is because you are not interested in converting the declarative SharePoint Designer workflow into a Visual Studio code-based workflow. You just want to wrap it in another deployment vehicle. The solution in Chapter 14 has some steps similar to this approach.

Further Reading

The following links are to resources that we think a reader interested in the material presented in this chapter would find useful:

- The Basics on Content Type Syndication in SharePoint 2010 `http://sharepoint.mindsharpblogs.com/Bill/archive/2010/01/23/The-Basics-on-Content-Type-Syndication-in-SharePoint-2010.aspx`

- Creating SharePoint 2010 Workflows with Visio 2010 `http://www.wictorwilen.se/Post/Creating-SharePoint-2010-workflows-with-Visio-2010.aspx`

- SharePoint Workflow Authoring in Visio Premium 2010 Part 1 `http://blogs.msdn.com/visio/archive/2009/11/23/sharepoint-workflow-authoring-in-visio-premium-2010-part-1.aspx`

- SharePoint Workflow Authoring in Visio Premium 2010 Part 2 `http://blogs.msdn.com/visio/archive/2010/01/19/sharepoint-workflow-authoring-in-visio-premium-2010-part-2.aspx`

- How to modify the web.config file in SharePoint using SPWebConfigModification `http://www.crsw.com/mark/Lists/Posts/Post.aspx?ID=32`

- How To: Programmatically Add and Remove web.config values `http://msdn.microsoft.com/en-us/library/cc768610.aspx`

- Visio Services Overview `http://technet.microsoft.com/en-us/library/ee663485(office.14).aspx`

CHAPTER 12

■ ■ ■

Rapid SharePoint Application Development Using Access

Microsoft Access has always been an excellent Rapid Application Development (RAD) tool for building data-centric desktop applications—but it has also been challenged when the need arises to move an application to the Web or to support a shared, multi-user environment. There are many reasons to move an application to the Web—centralized management of policy and data, centralized deployment for updates, and to enable browser-based access for users. Previous releases of Access have been able to meet some of these needs with mechanisms like linked tables, which allow data to be stored externally, or by using SharePoint for centralized storage of resources while retaining Access as the primary client application. With the release of Office 2010, the combination of SharePoint, Access, and Access Services now lets you publish an Access database application to the Web, requiring only a browser to use your Access Database applications. It also provides a much better experience when it comes to manageability.

Real-World Examples

All organizations need to track and manage information, and Access has been the tool of choice among business and power users because they could quickly build an end-to-end application—from the tables used to store the raw data, to the forms used to manage and interact with the data, to reporting. And by using linked tables, users can even build applications driven by data residing in repositories across the enterprise, even those external to Access. Access is extremely powerful, but it is also a challenge to manage and support for many IT departments. All too often, solutions written in Access become business-critical applications but reside outside the boundaries of what is managed by IT; many times, these solutions are unknown to the technical team until some sort of failure arises.

Solution Overview

Access targets two primary use cases—data workbenches and departmental tracking applications. Tracking applications were the focus of web databases in the 2010 release, and they are the focus of our solution for this chapter. We will use Access to build a fully featured Asset Tracking System that stores which assets exist in an organization, who owns them, and when the assets will be fully depreciated. When we finish building our application, we'll use the combination of Access, Access Services, and SharePoint to publish our solution to the Web, allowing users to interact with our application using only a browser.

Solution Walkthrough

This section will detail the major elements of the Asset Tracking System and the decisions we made as we developed it. The walkthrough will show you how to use Access to create a web-based, data-centric tracking application, including storage for the application data, forms to interact with the data and navigate the application, and reports. Once we have finished building our application in Access, we will share it by publishing our Asset Tracking System to the Web using SharePoint and Access Services. We won't write much code during this exercise, and the code we do write will be based on the Access macro language, but we expect you will be pleasantly surprised by just how much you can get done using Access as a RAD tool.

Create the Asset Tracking System Database

Create a Web Database

When you open Access you see the Backstage View, which allows you to create a new database. Take the time to browse through the available Office.com templates, as well as Access's included Sample templates. Among the Sample templates you'll notice an Assets Web Database template. Why are we not using that out-of-box sample? Well, we could use this template for our solution, but we want to start from scratch in order to walk through the creation of a web database end to end. The purpose of this chapter is to develop such a solution, but it is also to illustrate a common use case, and attaching people to things and reporting against this relationship is very common across most (if not all) organizations. Follow the steps below to create your Assets web database.

1. Select the Blank web database template. Using one of the web database templates ensures compatibility when we go to publish our database to SharePoint by enabling only features supported by Access Services and SharePoint.

2. Name your database **AssetTrackingSystem.accdb** and set the file system location to wherever you want to save your local copy of the database.

3. Your screen should look similar to Figure 12-1. Click the Create button to continue.

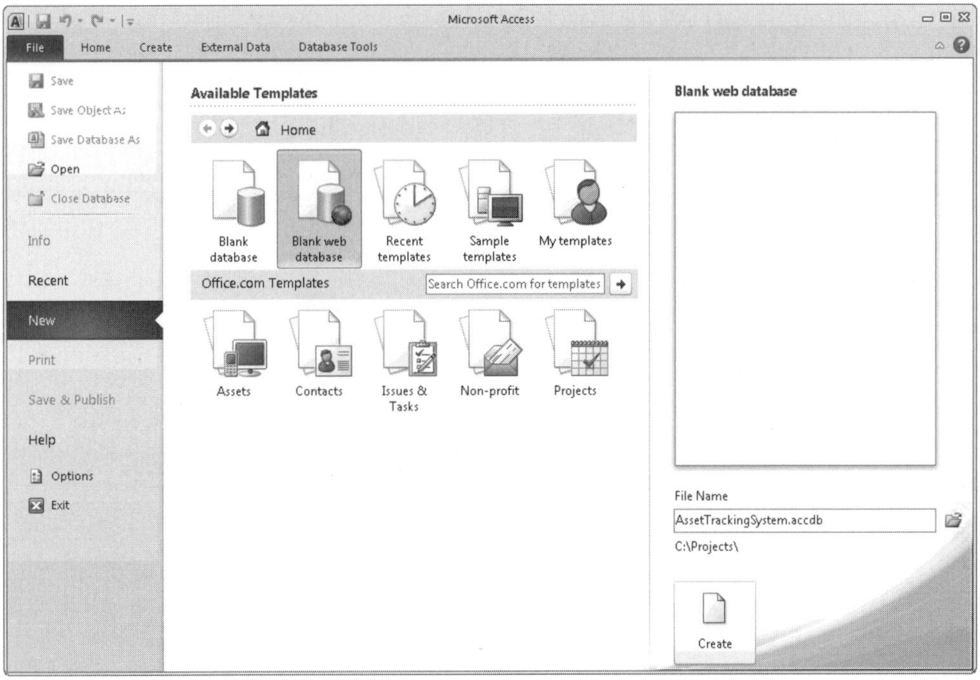

Figure 12-1. Creating the Assets database

Just as the template name implies, we now have a blank database. You actually get one table, named Table1, with one column, ID, and this table will open in datasheet view once the database is created; however if you close Table1, which you can do now, you'll notice the table was created but never saved, so now you truly do have a blank database. We now need to create and configure the three tables we'll be using to support tracking our assets. Once we publish our database to SharePoint, the tables we are getting ready to create will be saved as custom SharePoint lists; so, as you'll see, only SharePoint-compatible types will be allowed as fields for our tables. The following steps will walk you through getting the tables created and configured, beginning with the Owners table. Figure 12-2 shows a database diagram illustrating the tables we'll be building and using for our solution.

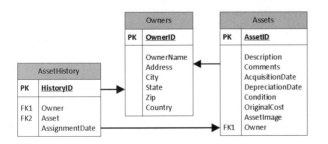

Figure 12-2. Database diagram for the Assets database

1. If you did not close the default Table1 created with the database, you can skip
    to step 2. Otherwise, click the Create tab on the ribbon and select Table. This
    will open a new table in datasheet view. In case you're wondering, design view
    is not supported for web objects. Instead, you must use options available on
    the ribbon or within the datasheet view to design and build your tables.

2. With the Fields tab of the ribbon selected, you should see a view similar to
    Figure 12-3. Right click on the ID column heading and select Rename Field;
    rename the field to **OwnerID** and press Enter.

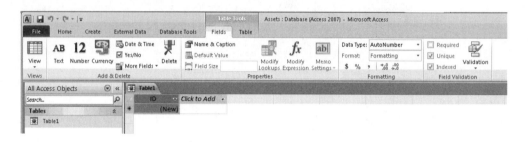

Figure 12-3. Creating a new table using the Fields tab on the ribbon

---

■ **Tip** After you finish editing the last column in a table, press Enter or Tab and Access will automatically bring up
the Add Column menu, reducing the number of necessary clicks and speeding creation of your new table.

---

3. Add a new column of type Text named **OwnerName** and press Enter.

4. Based on the diagram, the remaining columns in the Owners table are related
    to address information. Rather than creating each column individually, we can
    use the Quick Start data types to create multiple columns at once based on a
    template. With the Fields tab of the ribbon selected, choose More Fields and
    then click on Address in the Quick Start section of the drop-down menu. This
    adds the fields Address, City, State Province, Zip Postal, and Country Region;
    you can rename these fields to match those in the database diagram in Figure
    12-2 or keep the default names provided by the Quick Start template. Figure
    12-4 shows some of the additional Quick Start data types available with the
    default install.

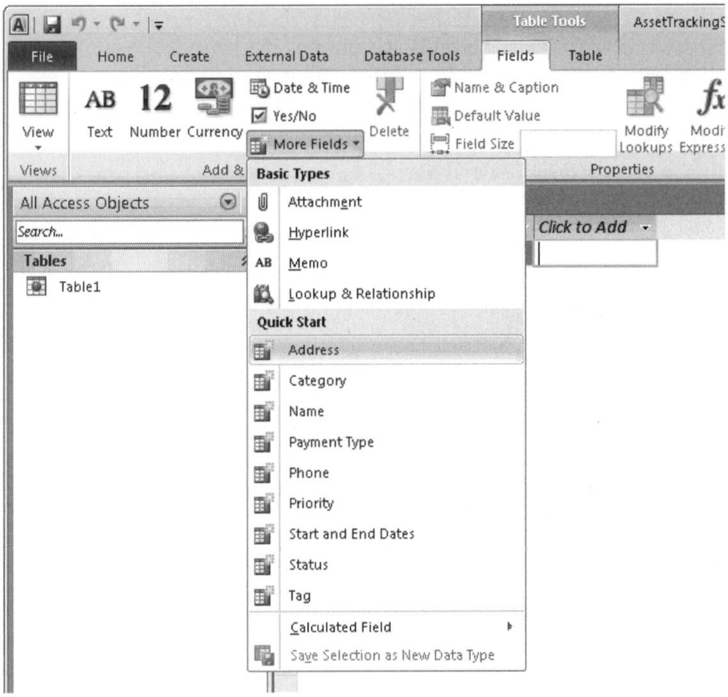

Figure 12-4. Adding a Quick Start data type

■ **Tip** To create your own Quick Start data type, select the columns you'd like to use as a template, click on the More Fields menu item found on the Fields tab of the ribbon, and select Save Selection as New Data Type.

---

5. Save the table by clicking the save icon above the ribbon or by right-clicking the Table1 tab in the editor window and selecting Save; name this table **Owners**. Close the Owners table

With the Owners table created, let's work on the Assets table, which will store the majority of the data we'll be tracking. The Assets table will be used to store details for each asset being tracked, including who owns the asset by referencing the OwnerID field from the Owners table.

1. Click the Create tab on the ribbon and select Table. Right click on the ID column heading and select Rename Field; rename the field to **AssetID** and press Enter.

2. Add a new column of type Text named **Description** and press Enter.

3. Add a new column of type Memo named **Comments** and press Enter. Click on the Comments column heading to select it and choose the Append Only option from the Memo Settings menu item on the Fields tab of the ribbon; this setting lets you keep a historical record of all comments for the asset that allows viewing all the comments together at once.

4. Add a new column of type Date & Time named **AcquisitionDate** and press Enter.

5. Add a column specifying the date the asset will be fully depreciated. We will use a very simple formula for depreciation here, assuming all assets are fully depreciated after the first day of the acquisition month plus three years; this lets us create a simple calculated value field. To add a new calculated value column, select the type Calculated Field with a subtype of Date/Time; this will display the Expression Builder dialog. Type the formula `DateSerial(Year([AcquisitionDate]) + 3, Month([AcquisitionDate]), 1)` noticing the IntelliSense as you type. Click the OK button to close the Expression Builder, Access will validate your expression to ensure it is web-compatible. Name your new column **DepreciationDate** and press Enter.

6. Add a new column of type Lookup & Relationship, which brings up the Lookup Wizard dialog as shown in Figure 12-5. Choose the option I will type in the values that I want and click Next. Keep the default of a single column and add the lookup values **Excellent**, **Good**, **Fair**, and **Poor**, then click Next to continue. On the final screen of the wizard enter **Condition** for the label of the lookup field and select the Limit to List check box. Click Finish. If you have not saved your Assets table, you'll be prompted to do so now. In this case, provide the table name **Assets** and click OK.

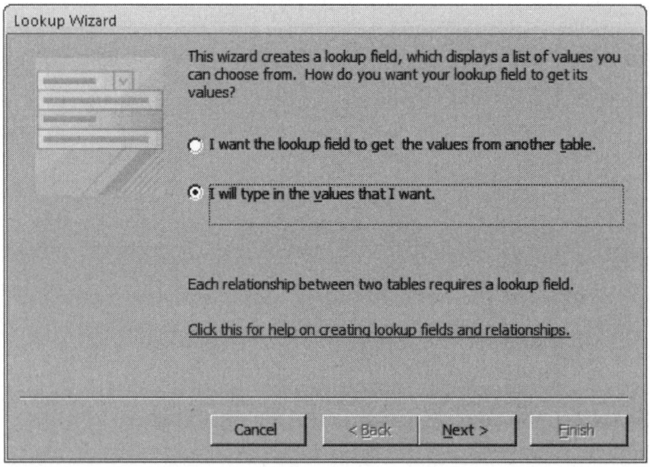

Figure 12-5. The Lookup Wizard dialog

7. Add a new column of type Currency named **OriginalCost** and press Enter.

8. Add a new column of type Attachment, which we'll use to store images of our assets. You can set the name of the attachment column by clicking the Name & Captions button on the Fields tab of the Ribbon and typing **AssetImage** for the Name.

We are just about done with the Assets table, except for adding the foreign key column for the asset owner. For this we need to associate the Owners table to the Assets table, and to implement referential integrity.

1. Add a new column of type Lookup & Relationship, which brings up the Lookup Wizard dialog. Choose the option I want the lookup field to get the values from another table and click Next.

2. Select Table: Owners and click Next.

3. Specify both the OwnerID and OwnerName as selected fields and click Next.

4. For sort order, select OwnerName, leave the order ascending, and click Next.

5. Ensure the Hide key column (Recommended) option is checked and click Next.

6. Enter **Owner** as the label of the lookup field and select the Enable Data Integrity check box with the Restrict Delete option enabled as shown in Figure 12-6. This ensures that users are unable to delete an owner from the Owners table if the record is identified as owning at least one asset. Save and close the Assets table.

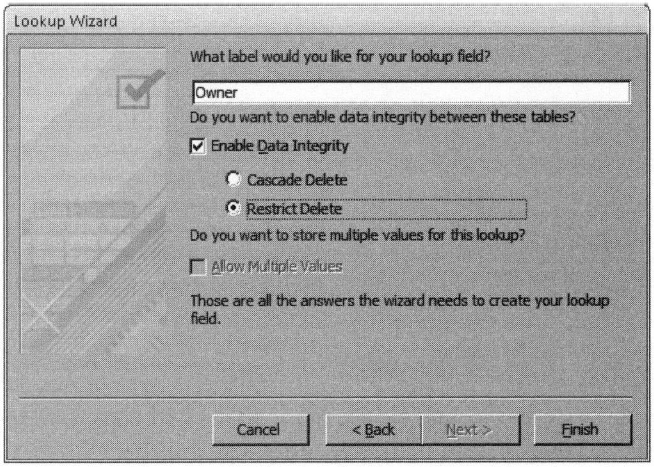

Figure 12-6. Setting options for the Owner lookup field.

■ **Note** Because all of the web tables in our database will end up being SharePoint lists, implementing referential integrity would have been difficult, if not impossible, without the new data integrity features that have been added to SharePoint 2010. For additional information on features that support relationships and constraints, see `http://msdn.microsoft.com/en-us/library/ee724401(v=office.14).aspx`.

The final table we need to create is the AssetHistory table, which will store the historical record of ownership for each asset. A bit later we will use data macros to automatically add records to this table any time a new asset is added to our system or if ownership of an asset is changed.

1. Click the Create tab on the ribbon and select Table. Right-click on the ID column heading and select Rename Field; rename the field to **AssetHistoryID** and press Enter.

2. Follow steps 1-6 above to create Lookup & Relationship columns for the Owner and Asset fields, associated to the Owners and Assets tables respectively. When prompted to save your table, provide the name **AssetHistory** and click OK.

3. Add a new column of type Date & Time named **AssignmentDate** and press Enter.

4. Save the **AssetHistory** table and then close it.

At this point we have created all of the tables we need to store data related to our assets. Now we need to build the user interface elements, such as forms, navigation, and reports, to provide a user-friendly way to interact with our data.

Add Some Forms

Forms let users interact with the tables in our database, supporting operations such as view, sort, list, filter, and add. For our Asset Tracking System, we'll create forms to work with the table data in a tabular form (the datasheet or list view) and forms to create and edit individual entries (the detail view). Furthermore, we'll add a navigation form to allow users to easily move between the various interface elements. Access will do much of the work for us by auto-generating most of what we need to create. After we publish our database to SharePoint, the forms will be saved as .ASPX pages, so ultimately we're using Access to help generate custom web forms. Let's start with simple datasheet and detail forms for our Owners table and a detail form for the Assets table.

1. Select the Owners table within the object window.

2. Select the Create tab on the ribbon and click the Datasheet button. Access automatically generates a new datasheet form based on the Owner table (since it is the currently selected table), then opens the form so you can edit the default configuration.

■ **Note** There are a few buttons on the Create tab prefixed with the word Client, such as Client Forms. This prefix denotes elements that will run only in the Access client; they are referred to as client-only objects and will not open in a browser. It is perfectly acceptable to create client-only objects in cases where you need enhanced functionality currently unavailable in Access Services, such as interaction with linked tables. You still get centralized storage of the objects in SharePoint; just be aware of the differences in how users will be able to interact with these objects.

3. Accept the defaults and save the form as **Owners**.

4. Select the Create tab on the ribbon, this time clicking the Form button. Access now generates a form with the detail for an individual item based on the Owner table.

5. Accept the defaults or experiment a bit and customize the layout. Save the form as **OwnerDetail**.

6. Select the Assets table within the object window.

7. Select the Create tab on the ribbon and click the Form button. Access now generates a form with the detail for an individual item based on the Assets table.

8. Accept the defaults or again feel free to experiment a bit. Save the form as **AssetDetail**. Figure 12-7 shows a slightly customized asset detail form with the default labels and controls repositioned and resized.

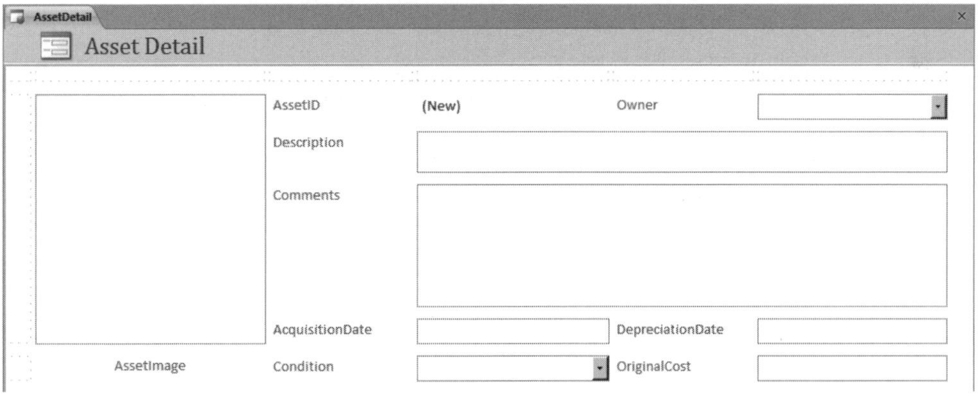

Figure 12-7. The AssetDetail form after adjusting the default field placement

The default Datasheet and Form templates we've used so far provide a quick way to generate some basic forms and include all the necessary functionality to navigate among records, even to search and filter the active dataset. We still need a tabular type form to view our list of assets, but this time let's build something with a bit more visual appeal than the simple datasheet we used for the Owners table.

1. Select the Create tab on the ribbon and click the Application Parts button. This brings up a menu displaying available prebuilt starter forms and quick start items, as shown in Figure 12-8. Select the List item from the Blank Forms section. Access will create and save a new form named List that should be visible in your object window. Depending on your security settings, you may get a warning that some active content has been disabled. Click the Enable Content button to continue.

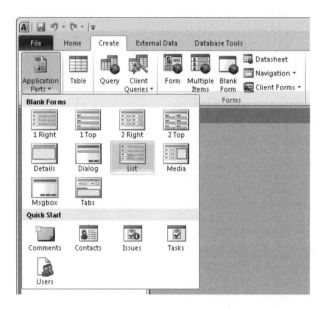

Figure 12-8. Menu showing availabile Application Parts

2. Right-click the List form in the object window, select Rename, and rename the form **Assets**.

3. Right-click the Assets form in the object window and select Layout View to open the form in design mode. Once the form is open, click the Design tab on the ribbon if it is not already the active selection.

4. The Application Parts templates don't automatically bind the form to a table so we need to set this binding behavior ourselves. If the property sheet is not already visible, open it by clicking the Property Sheet button on the ribbon. In the Property Sheet, select Form from the drop-down and then click the Data tab. On the Data tab select Assets for the Record Source.

5. Click the Add Existing Fields button on the ribbon to bring up the field selector. Drag one or more of the fields from the Assets table onto the form. Again, spend as much time as you want customizing the layout and other properties of the form, such as the caption. When you're done, save and close the form. Figure 12-9 shows a sample layout with the AssetImage, Description, AcquistionDate, and Condition fields added. Also included are the default Add New, edit, and delete buttons that are part of the Application Part template; we will add some substance to the buttons a bit later.

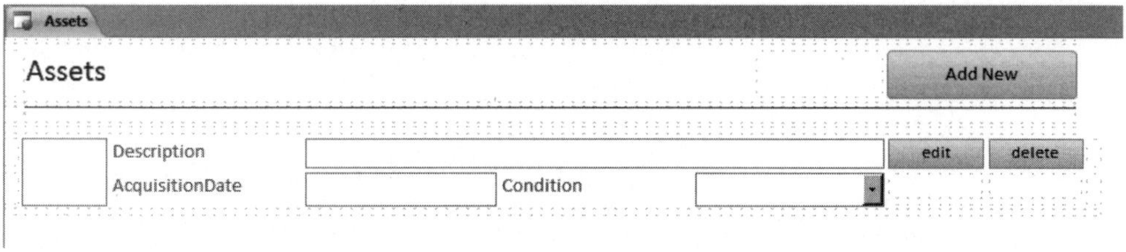

Figure 12-9. The Assets form created from the List Application Part template

We now have list and detail forms for two of our tables; we'll skip creating any forms for the AssetHistory table. As mentioned earlier, we will use data macros to create records in this table so we don't need to give users a form to add or update information. That said, we still need one more form to make it easier for users to navigate around our database application, and Access does a lot to get us started here as well. Let's create a navigation form that uses horizontal tabs to let users quickly move between the two list-view forms we just created; we'll also add a tab for the report we will be creating.

1. Select the Create tab on the ribbon and click the Navigation button to open the menu shown in Figure 12-10, which allows you to select the type of navigation form you want to create. Take a moment to look at the different options available and then select Horizontal Tabs, 2 Levels. Access will generate a new navigation form based on that selection.

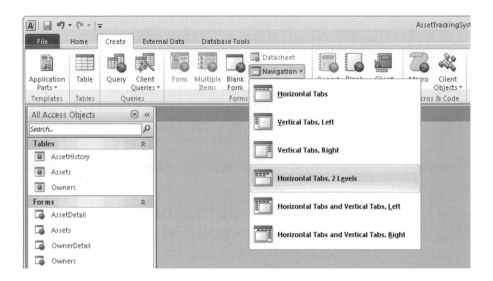

Figure 12-10. Options for creating a navigation form

2. Drag the Assets and Owners forms from the object window to the [Add New] tab of your newly created navigation form, which will create a new tab for each of the forms.

3. Click the [Add New] tab and type **Reports**, press Enter to create the new tab. We will use the second level of our two- level navigation control to list the available reports once we have them created.

4. Just to make the form a bit less generic, let's change the caption and the theme. For the caption, click the default title of the form, Navigation Form, and change it to **Asset Tracking System**. You can also change the default value by updating the Caption attribute in the properties window.

5. To change the theme, which will adjust elements such as the fonts and colors, click the Themes button on the Design tab of the ribbon to bring up the drop-down and make a selection. Changing the theme here will also set the theme for any of the other objects in our database where themes are supported, providing for a consistent look and feel.

6. Save your navigation form as **Main**.

■ **Note** We are only scratching the surface when it comes to developing forms, and this is really one of the more powerful features of Access as a RAD tool for web applications. It is worth spending some time looking at each of the different types of forms available on the Create tab and exploring the various ways you can customize attributes such as layout, color, etc. For some additional information related to creating forms in Access, take a look at http://office2010.microsoft.com/en-us/access-help/CH010369205.aspx.

Since we took the time to create a navigation form, we should set this form to open by default when a user accesses our application on the web or within Access. To set the default form, we need to update the database options.

1. Click the File tab on the Ribbon to open the Backstage View and click Options on the lower left side of the window to bring up the Access Options window.

2. Select Current Database from the list on the left to bring up the options specific to our Assets Tracking System database.

3. Set the Display Form and Web Display Form options to **Main** as shown in Figure 12-11. Click OK to save your changes; you'll be prompted to close and reopen the database before the changes take effect.

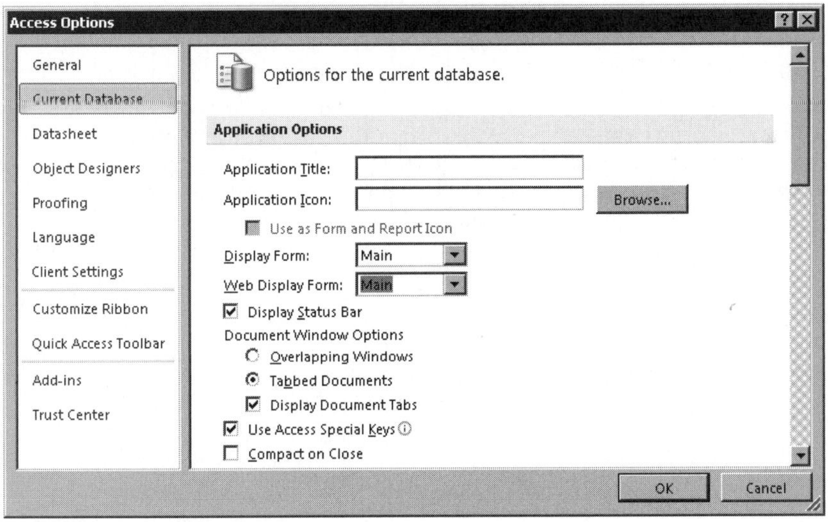

Figure 12-11. Setting options for the current database

283

What about the Code?

Since this is a web database containing web objects, we don't have the ability to write traditional VBA code. However, we can write macros, and Access actually provides a high degree of flexibility using this approach. Access supports two types of macros—UI macros and data macros. UI macros are associated with specific user interface elements, such as buttons, and are implemented as client-side JavaScript functions in the browser. Data macros are associated with tables, similar to traditional database triggers, and provide an excellent mechanism to ensure certain data-centric behaviors are executed regardless of the source of the action. When published to the web, data macros are implemented as custom SharePoint workflows.

Up to this point we've used the navigation form to allow users to navigate to the Assets and Owners forms, but we haven't provided a way for users to open the detail forms. While these forms by default allow users to edit and add items directly (this behavior can be modified by changing the Allow Edits and Allow Additions attributes of the form), a more user-friendly approach would be use the item detail form for these types of actions. Let's begin our exploration of macros by adding the ability to click on an item in our Owners form to bring up the corresponding OwnerDetail form in edit mode; additionally, clicking on an empty row should bring up the same OwnerDetail form in add mode.

1. Double-click the Owners form in the object window to open it.

2. Open the property sheet if it is not already open by clicking on the Property Sheet button on the Datasheet tab of the ribbon.

3. In the property sheet for the form, select OwnerID from the drop-down.

4. First we want to change the OwnerID column to be displayed as a hyperlink so users will know the element is clickable. Still in the property sheet, click the Format tab and set the Display As Hyperlink property to **Always**.

5. Next we need to create the macro that will bring up our detail item form when a user clicks on an OwnerID. Click on the Events tab on the property sheet to display the events we can add behaviors for; in this case we want to create a macro for the On Click event so select the On Click event in the property window, then click the ellipsis to the right of the property value to bring up the macro design surface shown in Figure 12-12.

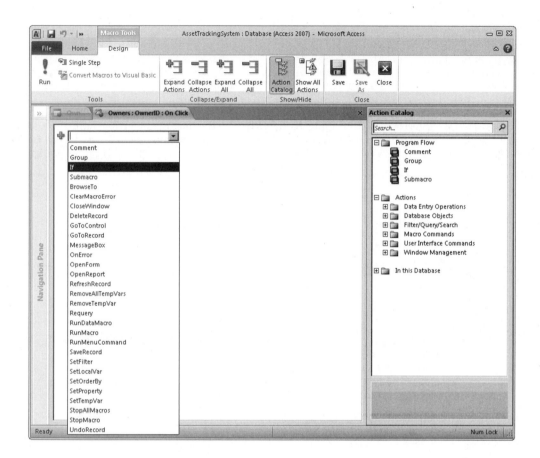

Figure 12-12. The macro design surface

■ **Note** Macros are how you "write code" in Access for web objects being published to SharePoint. One of the goals of Access Services was to enable business users, not developers, to publish databases to SharePoint without the intervention of IT. As a result, the Access team had to provide a safe no-code deployment model, and macros provide a safe and predictable set of actions. That said, macros can be very powerful, so don't underestimate them. For more information about macros in Access and what is possible check out http://office2010.microsoft.com/en-us/access-help/CH010369212.aspx.

The macro design surface lets you quickly build behaviors. Adding new actions, such as the If block shown in Figure 12-13, can be accomplished by typing the command if you know what it is, by selecting the command from the Add New Action drop-down on the design surface, or by double-clicking or dragging the command from the Action Catalog browser to the right of the design surface. Access will guide you through the creation of your macro using a fill-in-the-blank metaphor each time a new action is selected; and it provides IntelliSense, also shown in Figure 12-13, to speed development. The macro we'll build will help us accomplish three basic tasks. First, if edits have been made on the Owners form, we want to save those before continuing. Next, we'll open the item detail form in either edit or add mode, depending on which row the user clicked. Finally, once the item detail form window is closed, we need to refresh the Owners form to reflect our changes. Let's walk through each of these tasks.

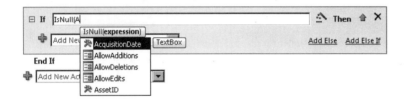

Figure 12-13. The macro design surface showing creation of an If action and IntelliSense

1. Start by adding a new **If** action with the condition `[Form].[Dirty]`; the `Dirty` property is a Boolean value set by Access that reflects whether the current record has unsaved edits. Within the If block add a **SaveRecord** action. The completed block is shown in Figure 12-14. Notice the comment block; you can insert comments using the Comment action type.

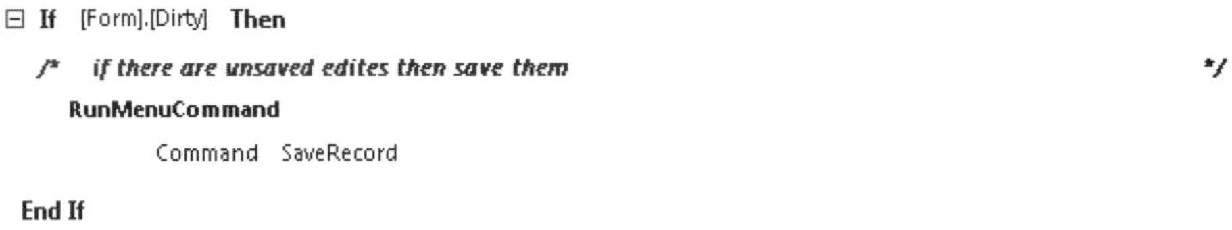

```
⊟ If  [Form].[Dirty]  Then

    /*    if there are unsaved edites then save them                        */
        RunMenuCommand

            Command    SaveRecord

    End If
```

Figure 12-14. Macro code to check if a save is necessary

2. Now we'll add a second If block. Add a new **If** action with the condition `IsNull(OwnerID)`. This will return true if the user clicks on (new) rather than on an existing row in the Owners form. Within the body of the If block add an **OpenForm** action with the Form Name `OwnerDetail`; Data Mode `Add`; and Window Mode `Dialog`, the dialog setting causes the form to open in a modal popup window. Finally, add a **Requery** action; this executes once the OwnerDetail form is closed to refresh the Owner form with the new record details. The Requery action will accept the control to refresh as an argument, which you can leave blank since we are refreshing the form. The completed block is shown in Figure 12-15.

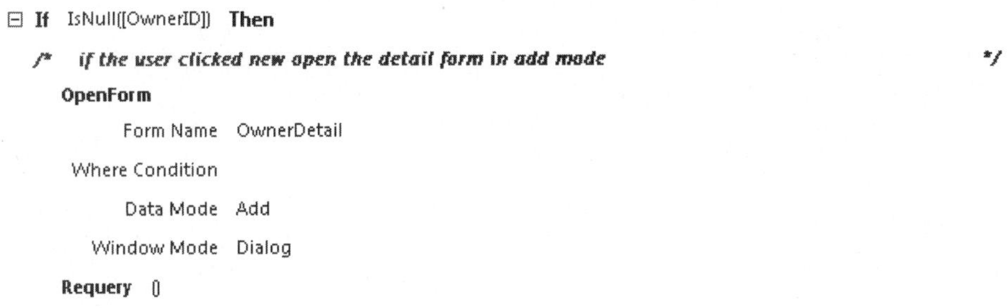

```
⊟ If   IsNull([OwnerID])  Then
    /*   if the user clicked new open the detail form in add mode                          */
        OpenForm
                Form Name   OwnerDetail
           Where Condition
                Data Mode   Add
              Window Mode   Dialog
        Requery  ()
```

Figure 12-15. Macro code to check for and handle adds

3. The last piece of the macro supports edits of existing records. Click the If block
    we just created to select and highlight the entire block, then click the Add Else
    link in the lower right of the selected region. Within the Else block add a
    SetTempVar action with the name `curOwnerID` and the Expression `[OwnerID]`.
    This will store the OwnerID the user clicked on in a temporary variable we will
    use as a filter. Next add an **OpenForm** action with the Form Name
    `OwnerDetail`, the Where Condition `[OwnerID] = [TempVars]![curOwnerID]`, the
    Data Mode `Edit` and the Window Mode `Dialog`. Lastly add a **RemoveTempVar**
    action with name `curOwnerID` and a **Requery** action to refresh the Owners form
    when the OwnerDetail form is closed. The completed block is shown in Figure
    12-16. Save the macro and close the designer then save and close the Owners
    form.

■ **Note** You may be wondering why we need the RemoveTempVar action. In the managed world we would expect
the resource to be released once execution of the macro is complete and the variable is out of scope. In Access,
however, temporary variables are global and stay in memory until released. This, along with the constraint that we
are limited to a maximum of 255 temporary variables at any one time, means removing a variable once we are
done with it is a best practice.

```
□ Else
    /*   else the user clicked a specific row so get the ID and pass as a filter to the form in edit mode    */
        SetTempVar
                    Name    curOwnerID
              Expression    = [OwnerID]
        OpenForm
               Form Name    OwnerDetail
         Where Condition    = [OwnerID] = [TempVars]![curOwnerID]
               Data Mode    Edit
             Window Mode    Dialog
        RemoveTempVar
                    Name    curOwnerID
        Requery    ()

    End If
```

Figure 12-16. Macro code to handle edits

We now need to take a similar approach for the Assets and AssetDetail forms, except we'll be adding behaviors for events attached to the default buttons, Add New, edit and delete, provided as part of the List template.

1. Right-click the Assets form in the object window and select Layout View.

2. Right-click the edit button and select Build Event…,which will open the macro design surface.

3. Again, start by adding a new **If** action with the condition `[Form].[Dirty]`. Within the If block add a **SaveRecord** action.

4. This time we don't need an If block since we are only dealing with edits. Add a **SetTempVar** action with the name **curAssetID** and the Expression `[AssetID]`. Next add an **OpenForm** action with the Form Name **AssetDetail**, the Where Condition `[AssetID]` = `[TempVars]![curAssetID]`, the Data Mode **Edit** and the Window Mode **Dialog**. Lastly add a **RemoveTempVar** action with name **curAssetID** and a **Requery** action to refresh the Assets form when the AssetDetail form is closed. The completed block for steps 3 and 4 is shown in Figure 12-17. Save the macro and close the designer.

```
□ If  [Form].[Dirty]  Then
    /*   if there are unsaved edits then save them                                    */
        RunMenuCommand
                Command   SaveRecord

  End If
/*   get the ID and pass to the form as a filter in edit mode                         */
    SetTempVar
                Name    curAssetID
        Expression   = [AssetID]
    OpenForm
            Form Name   AssetDetail
    Where Condition   = [AssetID]=[TempVars]![curAssetID]
          Data Mode   Edit
        Window Mode   Dialog
    RemoveTempVar
                Name    curAssetID
    Requery  ()
```

Figure 12-17. Macro code for editing assets

5. Right-click the delete button and select Build Event…,which will again open the macro design surface.

6. Add a **DeleteRecord** action. That's it for this one; the completed macro is shown in Figure 12-18. Save the macro and close the designer.

```
□ RunMenuCommand
      Command   DeleteRecord
```

Figure 12-18. Macro code for deleting assets

7. Right-click the Add New button and select Build Event…. This time you'll notice a default macro has been created to add a new record within the current form. We want to change this behavior to bring up the same details form we used for editing.

8. Remove the GoToRecord action and replace it with an **OpenForm** action with the Form Name **AssetDetail.** Leave the Where Condition blank and set the Data Mode to **Add** and the Window Mode **Dialog**. Below the OpenFom action add a **Requery** action to refresh the Assets form when the AssetDetail form is closed. The completed block is shown in Figure 12-19, including the error handler provided as part of the default macro. Save the macro and close the designer then save and close the Assets form.

```
⊟ OnError
                Go to   Macro Name
           Macro Name   ErrorHandler
  OpenForm
           Form Name    AssetDetail
      Where Condition
            Data Mode   Add
          Window Mode   Dialog
   Requery   ()

⊟ Submacro:  ErrorHandler
      MessageBox   (=[MacroError].[Description])
   End Submacro
```

Figure 12-19. Macro code for adding assets

So far we have built only UI macros. Let's now add one more macro, and this time we'll make it a data macro. As discussed earlier, data macros are somewhat analogous to triggers in SQL Server, with one key difference being data macros do not execute within the context of a transaction. This means we have no ability to treat the entire macro as a single atomic operation or to automatically rollback changes. However, just as is the case with triggers, data macros do provide an excellent means of associating business rules directly with the relevant data, ensuring consistency. Data macros are associated with a specific table and can be built as standalone reusable objects or can be triggered by the Before Change, Before Delete, After Insert, After Update, or After Delete events. In this case, we'll add an After Update data macro to the Assets table, which will create a new AssetHistory record any time a new owner is assigned to an asset. Repeat the following steps (minus adding the If block) to create an After Insert macro to capture the initial owner.

1. Double-click the Assets table to open it in Datasheet view.

2. Select the Table tab on the ribbon and then click the After Update button to open the macro design surface.

3. Add a new **If** action with the condition `Updated(['Owner'])`.

4. Within the If block, add a **CreateRecord** action using `AssetHistory` as the table name and `ah` for the Alias field.

5. Within the CreateRecord block (displayed as Create a Record In), add three **SetField** commands using the following values for the Name and Value attributes.

   - Name: `ah.Asset`

     Value =: `[Assets].[AssetID]`

   - Name: `ah.Owner`

     Value =: `[Assets].[Owner]`

- Name: `ah.AssignmentDate`

  Value =: `Now()`

6. The completed block is shown in Figure 12-20. Save the macro and close the designer.

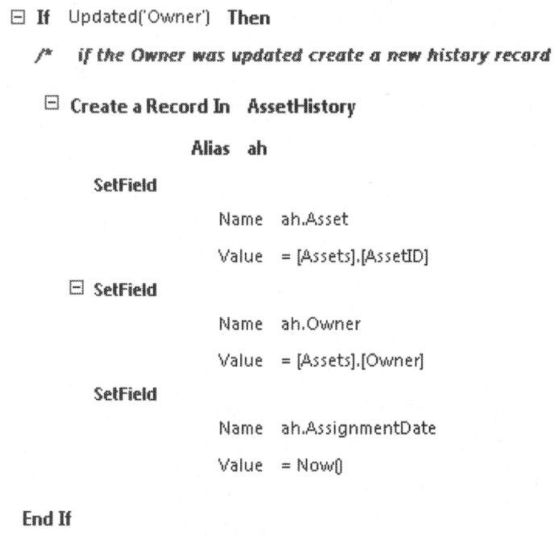

```
⊟ If   Updated('Owner')   Then
   /*   if the Owner was updated create a new history record

   ⊟ Create a Record In   AssetHistory

                 Alias   ah
         SetField
                    Name   ah.Asset
                    Value  = [Assets].[AssetID]
      ⊟ SetField
                    Name   ah.Owner
                    Value  = [Assets].[Owner]
         SetField
                    Name   ah.AssignmentDate
                    Value  = Now()

   End If
```

Figure 12-20. Macro code for creating the history record

Reporting is Key

We have created the tables to store our data and the forms to work with our data; now we need some reports to summarize our data. A great feature of Access is how it enables business users to quickly create very rich reports, and luckily this capability is available for web databases as well. In the case of web-based reports, Access Services relies on SQL Server Reporting Services to generate the output. Let's add a simple report to our Asset Tracking System to display the fully depreciated assets grouped by the owner of the asset.

■ **Note** Running reports in Access Services requires installation of the SQL Server 2008 R2 Reporting Services Add-In. The add-in can be run in connected or local mode. Connected mode requires a Reporting Services server and provides server features such as scheduling of reports. Local mode does not require a separate Reporting Services server but you can't access the server-only features. See `http://technet.microsoft.com/en-us/library/ee662542(office.14).aspx` for information on setting up and configuring the add-in.

---

1. First we need to create a new query that our report will be based on. Select the Create tab on the ribbon and click the Query button. This opens a new query in design view and brings up the Show Table dialog window. Select the Assets and Owners tables, click the Add button, then click the Close button.

2. In the lower section of the query designer, add the fields Description, AcquisitionDate, and DepreciationDate from the Assets table, and OwnerName from the Owners table; you can add the fields using the drop-down within the Field cell, by double-clicking the fields in each table, or by dragging the fields from the table to the lower section.

3. Add the expression <= Date() as the criteria for the DepreciationDate field and set the sort order to be **Ascending;** this will filter our results to return only assets that have met or surpassed their date of full depreciation.

4. Save your query as **DepreciatedAssets**. Your completed query in design view should look similar to Figure 12-21. Close the query designer.

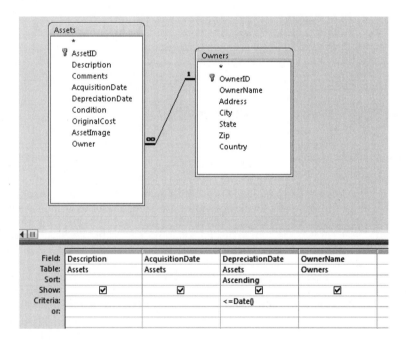

Figure 12-21. The query design surface for the DepreciatedAssets query

With the completed query we can now add a new report showing fully depreciated assets.

1. With the DepreciatedAssets query selected in the object navigation window, select the Create tab on the ribbon and this time click the Report button. Access will generate a new report based on the currently selected table or query, in this case the DepreciatedAssets query, and then open the report in design view.

2. As mentioned, we want to group our report by owner. Click the Add Group button in the Group, Sort, and Total section of the report design surface to bring up the group-on selector. If this section of the designer is not currently visible you can open it by clicking the Group & Sort button on the Design tab of the ribbon. Choose OwnerName from the drop-down. Click More to see the additional settings you can specify.

3. By default, our report includes a Totals field showing the number of all assets included in the report. Let's add another Totals field showing the total number of assets for each owner. On the report, select the cell just below the OwnerName column heading, then select the Design tab from the Report Layout Tools tab group of the ribbon. Click Totals from the Grouping & Totals section of the Ribbon and select Count Records as shown in Figure 12-22. This will add a new Totals field to the left of the default existing totals field; drag the newly created Totals field to the topmost cell under the Description heading. By moving the Totals cell here, we'll get the value for each grouping of owner.

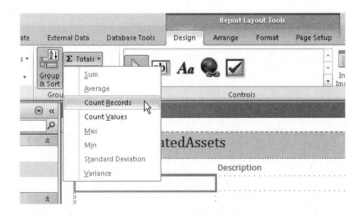

Figure 12-22. Adding a new Totals field to the DepreciatedAssets report

One other feature we can add to web reports is conditional formatting, which allows us to create some simple rules to change the formatting of a cell based on its value or an expression. Let's add some conditional formatting to the totals field we just added to change the background and font colors of the cell if the value is greater than or equal to 5; that is, the owner owns 5 of more fully depreciated assets.

1. With the new Totals cell we just created highlighted, select the Format tab from the Report Layout Tools tab group of the ribbon, then click the Conditional Formatting button to bring up the Conditional Formatting Rules Manager window.

2. Click the New Rule button to bring up the New Formatting Rule window. In the first two drop-downs of the rule builder, select Field Value Is and greater than or equal and then enter 5 in the text box. Next, use the formatting tools below the rule description to change the format of the cell for cases where the rule evaluates to true; we set the background color to blue and the font color to white. Your completed rule should look similar to Figure 12-23. Click OK to close the rule window and OK again to close the rule manager window.

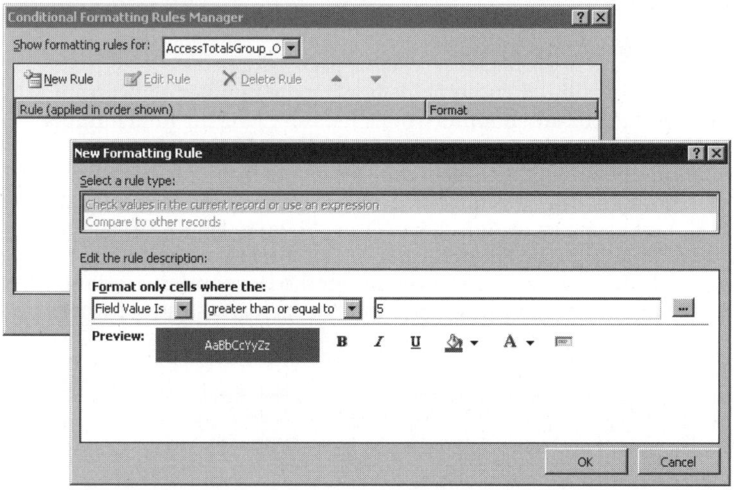

Figure 12-23. Setting up the conditional formatting rule

3. Save your report as **DepreciatedAssets**. Your completed report in design view should look similar to Figure 12-24. Take some time to customize the look of your report by adjusting cell size and margins, changing column headings, or by adding a custom title or logo. Again, Access provides the ability to quickly create some great-looking reports; for more information on building reports in Access, have a look at `http://office2010.microsoft.com/en-us/access-help/CH010369220.aspx`.

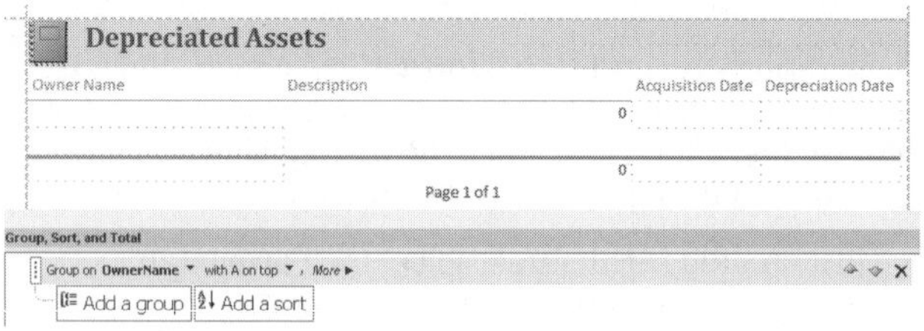

Figure 12-24. The report design surface for the DepreciatedAssets report

■ **Note** Access provides a live preview of the report while in design view, so if you have data in your database you'll see the data as it will look in context while you are designing your report, which is also the case with forms in design view. This really speeds the design process since you don't need to switch between views to see what the final result will look like. Add a few assets to your Asset Tracking System to see this in action.

4. Now let's add the report to the Main form so users will have quick access to it. Right-click the Main form in the object window and select Layout View. In the design window select the Reports tab; drag the DepreciatedAssets report from the object window to the [Add New] area on the heading below the tab group. Additional reports could be added to this area as well, providing users an easy way to navigate between reports. Save and close the Main form.

Publishing Our Asset Tracking System to SharePoint Using Access Services

Now for the moment we have all been waiting for—it is time to publish our Asset Tracking System to SharePoint via Access Services. Publishing our database entails Access launching the compatibility checker, which runs through a set of checks to ensure our web objects comply with all requirements and constraints, and then the creation of a new site where all the web objects will be created and managed. To make all of this magic happen, all you need is a SharePoint instance with Access Services and an existing site collection where you have rights to create a new site. Now let's walk though the publishing process so we can get our application to the web.

1. Click the File tab on the Ribbon to open Backstage View. The Info section of Backstage should be active by default; otherwise, select it now and click the Publish to Access Services button.

2. Set the Server URL to the location of the site collection where you'll be publishing your database and the Site Name to a unique site name within the site collection that will be used by Access Services during site creation.

■ **Note** You can click the Run Compatibility Checker button to confirm compatibility before publishing; however, Access will run through the checks as part of the publishing process so you will know if there are any issues. The compatibility checker is also a great tool to use during migration of an existing Access database to the web. The blog post at `http://blogs.msdn.com/access/archive/2009/12/21/access-2010-web-compatibly-checker.aspx` provides some additional information on how the tool works and how to address any identified issues.

3. Click the Publish to Access Services button to save and publish your database
    to the Web. Once this completes, a dialog window will be displayed with the
    link to your newly created site. Click the link to open your newly published
    Asset Tracking System in your browser, where you should see a view similar to
    Figure 12-25. Notice the Options drop-down, which lets you interact with your
    application in the context of the site beyond the functionality provided by the
    application itself; this is a reduced set of options compared with a traditional
    SharePoint site.

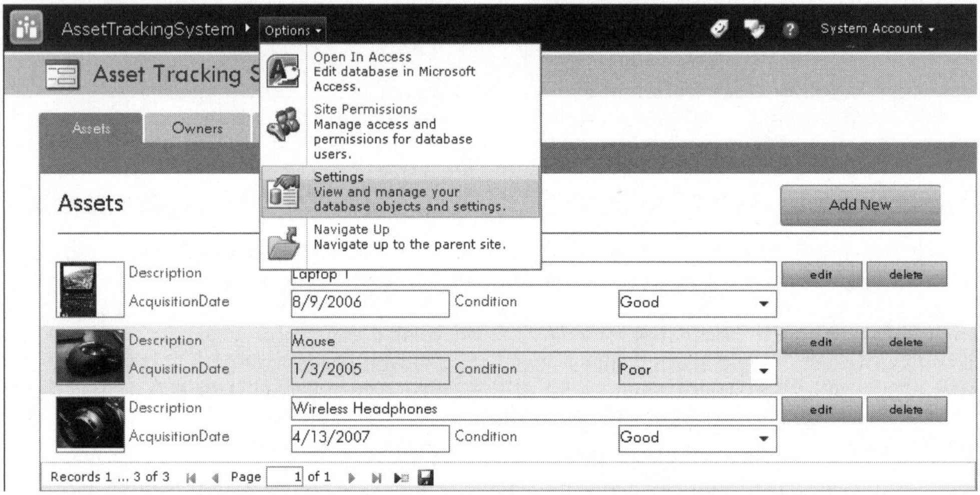

Figure 12-25. *The Asset Tracking System on the Web*

■ **Note** You can also open a form directly, without the SharePoint header, by using the form's URL. In this case, if
we wanted to open the Main form we could use `http://[server url]/[site name]/AccessServices/`
`Forms/Main.aspx`.

Now What?

There are likely several questions popping into your mind at this point related to the possibility of
working with and extending the Asset Tracking System beyond what is possible in Access. It is just a
SharePoint site after all, isn't it? It is, but there are some boundaries we must operate in. Any
modifications to the application, such as adding forms or modifying forms and reports, must still be
done in Access; any changes will then be synchronized back to SharePoint through Access Services.
Some changes, such as modification to table structure, require as well that you be online and connected
to the SharePoint site to ensure consistency. Many of the traditional mechanisms we have available to us

when working with normal SharePoint sites are not supported for sites created and managed by Access services; for example, SharePoint designer support is disabled for our site by default.

Fear not, there are still some options for customization; we do have the ability to interact with the lists (tables) using a few of the traditional approaches for customizing a SharePoint environment, such as building custom workflows in Visual Studio or writing custom event receivers. One point to remember here is that customizations developed in this way execute outside the boundaries of Access, so users running Access in a disconnected state will not trigger the events until synchronization occurs when the user is online and transitions to a connected state.

Also worth noting is the work the Access team has done to extend the capabilities offered by SharePoint; Access Services includes the Access Database Service, which provides enhanced caching, paging, filtering and sorting specific to Access applications.

Important Lessons

The Assets web database solution incorporated several key techniques worth highlighting as they could easily be reused in other projects.

> **Access as a RAD tool:** Using Access to develop SharePoint applications allows us to take advantage of the best of both worlds. Access provides the tools and the environment to quickly build data-centric applications, while SharePoint provides the ability to easily manage and secure and access those applications. We see limitless possibility with the combination of Access, Access Services, and SharePoint, especially with some of the options to customize the out-of-the-box experience as discussed in the Extension Points section below.

Extension Points

While coding this example, we thought of several variations to the solution we didn't incorporate. Mostly, these were not included because they distracted from the overall objective of the solution. We call them out now as extension points since they may be applicable to a specific project you are working on.

> **Add search capabilities:** Most of the default form templates provide a search box to filter the current dataset. If you are building custom forms you can quickly add this functionality by simply using a textbox, a button, and a custom macro to filter the result set, giving users the ability to search within the context of the specific dataset currently being worked with.

> **Add a custom workflow:** Ideally we want to automate and support integration where it makes sense as part of a business process, without the need for manual human intervention; this approach makes for a much more predictable and reliable process. Using a workflow is a great way to enable this automation, and by building custom SharePoint workflows in Visual Studio you can extend capabilities beyond what you can do with Access alone.

> **Add a custom event receiver:** To continue the integration and automation theme, you can also use custom event receivers to execute business logic based on certain events, such as a new asset being added to the Asset Tracking System—which is ultimately a new item being added to a SharePoint list.

Further Reading

The following links are to resources that we think a reader interested in the material presented in this chapter would find useful:

- Creating Web Databases with Access 2010 and Access Services `http://msdn.microsoft.com/en-us/library/ff402351(office.14).aspx`

- The official blog of the Microsoft Access product team `http://blogs.msdn.com/access`

- Set up and configure Access Services `http://technet.microsoft.com/en-us/library/ee748653(office.14).aspx`

- The Access Show on Channel 9 `http://channel9.msdn.com/shows/Access`

- Whitepaper: Improving the Reach and Manageability of Access `http://technet.microsoft.com/en-us/library/ff397963(office.14).aspx`

■ ■ ■

CHAPTER 13

Using Visio Services to Visualize Data

A picture is worth a thousand words, and Visio provides the canvas and the tools to create drawings that represent ideas and concepts ranging from network topologies to landscape design, and process diagrams to UML. Visio allows us to take complexity and model it visually making it much easier to share ideas and information concisely. Visio provides templates and shapes for many common scenarios and additional elements can be downloaded or even created and added to the toolbox. But we can go even further. What if we use these Visio drawings to surface data in a visual manner, bringing deeper understanding, context, and richness to our drawings? Using Visio you can connect the information stored across disparate repositories to shapes, and now the drawing is dynamic instead of static. With the release of SharePoint 2010 and Visio 2010 we now have the additional ability to publish our drawings to the web while still providing the dynamic and interactive capabilities to our users.

Real-World Examples

We are bombarded with data in every area of our daily lives; today, everything is captured, stored, and reported on in some sort of electronic fashion, which leads to huge repositories of information. Sifting through this information using traditional means can be tedious and time-consuming, making it extremely difficult to quickly understand the data and highlight data points that need attention. We need a way to visualize this information in a meaningful way in context, and this is exactly where Visio and Visio services come to the rescue. To use a simple example common in most organizations, typically there are diagrams for the network architecture, and there are repositories containing information related to the status and metrics of the network, but rarely are these two combined. Using Visio, however, we can easily link the system status and metric data to the network drawing, and associate data items to shapes in the diagram; this gives us a real-time view of the data in context, providing a much more meaningful view of the information. We can then save this amalgam, including the data links, to SharePoint as a web drawing and use Visio Services to render the information in a browser as well as to provide hooks to allow programmatic access to the drawing and its contents.

Solution Overview

The first goal of this solution is to detail how data can be linked to and surfaced in your Visio drawings. For this solution, we will start with a floor plan for an office, since this is a fairly universal concept typically conveyed using a drawing. Once the data has been linked we will look at the various ways we can associate and visualize specific data points within the shapes on our drawing; in this case offices, conference rooms, and printers.

Solution Walkthrough

The following section will detail the major elements of the solution and the decisions that were made in coding it. The walkthrough will begin by showing you how to connect external data sources to your floor-plan diagram, how to bind data to shapes within that diagram, and how to specify behaviors for the shapes based on specific data values. Once we've completed the diagram, we will publish it to SharePoint, allowing other users to view and interact with the diagram using only a browser. Then we will look at some of the options for adding interactivity to our diagram that enable users to interact with the data being surfaced through the floor plan. We highly recommend you download the accompanying code for this chapter from the Apress site so you can easily follow along and reuse some of the resources.

Creating the Floor Plan

The first thing we need is a diagram. As mentioned in the solution overview, we want to allow users to interact with our floor plan to find out who occupies a specific office, to reserve a conference room, and to get connection and status information for an office printer. We will highlight the key elements of the diagram necessary to successfully build the rest of the solution, in case you are interested in creating your own floor plan. If you'd rather skip creating the floor plan from scratch, you can use the prebuilt diagram (shown in Figure 13-1) contained in the download without missing anything critical to the solution; look for the file named FloorPlan.vsd in the chapter 13 sample files.

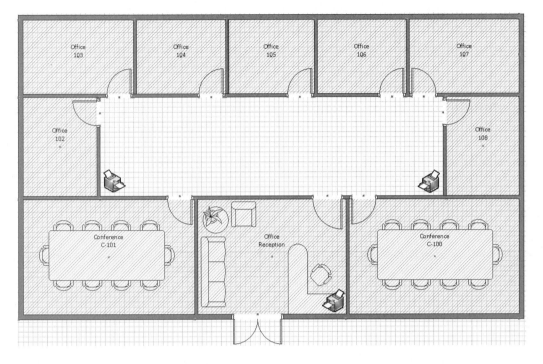

Figure 13-1. Sample floor plan diagram

■ **Note** An alternative to creating the floor plan by hand would be to start from an existing diagram, such as an image or CAD drawing, and simply overlay the shapes you'd like to represent on the drawing.

---

1. Open Visio and create a new drawing; we used the Floor Plan template for our sample but you are welcome to start from any of the predefined templates or even to use the blank drawing.

2. Create a drawing representing an office floor plan layout. The actual shapes you use to create the initial layout are unimportant; just be sure to define areas to represent offices, conference rooms, and space for printers.

When the floor plan is complete, we need to overlay the shapes we will be interacting with during the remainder of the solution, first for the rooms and then for the printers. Note that only the topmost shape is clickable once the drawing has been published to the Web, so you need to use the transparency setting of an overlay shape if you want to make an entire region clickable, rather than focusing on an individual shape as we'll do with the rooms on our floor plan.

1. Add a Space shape for each of the offices and conference rooms, resizing it to fill the entire area of the room. The space shape provides a large clickable area and is semitransparent by default, allowing you to view additional details of the drawing underneath. If you started with the Floor Plan template, the Space shape will be visible on the Walls, Shell and Structure stencil; otherwise, you can find this shape by browsing More Shapes ➤ Maps and Floor Plans ➤ Building Plan ➤ Walls, Shell and Structure.

2. Add one or more printers to your drawing. You can find the Printer shape by browsing More Shapes ➤ Network ➤ Computers and Monitors.

3. For each of your Space shapes, set the Space use property to either **Conference** or **Office** and the Name property equal to a unique room number, which will be mapped to the datasets we will be creating shortly. To set the property value, you can either right-click on each shape and select Properties to open the Shape Data window, or set the values using the Shape Data window found under the Task Panes drop-down on the View tab of the ribbon.

4. For each of your Printer shapes, set the Network Name property equal to a unique alphanumeric value, which again will be mapped to the datasets we create.

Setting up the Data

Next we need the data that we'll surface in our floor plan. For this solution, we'll create three very simple datasets; the first, for conference rooms, will be stored in a custom SharePoint list, and the other two, for offices and printers, will be stored in Excel. Use the following steps to create the **ConferenceRooms** custom list within SharePoint.

■ **Note** Since we are not focused on a specific data source, we are using an Excel spreadsheet and SharePoint list to simplify development of our solution. But don't take this as a limitation of options for data connections. Visio supports connecting to Excel workbooks, Access databases, SharePoint lists, SQL Server databases, or any other OLEDB or ODBC data source. And if that isn't enough you can create a custom data provider to consume data from other sources such as XML.

---

1. Open a browser and navigate to the local SharePoint site you'll be using to host this solution.

2. From the Site Actions menu select More Options, which will bring up the Create dialog shown in Figure 13-2. Select Custom List and name it **ConferenceRooms**. Click Create.

3. Once your **ConferenceRooms** list has been created, add two columns based on the following values for column name and column type, accepting the default values for the remaining settings.

- Column Name: **RoomNumber**

- Type: Single line of text

- Column Name: **ReservedBy**

- Type: Single line of text

4. Add new list items for each of the conference rooms in your floor plan, matching the RoomNumber in the list item to the Name used for the corresponding space shape in your diagram. If you used the sample floor plan, you will create two items corresponding to conference rooms C-101 and C-100 in the diagram. Title can be a value of your choosing and ReservedBy should be left blank for now.

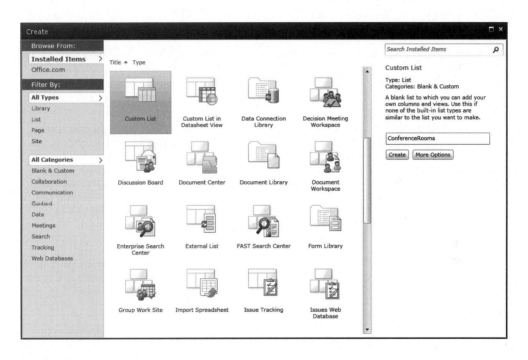

Figure 13-2. The Create dialog in SharePoint

For simplicity we will use Excel to store data related to offices and printers. In our solution, these two data sources will be used for reading values only, so feel free to use some other data repository such as SQL Server if you want to experiment with connecting to other data providers besides SharePoint and Excel. If you decide to go this route, use the settings in the steps below to build your data structures and adjust the steps in the Linking Data to our Shapes section accordingly.

1. Open Excel and create a new Blank Workbook. Rename Sheet1 and Sheet2 to **Offices** and **Printers** respectively. You can delete Sheet3.

2. In the **Offices** sheet we want to represent a table with two columns, **Office** and **Occupant**. Use these values as headings in the first row and then add a new item for each of the offices in your floor plan, matching the Office in the spreadsheet to the Name used for the corresponding space shape in your diagram. If you used the sample floor plan, you will create seven items corresponding to offices 102-108 in the diagram. We will be using the Occupant value to query against Profile database in SharePoint, so these values should map to actual users in your environment and be of the form **domain/user**. Sample values are shown in Table 13-1.

Table 13-1. The Offices Dataset

Office	Occupant
102	sample\chadwach
103	sample\edhild

3. In the **Printers** sheet we want to represent a table with four columns, **Network Name**, **Color**, **IP Address**, and **Status**. Again, use these values as headings in the first row and then add a new item for each of the printers in your floor plan, matching the Network Name in the spreadsheet to the Network Name used for the corresponding printer shape in your diagram. If you are using the sample floor plan, you'll create three items corresponding to the three printers in the diagram. For Color use the values **yes** or **no**. For Status use the values **online**, **offline**, or **error**. Sample values are shown in Table 13-2.

Table 13-2. The Printers Datase.

Network Name	Color	IP Address	Status
WEST	yes	192.168.0.200	online
EAST	no	192.168.0.201	offline
RECEPTION	no	192.168.0.202	error

4. Save the Excel spreadsheet to a document library in the local SharePoint site you're using to host this solution.

Linking Data to our Shapes

Now that we have a completed drawing and we've created related data, we want to link the two together. The drawing provides the right context for our data and the data gives life to what would otherwise be a static drawing.

1. Let's start with the printers dataset. Select the Data tab on the Ribbon and click the Link Data to Shapes button. This will bring up the Data Selector wizard shown in Figure 13-3. Choose the Microsoft Excel workbook option and click Next .

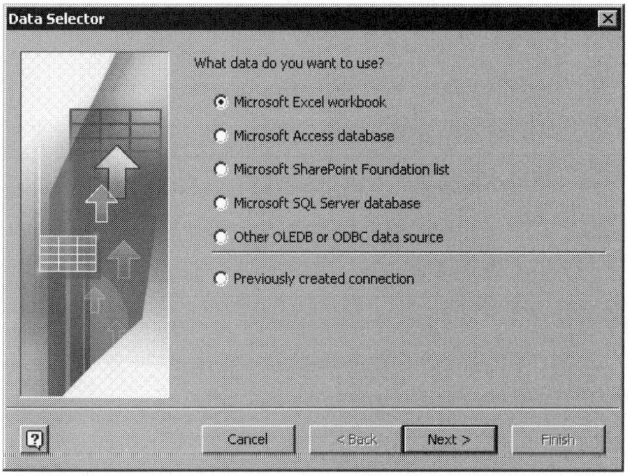

Figure 13-3. The data source selection screen of the Data Selector wizard

2. Next, for the workbook to import, enter the URL of the workbook you created in the previous section. Notice the warning in this step of the wizard stating the Excel workbook must be located on the same SharePoint site where our Web Drawing we will be published and that Excel Services must be enabled.

3. Select Printers$ as the worksheet to use. Make sure the First row of data contains column headings box is checked. Click Next.

4. Choose the Rows in my data are uniquely identified by the value(s) in the following column(s) option and ensure Network Name is checked. Click Finish.

Repeat steps 1-4 to link the offices dataset; select Offices$ for the worksheet in step 3 and check Office for the unique value in step 4.

1. Linking the conference rooms dataset is similar. Select the Data tab on the Ribbon and click the Link Data to Shapes button. This time choose the Microsoft SharePoint Foundation list option and click Next >.

2. Enter the URL of the SharePoint site where you created the ConferenceRooms list. Click Next.

3. Select ConferenceRooms as the list to use and choose the Link to List option. Click Finish.

The External Data window should have opened after linking the first dataset; if it isn't visible, select the External Data Window checkbox on the Data tab of the ribbon. You should see three tabs in this window, one for each of the linked datasets, with each tab providing a view of the rows and columns contained in the linked data. Right-clicking in the dataset window brings up options for linking and configuring each of the datasets. Figure 13-4 shows a view of the External Data window as well as the right-click menu.

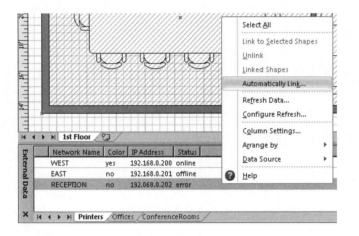

Figure 13-4. Working with the External Data window

After specifying the data sources, we need to link individual data items to shapes in our drawing, which will load the values in the dataset into corresponding attributes or a shape wherever the name of a column in the dataset matches the name of an attribute of our shape; for any column where a match is not found, a new attribute will be created for the shape. You can do this either manually by dragging a row of data to a shape or automatically by selecting Automatically Link… on the right-click menu or by clicking the Automatically Link button on the Data tab of the ribbon. Automatic linking will attempt to map the data in the dataset to the selected shapes wherever a matching value exists among pairs of column and attribute mappings you specify when setting up the link. For this solution we will use the automatically link wizard to pair data with our shapes.

1. By default, Visio will add a data graphic to each shape after linking occurs. We will add our own data graphic later, so we want to disable this behavior before linking occurs. To do this, select the Data tab on the ribbon and then click the Data Graphics button, which opens a menu. Make sure the Apply after Linking Data to Shapes option is not checked.

2. Next we need to rename one of the columns in our ConferenceRooms dataset. The ID column is used by SharePoint to store a unique ID for the row. We will need access to this value once we start writing some code, but Visio Services will not expose a column named ID as a property of the shape when viewed on the web, so we need to rename it within the context of our drawing. With the ConferenceRooms tab selected in the External Data window, right-click and select Column Settings. Highlight the ID column and click Rename; rename the column **RowID**. Figure 13-5 shows the column settings dialog after renaming the ID column.

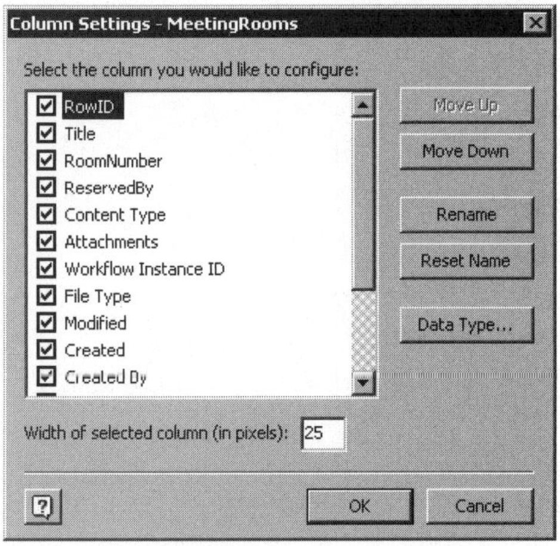

Figure 13-5. The column settings dialog

3. Now we are ready to link our datasets to our drawing. With the Printers tab selected in the External Data window, right-click on a row of data and select Automatically Link… to bring up the link wizard. Select the All shapes on this page option and click Next.

4. Next we need to map columns from our dataset to properties of our shapes; Visio will use these to determine which row of data aligns to which shape based on an equality check across these fields. Because the Network Name column in our dataset matches a property of one or more shapes on our diagram, the wizard should default to the correct selection in the drop-down for both the Data Column and the Shape Field, as shown in Figure 13-6. However, do double-check that the value is Network Name for both. Notice that you are able to add multiple mappings in this screen and of course the names do not have to match. Click Finish to complete the automatic linking process.

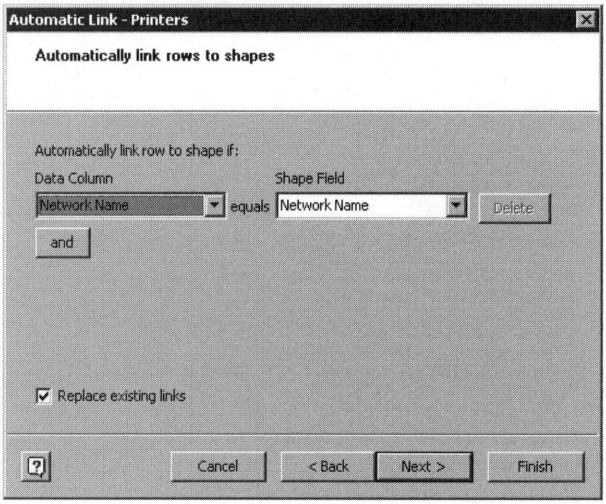

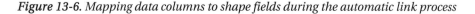

Figure 13-6. Mapping data columns to shape fields during the automatic link process

Once the automatic linking completes, right-click one of the printer shapes and select Properties. Notice that the Color and Status properties have been added as fields of the shape with values. Follow the previous steps 3-4 to automatically link the Offices and ConferenceRooms datasets; for the Offices dataset, map the Office column to the Name field and for the ConferenceRooms dataset, map the RoomNumber column to the Name field.

Giving Our Floor Plan Life

The real value of linking live data to our floor plan comes when we allow the data to be visualized in meaningful ways. Visio provides data graphics as a way to configure data-driven behavior associated with shapes. Information can be represented as text, data bars, or icon sets, or you can change the color of a shape based on a certain value or range of values. For our solution we will add custom data graphics to the printer shapes and to the conference rooms. For the printers, the data graphic will show the current status using icons, and will signify the ability to print in color using color by value. For the conference rooms, we'll indicate availability using color by value. Let's start with the printers.

1. Select one of the printer shapes on your drawing. Select the Data tab on the ribbon, then click the Data Graphics button to open the menu. Choose Create New Data Graphic… to open the New Data Graphic window.

2. First we will create the rules for the status icons. Select New Item to open the New Item window. For the Data field select Status and for the Displayed as option select Icon Set, which will present an additional drop-down for selecting specific icons. Choose the icon set beginning with the green checkmark; of the five icons in the set, we will use three, the checkmark for a status of online; the exclamation for a status of error; and the X for a status of offline. In the Rules for showing each icon section, set the conditions for each of the three icons. Your completed data graphic item should look like Figure 13-7. Click OK.

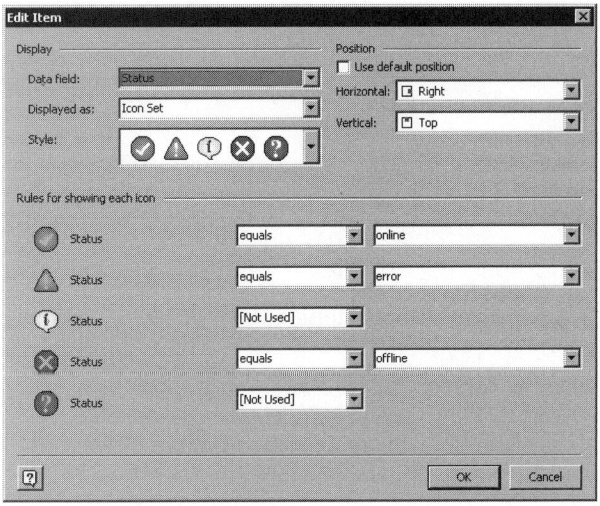

Figure 13-7. Creating a new data graphic item based on an icon set

3. Next we will create the rules to signify the capability to print in color. Keeping the New Data Graphic window open, select New Item to open the New Item window. For the Data field, select Color and for the Displayed as option, select Color by Value. This selection lets you configure color assignments in the lower half of the window; ensure there are two colors for the two values yes and no. Feel free to adjust the colors and click OK when you are done. Your completed New Data Graphic window should look like Figure 13-8. Click OK to close the window. Select yes if prompted to apply the data graphic to the selected shapes.

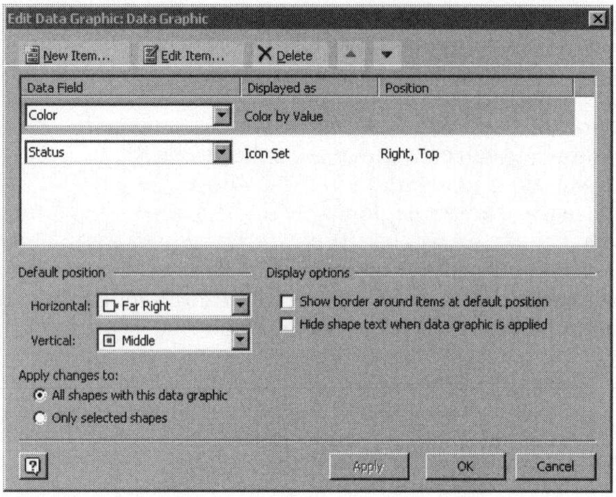

Figure 13-8. The completed new data graphic

4. Apply this data graphic to the rest of the printers in your drawing by selecting them and then choosing the data graphic you just created from the Available Data Graphics section in the Data Graphics dropdown on the ribbon.

All of your printers should now have a status icon and be colorized based on color printing abilities. The best part is, as the data changes—for example, when the status goes from offline to online—the shape will be updated accordingly. Now create a new data graphic to be used by the conference room space shapes to indicate availability.

1. Select one of the conference room space shapes on your drawing. Select the Data tab on the ribbon and then click the Data Graphics button to open the menu. Choose Create New Data Graphic… to open the New Data Graphic window.

2. Select New Item to open the New Item window. For the Data field, select ReservedBy and for the Displayed as option, select Color by Value. Click Insert to create a new color assignment row. Leave the value blank, which will evaluate to true anytime the ReservedBy field is empty, and select a color such as green to represent availability. Click OK.

3. Apply this data graphic to the rest of the conference rooms in your drawing by selecting them and then choosing the data graphic you just created from the Available Data Graphics section in the Data Graphics drop-down on the ribbon.

Assuming ReserveBy is empty for all rows in your ConferenceRooms dataset, your conference rooms should now be highlighted with the color you chose for the data graphic. We have now finished adding some simple but very effective data visualizations to our floor plan, providing users with a much richer experience than a static drawing would. However, there's one more thing to add before we publish our drawing; we need a legend to help users understand the meaning of our visualizations, and Visio can generate this for us automatically.

1. Select the Data tab of the ribbon once more and click the Insert Legend button to open the legend drop-down.

2. Choose one of the two options, Horizontal or Vertical, to insert a new legend based on the data graphics used in your drawing. Once the legend has been generated for your drawing, you can relocate it and modify the text and formatting to clarify meaning. Figure 13-9 shows the legend after we modified some of the text.

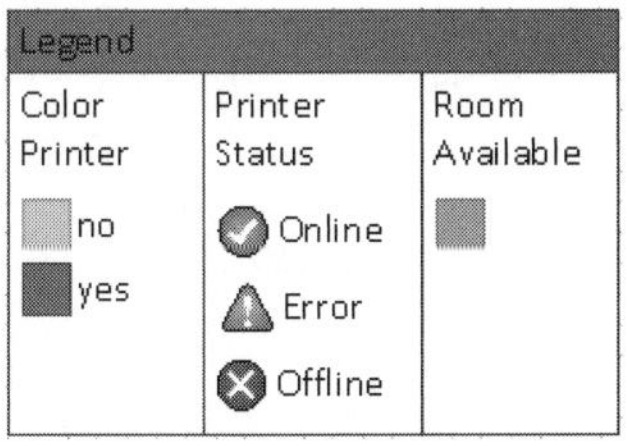

Figure 13-9. The Visio-supplied legend with modified text values

Sharing Your Floor Plan

With our floor plan complete, including data linking and visualizations, we can now save our drawing to SharePoint to enable delivery through a browser using Visio Services.

1. Select the File tab of the ribbon to open Backstage, then choose Save & Send on the left-hand side. Under the Save & Send heading select Save to SharePoint.

2. Click the Browse for a location option under Locations and the Web Drawing option under File Types. Make sure you select Web Drawing; otherwise you'll be saving a standard Visio drawing to a document library and Visio Services will not be able to render your floor plan in the browser.

3. Click Save As to open the Save As window, browse to a document library in the local SharePoint site you're using to host this solution, and save the file as **FloorPlan.vdw**.

4. When the save is complete, a new browser window will open to a view of the floor plan using Visio Web Access (VWA). You may get an alert that refresh is disabled, with the option to enable for this session or always. If you see this message, select Enable (always). Try zooming in and out and panning around to get a feel for how users can interact with your drawing. If your drawing has multiple pages, you will be able to navigate between them using the page drop-down just above the drawing space. Figure 13-10 shows the results of saving our Visio web drawing.

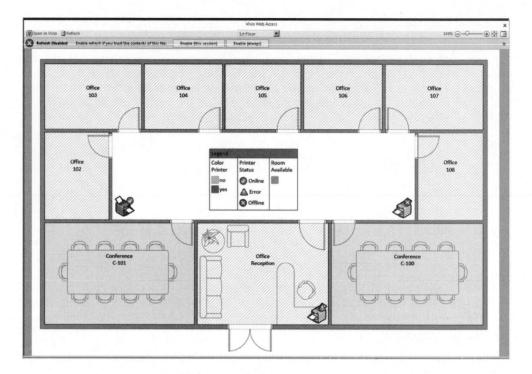

Figure 13-10. *The diagram after saving to SharePoint, rendered in the Visio Web Access control*

Adding More Interactivity

What we have accomplished up to this point is pretty amazing, considering we haven't written any code yet. We have created a floor-plan diagram in Visio, linked it to related data, provided users with rich visualizations based on the linked data that will update automatically based on current values, and saved the floor plan as a Visio Web Drawing to SharePoint, allowing users to view the diagram using only a browser. Now we want to look at how to go even further, using a bit of code to extend the available user interactions beyond what the Visio web access control provides out of the box. We will add the following: when a user clicks on a printer, show additional printer detail using an overlay on the drawing; allow a user to click on a conference room to reserve the space; when a user clicks on an office, query the SharePoint profile service to get additional user information for the current occupant of the office. To start, we will create a new SharePoint project in Visual Studio and then progressively add the necessary code to activate these features using the SharePoint and Visio Services JavaScript APIs. For a more detailed walkthrough of Visual Studio see chapter 3.

Setting up the Project

1. Launch Visual Studio 2010 and create a new project based on the SharePoint 2010 Empty SharePoint Project template, which you'll find by browsing the Installed Templates tree using the path Visual C# ➤ SharePoint ➤ 2010.

2. Name your project **FloorPlan** and leave the default choice of creating a new solution with the same name. Using the drop-down above the project types, ensure you are targeting the .NET Framework 3.5.

3. Next, the SharePoint Customization Wizard will prompt you for some information related to debugging and deployment. Enter the complete URL for the local SharePoint site you are using for this solution and select the Deploy as a full-trust solution option. Click Finish.

4. Right-click on the project and select Add ➤ New Item, which brings up the Add New Item window. Select the Visual Web Part template and name it **FloorPlanPart**. Click Add.

5. Expand the Features folder, then right-click on Feature1 and click Rename. Rename the feature to **FloorPlanFeature**. Your project should now look similar to Figure 13-11.

6. Double-click the FloorPlanFeature to open the Feature Designer window. Enter **Floor Plan Web Part** for the Title, **Floor plan interactive web part** for the Description, and ensure the Scope is set to **Site**. The scope defines the level at which our feature will be available in the SharePoint hierarchy; the options are Web for a site-level feature, Site for a site collection-level feature, Farm for a farm-wide feature, and WebApplication, which applies to all sites contained within the associated web application. Features containing web parts require a scope of at least Site. Close the Feature Designer window.

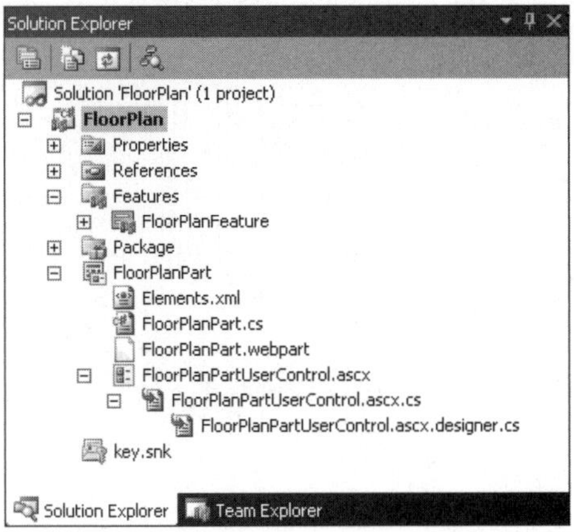

Figure 13-11. The FloorPlan project

Writing Some Code

The `FloorPlanPartUserControl.ascx` file should be open in the source window for editing. If it isn't visible, double-click the FloorPlanPart node in the Project Explorer to open it. This is the file where we'll write all the code to interact with our floor plan, and for this solution, all the code we write will be JavaScript or HTML. The first thing we need to do is add some references to required script libraries.

On the first blank line in the file, add a script reference to `sp.js` using the SharePoint `ScriptLink` control, shown in Listing 13-1, to gain client-side script access to many of the SharePoint APIs. We will use this reference to update the ReservedBy value in our ConferenceRooms list.

Listing 13-1. Setting up the Client-Side Script References

```
<SharePoint:ScriptLink runat="server" Name="sp.js" LoadAfterUI="true" Localizable="false" />
```

■ **Note** Most, if not all, of the JavaScript files provided with SharePoint are compressed to make transferring these files over the wire as efficient as possible, but this format makes them nearly impossible to use for debugging. To mitigate this issue, many of the script files are also provided as corresponding debug versions for developers; for example the `sp.js` file referenced in Listing 13-1 has a corresponding debug file named `sp.debug.js`. For more information on the ECMA script object model and associated script files, see `http://msdn.microsoft.com/en-us/library/ee538253(v=office.14).aspx`.

Add a service reference to the SharePoint user profile web service using the ASP.Net `ScriptManagerProxy` control; this reference instructs the ASP.NET runtime to evaluate the path attribute to generate a client-side proxy. Notice we are using the `ScriptManagerProxy` as opposed to the `ScriptManager`. This is because the default SharePoint templates include the `ScriptManager` tag in the MasterPage and only one instance of this control is allowed. Listing 13-2 shows the code to be inserted. We will use this reference to get user details for office occupants.

Listing 13-2. Setting up the User Profile Service Reference

```
<asp:ScriptManagerProxy runat="server">
    <Services>
        <asp:ServiceReference Path="/_vti_bin/userprofileservice.asmx" />
    </Services>
</asp:ScriptManagerProxy>
```

We will use CSS to add some styling and visibility to the content of our web part. Add the style tags and CSS shown in Listing 13-3.

Listing 13-3. Setting CSS Declarations

```
<style type="text/css">
    .heading {padding:5px;background:#000000;color:#FFFFFF;font-weight:bold;↵
text-align:center;margin-bottom:10px;}
    .hidden {position:absolute;visibility:hidden;}
    .visible {position:relative;visibility:visible;}
    #userPhoto {float:left;padding-right:5px;}
</style>
```

Now let's move on to the code. Visio services exposes four object types to the client—**VwaContol,** which represents the Visio web access web part; **VwaPage,** which represents the currently displayed page of the drawing being rendered; **Shapes,** which is a collection of all the shapes on the current page; and **Shape,** which represents an individual shape in the Shapes collection. For more information on the Visio Client object model see http://msdn.microsoft.com/en-us/library/ff464325(v=office.14).aspx.

Create a script block and add the code shown in Listing 13-4. The script declares three global variables we will use to interact with our diagram and wires up an event handler for the **Sys.Application.load** event, which is part of ASP.Net AJAX and fires once all scripts and objects have been parsed and loaded.

Listing 13-4. Variable Declarations

```
<script language="ecmascript" type="text/ecmascript">
    var vwaControl; // Visio Web Access contol
    var vwaPage; // current page in the diagram
    var vwaShapes; // shape collection

    //ajax call ensures webpart has rendered
    Sys.Application.add_load(onApplicationLoad);
</script>
```

Implement the **onApplicationLoad** event handler to handle the **load** event, as shown in Listing 13-5. This code will initialize the global variables we declared earlier, as well as wire up event handlers for our diagram to handle clicks, **onshapeselectchanged**, and mouse-over, **shapemouseenter** and **shapemouseleave**. The ID of the Visio Web Access web part, **WebPartWPQ2** in the code listing, is required in order to connect to the correct web part instance. This ID is auto-generated by SharePoint, with the numeric value determined by the order web parts are added to a page, beginning with 2 (the Search web part always gets 1). This could be a configurable value for our FloorPlanPart web part but, to simplify the walkthrough, we will leave this as an exercise beyond the scope of this chapter. If you follow the steps in the section titled Deploying our Solution, ensuring the Visio Web Access web part is added to the page first, **WebPartWPQ2** will be the correct value.

Listing 13-5. The onApplicationLoad Event Handler

```
function onApplicationLoad() {
    // get the VWA control on the page
    vwaControl = new Vwa.VwaControl('WebPartWPQ2');
```

```
    // add handler which will fire once the diagram has loaded
    vwaControl.addHandler('diagramcomplete', onDiagramComplete);

    // wire up handlers for mouse events
    vwaControl.addHandler('shapeselectionchanged', onShapeSelectionChanged);
    vwaControl.addHandler('shapemouseenter', onShapeMouseEnter);
    vwaControl.addHandler('shapemouseleave', onShapeMouseLeave);
}
```

Finally, implement the **onDiagramComplete** event handler, as shown in Listing 13-6. This code will initialize the variables referencing the current page and the shapes on the page and will fire once the diagram completes loading. It is important to note this code will run anytime the diagram loads including after a call to the refreshDiagram method of the control.

Listing 13-6. The onDiagramComplete Event Handler

```
function onDiagramComplete() {
    vwaPage = vwaControl.getActivePage(); // page
    vwaShapes = vwaPage.getShapes(); // shape collection
}
```

Adding an Overlay

Next we want to add an overlay in response to a user moving the cursor over a printer shape. Visio Services supports two types of overlays corresponding to the two types of diagram renderings; XAML for Silverlight-rendered drawings and HTML DIV tags for PNG-rendered drawings. Why do we have two different formats for rendering drawings you ask? This behavior is to support users who don't have Silverlight installed, in which case Visio Services will fall back to returning a PNG. You can also configure the web part to return PNG by default and use the API to determine the current display mode. For our drawing, we will assume you are using the default Silverlight rendering, so we will use XAML to add an overlay to the printers to display the network name and IP address as shown in Figure 13-12.

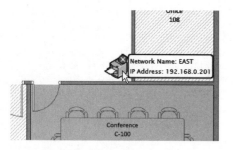

Figure 13-12. The overlay shown when a user moves the mouse over a printer

Add the **onShapeMouseEnter** event handler to handle the **shapemouseenter** event using the code in Listing 13-7. In the code, we first get a reference to the shape that triggered the event; we check to see if it was a printer shape by inspecting the internal name property. If it was a printer shape, we build the

XAML string, including the properties of the printer shape, and call the **addOverlay** method to add the overlay to the drawing. The arguments to **addOverlay** are the name of the overlay, the XAML string, horizontal alignment, vertical alignment, width, and height. As mentioned, we are assuming Silverlight only rendering for our solution, but you can add a check for PNG rendering using the **getDisplayMode()** method of the Visio web access control, the **vwaControl** variable in our case, and if it is a PNG you can pass DHTML instead of the XAML.

Listing 13-7. *The ShapeMouseEnter Event Handler*

```
function onShapeMouseEnter(source, args) {
    var shape = vwaShapes.getItemById(args); // shape associated with the event

    // if this shape is a printer shape
    if (shape.getName().substring(0, 7) == 'Printer') {
        var shapeData = shape.getShapeData(); // load data related to the shape

        // define the XAML overlay
        var overLay = '<Canvas>' +
            '<Rectangle Fill="Black" Height="54" Width="200" />' +
            '<Rectangle Fill="White" Height="50" Width="196" Margin="2,2" />' +
            '<StackPanel Margin="5,5">' +
            '<TextBlock Text ="Network Name: ' + shapeData[0].value + '" />' +
            '<TextBlock Text ="IP Address: ' + shapeData[1].value + '" />' +
            '</StackPanel>' +
            '</Canvas>';

        shape.addOverlay('printerOverlay', overLay, 2, 1, 200, 54); // add overlay
    }
}
```

When the user moves the cursor off of the printer shape, we need to remove the overlay. Use the code in Listing 13-8 to implement the **shapemouseleave** event. Again, we first get a reference to the shape that triggered the event and check to see if it was a printer shape.

Listing 13-8. *The ShapeMouseLeave Event Handler*

```
function onShapeMouseLeave(source, args) {
    var shape = vwaShapes.getItemById(args); // shape associated with the event

    // if this shape is a printer shape
    if (shape.getName().substring(0, 7) == 'Printer') {
        shape.removeOverlay('printerOverlay');  // remove the overlay from the drawing
    }
}
```

Adding a UI

Before we write a bit more code to handle shape selection (aka the click event), let's add some HTML to our web part to create a very simple UI to present information related to the space shapes, offices, and conference rooms contained in our floor plan. The UI will provide user information, such as the name and phone number, for office occupants, as well as the ability to update the *ReservedBy* attribute of a conference room.

Insert the HTML in Listing 13-9 below the closing `</script>` tag. We will show the `userInfo` div when an office is selected, the `roomInfo` div when a conference room is selected, and the `nothingSelected` div otherwise.

Listing 13-9. The ShapeMouseLeave Event Handler

```
<div style="position:relative;">
<div id="nothingSelected" class="visible" >
    <div class="heading">Select a Room</div>
    <div>
        Select an office to view occupant details or a
        conference room to view reservation details.
    </div>
</div>

<div id="officeInfo" class="hidden">
    <div class="heading">Office #<span id="officeNum"></span></div>
    <div id="notOccupied" class="hidden">Not Occupied</div>
    <div id="userInfo" class="hidden">
        <div><img id="userPhoto" src="" alt="user photo" /></div>
        <div>Name: <span id="userName"></span></div>
        <div>Phone: <span id="userPhone"></span></div>
    </div>
</div>

<div id="roomInfo" class="hidden">
    <input type="hidden" id="roomId" />
    <div class="heading"><span id="roomTitle"></span> Reservation</div>
    <div>Reserved By: <input type="text" id="reservedBy" value="" /></div>
    <div style="padding:10px;text-align:right;">
        <input type="button" id="resvSubmit" value="Save" onclick="updateReservation();" />
    </div>
</div>
</div>
```

Responding to Clicks

The last bit of code to write is for the `onShapeSelectionChanged` method to handle shape selection changes, for the `updateReservation` method to handle the click event of the button in the `roomInfo` div, and for related handlers to support asynchronous callbacks.

Insert the code in Listing 13-10 above the closing `</script>` tag. This is a big block of code, but it is fairly simple. First we get a reference to the shape that triggered the event and check to see if it was a space shape by inspecting the internal name property. If it was a space shape, we evaluate the type of space shape and act accordingly. If the shape represents an office, we call the `GetUserProfileByName` method of the `UserProfileService` service (this is the proxy the ASP.NET runtime generated for us), passing in the occupant attribute of the shape as well as call back methods for success and failure. If the shape represents a conference room, we make the `roomInfo` div visible, allowing users to reserve the room. You will notice we are using numeric indexing, such as `shapeData[5].value`, to retrieve values for specific attributes of our shape rather than textual keys, such as `shapeData['officeNum'].value`. This is because the shape data is simply an array of objects representing the attributes. If you want to make the code a bit more readable you could use global constants with descriptive names as the index values, such as `var officeNum = 5;`.

Listing 13-10. The ShapeMouseLeave Event Handler

```
function onShapeSelectionChanged(source, args) {
    var shape = vwaShapes.getItemById(args); // shape associated with the event

    // hide all divs
        document.getElementById('nothingSelected').className = 'hidden';
        document.getElementById('officeInfo').className = 'hidden';
        document.getElementById('roomInfo').className = 'hidden';
        document.getElementById('userInfo').className = 'hidden';
        document.getElementById('notOccupied').className = 'hidden';

    // if this shape is a space shape
    if (shape.getName().substring(0, 5) == 'Space') {
        var shapeData = shape.getShapeData(); // load data related to the shape

        // if this is an office show occupant details
        if (shapeData[0].value == 'Office') {
            document.getElementById('officeNum').innerText = shapeData[5].value;
            document.getElementById('officeInfo').className = 'visible';
                if (shapeData[6].value != "") {
                    Microsoft.Office.Server.UserProfiles.UserProfileService.↵
                    GetUserProfileByName(shapeData[6].value, ↵
                    onProfileRequestSuccess, onProfileRequestFailed);
                }
                else {
                    document.getElementById('notOccupied').className = 'visible';
                }           }
        // else if this is a conference room show reserve dialog
        else if (shapeData[0].value == 'Conference') {
            document.getElementById('reservedBy').value = shapeData[8].value;
            document.getElementById('roomTitle').innerText = shapeData[6].value;
            document.getElementById('roomId').value = shapeData[5].value;
            document.getElementById('roomInfo').className = 'visible';
        }
    }
    // else not a space shape
    else document.getElementById('nothingSelected').className = visible;
}
```

As we mentioned, we provided the call to the `GetUserProfileByName` method callback handlers. This is because the call will occur asynchronously, but we do need to act on the response once we receive it. The code in Listing 13-11 provides implementation for these two callbacks; `onProfileRequestSuccess` uses the return value to set user information and `onProfileRequestFailed` alerts the user if the call fails.

Listing 13-11. Callbacks for the GetUserProfileByName Call

```
function onProfileRequestSuccess(results) {
    document.getElementById('userPhoto').src = ↵
        results[15].Values[0] == null ? "" : results[15].Values[0].Value;
    document.getElementById('userName').innerText = ↵
        results[6].Values[0] == null ? "" : results[6].Values[0].Value;
    document.getElementById('userPhone').innerText = ↵
        results[8].Values[0] == null ? "" : results[8].Values[0].Value;
    document.getElementById('userInfo').className = 'visible';
}

function onProfileRequestFailed(results) {
    alert('Your request for profile details failed');
    document.getElementById('nothingSelected').className = 'visible';
}
```

If the user clicks on a conference room, we have made the `roomInfo` div visible, which provides the ability to see who has the room reserved and to change this value. This is a very simple implementation, and this type of feature would more likely be tied into a scheduling system. What we want to show here is the ability to write a value back to a data source, in this case our SharePoint list, and then to immediately reflect the update on the diagram. To do this, we use the SharePoint ECMA script client object model. Insert the code from Listing 13-12.

■ **Note** Immediately reflecting the update on the diagram will depend on the configuration of Visio Services in your environment. The farm administrator can set the minimum cache age for Visio Services (the default value is 5 minutes) to reduce the impact on performance. For more information see `http://technet.microsoft.com/en-us/library/ff356849(office.14).aspx`.

Listing 13-12. The updateReservation Event Handle

```
function updateReservation() {
    document.getElementById("resvSubmit").disabled = true; // disable save button

    // define commands, these will not execute until we call executeQueryAsync
    // get current SharePoint context
    var clientContext = SP.ClientContext.get_current();
    // get the current SharePoint site
    var web = clientContext.get_web();
    // get reference to ConferenceRooms list
    var list = web.get_lists().getByTitle('ConferenceRooms');
    // get item
    var item = list.getItemById(parseInt(document.getElementById('roomId').value));
```

```
    // set new value
    item.set_item('ReservedBy', document.getElementById('reservedBy').value);
    item.update(); // update item

    // execute commands and set callbacks
    clientContext.executeQueryAsync(Function.createDelegate(this, this.onReserveSuccess),↵
        Function.createDelegate(this, this.onReserveFailed));
}
```

The final code block shown in Listing 13-13 implements the callbacks required by the call to executeQueryAsync, which we used to update the ConferenceRooms list; onReserveSuccess refreshes the diagram and enables the save button while onReserveFailed alerts the user if the update fails.

Listing 13-13. Callbacks for the executeQueryAsync Call

```
function onReserveSuccess(sender, args) {
    vwaControl.refreshDiagram(); // refresh the diagram
    // reenable the button for the user
    document.getElementById("resvSubmit").disabled = false;
}

function onReserveFailed(sender, args) {
    alert('Reservation update failed');
    // reenable the button for the user
    document.getElementById("resvSubmit").disabled = false;
}
```

The Home Stretch

With our web part complete, we are ready to pull all the parts together. First we will build and deploy our FloorPlanPart web part feature to the SharePoint environment. Next we will create a new page on the SharePoint site and choose the layout template. Finally, we will add the Visio Web Access web part and our FloorPlanPart web part to the page.

1. In Solution Explorer, right-click on the FloorPlan project and choose Deploy. This will build, deploy, and activate your feature on the SharePoint site you specified during project creation.

2. Open a browser and navigate to the local SharePoint site you are using to host this solution.

3. From the Site Actions menu, select New Page to bring up the New Page dialog. Enter **OfficeFloorPlan** for the New Page Name and click Create.

4. This creates a new page and opens in edit mode. Select the Text Layout drop-down and choose the One column with Sidebar layout. Click into the column on the left to make sure it is in focus, then click the Insert tab on the ribbon.

5. On the Insert tab, click the Web Part button to open the web part task pane. Under Categories select Business Data, then select Visio Web Access under Web Parts as shown in Figure 13-13. Click Add.

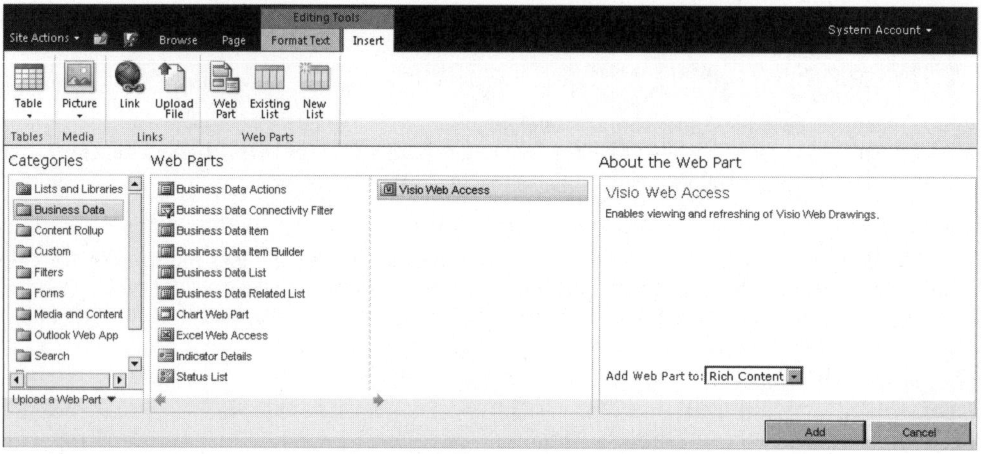

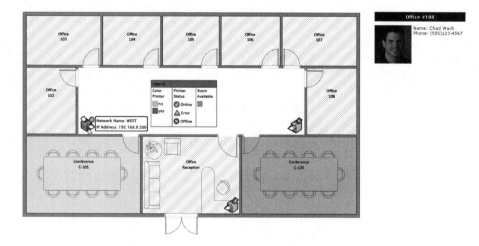

Figure 13-13. Inserting the Visio Web Access web part

6. Configure the diagram URL for the Visio Web Access web part to point to the OfficeFloorPlan.vdw file we saved to the site earlier.

7. Click into the column on the right to make sure it is in focus. On the Insert tab click the Web Part button to open the web part task pane. Under Categories select Custom, then select FloorPlanPart under Web Parts. Click Add.

8. Save the OfficeFloorPlan page.

Figure 13-14 shows the result of our page with the two web parts after clicking on an office to view occupant details.

Figure 13-14. Our custom OfficeFloorPlan page

Important Lessons

The Visio Services floor plan solution incorporated several key techniques worth highlighting as they can easily be reused in other projects.

Client object model: The client object model now provided by SharePoint supplies an extremely rich extension model in many different environments, script, .NET, and Silverlight. We used this approach to write a value back to a SharePoint list asynchronously, and this same approach could be taken much further.

Visual web parts: Our visual web part was very simple, but the ability to create web parts using the same technique developers have become accustomed to in developing for ASP.NET is greatly appreciated and can be reused across many projects and scenarios.

Extension Points

While coding this example, we thought of several variations that we didn't incorporate. Mostly, these were not included because they distracted from the overall objective of the solution. We call them out now as extension points since they may be applicable to a specific project you are working on.

Add a custom data provider: Out of the box Visio supports the most common types of data connections, but Visio Services also provides an interface that supports custom data providers. A custom provider could be written to consume data from XML or flat files, for example. To extend our solution you could create a custom data provider to read printer information directly from Active Directory.

Use web part data connections: For a no-code approach, Visio Web Access does support web part data connections. With this approach, you can, for example, use a selector to select all shapes on a diagram of a specific type, such as all offices, or that have a specific attribute value, such as all available offices.

Tie the room reservation into a scheduling system: We kept the code related to reserving a conference room very simple. However, this is a common pattern and the act of reserving a space could be tied into a calendar and a resourced-based scheduling system.

Further Reading

The following links are to resources that we think a reader interested in the material presented in this chapter would find useful:

- The official blog of the Microsoft Visio product team `http://blogs.msdn.com/visio`

- Embedding a Web Drawing in a SharePoint Page `http://blogs.msdn.com/visio/archive/2009/11/05/embedding-a-web-drawing-into-a-sharepoint-page.aspx`

- Visio Services in SharePoint Server `http://msdn.microsoft.com/en-us/library/ff408345(v=office.14).aspx`

- Creating a Custom Data Provider with Visio Services `http://msdn.microsoft.com/en-us/library/ff394595(v=office.14).aspx`

■ ■ ■

CHAPTER 14

Building Mashups

If you think about Web 2.0, chances are you'll think about mashups—the aggregation of various types of content. Typically, mashups take data from multiple sources and combine them into a single presentation. The goal is to create a whole that is more than the sum of the individual parts, enabling users to gain insight that would be difficult to achieve by examining each stack of information separately. In this chapter, we will detail how, as a developer, you can take advantage of SharePoint to build a mashup. This solution will combine data from multiple sources: a SharePoint list, a geocoded RSS feed, and a KML (Keyhole Markup Language) file. The result will be an interactive map containing the aggregate data.

Real-World Examples

Many organizations we've met with have expressed an interest in bringing together data from siloed resources into a single composite. One military group responsible for responding to base emergencies would like to see weather information, emergency vehicle location, and building information on a single interface. Other military groups, who use lots of applications in war gaming where they simulate possible events and responses, realize they could benefit from this type of solution. A university we met with would like to bring together data about their applicants and registration events. Lots of commercial customers understand the advantage of seeing sales data overlaid with store locations, sales districts, etc. In fact, this is becoming such a trend that major software companies such as Google, Yahoo, and Microsoft are all investing in ways for organizations to publish their data and for consumers to retrieve and analyze it. Feedburner, purchased by Google, provides a platform for content publishers to expose their content through RSS feeds. Yahoo Pipes is a web-based application that enables users to aggregate feeds into mashups. Microsoft announced a project code-named Dallas that looks to establish a marketplace for such data exchanges. For more information on Dallas, or to create a developer account, visit http://www.microsoft.com/windowsazure/dallas/. We will not use Dallas in this chapter as at the time of this writing it is still in an early beta stage, however, the same techniques used here could easily be applied to its datasets.

Solution Overview

To provide some context for our solution, we decided to create a composite that shows national parks in the United States, a user-maintained SharePoint list of campgrounds, and a newsfeed about wildlife disease alerts. Together these data sources could be used by an organization planning the placement of new campgrounds, a user arranging a camping trip, or park service personnel looking for trends. Each of these data sources is public information and is stored in a different format, making them good examples for showing how to retrieve data for mashups. Our solution will leverage the Bing Maps Silverlight Control SDK to provide the interactive map surface to layer the data; this control will be the main focus of our Silverlight mashup solution.

The national parks data will be loaded via a KML file, and the wildlife newsfeed is available as a geocoded RSS feed. We will write code using SharePoint's client library for Silverlight to retrieve campground information that will be stored in a customized contact list. The customizations will include new fields for Latitude, Longitude, and Geocoded Status. The good news is that we will not require users to use some other tool to translate addresses of campgrounds into coordinates. Instead, we'll include an event handler that calls a Bing Maps web service to geocode the campground's address. Since the geocoded contacts list is a piece of functionality that is obviously reusable, we will deploy it as a SharePoint feature so that any site administrator can simply turn it on to add this capability to his site. The actual Silverlight map, which is site-specific, will be deployed as a SharePoint sandboxed solution.

Solution Walkthrough

This section covers the major elements of the solution and the decisions that were made in coding it. The walkthrough shows you how to create the Silverlight application, install the Bing Maps Silverlight control, and lay out the mashup's user controls. We will describe how to consume the geocoded RSS feed and place red circles for each wildlife disease alert onto the map's interface. You'll learn how to parse the KML file of US national parks. For each park, we will place a custom icon at the park's location and support a mouse-over event that displays the selected park's name. You'll see how to retrieve data from a SharePoint list from within the Silverlight mashup and use it to place push pins onto the map for each campground, including a mouse-over for the name of the campground. You'll then build a set of reusable customizations as a SharePoint feature to support an extended contact list that provides geocoding of the contacts' addresses. Finally, we will deploy the mashup as a sandboxed solution and show you how to wire everything up on a test site.

Getting the Bing Maps Silverlight SDK

Before diving into Visual Studio 2010 and building the mashup application, you need to establish a Bing Maps developer account, then download and install the Bing Maps Silverlight Control SDK. To create a free developer account, visit the Bing Maps Account Center (`https://www.bingmapsportal.com`). On the left-hand menu, you'll see options to create your account and a Bing Maps key. This key is a string the solution needs to pass to Bing whenever you use its functionality, such as displaying a map or asking it to geocode an address.

Register your account with the system using a Windows Live ID. To create the key, you have to specify an application name as well as a URL. We named our application **SharePointDevSample** and used the URL of our main SharePoint site collection, `http://edhild3/sites/mashup`. Remember to use your key as you build out the application. If you download the solution from the Apress web site, you still have to generate an application key and replace it where necessary in the solution. We will be sure to highlight those locations as we go along.

Next, you need to download and install the Bing Maps Silverlight Control SDK into your development environment as this control provides the map for our mashup. You can find the SDK at `http://www.microsoft.com/downloads/details.aspx?displaylang=en&FamilyID=beb29d27-6f0c-494f-b028-1e0e3187e830`.

In case you haven't yet ventured into development with Bing Maps, we have collected some very useful links that will give you a solid introduction. Since map development isn't something all SharePoint developers have in their tool belt, we will be sure to explain everything we are doing in this area. However, we are just scratching the surface with this example, so if you want to know more about this topic, these links are the place to start. The best link of the group is the Interactive SDK, which allows you to specify an action you want to do with the map and then shows you the necessary code to make it happen.

- Bing Maps Platform Overview

  ```
  http://www.microsoft.com/maps/developers/
  ```

- Bing Silverlight Map Control Interactive SDK

  ```
  http://www.microsoft.com/maps/isdk/silverlight/
  ```

- Bing Maps SDKs

  ```
  http://msdn.microsoft.com/en-us/library/dd877180.aspx
  ```

- Bing Maps Silverlight Control Code Samples from PDC 2009

  ```
  http://blogs.msdn.com/veplatform/archive/2009/11/20/bing-maps-silverlight-control-
  code-samples-available-from-pdc09.aspx
  ```

Create the Silverlight Mashup Application

We will start building this solution with a Silverlight application, which is the mashup itself. Simply start Visual Studio and create a new project. Under the C# language node, select Silverlight to display the Silverlight project templates, then choose Silverlight Application. Name the project **MashupMap**. Leave the default option of creating a directory for the solution and confirm that the .NET framework drop-down at the top of the dialog is set to .NET Framework 3.5. This lets us use Silverlight version 3 for the mashup, which is supported by SharePoint. Your New Project dialog should look like Figure 14-1.

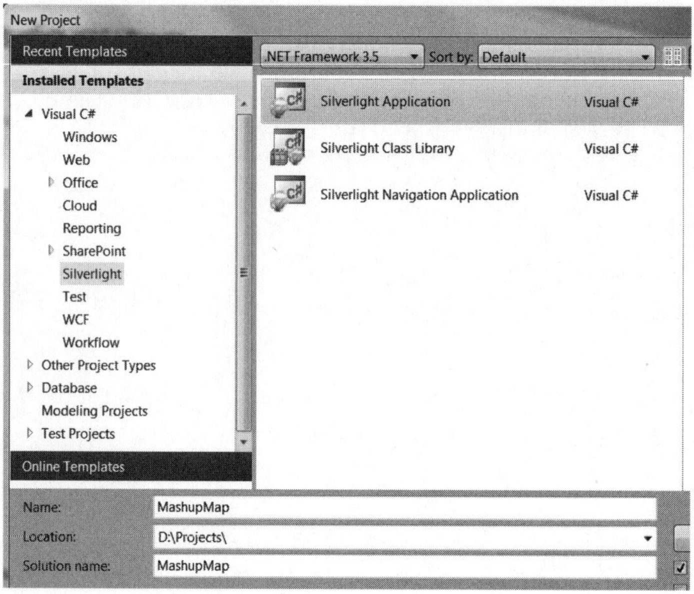

Figure 14-1. Creating the Mashup Silverlight Project

When you click OK, the New Silverlight Application wizard will ask you about a few configuration options for the project.

■ **Note** You may get prompted by Visual Studio 2010 that you need to download the Silverlight Development environment. If so, download the installer Visual Studio directs you to, install it, and retry creating the project.

The first set is about how the Silverlight application is going to be hosted. Though eventually the mashup will be hosted in SharePoint, having an ASP.NET test harness can be useful for debugging early in the process. Leave the default options to create a companion ASP.NET web application. Confirm under the Options heading that the target Silverlight version is Silverlight 3. Click OK.

After the new project is created, your solution already contains a few files, visible in the Solution Explorer window of Visual Studio. One file in the Silverlight project, `MainPage.xaml`, is our design surface where we will lay out the controls that make up the mashup user interface. In the ASP.NET testing web site that was created for you, you'll see a `ClientBin` folder. This is where the mashup application will be deployed as a Silverlight package (`.xap`) file when you are debugging, before you publish the mashup to SharePoint. The HTML and ASPX pages there are simply test harnesses that load the Silverlight application onto the page.

Before jumping into the code, let's get a few other items out of the way. First, there are some assemblies we need to add references to in the MashupMap project:

- **Microsoft.Maps.MapControl and Microsoft.Maps.MapControl.Common:** These two assemblies are part of the Bing Maps Silverlight Control SDK and include the control and classes we'll need to build the mashup. Assuming you installed the SDK as described above, you'll find these assemblies at `C:\Program Files (x86)\Bing Maps Silverlight Control\V1\Libraries`.

- **System.ServiceModel.Syndication:** This assembly contains classes such as SyndicationFeed that we'll use to work with the RSS data source.

- **System.Xml.Linq:** This assembly will allow us to use LINQ-style queries to parse the XML content we get back from some of our data sources.

- **System.Windows.Controls.Data.Input:** This assembly contains some of the controls we will use in our markup such as the Label control. Normally this will add automatically as you drag controls onto the design surface, but if you are just copying our XAML, you will need to add the reference.

- **Microsoft.SharePoint.Client.Silverlight and Microsoft.SharePoint.Client. Silverlight.Runtime:** These assemblies represent the client-side library and runtime for Silverlight applications. As discussed in Chapter 3, SharePoint 2010 provides several different types of client-side libraries, enabling communication from solutions not running on the SharePoint server. Our Silverlight application runs within the context of the browser's Silverlight plug-in, so it is not on the server. You'll find these assemblies at `C:\Program Files\Common Files\Microsoft Shared\Web Server Extensions\14\TEMPLATE\LAYOUTS\ClientBin\`.

Now that the appropriate references have been added, you can add the `using` statements into the code file we'll be modifying. Listing 14-1 indicates the `using` statements that need to be added to the code-behind file of the user control, `MainPage.xaml.cs`.

Listing 14-1. Using Statements

```
using SP = Microsoft.SharePoint.Client;
using Microsoft.SharePoint.Client;
using Microsoft.Maps.MapControl;
using System.Xml;
using System.ServiceModel.Syndication;
using System.IO;
```

Switching to the designer for `MainPage.xaml`, we can begin to lay out the user interface for our Silverlight mashup. This includes the Bing maps control with a tools column on the right-hand side that enables the user to hide or show any of the data sources on the map, as well as re-query the wildlife disease alerts RSS feed. Figure 14-2 shows the result we are looking for.

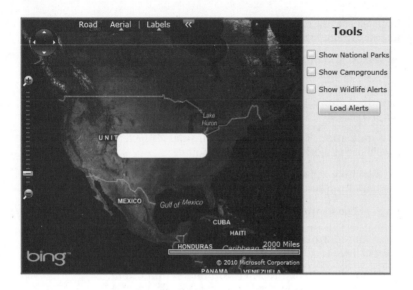

Figure 14-2. The Mashup Interface

When building a Silverlight user interface, you can either lay out the Silverlight XAML yourself in Visual Studio or use a design tool like Microsoft's Expression Blend 3. Blend gives you more of a designer's experience, allowing you to drag controls, set their properties, control animations, and rendering preferences such as brushes, gradients, and fills. With Visual Studio, on the other hand, you'll find yourself frequently editing the XML markup. There are many references on Silverlight user interface design, so we won't turn this chapter into that. If you want the exact interface we built, just grab the markup from the code download, but do feel free to design your own. You will have to at least build your project once to see the interface since our XAML markup includes references to the project assembly. You may also want to comment out the KMLElementCollection markup and the ParkLayer until we add that functionality later. We will detail the crucial elements of the markup as we go through the chapter. Already, as shown in Listing 14-2, the definition of the namespaces includes some that are not in the default markup.

Listing 14-2. Namespaces for the Silverlight User Control

```
<UserControl xmlns:my="clr-namespace:System.Windows.Controls;assembly=↩
  System.Windows.Controls.Data.Input"  x:Class="MashupMap.MainPage"
  xmlns="http://schemas.microsoft.com/winfx/2006/xaml/presentation"
  xmlns:x="http://schemas.microsoft.com/winfx/2006/xaml"
  xmlns:d="http://schemas.microsoft.com/expression/blend/2008"
  xmlns:mc="http://schemas.openxmlformats.org/markup-compatibility/2006"
  xmlns:m="clr-namespace:Microsoft.Maps.MapControl;↩
          assembly=Microsoft.Maps.MapControl"
  xmlns:db="clr-namespace:MashupMap"
  mc:Ignorable="d"
  d:DesignHeight="400" d:DesignWidth="600" Loaded="UserControl_Loaded">
```

The two namespaces that are new here are **m** and **db**. The **m** namespace is for the Bing Maps control and enables us to add it to the markup. The **db** namespace is for this project itself. By placing it here, we will be able to databind controls to the classes in our solution. This technique will be used for the national parks data source later in this chapter. Notice that we have specified the height and width of the control as well as an event handler for the control's loaded event, which we'll write code for in the code-behind.

The layout of the mashup is a grid with two columns; Listing 14-3 shows the beginning of the XAML for this layout. The first column contains the Bing Maps control. Notice that you need to specify the application key you generated at the Bing Maps Account Center. Within the map declaration, you also specify that you want the mode of the map to show an aerial view with labels. By combining the zoom level with a center location, we focus the map on the United States. You may be wondering how we picked this location. The interactive SDK includes an example of how to center the map to specific locations. The United States was one of the choices and we just copied the resulting markup from the SDK into our Silverlight control. For right now, we'll ignore the markup within the map control that defines layers for our data. We will cover it later in this chapter as we focus on each of the data sources.

Listing 14-3. XAML Layout of the Mashup User Interface

```
<Grid x:Name="LayoutRoot" Background="White" Width="600" Height="400">
  <Grid.ColumnDefinitions>
    <ColumnDefinition Width="458*" />
    <ColumnDefinition Width="142*" />
  </Grid.ColumnDefinitions>
  <m:Map x:Name="mapControl" Grid.Column="0"
         CredentialsProvider="YOUR BING MAPS KEY" Mode="AerialWithLabels"
         Center="39.3683,-95.2734,4.0" ZoomLevel="3" >
...
  </m:Map>
```

The second half the XAML for the mashup is shown in Listing 14-4. The main component is a stackpanel control that renders the user interface for the tools area. The stackpanel control takes its nested controls and arranges them horizontally or vertically. The checkbox controls are a bit interesting here in that we have specified event handlers for both the **Checked** and **Unchecked** events. The easiest way to specify these event handlers is to place your cursor on the control in the XAML and use Visual Studio's properties window to browse that control's events. Double-clicking on an event will wire up an event handler in the code-behind file. Note that in Silverlight, unlike ASP.NET, there are two separate events for the checkbox, as opposed to one where you respond to both cases.

Listing 14-4. XAML Layout of Tools Area of the Mashup

```
<StackPanel Grid.Column="1" Height="400" HorizontalAlignment="Left"
            Name="stackPanel1" VerticalAlignment="Top" Width="142"
            Background="Beige" >
  <my:Label Content="Tools" FontSize="16" FontWeight="Bold"
            HorizontalAlignment="Center" Margin="0,10,0,10" />
  <CheckBox x:Name="ShowParks" Content="Show National Parks" Margin="5,5,0,5"
            Checked="ShowParks_Checked" Unchecked="ShowParks_Unchecked" />
  <CheckBox x:Name="ShowContacts" Content="Show Campgrounds" Margin="5,5,0,5"
            Checked="ShowContacts_Checked" Unchecked="ShowContacts_Unchecked" />
```

```
    <CheckBox x:Name="ShowWildlifeAlerts" Content="Show Wildlife Alerts"
            Margin="5,5,0,5" Checked="ShowWildlifeAlerts_Checked"
            Unchecked="ShowWildlifeAlerts_Unchecked" />
    <Button x:Name="loadFeed" Content="Load Alerts" Width="100" Margin="5,5,0,5"
          Click="loadFeed_Click" />
  </StackPanel>
</Grid>
```

In the next few sections, we'll add a data source to the mashup. This will include more detail on the XAML for the map layers. Think of each map layer as a transparent sheet of paper that we are drawing on with a marker and then placing on top of the map's surface. As each layer is placed on top of the map, it is also being placed on top of other layers. This is why the `InfoLayer` that represents the flyout for the mouse-over event is defined last—it needs to be able to be seen above any of the other visualizations.

We will also explore the code for loading and parsing data, as well as for interacting with the tools controls. Though we will not be walking through the layers in the same order they are set in the XAML, the order does matter.

Retrieve and Parse the Geocoded RSS Feed

RSS stands for "Really Simple Syndication." It has become a popular way to publish content that is frequently added to or updated. The publishers don't want to burden users with continually having to point their browsers back to a specific site to see updates. Instead, users subscribe to the RSS feed, causing short summaries to be pulled by the user on a regular basis. The feed can be rendered in RSS readers such as a desktop gadget in Windows 7 or Windows Vista, Microsoft Outlook, or even other web sites. An RSS feed is said to be geocoded when it includes coordinates (latitude and longitude) specifying the location that is referenced or referred to in the content. For this example, we will use wildlife disease alerts from the National Biological Information Infrastructure (NBII). You can read more about the Wildlife Disease Information Node of this organization at `http://www.nbii.gov/images/uploaded/ 8496_1258549821937_WDIN-DiseaseNewsMap.pdf`. Their geocoded RSS feed is exposed through Feedburner and can be accessed at the following URL `http://feeds.feedburner.com/wdinNewsDigestGeoRSS`. Feedburner is a tool that provides enhanced services for publishers beyond simply making their information available. It includes traffic analysis and publicizing features, among many others. Listing 14-5 shows just one item from the feed. Notice that it includes information about the content as well as coordinates specifying the location.

Listing 14-5. A Wildlife Disease Alert RSS Item

```
<item>
  <title>Wild deer disease surveillance continues; new bovine TB positive deer
      Confirmed (Minnesota, United States)
  </title>
  <link>http://feedproxy.google.com/~r/wdinNewsDigestGeoRSS/~3/sGOgnVzDSnA/</link>
  <pubDate>Mon, 21 Dec 2009 00:00:00 -0600</pubDate>
  <description>Published by Minnesota Department of Natural Resources -
    www.dnr.state.mn.us on  12/21/2009 - With test results for the entire fall
    sample of hunter-harvested deer in northwestern Minnesota pending, tissue
    samples from one suspect deer submitted for expedited testing have come back
    positive for bovine tuberculosis (TB).&lt;img
```

```
        src="http://feeds.feedburner.com/~r/wdinNewsDigestGeoRSS/~4/sGOgnVzDSnA"
        height="1" width="1"/&gt;
</description>
<source>Minnesota Department of Natural Resources - www.dnr.state.mn.us
</source>
<guid isPermaLink="false">http://news.dnr.state.mn.us/index.php/2009/12/21/wild↵
    -deer-disease-surveillance-continues-new-bovine-tb-positive-deer-confirmed/
</guid>
<georss:point>46.3478823547 -94.1990570584</georss:point>
<feedburner:origLink>http://news.dnr.state.mn.us/index.php/2009/12/21/wild-deer-↵
    disease-surveillance-continues-new-bovine-tb-positive-deer-confirmed/
</feedburner:origLink>
</item>
```

■ **Note** Just in case you are modifying the examples as you go along to access some other data source, you need to be aware that Silverlight has a security feature that can cause problems loading data you don't own. This feature requires that the data source publish a policy allowing its data to be consumed from another domain. Many web sites lack this policy, though major syndicators usually include it, which is why we are using Feedburner as the source in this example. For more information, see `http://timheuer.com/blog/archive/2008/06/03/use-silverlight-with-any-feed-without-cross-domain-files.aspx`.

With an understanding of our data source, let's move on to getting the data onto our map. For this example, we simply want to have a red circle placed at the coordinates specified by the alert. Our first step is to add a layer to the map control, which you can do using the XAML in Listing 14-6. Notice that the default visibility is set to `collapsed`, which will hide the layer and its contents until a user asks to see it on the map.

Listing 14-6. The MapLayer for Wildlife Alerts

```
<m:MapLayer x:Name="AlertLayer" Visibility="Collapsed">
</m:MapLayer>
```

We decided with this data source that we would retrieve the data on demand for the user. There wasn't a strong reason for this choice, other than to provide a different behavior from the other data sources that we'll load automatically when the mashup is loaded for the user. The initial request is made when the user clicks the Load Alerts button (`loadFeed`) in the tools area of the mashup. The `loadFeed` event handler is shown in Listing 14-7. We use a Boolean variable to track whether we've previously loaded the data. If we have, the first thing the event handler does is clear any controls we had loaded into the layer, thus removing any red circles from a previous request. The event handler then creates a `WebClient` object to fetch the data. It is important to note that Silverlight is an asynchronous environment. This is why we specify a method (`wc_OpenReadCompleted`) to be called when the data has been retrieved and is ready for parsing.

Listing 14-7. The Load Feed Button's Click Event Handler

```
private bool alertsLoaded = false;
private void loadFeed_Click(object sender, RoutedEventArgs e)
{
  if (alertsLoaded) AlertLayer.Children.Clear();
  WebClient wc = new WebClient();
  wc.OpenReadCompleted += new OpenReadCompletedEventHandler(wc_OpenReadCompleted);

  Uri feedUri = new Uri("http://feeds.feedburner.com/wdinNewsDigestGeoRSS",
                          UriKind.Absolute);
  wc.OpenReadAsync(feedUri);
}
```

Once the RSS feed's data has been retrieved, control switches to the web client's `OpenReadCompleted` method, shown in Listing 14-8. We check to make sure that there wasn't an error getting the data, then load the resulting XML data into a `SyndicationFeed` object that makes it easy for us to retrieve common properties of the items in the RSS feed. (We include a link in the Further Reading section of this chapter about the syndication object if you are interested in digging deeper.) For each item we construct a circle—an ellipse object whose height and width are equal—and place it on the map at the corresponding location. Note that in order to retrieve the latitude and longitude values, we had to do a bit more work as the `SyndicationFeed` and `SyndicationItem` objects are fairly generic. The point data is accessible through the item's `ElementExtensions` collection, but then we had to split the coordinates up as they are stored as a single string in the feed. The most important line of code here is when the ellipse object is added to the alert map layer at the specified location. At the end of the method, we simply record that we have parsed the feed and check the corresponding box on the mashup tools.

Listing 14-8. Parsing the Geocoded RSS Feed

```
void wc_OpenReadCompleted(object sender, OpenReadCompletedEventArgs e)
{
  if (e.Error != null)
  {
    MessageBox.Show("Error: " + e.Error.Message.ToString());
    return;
  }
  using (Stream s = e.Result)
  {
    SyndicationFeed feed;
    using (XmlReader reader = XmlReader.Create(s))
    {
      feed = SyndicationFeed.Load(reader);
      foreach (SyndicationItem feedItem in feed.Items)
      {
        Ellipse ell = new Ellipse();
        ell.Height = 10;
        ell.Width = 10;
        ell.Fill = new SolidColorBrush(Colors.Red);
        string point = feedItem.ElementExtensions[0].GetObject<String>();
        string[] pointParts = point.Split(' ');
```

```
        Location loc = new Location(double.Parse(pointParts[0]),
                        double.Parse(pointParts[1]));
        AlertLayer.AddChild(ell, loc);
      }
    }
  }
  alertsLoaded = true;
  ShowWildlifeAlerts.IsChecked = true;
}
```

The last action our code took after loading and parsing the RSS feed was to mark the checkbox in the tools area for Wildlife Alerts. Since our mashup should be flexible enough to allow the user to see any combination of data, this checkbox is also used to hide or subsequently show again this layer of data. Listing 14-9 shows both the Checked and Unchecked event handlers for the checkbox for hiding or showing the map layer.

Listing 14-9. Responding to the ShowWildlifeAlerts checkbox

```
private void ShowWildlifeAlerts_Checked(object sender, RoutedEventArgs e)
{
  if (!alertsLoaded)
  {
    MessageBox.Show("Please load the wildlife alerts feed");
    ShowWildlifeAlerts.IsChecked = false;
  }
  else
  {
    AlertLayer.Visibility = Visibility.Visible;
  }
}
private void ShowWildlifeAlerts_Unchecked(object sender, RoutedEventArgs e)
{
  AlertLayer.Visibility = Visibility.Collapsed;
}
```

At this point, you can debug your solution using the ASP.NET test harness that was created along with your Silverlight application. Simply pressing F5 will bring up the ASPX page with your Silverlight mashup map loaded. Click the load button and make sure your alert circles display correctly on the map. The result should look like Figure 14-3.

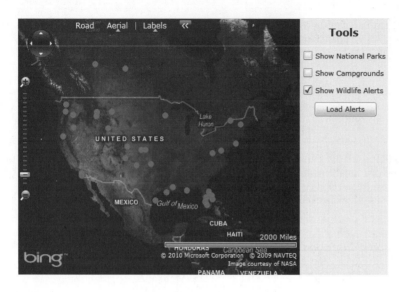

Figure 14-3. The Mashup with Wildlife Alerts

Retrieve and Parse the KML file

KML stands for Keyhole Markup Language, an XML schema for geographic information whose popularity is driven by the primary viewer—Google Earth. For this example, we will download a KML file from the Discovery Channel that contains information about national parks in the United States. You can obtain this file from `http://dsc.discovery.com/utilities/googleearth/nationalparks/nationalparks.kml`. Unlike in the previous example, this time we will download this file for our solution instead of requesting it online. This has to do with the security policy we noted earlier and with the fact that this list is not nearly as volatile as the previous example. You can grab our copy of this file from the code download or from the Discovery Channel directly. When we saved it, we named the file `nationalparks.xml`. You need to place the file in the `ClientBin` folder of the ASP.NET test harness application if you want to be able to debug this portion of the solution. We will address loading this file into the SharePoint site a bit later. In KML markup, the parks are Placemark items. You'll notice the latitude and longitude values show up twice in this file. This is because KML allows for the definition of the placemark as well as for controlling the position of the viewer's virtual camera (`LookAt`). Listing 14-10 shows an example placemark from the file (we truncated the description).

Listing 14-10. A National Park KML Item

```
<Placemark>
<name>Glacier National Park</name>
<description><![CDATA[<a href="http://www.discovery.com/googleearth/?dcitc=w02-530-
    aj-0000&autoplay=true&blid=169202840&bctid=16938864"><img
    src="http://dsc.discovery.com/utilities/googleearth/nationalparks/gallery/
    glacierpark.jpg" width="320" height="240" border="0" alt="Glacier National Park"
    /></a><br /><font size="3" color="#000000">Picture: PhotoDisc/Getty Images
```

```
    |</font><br /> <br /><font size="4"><strong>Inside Glacier National
    Park</strong></font><br />Explore through video the gem of …]]>
</description>
<Snippet>Glacier</Snippet>
<LookAt>
    <longitude>-113.654822</longitude>
    <latitude>48.756675</latitude>
    <range>9444</range>
    <tilt>0</tilt>
    <heading>0</heading>
</LookAt>
<styleUrl>#discoveryPOIMap</styleUrl>
<Point>
    <coordinates>-113.654822,48.756675,0</coordinates>
</Point>
</Placemark>
```

This time, instead of loading on demand, we simply load the file when the Silverlight application loads. To accomplish this we need a new layer for the parks, and we will use a databinding technique to get icons placed onto the layer for each of the national parks in the KML file. Let's start with the map layer, which is shown in Listing 14-11.

Listing 14-11. The MapLayer for National Parks

```
<m:MapLayer x:Name="ParkLayer" Visibility="Collapsed">
    <m:MapItemsControl x:Name="Parks"
      ItemTemplate="{StaticResource ElementTemplate}"
      ItemsSource="{StaticResource KMLElements}">
    </m:MapItemsControl>
</m:MapLayer>
```

Just like the last layer, this one starts hidden from the user. However, in this map layer there is a declaration of a map items control that will represent the shapes we put on the map for the national parks. In this case, we have specified both a data source and a XAML template that should be used for each item in the collection. These are Silverlight resource elements and are defined in the Resources area of the user control. The XAML is shown in Listing 14-12.

Listing 14-12. Resource XAML Content for Databinding

```
<UserControl.Resources>
  <DataTemplate x:Key="ElementTemplate">
    <Image Width="29" Height="34" Source="nationalparksml.png"
           m:MapLayer.Position="{Binding Location}" Tag="{Binding Name}"
           MouseEnter="Park_MouseEnter" MouseLeave="Park_MouseLeave" />
  </DataTemplate>
  <db:KMLElementCollection x:Key="KMLElements" Source="nationalparks.xml" />
</UserControl.Resources>
```

Let's focus first on the db:KMLElementCollection element. Remember that the db namespace alias is actually set to be the namespace of our solution. This means that in our code download you will see a KMLElementCollection class that takes the responsibility of parsing the national parks KML file. This class was one we found in code samples from Microsoft's Professional Developer Conference in 2009, where the Bing Maps Silverlight Control SDK was announced. You can get this code and many other examples from http://blogs.msdn.com/veplatform/archive/2009/11/20/bing-maps-silverlight-control-code-samples-available-from-pdc09.aspx.

This class parses the XML of the file and creates a collection of KMLElement objects. For each national park, we add the XAML in the DataTemplate to our map layer. In this case, the data template is using an image control to place an icon at the specified coordinates. You can grab the nationalparksml.png icon file from our code download. Notice that the position of the image is bound to the Location property of the KMLElement object and its tag is bound to the Name property. We will use the tag later in the MouseEnter and MouseLeave events. The picture file itself should be added to the root of the Silverlight project. Make sure that its Build Action property is set to Resource so that the file is included in the Silverlight .xap package.

■ **Note** You will not be able to place a GIF onto a map layer with the image control. We used a PNG format since we want to display a transparent background. JPGs are also common.

Since the data source and template are declaratively defined in the XAML, the KMLElementsCollection class will take care of getting our icons into the map layer when the mashup is first loaded. Of course, we hide that layer until the user clicks the checkbox to show this data. The code for hiding and showing the layer is very similar to the previous RSS source so we won't duplicate it here. The more interesting code relates to how we handle displaying the title of the national park when the user hovers over the icon on the map. Moreover, we will need this type of functionality for the campgrounds stored in a SharePoint list later, so it is important that the code is reusable and not specific to the parks. For that reason, in our code download, there's an InfoLayer map layer that is defined last in the XAML (meaning it is the top-most layer). Inside this layer we placed a Border object and a TextBlock control that we will use to display text for a mouse-over. We will dynamically hide, show, and position this content when needed. Notice that the layer is always visible, but the infoBox control is hidden by default. The XAML for the map layer is shown in Listing 14-13.

Listing 14-13. The MapLayer for Mouse Over Displays

```
<m:MapLayer x:Name="InfoLayer" >
  <Border x:Name="infoBox" Background="White" Height="40" Width="150"
          Visibility="Collapsed" CornerRadius="10"  >
    <TextBlock x:Name="pinInfo" FontSize="10" Foreground="Black"
               FontWeight="Normal"  HorizontalAlignment="Left"
               Margin="5,5,0,0"  TextWrapping="Wrap"  />
  </Border>
</m:MapLayer>
```

Remember in the DataTemplate we specified event handlers for the `MouseEnter` and `MouseLeave` events of the image that represents the national park? These event handlers will hide, show, and position the `infoBox`, as well as place the name of the national park in the `TextBlock`. Listing 14-14 shows the `Park_MouseEnter` event handler, which gets a reference to the corresponding map element (pin) and sets the position of the `infoBox` to be that of the pin with a small offset. The tag is then retrieved and placed as the contents of the `TextBlock` and then shown to the user. Listing 14-14 also includes the `Park_MouseLeave` event handler, which hides the `infoBox`.

Listing 14-14. Showing the Title of the Park in the Flyout

```
private void Park_MouseEnter(object sender, MouseEventArgs e)
{
  FrameworkElement pin = sender as FrameworkElement;
  MapLayer.SetPosition(infoBox, MapLayer.GetPosition(pin));
  MapLayer.SetPositionOffset(infoBox, new Point(20, -15));
  pinInfo.Text = pin.Tag as string;
  infoBox.Visibility = Visibility.Visible;
}
private void Park_MouseLeave(object sender, MouseEventArgs e)
{
  infoBox.Visibility = Visibility.Collapsed;
}
```

With this, we've finished getting the national parks KML data source onto our mashup. Double-check that you have the icon as a resource in the Silverlight project, the XML file in the `ClientBin` folder of the ASP.NET test harness, and the `KMLElementsCollection` code file in the solution. Running the ASP.NET test application and clicking the checkbox to show the national parks should result in something like Figure 14-4. Note that we are not showing the RSS feed data, but there is no reason why you couldn't combine them at this point.

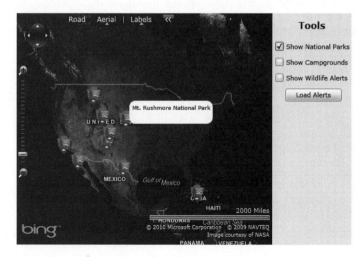

Figure 14-4. The Mashup with National Parks

Add the SharePoint List to the Mashup

The last data source for our mashup will be a SharePoint list of campgrounds. We will create this list by extending the out-of-the-box SharePoint contact list, adding three new fields in the process: Latitude, Longitude, and Geocoded Status. To accomplish this, we will create a new content type, site columns, and a list definition. We will also add an event handler so that when a user adds a contact, the system will use a Bing Maps web service to convert the contact's address into coordinates. However, we will postpone making these SharePoint customizations until a bit later in the chapter and, for now, assume we have such a list to complete the mashup and that the list is in the same SharePoint site. We begin with the code in Listing 14-15, which is the layer that will contain pushpins for each of the campgrounds.

Listing 14-15. The MapLayer for Campgrounds

```
<m:MapLayer x:Name="PinLayer" Visibility="Collapsed" >
</m:MapLayer>
```

We will have to interact with a few SharePoint objects in order to get the campground data. The code in Listing 14-16 declares some variables to store the references to these SharePoint objects as field-level variables in the `MainPage.xaml.cs` file. Don't forget, though, that these are not server-side objects but rather objects from SharePoint's client-side libraries for Silverlight.

Listing 14-16. SharePoint Client-Side Objects

```
SP.ClientContext context = null;
SP.Web web = null;
SP.List campgroundList = null;
SP.ListItemCollection campgroundItems = null;
```

We want to load the campground list items automatically when the mashup is loaded. Therefore, the code in Listing 14-17 issues the query for data in the `UserControl_Loaded` method of the mashup. Notice that the first thing we do is retrieve the current SharePoint context so we can then get a reference to the SharePoint site (`web`) where the user is viewing the mashup. This technique is one that SharePoint developers will recognize because it is the same technique used in server-side code. However, this code is client-side since the Silverlight application runs within the user's browser, not the SharePoint server. The client-side libraries were designed so that developers versed in server-side code would be able to make an easy transition.

Listing 14-17. Requesting Geocoded Campground List Items

```
private void UserControl_Loaded(object sender, RoutedEventArgs e)
{
  context = SP.ClientContext.Current;
  web = context.Web;
  campgroundList = web.Lists.GetByTitle("Campgrounds");
  SP.CamlQuery query = new SP.CamlQuery();
  query.ViewXml = "<View><Query><Where><Eq>" +
      "<FieldRef Name='GeocodeStatus'/><Value Type='Choice'>Geocoded</Value>" +
      "</Eq></Where></Query></View>";
```

```
    campgroundItems = campgroundList.GetItems(query);
    context.Load(campgroundItems);
    context.ExecuteQueryAsync(requestSucceeded, requestFailed);
}
```

After obtaining a reference to the current site, we use the `SP.Web` object's `Lists` collection to find our campground list. It is worth pointing out that client-side libraries do not actually perform any operations against the server until an execute method is called. This is somewhat similar to a developer's experience with an ADO.NET command object. With a command object, you specify the stored procedure you want to call, define the connection, and hook up all the parameters for the query. But nothing really happens until the command object is executed. With SharePoint client-side libraries, you specify actions you want performed and then the context's object execute methods cause the round-trip with the server. In this example, we specify a CAML query to return campground list items where the `GeocodeStatus` choice column has a value of **Geocoded**. This is a column we will use to signal that our geocoded process with Bing Maps was successful. Last but not least, the method executes the query. Like all of our other requests for data sources, this one happens asynchronously so we specify two methods to route control to depending on whether or not the query is successful.

Since our query for the SharePoint list items is asynchronous, we have a little bit of work to do to make sure our handling of the response runs in a client thread that has access to our user controls. Listing 14-18 shows the code. These techniques are similar to those used by Windows Forms developers. Notice that both the `requestSucceeded` and `requestFailed` methods make use of an `UpdateUIMethod` delegate. By using the delegate, we can make sure that either the `AddCampgroundPins` or `CampgroundsNotFound` methods run in the appropriate thread.

Listing 14-18. Managing Threading of the Completed Request

```
private delegate void UpdateUIMethod();

private void requestSucceeded(object sender, SP.ClientRequestSucceededEventArgs e)
{
    UpdateUIMethod updateUI = AddCampgroundPins;
    this.Dispatcher.BeginInvoke(updateUI);
}
private void requestFailed(object sender, SP.ClientRequestFailedEventArgs e)
{
    UpdateUIMethod updateUI = CampgroundsNotFound;
    this.Dispatcher.BeginInvoke(updateUI);
}
```

The `CampgroundsNotFound` method simply displays a message box with an error message. More interesting is the `AddCampgroundPins` method, shown in Listing 14-19, which adds new push pin shapes to our map layer. With this data source we are using columns of the list item to control the pin. The `Latitude` and `Longitude` fields specify where the pin should be placed. We use the `Company` column, which will store the name of the campground, as the pin's tag so that it will be displayed when the user places the mouse over the pin.

Listing 14-19. Adding Push Pins for the Campgrounds

```
private void AddCampgroundPins()
{
  foreach (SP.ListItem item in campgroundItems)
  {
    Pushpin pin = new Pushpin();
    pin.Tag = item["Company"].ToString();
    double latitude = (double)item["Latitude"];
    double longitude = (double)item["Longitude"];
    Location loc = new Location(latitude, longitude);
    pin.Location = loc;
    pin.MouseEnter += new MouseEventHandler(pin_MouseEnter);
    pin.MouseLeave += new MouseEventHandler(pin_MouseLeave);
    PinLayer.Children.Add(pin);
  }
}
```

We won't go over the remaining code in the code download because it processes the pin's mouse events in the same manner as the flyouts we made for the national parks. In fact, it uses the same `infoBox`. And we won't cover the checkboxes for hiding and showing this map layer as they use the same technique described earlier. This time you can't use the ASP.NET test harness to debug you code since this data source is expected to be in the same SharePoint site as the mashup.

In the next section of the chapter, we will walk you through building a deployment vehicle, and then show how to get a geocoded campground list a bit later. To keep you going, Figure 14-5 shows the mashup with all three data sources and a flyover for a specific campground.

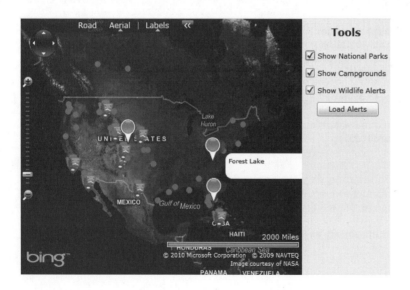

Figure 14-5. The Mashup with All Three Data Sources

Deploy the Mashup as a Sandboxed Solution

Since sandboxed solutions are new in SharePoint 2010, we will take a moment to explain what they are. Sandboxed solutions are SharePoint customizations whose code runs in a managed environment, isolated from SharePoint itself. This means that their assemblies are not deployed to the global assembly cache of the web front-end servers, They cannot crash the `w3wp.exe` worker processes that keep SharePoint up and running. These new type of solutions are intended to provide some sanity for IT pros who are responsible for maintaining environments that have evolved to support rapid application development. Too often with SharePoint 2007, developers deployed custom code that ran with full trust on the SharePoint servers and even within the same processes as the product itself. It only took one poorly written web part to impact the performance of the entire farm, and it was usually the IT pro's phone that rang first when the intranet was down, not the developer's. Sandboxed solutions are meant to provide a middle ground where IT pros can manage a stable server environment, yet developers can still provide customizations. If a sandboxed solution behaves poorly, such as erroring too frequently, the IT pro simply sets a threshold number of times it can fail before SharePoint no longer loads the customization. In this case, the SharePoint servers are still up and it is the developer who gets the call as to why his customizations are no longer on the site.

There are lots of things to learn about sandboxed solutions and we have included a link in the Further Reading section of this chapter. For now, consider them site-collection-specific solutions as opposed to enterprise SharePoint customizations. In fact, this is the main reason we have chosen to deploy the mashup as a sandboxed solution. It doesn't have code that will run on the server, but it does rely on aspects of the site it is running in. Sandboxed solutions also run with their own `web.config` file and have limits on which parts of the SharePoint object model they can call. Administrators can also place resource restrictions on them, such as CPU or memory utilization.

For this project, we will use a sandboxed solution to deploy the Silverlight mashup and the national parks XML file to a SharePoint site. Right-click on the solution in Visual Studio's Solution Explorer and choose **Add New Project**. Expand the Visual C# node, the SharePoint node, and select the 2010 node to display the SharePoint 2010 project templates. Select the **Empty SharePoint Project** template and make sure that the .NET Framework 3.5 is selected in the top drop-down. Name the project **MapFeature**. Your Add New Project dialog should look like Figure 14-6. Click OK.

Figure 14-6. Adding the MapFeature SharePoint Project

The SharePoint Customization Wizard will start, and begin by asking you which SharePoint site you want to use for debugging. Any normal team site will do, but make sure that whichever one you choose you continue to use for other SharePoint projects we create in this chapter. In our environment we specified `http://edhild3/sites/mashup`. The rest of the dialog asks you whether or not this is a sandboxed solution. Choose the option to **Deploy as a sandboxed solution**. In this solution, we aren't going to write any new code, but rather create a SharePoint feature that places our Silverlight application and national parks XML file into a specific place in the site. To do this we will use a Module customization that allows us to add content to the site when the feature is activated. Use the following steps to add this to your MapFeature project.

1. Right-click on the MapFeature project and choose **Add ➤ New Item**.

2. Select the Module project item template and name it **MashupMapModule**. Click **Add**.

3. The previous step defines a new Feature in the project and associates the MashupModule with it. This module will have some sample markup in its `Elements.xml` file that places a `sample.txt` file into the SharePoint site. Expand the MashupMapModule node in the project to find both these files.

4. Delete the `Sample.txt` file from your project. Notice that the reference to it is now removed from the module's Elements file.

5. Now right-click on the `nationalparks.xml` file in Visual Studio's Solution Explorer window. This file should still be in the `ClientBin` folder of the Silverlight ASP.NET test harness application. Select **Copy** from the context menu.

6. Right-click on the MashupMapModule node of the MapFeature project and choose **Paste**. Notice that not only is the file copied, but the `Elements.xml` file now also includes markup for it.

7. Getting the Silverlight application here is a bit more interesting as we want to be sure we have the latest compiled version. Select the MashupMapModule node and locate its Project Output References property in Visual Studio's Properties window. Click the ellipses "**…**" button.

8. In the Project Output References dialog, click **Add**. Select **MashupMap** from the Project Name property and specify the Deployment Type as **ElementFile**. This dialog should look like Figure 14-7. Click **OK**. Notice the Silverlight `.xap` package is added to the `Elements.xml` file.

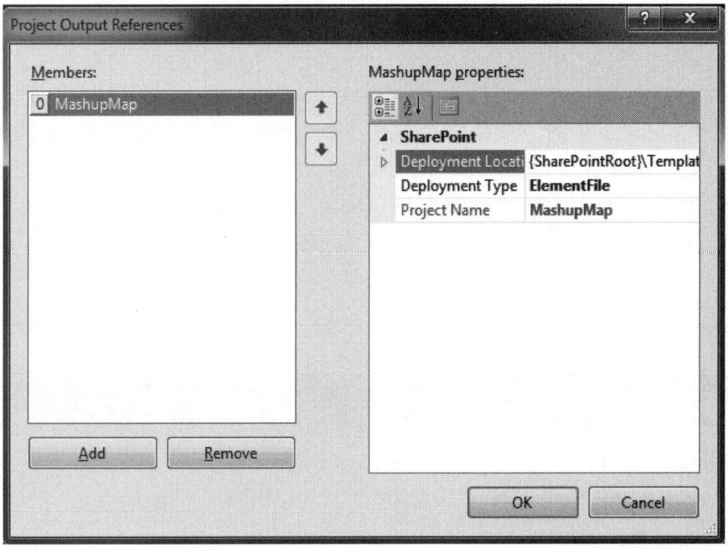

Figure 14-7. Adding the Silverlight Project's Output to the Module

We do want to tweak the XML markup in this module just a bit. If we left it as is, a new folder with the same name of the module would be created in the site and our files would be placed there. Though this is fine and is normally done in production environments, it does make it difficult to confirm that everything worked, since this folder is not part of the SharePoint user interface and can only be seen with a tool such as SharePoint Designer. Instead, let's have our two files placed in the Shared Documents document library of the site. Obviously, this is not a good place if we give users permission to edit this library, but putting our files in a library will let us see that they have been successfully deployed. Listing 14-20 shows the modified elements file for the module.

Listing 14-20. The Module's Elements file to Deploy the Files to a Document Library

```
<Elements xmlns="http://schemas.microsoft.com/sharepoint/">
  <Module Name="MashupMapModule">
  <File Path="MashupMapModule\nationalparks.xml"
       Url="Shared Documents/nationalparks.xml"  />
  <File Path="MashupMapModule\MashupMap.xap"
       Url="Shared Documents/MashupMap.xap" />
</Module>
</Elements>
```

You can now deploy this feature. Unlike enterprise solutions that are deployed to the server and activated through an interface like Site Features or Site Collection Features, sandboxed solutions are deployed to the site collection's Solutions gallery, which you find in the Site Settings administration area of the top-level site. Confirm that your MapFeature solution made it there and that it was activated. Your screen should look like Figure 14-8.

■ **Note** We have seen environments that generate an error when deploying a sandboxed solution. The error is usually something like: "Error occurred in deployment step 'Activate Features': Cannot start service SPUserCodeV4 on computer 'servername'". This error occurs when the service that hosts sandboxed solutions is not started on the SharePoint Server. You can find more information at `http://www.dotnetmafia.com/blogs/dotnettipoftheday/archive/2009/11/30/troubleshooting-sandboxed-solutions-in-sharepoint-2010.aspx`.

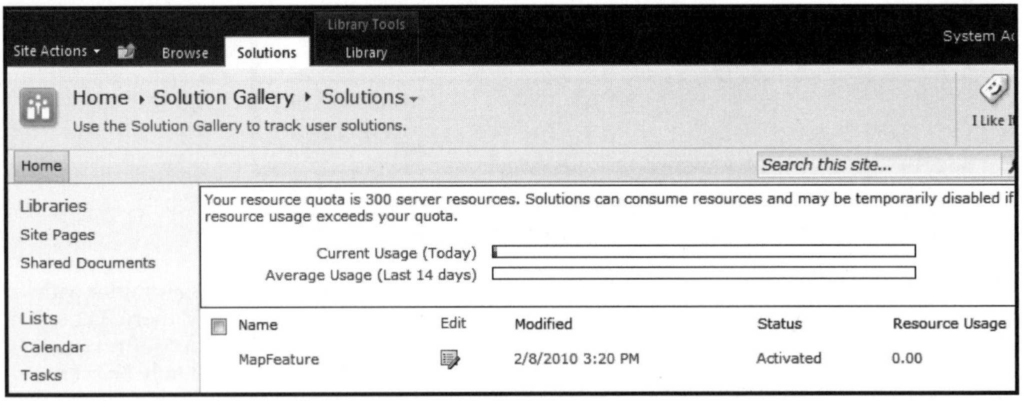

Figure 14-8. The Deployed Site's Solutions Gallery

If the deployment was successful, you should see the `MashupMap.xap` Silverlight application package and the `nationalparks.xml` file in the Shared Documents library of the site. Of course, we can't use them yet as we have not created the campgrounds list. That's the next section of the chapter.

■ **Note** Not that this particular sandboxed solution did not contain any server-side code, but if it did, you might find yourself stuck debugging it. This is because the code is not deployed to your normal `w3wp.exe` process. Instead, you should attach Visual Studio to the `SPUCProcess.exe` process.

Create a Geocoded Contacts List Feature

To complete the solution, we are going to create a set of SharePoint customizations that enable any site administrator to access an extended contacts list definition that geocodes the address of each contact. Since this functionality is likely to be used by many different sites for many different reasons, we will deploy it as a SharePoint enterprise solution rather than a sandboxed solution. We will create this functionality by first defining a new content type called GeocodeContact, which is derived from the contact content type with the additional columns of Latitude, Longitude, and GeocodeStatus. We will then create a new list definition based on the content type called GeocodedContacts. Finally, we will create a list event handler for that list definition that incorporates Bing Maps' Geocode web service to convert contact addresses into coordinates.

Add another project to your MashupMap solution. Name the project **GeocodeFeature** and choose the **Empty SharePoint Project** template. This time choose the **Deploy as a farm solution** option and make sure you are targeting the same SharePoint site you've been using thus far.

To create the new content type, **Add** a **New Item** to the project. From the SharePoint project item templates, select Content Type and name it **GeocodeContact**. From the SharePoint Customization Wizard, choose the base content type to extend—in this case, it's the Contact content type. This will add a new `Elements.xml` file to the project containing the XML markup for the content type. It is here that we will define our new site columns and add them to the content type. Listing 14-21 contains the XML for the three site columns we want to add. This markup should be placed just before the content type.

Listing 14-21. Defining New Site Columns for the Content Type

```
<Field
    ID="{673EC61F-5CC3-41ae-A974-DE547EDB5FC7}"
    SourceID="http://schemas.microsoft.com/sharepoint/v3/fields"
    Name="Latitude"
    StaticName="Latitude"
    Type="Number"
    Group="Geocode Group"
    DisplayName="Latitude">
</Field>
<Field
    ID="{318A3DE7-4783-4a8b-A9D2-FE1A59E6CCBA}"
    SourceID="http://schemas.microsoft.com/sharepoint/v3/fields"
    Name="Longitude"
    StaticName="Longitude"
```

```
        Type="Number"
        Group="Geocode Group"
        DisplayName="Longitude">
</Field>
<Field
    ID="{E9DBD6FD-A198-4eca-85A6-65825DE56066}"
    SourceID="http://schemas.microsoft.com/sharepoint/v3/fields"
    Name="GeocodeStatus"
    StaticName="GeocodeStatus"
    Type="Choice"
    FillInChoice="FALSE"
    Group="Geocode Group"
    DisplayName="GeocodeStatus">
    <CHOICES>
      <CHOICE>Not Geoencoded</CHOICE>
      <CHOICE>Geocoded</CHOICE>
    </CHOICES>
    <Default>Not Geoencoded</Default>
</Field>
```

Our additional site columns are Latitude, Longitude, and GeocodeStatus. Both Latitude and Longitude are numbers representing Bing Maps coordinates. The GeocodeStatus column is a choice field that will let us know if the conversion of the address by Bing was successful. Remember that we are filtering in the mashup for contacts that have only a value of Geocoded in this column. In case you are wondering, the values of the GUIDs here simply have to be unique. If you are interested in knowing more about the schema used to define these or other site columns, visit `http://msdn.microsoft.com/en-us/library/ms196289.aspx`.

With the site columns defined, we will now focus on the content type. In our solution, we cleaned up the name a bit but the most important addition is the inclusion of the columns we just defined. Note that you can tell by looking at the ID attribute that this content type is indeed derived from the out-of-the-box contact content type. With SharePoint content types, the IDs just extend down the inheritance tree. The parent content type is obviously a contact since the ID starts with 0x0106. As the code shows in Listing 14-22, each site column needs to be referenced in the content type. Make sure your GUIDs match up.

Listing 14-22. The GeocodeContact Content Type

```
<ContentType ID="0x0106008d5ceaa8cb464dca9ba7a3e4ae9362a2"
             Name="GeocodeContact"
             Group="Custom Content Types"
             Description="My Content Type"
             Inherits="TRUE"
             Version="0">
  <FieldRefs>
    <FieldRef ID="{673EC61F-5CC3-41ae-A974-DE547EDB5FC7}" Name="Latitude" />
    <FieldRef ID="{318A3DE7-4783-4a8b-A9D2-FE1A59E6CCBA}" Name="Longitude" />
    <FieldRef ID="{E9DBD6FD-A198-4eca-85A6-65825DE56066}" Name="GeocodeStatus" />
  </FieldRefs>
</ContentType>
```

If you are so inclined, you could build and deploy the solution at this point. In the Site Settings area of your test site, you should be able to find the new site columns in their gallery (as shown in Figure 14-9) and the new GeocodeContact content type.

Geocode Group

GeocodeStatus	Choice	Home
Latitude	Number	Home
Longitude	Number	Home

Figure 14-9. The Deployed New Site Columns

Now go back to your GeocodeFeature project in Visual Studio and **Add** a **New Item**. This time, choose the **List Definition from Content Type** item template. Name the item **GeocodedContacts**. In the SharePoint Customization Wizard dialog, you will be asked to select the content type from which to base the list definition. As shown in Figure 14-10, choose the **GeocodeContact** type we defined in the same project. You should see the project name before the name of the content type. Name the list definition **GeocodedContacts** and uncheck the option to create an instance of this list definition upon activation of the feature.

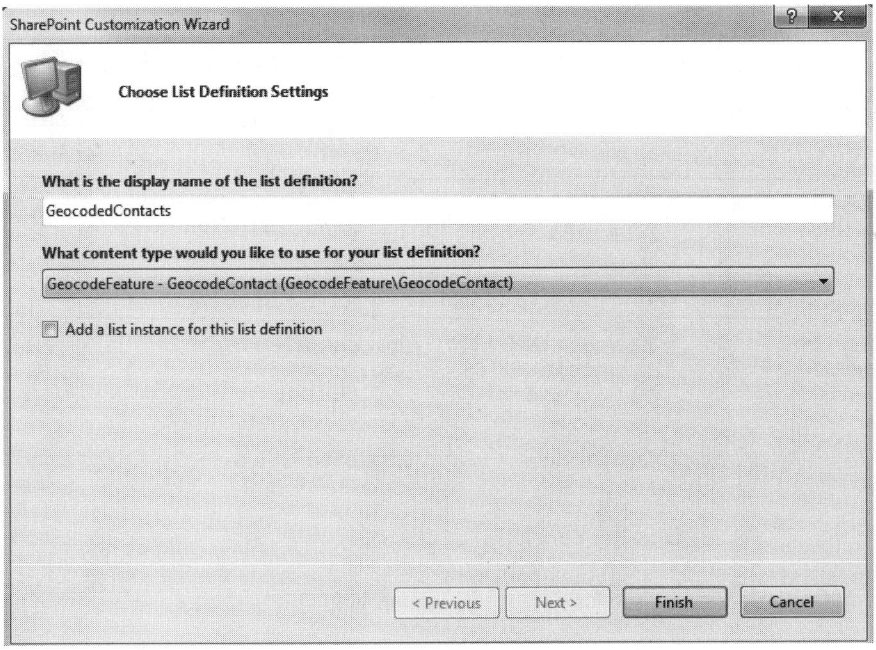

Figure 14-10. Creating a List Definition from a Content Type

Completing this wizard adds a new `Elements.xml` file to the project. This time it includes markup for the list template. As shown in Listing 14-23, we cleaned up a few of the properties to make them easier to read.

Listing 14-23. The GeocodedContacts List Definition

```
<ListTemplate
    Name="GeocodedContacts"
    Type="10000"
    BaseType="0"
    OnQuickLaunch="TRUE"
    SecurityBits="11"
    Sequence="330"
    DisplayName="GeocodedContacts"
    Description="Geocoded Contacts"
    Image="/_layouts/images/itcontct.png"/>
```

The last SharePoint customization we will include in this project is the list event handler that will respond to new or updated contacts within the list. Any time there is an addition or edit, we will make a call to Bing Maps' web service to convert the address to coordinates. Since we are not requiring any user to get involved and we want this activity to happen right after an item has been added, we chose to implement this customization as an event handler instead of a workflow. Within the same GeocodeFeature project, **Add** a **New Item**. Select the **Event Receiver** template and name the item **GeocodeReceiver**. In the SharePoint Customization Wizard you will be asked to configure the type of events you want to respond to. For our solution, we will respond to **List Item Events** and the event source is the **GeocodedContacts** list definition we created earlier. In terms of events, we want to make sure that our geocoding operation occurs synchronously with the edit or addition of the item so that the coordinates are immediately available for the mashup. Therefore, select both the **An item is being added** and the **An item is being updated** events.

With the customization added, use the following steps to add a reference to the Bing Maps' Geocode web service.

1. Right-click on the GeocodeFeature project and select **Add Service Reference**.

2. In the address box, specify the following URL: `http://dev.virtualearth.net/webservices/v1/geocodeservice/geocodeservice.svc?wsdl`.

3. Click **Go**.

4. In the Namespace textbox, replace the default value with **GeocodeService**.

5. Click **OK**.

Now switch over to the class file that was added for the event receiver. This file should be named `GeocodeReceiver.cs`. Add the `using` statements shown in Listing 14-24 to the top of the file so that you can use WCF classes and the Geocode web service without fully qualifying their names.

Listing 14-24. Using Statements for the Event Receiver

```
using GeocodeFeature.GeocodeService;
using System.ServiceModel;
```

This class file should already be stubbed out with methods for the **ItemAdding** and **ItemUpdating** events or the contact item. The code in Listing 14-25 shows how we injected our own processing before the addition or edit is committed to the SharePoint server.

Listing 14-25. Modifying an Item in the Event Receiver

```
public override void ItemAdding(SPItemEventProperties properties)
{
  GeoCodeItem(properties);
  base.ItemAdding(properties);
}
public override void ItemUpdating(SPItemEventProperties properties)
{
  GeoCodeItem(properties);
  base.ItemUpdating(properties);
}
```

All of the work of communicating with Bing Maps happens in the **GeoCodeItem** method. The beginning of this method is shown in Listing 14-26. Notice that the request to the web service includes your application key you used earlier in the mashup. The heart of the request is a **GeocodeRequest** object that we populate with the address of the contact item. We got the names of these fields by looking at the fields of the contact content type. The last portion of Listing 14-26 simply specifies that we are interested only in high confidence results from Bing.

Listing 14-26. Setting up the Geocode Request

```
private void GeoCodeItem(SPItemEventProperties properties)
{
    string bingMapsKey = "YOUR KEY HERE";
    GeocodeRequest geocodeRequest = new GeocodeRequest();
    // Set the credentials using a valid Bing Maps key
    geocodeRequest.Credentials = new GeocodeService.Credentials();
    geocodeRequest.Credentials.ApplicationId = bingMapsKey;
    // Set the full address query
    string addressTemplate = "{0},{1},{2},{3}";
    geocodeRequest.Query = string.Format(addressTemplate,
        properties.AfterProperties["WorkAddress"].ToString(),
        properties.AfterProperties["WorkCity"].ToString(),
        properties.AfterProperties["WorkState"].ToString(),
        properties.AfterProperties["WorkZip"].ToString());
    // Set the options to only return high confidence results
    ConfidenceFilter[] filters = new ConfidenceFilter[1];
    filters[0] = new ConfidenceFilter();
```

351

```
filters[0].MinimumConfidence = GeocodeService.Confidence.High;
GeocodeOptions geocodeOptions = new GeocodeOptions();
geocodeOptions.Filters = filters;
geocodeRequest.Options = geocodeOptions;
```

Next, the method continues by executing the request. Since our event handler will be deployed to the global assembly cache and we don't want to modify SharePoint's `web.config` file, we will setup the WCF binding and endpoint explicitly instead of relying on a configuration file. This is the code that is shown in Listing 14-27.

Listing 14-27. Configuring the Proxy and Executing the Geocode Request

```
// Make the geocode request
BasicHttpBinding binding1 = new BasicHttpBinding();
EndpointAddress addr = new EndpointAddress(
    "http://dev.virtualearth.net/webservices/v1/geocodeservice/GeocodeService.svc");
GeocodeServiceClient geocodeService = new GeocodeServiceClient(binding1, addr);
GeocodeResponse geocodeResponse = geocodeService.Geocode(geocodeRequest);
```

The remainder of the GeoCodeItem method checks to see if there was a response. In this case, we are expecting a single set of coordinates. The code in Listing 14-28 gets these return values and modifies the list item to have these values before it is committed to the server.

Listing 14-28. Retrieving the Result of the Geocode Request

```
// The result is a GeocodeResponse object
if (geocodeResponse.Results.Length > 0)
{
  properties.AfterProperties["Latitude"] =
    geocodeResponse.Results[0].Locations[0].Latitude;
  properties.AfterProperties["Longitude"] =
    geocodeResponse.Results[0].Locations[0].Longitude;
  properties.AfterProperties["GeocodeStatus"] = "Geocoded";
}
}
```

You are now finished with the GeocodeFeature project. Build and deploy the SharePoint customizations to the site. We will now walk you through just a few final items to make the mashup complete.

Setting up the SharePoint Site

With both your SharePoint features deployed, there are only a few items to bring the entire solution to life. Using the same SharePoint site, create an instance of the GeocodedContacts list definition named **Campgrounds**. Go ahead and populate it with a few items specifying the name of a campground in the company field and its full address. You will have to specify a first and last name of a contact. If you want some data to use as a source, we found a nice collection at the organization known as 1000 trails: http://1000trails.com/index.asp.

One other small change we made is that we didn't think it was appropriate to display the fields for Latitude, Longitude, and GeocodeStatus to the user on the item edit form as these are really there only for our event code. Fortunately, in SharePoint 2010, a list's forms can be quickly modified using InfoPath. Use the following steps to change the campground's list form.

1. With the Campgrounds list open, click **List** on the ribbon and choose the **Customize Form** button in the Customize List group.

2. InfoPath will load the list's form into the form designer with the list of list columns displayed off to the right. Delete the three rows from the design surface of the form to hide our Latitude, Longitude, and GeocodeStatus fields from the user. The form should look like Figure 14-11.

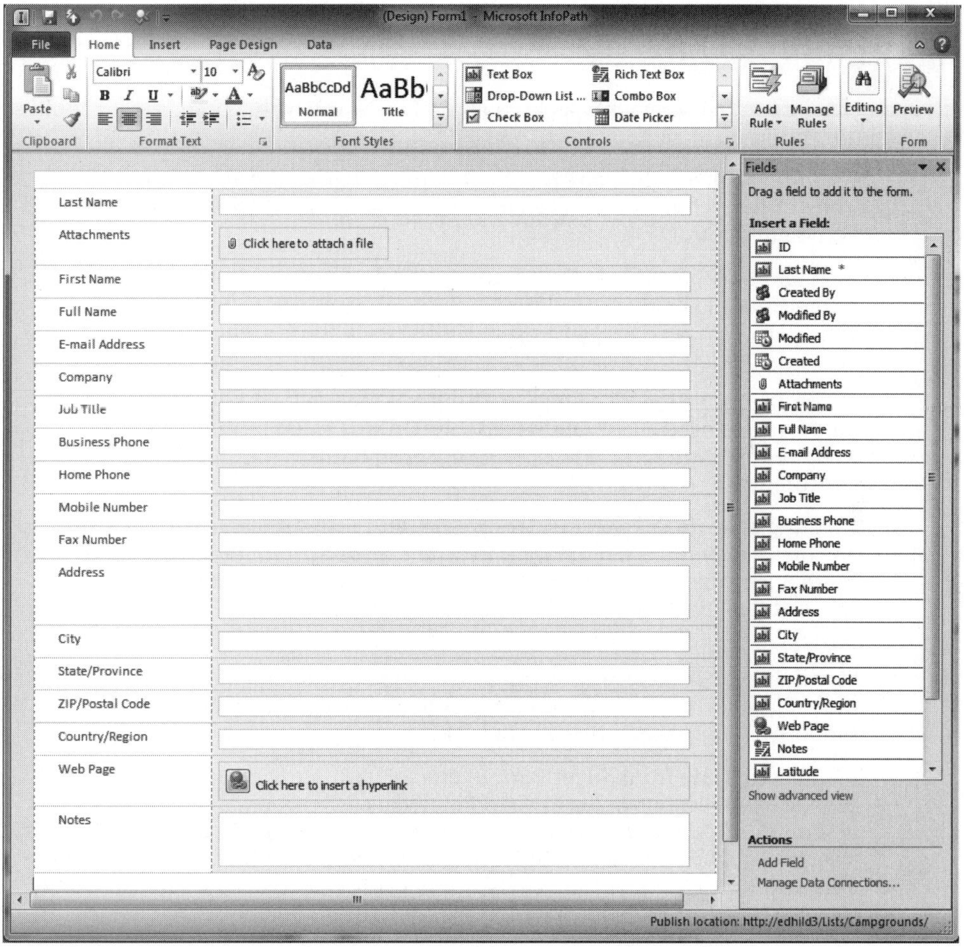

Figure 14-11. Using InfoPath to Modify the Campground List's Form

3. In the very top-left corner of InfoPath there is a Quick Publish button immediately to the right of the save option. Click it to commit the changed form back to the list. Now when you edit an item, our three fields won't confuse the user into thinking they are responsible for those values.

Lastly, you will need a place to display the mashup. On any page of your SharePoint site, or a new page if you prefer, add the Silverlight Web Part that is in the Media and Content category. When you add the web part, you are asked for the URL of the Silverlight application package. You can also find this setting by editing the web part to pull up its properties and click the Configure button. Since our module deployed it to the Shared Documents library, this value should be `/sites/mashup/Shared Documents/MashupMap.xap`. You're done! If you don't see the whole Silverlight control, just adjust the size of the web part through its properties to match that of the XAML markup (Height:400, Width:600). Test everything to make sure you can load all three data sources onto the mashup.

Important Lessons

This chapter incorporated several key techniques that are worth highlighting as they could easily be reused in other projects.

Bing Maps Silverlight Control: The solution detailed how to layer shapes, icons, and pins into different layers of an interactive map using the Bing Maps Silverlight Control SDK.

Bing Maps Web Services: The solution used the Geocode web service provided by Bing Maps to convert an address into coordinates. There are several other Bing Maps Web Services and we included a link in the Further Reading section of the chapter.

Sandboxed Solutions: The mashup itself was really a site-specific solution. We therefore deployed it as a sandboxed solution so it could be managed in a restricted area without the risk of causing great harm to the SharePoint environment.

Creating a Content Type, List Definition, and Event Receiver in a Feature: As a developer, you will often want to extend an out-of-the-box SharePoint content type, create a list based on your changes, and attach an event receiver. This solution included these three steps in concert, all defined within a single feature.

Modifying a List's Form with InfoPath: When you are not quite happy with the out-of-the-box list form and want to give your users a better experience, simply customize the form using InfoPath.

Requesting Data from Silverlight: In this solution, we showed you how from a Silverlight application living in SharePoint you can retrieve data from a variety of sources. We showed you how to load data from a RSS feed, consume a local KML file, and how to query SharePoint lists using SharePoint's client-side libraries.

Extension Points

While coding this example, we thought of several variations to the solution that we didn't incorporate. Mostly, these were not included because they distracted from the overall objective of the solution. We call them out now as extension points since they may be applicable to a specific project you are working on.

Pull in data from an Excel Services spreadsheet: As shown in Chapters 5 and 10, Excel Services now provides a REST API for retrieving elements of the spreadsheet. These elements could be charts or even named ranges. You could use them as yet another data source, either pulling in a chart as an overlay (inserting it as an image similarly to the park icon) or retrieving a table of data for a new map layer.

Store your Bing Maps Key separately, not as a literal string in code: In this chapter the Bing Maps key was hard-coded into the solution, which is definitely not a best practice. You could place this value in a resource file for both the Silverlight solution and the feature. Another possibility would be to store it in the `web.config` file. Chapter 11 shows an example of how to have your feature write configuration modifications to the `web.config` file automatically.

Draw polygons on the map: We had thought of drawing large polygons on the map as a layer to signify regions of responsibility, something similar to sales districts: Northeast, Southeast, Heartland, Northwest, Southwest. However, the bottom line is that we could only go so far with the "context" for this chapter. We recommend looking at the Interactive SDK and spending some time with the additional things you can do with the map.

Further Reading

The following links are to resources we think a reader interested in the material presented in this chapter would find useful:

- Develop a Sandboxed Silverlight 3.0 Web Part for SharePoint 2010 `http://sptechpoint.wordpress.com/2010/01/12/develop-a-sandboxed-silverlight-3-0-web-part-for-sharepoint-2010/`

- Using Bing Maps in SharePoint `http://cm-bloggers.blogspot.com/2009/06/using-microsoft-bing-maps-in-sharepoint.html`

- SharePoint 2010, the Client Object Models and Bing Maps `http://www.tonstegeman.com/Blog/Lists/Posts/Post.aspx?List=70640fe5%2D28d9%2D464f%2Db1c9%2D91e07c8f7e47&ID=123`

- Deep Dive on Bing Maps Silverlight Control `http://microsoftpdc.com/Sessions/CL36`

- Reading and Displaying RSS Feed in a Silverlight Datagrid `http://www.dotnetcurry.com/ShowArticle.aspx?ID=252&AspxAutoDetectCookieSupport=1`

- Data Retrieval Overview `http://msdn.microsoft.com/en-us/library/ee539350(office.14).aspx`

- How To: Retrieve List Items `http://msdn.microsoft.com/en-us/library/ee534956(office.14).aspx`

- Working with BeforeProperties and AfterProperties on SPItemEventReceiver `http://www.synergyonline.com/blog/blog-moss/Lists/Posts/Post.aspx?ID=25`

- Bing Maps Web Services SDK `http://msdn.microsoft.com/en-us/library/cc980922.aspx`

- Syndication Feed Class `http://msdn.microsoft.com/en-us/library/system.servicemodel.syndication.syndicationfeed.aspx`

- Sandboxed Solutions `http://msdn.microsoft.com/en-us/magazine/ee335711.aspx`

CHAPTER 15

■ ■ ■

Realizing the Vision

Today, many organizations lose productivity because their workers find it difficult to locate, use, and share the information they need. Software developers build solutions to try to reduce this loss. However, by not incorporating their applications into tools familiar to the user, they can often increase user workload.

Consider a solution that helps educators generate and track student learning plans. A developer may read the requirements for standardization, compliance, and promotion of best practices, and as a result, deliver a Windows application that provides the teachers with a wizard-like approach that stores the plans in a central database. This solution would standardize the plans and provide a vehicle for enforcing regulations for how frequently they are reviewed and updated. By using a wizard approach, the application breaks the plan into sections, providing thought-provoking instructions and best practices for each area. A school system could reasonably expect the application to not only meet its goals for standardization, but also to increase the quality of the plans' content.

However, often such solutions actually burden the user with extra work. After the deployment of new systems, it is not easy to motivate users to adjust their behaviors. Even if an organization sets the policy that all plans are to be constructed the new way, the teachers are just as likely to continue to use their old document templates to construct plans and then copy/paste their contents into the wizard tool to be compliant. Such behavior bypasses the best practices and instructions the wizard provides, and reduces the likelihood that the quality of the plans will improve. Even worse, it increases the amount of time teachers spend working on each plan.

One of the reasons for the increased user workload is that applications typically don't provide a familiar environment. Continuing with our teaching example, it's highly likely the teachers were comfortable with Microsoft Word and, in fact, with all or most of the Microsoft Office apps. Word, Excel, Outlook, and PowerPoint have been on users' desktops for over a decade and have a well-established connection, level of comfort, and high adoption rate. Developers today quickly limit the architecture options for their solutions to either the Web or Windows, and they also need to view Office as a development platform. Instead of building a new application that is separate from Office, the developers in the teaching example should have extended Microsoft Word to incorporate the new application's requirements. By developing with Office, what was once viewed as a separate, siloed system that requires special training is instead just a new feature of a familiar tool.

This example application could now be developed within Microsoft Word. An add-in could use a task pane to display the best practices and instructions sensitive to the user's position in the document. By using the Open XML file format as well as Word's support for XML schemas, the plan document could easily be parsed into the central database. Going one step further, SharePoint could provide search services across the repository, versioning of the plans, and a workflow system for approvals. Such a solution would meet the goals of the school system without moving users away from the tool they had always used to maintain the plans.

Viewing SharePoint as a Set of Services

From reading this book, you might think we look at the world through SharePoint-coated glasses, that every customer we talk to hears the word SharePoint in the answer, and that we recommend every solution be built on top of it. The funny thing is that most customers are eager to have their application "built on top of SharePoint" without really understanding what SharePoint has to offer. When working with customers, the challenge is to get them to quantify the SharePoint services their application needs. Simply porting an ASP.NET application to SharePoint doesn't justify the cost if it won't provide any additional functionality.

In this vein, we'd like to highlight the various services that SharePoint provides. When considering your applications, use these lists and ask yourself, "What does my solution need?" Even if there are services your application can leverage, consider how much custom developing this feature would cost you, compared with the product's cost. Are there any future advantages? In other words, by tying yourself to the product, will your solution benefit from product enhancements over time? Table 15-1 includes some of the important services in SharePoint Foundation; Table 15-2 details additional services provided by Microsoft SharePoint Server.

Table 15-1. Services Offered by SharePoint Foundation

Service	Description
Team sites	SharePoint Foundation can be viewed as a provisioning engine that creates web-based workspaces for teams of users to execute share information. Often these sites represent an instance of a business process. In addition to using the out-of-the-box site templates, you can create your own that contain the necessary functionality for the team.
Document libraries	Document libraries provide storage containers for files, including support for item-level security, versioning, and metadata.
Lists	Lists are a large component of SharePoint and can provide features such as calendars, tasks, and discussion threads to your application. Their flexibility makes them great for storing rows of information, and in the 2010 release they gain some behaviors of a relational system, such as foreign-key constraints.
Workflow	SharePoint hosts Windows Workflow Foundation. You can use the out-of-the-box templates or create your own with SharePoint Designer or Visual Studio 2010. This allows you to leverage the workflow engine without having to implement it in a hosting application. SharePoint's implementation includes user interfaces for interacting with the workflow, including tasks and auditing.
Web parts	You can build web parts with just ASP.NET. However, SharePoint provides many of them out of the box and generates one for each of your lists and libraries.
Search	SharePoint Foundation provides a search engine that allows users to search within the site for information.

Service	Description
RSS	SharePoint lists and libraries can easily be set up to be RSS providers, which allows site content to be pulled and aggregated into other RSS viewers, such as Internet Explorer, Windows gadgets, and Outlook.
Integration	The Business Connectivity Services (BCS) in SharePoint Foundation allow you to connect to external data sources to bring their data into the SharePoint environment as external lists or external data columns.
Alerts	SharePoint provides an alerting structure so users can sign up for notifications about changes to items or new items being added to a list or library.

Table 15-2. Services Offered by Microsoft SharePoint Server 2010

Service	Description
Secure Store Service	The Secure Store Service in SharePoint Server gives developers a solution for securely storing and encrypting alternate credentials for users to access external applications.
Enterprise search	SharePoint Server includes the enterprise search service which supports the indexing of content both inside and outside of SharePoint. This can include sources such as file shares, web sites, Exchange public folders, and custom database or web-service applications through the use of the Business Connectivity Services.
Web content management	The web content management features of SharePoint Server let users maintain HTML portions of site pages with restrictions so they are forced to comply with an organization's style guidelines.
Records management	Records management is about applying retention policies to content so that documents can be reviewed or removed when they expire. This service also includes labeling and bar-coding functionality to link physical documents to the electronic ones. This functionality can be used to route records to a central location or in-place in the site collection where the file resides.
Excel Services	Excel Services offers many different types of services. It can be used as a calculation engine or a data-visualization service, and it helps the distribution of spreadsheet-driven processes.
Performance Point Services	Performance Point Services enables the connection of data-visualization components into an interactive, action-driven dashboard. This allows users to focus on certain indicators to create more detailed and specific reports, giving users more insight into their data.

Continued

Service	Description
Forms Services	InfoPath Forms Services enhances Microsoft's electronic forms strategy. For developers, this service can decouple the data-entry mechanism from a custom application, allowing the organization to support the form UI. The forms can now be displayed in either thin/web browser or thick/InfoPath interfaces.
Data Connection Libraries	Data connection libraries allow you to publish necessary connection information to an external source as a single file. Such files allow users to reuse the information to establish connections to corresponding data sources and to visualize data in spreadsheets or incorporate it into forms.
Personalization	SharePoint Server lets you personalize its interface for specific audiences or user roles. A SharePoint audience is established by defining a set of rules based on user properties gathered into the user profile store. These rules are compiled, evaluating which users should be placed into the audience.
My Sites and Social Networking	The My Sites of SharePoint Server provide a personal dashboard for users to maintain their own workspace. In addition, they can serve as profile pages. Powering the My Sites is a user-profile store whose fields can be populated from Active Directory, other applications, or the users themselves. This profile directory is also available through a web service, making it accessible to custom applications.
Integration	The Business Connectivity Services of SharePoint Server extends the functionality provided by SharePoint Foundation. With the server product, you gain the ability to include external data in your search, view the data with external data web parts and profile pages, as well as use the external data in workflows. The BCS can also use the Secure Store Service and provides the rich-client integration features that enable pulling and even updating the data in Microsoft Office.
Taxonomy Service	SharePoint Server provides a term store where both users and enterprises can create flat or hierarchical vocabularies for metadata properties.
Document Sets	Document sets in SharePoint Server allow users to manage a collection of files as single item.
Word Automation	The Word Automation Services supports server-side conversion of documents that the Microsoft Word client application supports, such as converting Word documents to PDFs.

A Real-World Example

Here's a real-world example of evaluating whether a solution should be built on top of SharePoint. An RFP (request for proposal) that once came across my desk (well before the 2010 release) asked for a solution to be built that allowed teams of lawyers to share information regarding cases they were working on. Each case included content like a shared calendar, documents, contact information, and other lists. Microsoft Office was cited as the preferred application for maintaining the content. This sounds like an obvious SharePoint opportunity; however, there were no requirements that it be a web-based solution. In fact, the customer envisioned the solution as a desktop tool so that the lawyers could take the content to court with them.

In creating the response, I didn't want our developers to have to build an entire structure that stored the documents, as well as construct features to provide security, versioning, and metadata. So we proposed SharePoint as a server, and a rich client application that interacted with it. Each case would get its own team site, even though users would never see its web interface. They would simply select the case they wanted to work on, and we would pull the site content into a local data store for the application. (If we had access to the SharePoint 2010 technologies, we would certainly have looked long and hard at SharePoint Workspaces for this client.) Our concept allowed us to propose a shorter development time for the application, as well as a lower cost, and we won the job. During the follow-up requirements confirmation, additional requests were made, including the capability for the lawyers' assistants to search across all cases for information, and for lawyers outside their organization to have access to the information, but not by installing the tool. As you can guess, it was a good thing we had SharePoint in the design. None of these changes were difficult because SharePoint provided the enterprise search service and could be set up to support an extranet web-based scenario.

A Thank-You

This book set an ambitious goal of introducing Microsoft Office as a solution platform for developers. We made our case by examining common problems our customers encounter on a routine basis. Very likely, some of these problems sounded familiar. The best developers are those with a lot of experience and a wide range of tools that they can apply to new problems. We hope that, through this book, you have learned from our experiences and gained a few new tools. By no means do we think this story is complete; this platform is still new and the community is still exploring ways to leverage it. If you made it to this page of the book (and just didn't flip to the end!), we appreciate your time. We challenge you to extend the techniques we've covered to apply them to your needs. Please share your experiences as we have so that this development platform evolves and matures. We will continue to have this conversation. Follow along through Ed Hild's and Chad Wach's blogs, where they discuss new ways to build solutions with Microsoft Office, SharePoint, and .NET code:

- Ed Hild's Blog: `http://blogs.msdn.com/edhild`

- Chad Wach's Blog: `http://chad.wach.us/blog`

Index

Microsoft SharePoint. *See* SharePoint 2010

Microsoft Visio. *See also* Visio Services

    automatic linking, 306–8

    Floor Plan template, 301

    proposing workflow using Visio, 240–43, 266

Microsoft Word

    AltChunks in, 155

    automation services, 156–60, 360

    extending templates with VSTO, 133–35

    merging list data into, 101–26

        extension points, 125

        key techniques, 124

        performing the merge, 122–24

        solution overview, 102

        walkthrough, 102–24

    task panes, 135–40

    Trust Settings, 144

Microsoft.Maps.MapControl assembly, 329

Microsoft.Maps.MapControl.Common assembly, 329

Microsoft.Office.Word.Server assembly, 158

Microsoft.SharePoint.Client.Silverlight assembly, 329

Microsoft.SharePoint.Client.Silverlight.Runtime assembly, 329

Microsoft.SharePoint.Linq assembly, 148, 193

Model-View-Controller (MVC) pattern, 171

MSSQLFT search queries, 137

multi-project deployment, 63

MVC (Model-View-Controller) pattern, 171

My Sites, 360

■ N

named arguments (C#), 63

named parameters (C#), 62

National Biological Information Infrastructure (NBII), 332

navigation forms (Access databases), 278, 281

.NET Framework 4.0, 62

New Data Graphic window (Visio), 309

new projects, creating, 30

Notes pages (PowerPoint), 212

■ O

OBA (Open Business Applications), 4

Objectives lists

    building slides from, 176–77

    searching for, 173

Office development, 41–65

    deployment guidelines, 64

    enhancements with Office 2010, 60–63

    history of, 41–42

    importance of, 42

    opportunities for, 42–53

        managed code, 51

        Open XML. *See* Open XML format

    with VSTO. *See* Visual Studio Tools for Office

office floor plan, visualizing, 299–324

    extension points, 323

    key techniques, 323

    solution overview, 300

    walkthrough, 300–322

        adding interactivity, 312–21

        applying custom data graphics, 308–11

        creating floor plan, 300–302

■ X

■ Y

You Need the Companion eBook

Your purchase of this book entitles you to buy the companion PDF-version eBook for only $10. Take the weightless companion with you anywhere.

We believe this Apress title will prove so indispensable that you'll want to carry it with you everywhere, which is why we are offering the companion eBook (in PDF format) for $10 to customers who purchase this book now. Convenient and fully searchable, the PDF version of any content-rich, page-heavy Apress book makes a valuable addition to your programming library. You can easily find and copy code—or perform examples by quickly toggling between instructions and the application. Even simultaneously tackling a donut, diet soda, and complex code becomes simplified with hands-free eBooks!

Once you purchase your book, getting the $10 companion eBook is simple:

❶ Visit **www.apress.com/promo/tendollars/**.

❷ Complete a basic registration form to receive a randomly generated question about this title.

❸ Answer the question correctly in 60 seconds, and you will receive a promotional code to redeem for the $10.00 eBook.

Apress®
THE EXPERT'S VOICE™